STUDIES IN WELSH HISTORY

Editors

RALPH A. GRIFFITHS CHRIS WILLIAMS
ERYN M. WHITE

27

THE POLITICS OF THE PRINCIPALITY:

WALES, *c.*1603–1642

THE POLITICS OF THE PRINCIPALITY: WALES, c.1603–1642

by
LLOYD BOWEN

*Published on behalf of the
History and Law Committee
of the Board of Celtic Studies*

CARDIFF
UNIVERSITY OF WALES PRESS
2007

© Lloyd Bowen, 2007

British Library Cataloguing-in-Publication Data
A catalogue record for his book is available from the British Library.

ISBN-10 0-7083-1906-8
ISBN-13 978-0-7083-1906-2

All rights reserved. No part of this book may be reproduced, stored in a retrieval system, or transmitted, in any form or by any means, electronic, mechanical, photocopying, recording or otherwise, without clearance from the University of Wales Press, 10 Columbus Walk, Brigantine Place, Cardiff, CF10 4UP.
www.wales.ac.uk/press

The right of Lloyd Bowen to be identified as author of this work has been asserted by him in accordance with sections 77 and 78 of the Copyright, Designs and Patents Act 1988.

Printed in Wales by Dinefwr Press, Llandybïe

EDITORS' FOREWORD

Since the foundation of the series in 1977, the study of Wales's history has attracted growing attention among historians internationally and continues to enjoy a vigorous popularity. Not only are approaches, both traditional and new, to the study of history in general being successfully applied in a Welsh context, but Wales's historical experience is increasingly appreciated by writers on British, European and world history. These advances have been especially marked in the university institutions in Wales itself.

In order to make more widely available the conclusions of original research, much of it of limited accessibility in postgraduate dissertations and theses, in 1977 the History and Law Committee of the Board of Celtic Studies inaugurated this series of monographs, *Studies in Welsh History*. It was anticipated that many of the volumes would originate in research conducted in the University of Wales or under the auspices of the Board of Celtic Studies, and so it has proved. But the series does not exclude significant contributions made by researchers in other universities and elsewhere. Its primary aim is to serve historical scholarship and to encourage the study of Welsh history.

For Nicki and Taliesin with love

CONTENTS

Editors' foreword		v
Acknowledgements		ix
Abbreviations		xi
Introduction		1
1	The Politics of Parliamentary Election in Early Stuart Wales	12
2	Welsh Parliamentary Business, 1604–1629	39
3	The Burdens of War: Wales in the 1620s	85
4	Wales and the Personal Rule (I): Ship Money	152
5	Wales and the Personal Rule (II): Religion	207
6	Civil War Allegiance and Welsh Political Culture	235
Conclusion: A 'Welsh Politics'?		262
Bibliography		279
Index		299

ACKNOWLEDGEMENTS

In the indecent time it has taken to complete this book, I have incurred many debts, personal, professional and financial. This study began as a doctoral dissertation at Cardiff University, and would not have been possible without the financial support of the British Academy (now the AHRC). I am also most grateful to the trustees of the Huntington Library, who awarded me a Fletcher Jones Foundation Fellowship to consult the papers of John Egerton, first earl of Bridgwater, in such delightful surroundings.

I should also like to thank the archivists and librarians who have produced documents and answered enquiries with such professionalism and courtesy. These institutions can be found in the bibliography, but I should like to give particular thanks to the staff of the National Library of Wales, Aberystwyth, and the National Archives, Kew (the Public Record Office to true believers, of course), whose services were called on most heavily in this research.

My doctoral studies were pursued under the supervision of Anthony Johnson, and I am indebted to him for his guidance and advice. My two examiners, John Morrill and John Gwynfor Jones, offered encouragement and invaluable comments on the text, and I remain grateful for their continuing support.

I was most fortunate in having colleagues at the History of Parliament Trust who encouraged the asking of new questions of this material. Simon Healy, Paul Hunneyball, Patrick Little, Jason Peacey, Stephen Roberts and David Scott were all (often unwittingly) important in helping refine my ideas on early Stuart Wales.

My colleagues at Cardiff University have provided a stimulating atmosphere within which the arguments in this book have been developed. I am especially grateful to Garthine Walker and Kevin Passmore who have contributed more to this book than they realize, and who helped me understand what the research and writing of history was really all about. For this and all those coffees I will always be grateful.

The generosity of the community of early modern historians was made clear to me when several scholars agreed to read and comment upon parts of the manuscript, having receiving unsolicited emails and letters requesting another perspective. For this I am indebted to Kenneth Fincham, Madeline Gray, Philip Jenkins and Barrie Williams. Tom Cogswell went above and beyond the call of duty in his encouragement and detailed discussion of the 1620s for which I am extremely thankful. Stephen Roberts was generous enough to read the whole manuscript and offer many valuable observations. Mark Stoyle's work has provided an important context for some of the arguments here, and his discussions of parts of the manuscript have been both generous and rewarding.

I am grateful to my editors, Ralph Griffiths and Eryn White, for their close attention to the book. I should like to thank Ralph in particular for his meticulous reading and sage advice, and for making my prose a consumable commodity.

Thankfully the input of my friends has been negligible. Their fair-weather support has been given grudgingly and has, if anything, hindered rather than helped the production of this volume. Dark Skies, Dar and Dids have constituted a triumvirate of indifference which constantly undermined my confidence; the lush winnuts didn't help. By contrast, Suzy has always been enormously generous in helping me stay in London and Oxford – many thanks.

My family have been the ones who have had to live with the shadow of this book over them, and they have always remained steadfast in their support. To my mam and dad I owe everything; without them I would never have embarked upon, let alone completed, this book. Alun and Mair have always helped in any way they could, for which I am most thankful. The greatest discovery in the researching of this book was Nicki. Her limitless patience and humbling love have been the most important constants throughout the perambulations and peregrinations during which this study took shape. The book is dedicated to her and our wonderful son, Taliesin, but this is poor recompense for everything they have given me. My greatest debt always will be to you.

ABBREVIATIONS

Unless indicated otherwise, the place of publication is London

Add.	Additional Manuscript
APC	*Acts of the Privy Council*
BBCS	*Bulletin of the Board of Celtic Studies*
BL	British Library
Bowen, thesis	L. Bowen, 'Wales in British politics, c.1603–42' (Ph.D. thesis, University of Wales, 1999)
CWP	J. G. Ballinger (ed.), *Calendar of the Wynn (of Gwydir) Papers, 1515–1690* (Cardiff, 1926)
CD1621	W. Notestein, F. H. Relf, and H. Simpson (eds), *Commons Debates, 1621* (New Haven, 1935), 7 vols.
CD1628	R. C. Johnson, M. J. Cole and W. B. Bidwell (eds), *Commons Debates, 1628* (New Haven, 1977–8), 4 vols.
CJ	*Journal of the House of Commons* (unless specified, all references are to volume 1)
CSPD	*Calendar of State Papers, Domestic*
Dodd, 'Apprenticeship'	A. H. Dodd, 'Wales's parliamentary apprenticeship (1536–1625)', *TCS*, 1942
Dodd, 'Parliaments, 1625–29'	A. H. Dodd, 'Wales in the parliaments of Charles I, I. (1625–1629)', *TCS*, 1945
Dodd, 'Parliaments, 1640–42'	A. H. Dodd, 'Wales in the parliaments of Charles I, II. (1640–42)', *TCS*, 1946–7
Dodd, 'Pattern of politics'	A.H. Dodd, 'The pattern of politics in Stuart Wales', *TCS*, 1948

Dodd, *Studies*	A. H. Dodd, *Studies in Stuart Wales* (Cardiff, 1952; 2nd edn, 1971)
DWB	J. E. Lloyd et al. (eds), *Dictionary of Welsh Biography Down to 1940* (1959)
HMC	Historical Manuscripts Commission
LJ	*Journals of the House of Lords*
NLW	National Library of Wales
NLWJ	*National Library of Wales Journal*
PP1625	M. Jansson and W. B. Bidwell (eds), *Proceedings in Parliament, 1625* (New Haven, 1987)
PP1626	M. Jansson and W. B. Bidwell (eds), *Proceedings in Parliament, 1626* (New Haven, 1992–6), 4 vols.
RO	Record Office
Russell, *Parliaments*	C. Russell, *Parliaments and English Politics, 1621–1629* (Oxford, 1979)
SR	*Statutes of the Realm* (1810–28), 11 vols.
TCS	*Transactions of the Honourable Society of Cymmrodorion*
TNA	National Archives (formerly The Public Record Office)
WHR	*Welsh History Review*

INTRODUCTION

Early seventeenth-century Wales has not fared well at the hands of modern historians. Few have been attracted to a period lacking most of those characteristics which preoccupy much Welsh historical writing and which are often seen as representative of Wales's 'true' national character in the form of a democratic, plebeian culture leavened with nonconformist energies and a nationalistic, resistive edge working at the bonds of encroaching English influence. When Gwyn Alf Williams introduced Michael Foot at a historical meeting during the 1970s, he articulated the unease of many Welsh historians with Stuart Wales, noting that Foot possessed

> a certain 17th century thundercloud around his head, I don't mean the Welsh 17th century, I mean the good seed, the English 17th century, which taught kings that they had a bone in their necks and that the 'poorest he' in England had rights along with the 'richest he'.[1]

With few such values immediately apparent in pre-Civil War Wales, it has remained very much a 'Cinderella' subject and a period 'seldom studied for its own sake by Welsh historians'.[2] For most Welsh writers, the early seventeenth century is sandwiched uncomfortably between the rule of the Welsh Tudors who had passed the Acts of Union integrating the country into the political structures of England, and the heroic phase of early Welsh nonconformity which prefigured the dynamic evangelical revivals of the eighteenth century.

This neglect has been mirrored in the wider historiography of seventeenth-century England, with most recent scholars failing to integrate Wales satisfactorily into their accounts.

---

[1] *Llafur*, 1(3) (1974), 18–19. I am grateful to Neil Evans for this reference.
[2] G. Williams, review of G. D. Owen, *Wales in the Reign of James I*, *WHR*, 15 (1990–1), 130; M. Gray, review of the same volume, *Journal of Welsh Ecclesiastical History*, 6 (1989), 76. G. D. Owen's book is a notable exception to this general neglect of early Stuart Wales, but is a rather idiosyncratic work which offers some valuable Welsh materials from the National Archives but does not shape these into an analytical framework; the book lacks a conclusion.

Thus, one of the most influential works on the high politics of the 1620s is tellingly entitled *Parliament and English Politics, 1621–1629*, and despite Conrad Russell's keen ear for the provincial voice in parliament, 'Wales' only garners two citations in his index. The influential 'county community' approaches of the 1960s and 1970s, meanwhile, almost completely ignored the Welsh experience.[3] Similarly, the influential revisionist wave which broke in the 1970s, of which Russell's book was perhaps the most important text, failed to reach the shores of Welsh history, as have the 'post-revisionist' reassessments which currently dominate the field. The impulses of the 'New British History' have generated more interest in the Welsh experience, although here, too, interest fades rapidly after the most obviously 'British' episode of Wales's incorporation within the English state in 1536–43. As Stephen Roberts commented trenchantly in a recent article on the Civil War in south Wales, 'current interest in early modern Welsh cultural and social history is built on the thin sands of an inadequate political history base'.[4]

Despite its comparative neglect, Stuart Wales did find its historian in the person of A. H. Dodd. He produced a series of pioneering studies in the 1940s and 1950s examining the parliamentary history of Tudor and Stuart Wales, and he wrote what has become the standard text for the period, *Studies in Stuart Wales*, which first appeared in 1952. Dodd's work was remarkable in its ambition and willingness to use manuscript materials in concert with parliamentary journals and diaries to describe the political preoccupations of Wales's MPs. In many ways he fulfils the role of the principality's S. R. Gardiner, the historian who opened up the dark terrain of early seventeenth-century England in his massive *History of England from the Accession of James I to the Outbreak of the Civil War*. Yet the willingness to revise Gardiner and adopt new approaches to the political history of early seventeenth-century England, which have been so influential since the revisionist reinterpretations

---

[3] H. A. Lloyd's volume on south-west Wales, though providing a useful chapter on politics, was much more concerned with the socio-economic interests of the region's gentry, reflecting, perhaps, the interests of his supervisor, Hugh Trevor-Roper: H. A. Lloyd, *The Gentry of South-West Wales, 1540–1640* (Cardiff, 1968).

[4] S. Roberts, 'How the west was won: parliamentary politics, religion and the military in south Wales, 1642–9', *WHR*, 21 (2002–3), 648.

of the mid-1970s, has not found their corollary in Wales. For the most part, Dodd's work remains the standard point of reference for dealing with Stuart Wales and his conclusions serve as the basis for almost all assessments made about the principality in the pre-Civil War era.[5] Yet Dodd's approach was very much formed within the prevailing Whig/Gardinerian view of the early seventeenth century, which portrayed parliament as a 'rising' institution ranged against corrupt and unconstitutional monarchs. Parliament embodied forces of progress and modernity while the monarchy personified the reactionary legacy of the late medieval period. The early seventeenth century was essentially a prelude to the inevitable constitutional clash between these two forces in the Civil War of the 1640s. Dodd's work placed early seventeenth-century Wales and its MPs firmly within this teleological schema of 'opposition' and 'party', and there they have stayed, frozen in a kind of historiographical amber.

As a result of Dodd's continued influence and the unease of most historians of England at venturing beyond Offa's Dyke, Wales has been insulated from the insights offered by revisionist and post-revisionist reinterpretations of early Stuart history, which have challenged and developed many of the accepted notions about the nature of politics in this period. This study seeks to reconnect Wales with this recent historiography and to build upon and extend Dodd's analysis of early Stuart Welsh politics by drawing on the techniques and interpretations of recent approaches. It also utilizes previously unused sources in its discussion of early Stuart Welsh politics, as well as evidence which has long been deployed in studies of early Stuart England but has never been systematically used for Wales: for example, the Privy Council registers of the 1630s have not been used previously to examine Wales's experience of ship money.

This book investigates the political culture of early Stuart Wales by examining the interaction of the centre and the

---

[5] See, for example, the influential textbook by J. G. Jones, *Early Modern Wales*, c.*1525–1640* (Basingstoke, 1994), ch. 5. Philip Jenkins recognized Dodd's enduring influence when he noted how the 'high politics of Stuart and Georgian Wales have never really been fashionable despite the magnificent precedent set by A.H. Dodd': P. Jenkins, *A History of Modern Wales, 1536–1990* (Harlow, 1992), p. 418.

periphery, often through the institution of parliament. However, it is wary of the idea, prevalent in much Whig and revisionist literature and a key component of Dodd's approach, that politics was restricted to Westminster and Whitehall, the preserve of a small number of courtiers and MPs. It seeks rather to present parliament and the politics of the centre as one component of a broader political sphere encompassing patronal networks, factional ties and the interests of electorates in Wales. This is not a study of popular politics in early Stuart Wales, but it does attempt to demonstrate how the interplay between centre and locality operated within a series of overlapping political communities which included a modest blacksmith in Llantrisant, Glamorgan, as well as the duke of Buckingham.

In exploring the composite political culture of the early Stuart principality, this book tackles the experiences of a disparate set of thirteen counties bound together by common cultural and linguistic heritages and administrative provisions.[6] This has proved a difficult balancing act of providing adequate coverage of each county while retaining a coherent analytical structure. Although the book follows a broadly chronological arrangement, it adopts an episodic approach, examining what the experience of parliamentary lobbying or of paying ship money can reveal about the prevailing assumptions and discourses which shaped and informed Wales's political culture. The chapters may be seen as discrete but interlinked cross-sections through the complex nexuses of centre–locality interactions which, when reassembled, offer a rounded, if incomplete, view of the channels and processes through which early Stuart Welsh political culture operated. Such an approach does not collapse the experiences of thirteen shires into a monolithic 'national' view of Welsh politics, but retains enough of its integrity to avoid fracturing into a rough composite of thirteen county narratives. It is an attempt to offer a regional history which acknowledges the integration of a distinct cultural region within the early modern British

---

[6] Monmouthshire is included here as one of the Welsh counties, though for most administrative purposes it was part of England after the Acts of Union. Culturally it remained very much Welsh in character.

state and recognizes the degree to which its political life operated through British structures; it also remains sensitive to the particularist and distinctive elements which helped to mould its political culture. Through such an approach, the book seeks to move beyond the simple dichotomies of central versus local politics in order to explore the manner in which the interactions between London and the Welsh counties constituted a regional politics at once fully integrated within a wider British context, and yet composed of a distinctive collection of cultural, linguistic, topographical, social and economic elements.

Early Stuart Welsh politics has to be understood within this broader British framework because of the Acts of Union passed in 1536 and 1543, by which Wales was integrated into the political and administrative structures of the English realm. The Henrician settlement provided for the extension of the English machinery of government throughout Wales, with the creation of new shires from medieval marcher lordships and the introduction of justices of the peace and quarter sessions in all counties. Importantly, the union statutes also enfranchised the Welsh shires and boroughs, meaning that, from 1543, they elected members to the national parliaments who participated in the formulation of legislation that was now equally applicable to both Wales and England.[7] Wales retained a degree of political and administrative distinctiveness after the union, however, in the form of the Courts of Great Sessions and the Council in the Marches of Wales. The former were equivalent to the English assize courts, although unlike their English counterparts they exercised an equity as well as a criminal jurisdiction. The Council in the Marches began life as a princely council-cum-household, but was given an important institutional role under the union settlement. Comprising a body of officials and lawyers headed by a centrally appointed lord president whose powers were defined by sets of royal instructions, the Council in the Marches acted essentially as an executive arm of the Privy Council. Its wide jurisdiction encompassed the whole of Wales, along with the

---

[7] For a more detailed discussion of the electoral arrangements in early modern Wales, see below, pp. 12–13.

four western English counties of Shropshire, Herefordshire, Worcestershire and Gloucestershire. Normally based in the Shropshire town of Ludlow, the Council also acted as a regional law court which possessed extensive criminal and civil jurisdictions.

It may be suggested that it was the union settlement which provided Wales with the political integrity it enjoyed thereafter, forging a uniform administrative region from the patchwork jurisdictions of the marcher lordships and the principality counties of the late medieval era. However, we should acknowledge the profound and continuing divisions within Wales which renders the investigation of a 'politics of the principality' problematic. Perhaps the most significant of these internal discontinuities was the barrier of geography which militated against easy communications across the central massif and the construction of a single political identity.[8] The mountainous heart of Wales presented a formidable obstacle to political integration, and communications were predominantly east–west rather than north–south, with some areas even looking across the border to English towns like Shrewsbury and Bristol as economic centres rather than to any part of Wales. It was for such reasons that the historical developments of north and south Wales had been separate and such divisions endured beyond the early modern period. In addition, Wales had never been a unified kingdom under one ruler, and the region possessed no institutions which could provide a focus for any 'national' political sentiment: Wales had no parliament of its own, and particularistic bodies such as the Council in the Marches of Wales and the Courts of Great Sessions were populated largely by centrally appointed English officials and never formed the focus for any kind of distinctively Welsh political movement.

Despite these tendencies towards heterogeneity, there were a number of factors which allowed those living within the geographical area of Wales to consider themselves as a distinct people, and which rendered them separate in the eyes of

[8] See Jenkins, *Modern Wales*, pp. 1–13; idem, 'A new history of Wales', *Historical Journal*, 32 (1989), 389–90; idem, 'Seventeenth century Wales: definition and identity', in B. Bradshaw and P. Roberts (eds), *British Consciousness and Identity: The Making of Britain, 1533–1707* (Cambridge, 1998), pp. 213–35.

others also. The most important of these factors was the Welsh language which the vast majority of the population spoke throughout the thirteen shires. This not only formed a powerful bond within local communities, but helped to define Wales as a country with a cultural make-up quite distinct from that of England.[9] This was reinforced by the mythologies of Wales's history which were important in helping to foster the notion of the Welsh as a separate and identifiable people, the 'Britons' or *Cymry*, with their own unique heritage.[10] This was a potent piece of rhetoric which surprisingly had few implications for a politics of separation, but rather cultivated an attachment to the British polity and its monarchy which was seen as descending from British stock. When James I succeeded to the throne in 1603, for example, his British 'project' found a resonance with a number of Welsh authors and politicians such as Sir William Maurice of Clenennau, who saw in the union plans the fulfilment of an ancient prophecy concerning a British dynasty reuniting the island.[11] Such ideas of Britishness were also important in helping to legitimate and inculturate the Church of England in Wales; it was presented to the Welsh people as the reintroduction of an ancient British church which the Welsh had preserved inviolate until the introduction of Catholic corruptions by the Saxons. Elements such as these gave the idea of 'Wales' an important place in the mental worlds of its inhabitants, and also allowed this 'imagined community' to have some purchase in the political discourse of the period.[12] In addition, the Welsh were defined and identified by the English as a

[9] G. H. Jenkins, R. Suggett and E. M. White, 'The Welsh language in early modern Wales', in G. H. Jenkins (ed.), *The Welsh Language Before the Industrial Revolution* (Cardiff, 1997), pp. 45–6.
[10] G. Williams, *Renewal and Reformation: Wales, c.1415–1642* (Oxford, 1993), pp. 451–9; P. R. Roberts, 'Tudor Wales, national identity and the British inheritance', in Bradshaw and Roberts, *British Consciousness and Identity*, pp. 8–42; R. R. Davies, 'The peoples of Britain and Ireland, 1100–1400. IV. Language and historical mythology', *Transactions of the Royal Historical Society*, 6th series, 7 (1997), 15–24.
[11] See below, pp. 70–3.
[12] For parallel discussions of the relationship between cultural distinctiveness and political particularism in areas usually considered wholly English by the sixteenth century, see T. Thornton, *Cheshire and the Tudor State, 1480–1560* (Woodbridge, 2000); M. Stoyle, *West Britons: Cornish Identities and the Early Modern British State* (Exeter, 2002).

separate cultural group. Drawing on a long tradition of antagonism and difference, the English continued to conceive of the Welsh as a separate people despite the political and administrative unification, and this perception of ethnic division seems to have had some political ramifications, for example, in configuring the patterns of allegiance demonstrated by most of the principality in the initial stages of the Civil War.[13]

The following chapters examine how this distinct but heterogeneous country experienced and interacted with the early Stuart state, and consider the manner in which these interactions reflect a discrete but wholly assimilated political culture in early seventeenth-century Britain. Chapter 1 opens the analysis with a discussion of the dynamics of parliamentary elections in Wales, and this is extended in Chapter 2 in an examination of sectional interests in early Stuart parliaments. It is contended that the electoral landscape of early Stuart Wales was composed of hierarchical structures of gentry patronage but that these were tempered by important considerations of reciprocity and service. These notions of service extended to parliament, and Chapter 2 describes the way such rhetorics of service and obligation were translated into the lobbying activities of particular Welsh interest groups who pressed for action on issues such as the rebuilding of Chepstow Bridge and the trade in Welsh cottons. It thus concentrates on economic and regional interests in Wales which sought to utilize parliament as a place where they could discharge business. In addition, the possible existence of a Welsh interest group in the Commons is considered.

Another level of business discussed in parliament was international politics and foreign affairs, and the outbreak of the Thirty Years' War meant that the parliaments of the 1620s were intimately concerned with such issues. Once more, this study attempts to place the activity of Welsh members on such questions as the defence of the Palatinate and the outbreak of war with Spain beside responses within the principality more generally. The impact of war on society in Wales is considered in Chapter 3 through its most obvious forms of demands for

[13] See below, pp. 242–3, 258–60.

money and men. The increased political temperature over war policy in the parliaments of the 1620s was mirrored in many areas of the country by the responses to these demands, responses which became increasingly politicized as the unpopular war continued. The analysis of expedients such as benevolences and the forced loan imposed in the shires of Wales attempts to reveal the patterns of compliance and dissent in relation to these politically charged levies.

Perhaps the least studied period in early Stuart Wales has been that of Charles I's personal rule during the 1630s. This crucial era requires investigation, not only to achieve a better understanding of the decade in its own terms, but also to provide an adequate context in which to judge Welsh attitudes towards the political breakdown of 1640–2. The relationship between the regional and the national provides the basis of the analysis pursued in Chapter 4, where the central fiscal expedient of the period, ship money, is examined. Patterns of payment and the nature of the difficulties ship money encountered in Wales provide a means by which the political temperature of the principality can be taken and the degree to which the country had become alienated from Caroline rule can be assessed. It is suggested that, whereas previous studies have concentrated almost exclusively on the difficulties which collecting ship money faced elsewhere, the Welsh experience reveals a pattern of compliance and acquiescence which also demands explanation.

Crucially, the personal rule was also a period when the contentious religious policies of Archbishop William Laud were implemented throughout the kingdom. Consideration of religion in a Welsh context during the 1630s has hitherto centred on the few nonconformists who appeared in the eastern parts of Wales most open to English influences, without giving adequate consideration to moderate Church of England Protestantism and its fortunes. In Chapter 5 an attempt has been made to demonstrate that, rather than being a period of incipient puritan activism, the 1630s in Wales witnessed Laudian policies being implemented without significant resistance or comment. The somewhat conservative nature of Welsh religion appears to have conditioned this response, meshing more easily with the symbolic and clericocentric Anglicanism of Laud than with the Word-based piety of the puritans. Although the extent to which Laudianism was actively supported and promoted in Wales is impossible to ascertain accurately, the view that this kind of conservative attachment to the Church of England was a much more vital force than has been previously allowed helps us to understand the widespread support for the king in 1642.

The final chapter explores these patterns of political allegiance in Wales at the beginning of the first Civil War. The principality's support for the king in 1642 has been explained inadequately hitherto in terms of allegiance to the Tudors being transferred to the Stuart kings, or in terms of the royalist gentry conditioning the responses of their tenants. This chapter suggests that the tenor of religious sensibilities in Wales, along with closely related factors of ethnic, cultural and linguistic distinctiveness, are essential elements in constructing a more satisfactory explanation for the emergence of royalist Wales. Although the revisionist historiographical emphasis on consensus and the absence of ideological division in the early Stuart period meshes well with the Welsh experience as it is described here, it is also suggested that its emphasis on high politics and willingness to de-emphasize continuities between the politics of the 1620s and that of the 1640s is limiting. It is rather argued that meaningful connections between the politics of the 1620s and the 1640s can be made in Wales. Unlike most recent research, which concentrates on the presence of ideological division and opposition in pre-Civil War England, however, this study identifies continuities of a more conservative kind across these decades, and, indeed, argues that such continuities help to explain the popular royalism evident in regions such as Wales and Cornwall.

This examination of early seventeenth-century Welsh political culture suggests that previous studies have been either too eager to subsume completely a Welsh political identity in an expanding Stuart state, or too keen to ascribe a coherence and purpose to Welsh politics which are not reflected in the evidence. Rather it proposes that a more fruitful approach is to consider the manner in which a particularist, but not nationalist, Welsh political culture could emerge as a product of the country's remarkably successful reconciliation with, and accommodation to, the British state. Although cognizant of the fragmented nature of political life in early seventeenth-century Wales, this study argues that Welsh politics may have been more than simply the sum of its localist parts. Throughout the book, the politics of early Stuart Wales is shown to be dynamic and shifting, and is presented not only through the actions of MPs in parliament but also in the attitudes and responses of their constituents in the Welsh shires and towns. Welsh politics is conceived, therefore, not as the consistent expression of values and principles by its MPs, but rather as the outcome of a number of forces operating at local, regional and national levels. It is also suggested that the counties of Wales were qualitatively different in their reactions from those of England, and were capable of articulating distinctive responses to political issues. Political expression in early Stuart Wales thus possessed an inchoate national character without developing into a politics of nationhood.

1
THE POLITICS OF PARLIAMENTARY ELECTION IN EARLY STUART WALES

The pursuit of power and the affirmation of social status in early modern Wales were perhaps most evident at elections to the intermittent parliaments which sat at Westminster. The following overview examines what these elections to the parliaments called between 1604 and 1640 reveal about the political culture of early Stuart Wales, and provides a context for the next chapter which examines the prosecution of Welsh business in parliament during this period.[1]

Elections were occasions when the political assumptions of the élites in Welsh constituencies may be glimpsed through the exercise of patronage, requests for favour and the negotiation of power among local oligarchies. This study explores the manner in which the power of regional élites was mediated and articulated at this crucial interface between local and national politics. Elections offer insights into the socio-political structures of Welsh constituencies, and the ways in which these interacted with the broader political developments of the early Stuart period.

Under the enfranchisement provisions of the union legislation, most Welsh counties returned one member, unlike their English counterparts, although Monmouthshire returned two. One member was also elected for each shire town, although Merioneth had no borough representative, and Pembrokeshire contained the county borough of Haverfordwest which elected a member in addition to the member for the county town of Pembroke. Elections in Wales could be particularly bitter and contested affairs because the paucity of available seats meant that there was little possibility of sharing representation as was the case in English shires. In total, twenty-seven members were returned at each election. The county franchise followed the English

---

[1] A detailed analysis of Welsh elections is presented in Bowen, thesis, 11–108.

model in allowing the forty-shilling freeholder to vote, but the borough franchise was more complex. Here a unique system prevailed whereby the 'ancient boroughs' or 'out-boroughs' of the county were allowed to participate in the election of the borough member, and were also liable (in theory at least) to contribute to his wages. The system was not uniform, however, as some out-boroughs had been excluded from voting before the accession of James I, while elsewhere such towns maintained their participatory rights.

The politics of parliamentary elections in early Stuart Wales exhibits a good deal of diversity of practice across the principality, and the relative balances of power and influence within constituencies were constantly shifting. The complexion of electoral politics in any constituency changed over time, and the image of a static system of aristocratic patronage or gentry dominance in any one county or borough fails to take account of these subtleties. Consequently the typologies within which elections are examined here provide a general framework for discussion.

The exercise of political choice in parliamentary elections cannot be understood without recognizing that it was integrated into the web of local socio-political relationships. The operation of parliamentary patronage by the aristocracy is a well-known aspect of this process, but in most of Wales during the early seventeenth century noble presence had become attenuated.[2] It was effectively limited to the southern and eastern parts of the country where the powerful Herbert dynasty held sway, and also in Monmouthshire where the only resident aristocratic family in Wales, the earls of Worcester at Raglan Castle, exerted influence. In addition, the Devereux interest of the earls of Essex continued to have some electoral weight in Pembrokeshire, Radnorshire and Breconshire, though it was reduced severely after the first earl's rising in 1601; the limited influence of the earls of Derby and Ellesmere continued to reach into Flintshire in the seventeenth century. Although such individuals were

---

[2] P. R. Roberts, 'The English crown, the principality of Wales and the Council in the Marches, 1534–1641', in B. Bradshaw and J. Morrill (eds), *The British Problem, c.1534–1707* (Basingstoke, 1996), pp. 134–5.

elevated socially far above those whom they helped into parliament, it would be a mistake to interpret the exercise of their patronage as an uni-directional process, with a powerful noble placing associates in shire or borough seats like so many political pawns.[3] Such an interpretation ignores the essential elements of reciprocal and mutual benefit for both parties in the construction of webs of influence and interdependence. Although elections ultimately were concerned with the distribution of local power, the establishing of good governance, cultivation of beneficial contacts, connecting local élites to central authority and securing the approbation of nationally powerful figures were all elements in the operation of electoral patronage. Power was intimately connected with ideas of honour in early modern England and Wales, and electoral patronage cut both ways in a recirculation of honour and mutually reinforcing ties of affinity and service.[4]

The case of William Herbert, third earl of Pembroke, in Glamorgan is important in understanding this practice in a Welsh context.[5] The house of Herbert held an enormous amount of land in this county with which it had particularly close historical ties; indeed, the second earl's widow, Mary, continued to reside at Cardiff in the early part of James's reign.[6] The Herbert interests here were translated into a potent political influence at parliamentary elections. Yet some examples demonstrate the kinds of discourses and languages which framed this political process, and reveal the manner in which elements of mutuality and interdependence characterized such patronal relationships. In 1626, Sir John Stradling of St Donat's was returned as the county member, his indenture being witnessed by many of the county's leading gentry families, a potent symbol of a

[3] This is a tendency in J. K. Gruenfelder, *Influence in Early Stuart Elections, 1604–1640* (Columbus, Oh, 1981).

[4] I. Atherton, *Ambition and Failure in Early Stuart England: The Career of John, First Viscount Scudamore* (Manchester, 1999), p. 257.

[5] A pioneering, though now dated, study of the electoral patronage of the 3rd and 4th earls is V.A. Rowe, 'The influence of the earls of Pembroke on parliamentary elections, 1625–41', *English Historical Review*, 50 (1935), 242–56. See also B. O'Farrell, 'Politician, patron, poet, William Herbert, 3rd earl of Pembroke' (Ph.D. thesis, University of California, 1966), ch. 4.

[6] TNA, STAC 8/183/35–6.

community of support.[7] Yet Stradling was also associated closely with Pembroke, having been returned the previous year by the earl's influence at Old Sarum. A tract which Stradling wrote in 1625 reveals the kind of political relationship which was being constructed. He dedicated the tract to Pembroke, and deployed the language of clientage, describing the earl's 'experienced favours towards me' and lauding the 'noblenes of your heriock disposition'.[8] These kinds of sentiments were the currency in which the socio-political mutual exchange of patronage was conducted, and Stradling's return as the Glamorgan knight in 1626 may be interpreted as another component in this process.[9] This is not to deny the agency of local gentry figures in the election, but rather to suggest that a community of interest was being established through such transactions. In acting as Stradling's patron, Pembroke was helping to ensure his client's assistance in parliament; at the same time, this political transaction meant that those gentry who endorsed Stradling's election became parties to the connection which helped to bind the constituency to the earl. The return of Pembroke's client also ensured that the Glamorgan gentry had the ear of a particularly powerful noble, who possessed significant influence at the Court and in the Privy Council as lord chamberlain and later lord steward.

This process is even more visible in the election of borough members at Cardiff. Pembroke had a more immediate and pervasive influence over Cardiff as lord of the manor than he could ever have hoped to exercise over the powerful gentry electorate of the shire, and indeed the candidates returned for Cardiff in this period have been described as a 'roll call of Pembroke's clients'.[10] Evidence suggests, however, that this seat was bestowed with more than a nod towards conventions of reciprocity and assent.

[7] TNA, C219/40/18.
[8] NLW, MS 5666C.
[9] Cf. Dodd, *Studies*, pp. 181–2, who maintains that gentry interests were the most important factor in Glamorgan's elections, and downplays the role of the earl. Although members of gentry families would probably have been elected in any case, it is significant that almost all of those returned in this period can be associated directly with the house of Herbert.
[10] Gruenfelder, *Influence*, p. 126.

In 1620, William Herbert of Grey Friars wrote to his cousin and namesake of Cogan Pill, informing him that the countess of Pembroke had written to 'hir bailiffe and townes men of Cardif that they should make choyce of me for their burges the next parlament; who weere very willinge and reddy to performe that I should bee before anie other'. He continued by explaining

> how much bound I am to that noble earle my Lord Chamberlaine, for that he defended me from a great deale of troble and chardge, for the which both my self and all myne will daily praie for him. And alsoe if his honor had anie cause to comand me, my life and all that I have shalbe reddy to doe him service to the uttermost of my power, with as good a will as anie man that breathes.[11]

Through the agency of his wife, the earl obtained not only the return of a kinsman, but also strengthened the ties that existed between them.[12] The binary and reciprocal nature of the election process may be seen in Herbert's reference to his evident desire to serve the earl in return for the honour of being chosen as his nominee. That the assent of the electorate was something more than a closed corporation affirming the candidate proposed by its most powerful patron, however, is suggested by the original writs surviving for Cardiff and the out-boroughs which participated in the election.

The Cardiff return shows that around one hundred inhabitants endorsed the choice of William Herbert of Grey Friars.[13] Even more interesting are the returns which survive for Llantrisant and Cowbridge, two of the seven out-boroughs which would have contributed (at least in theory) to Herbert's wages. The Llantrisant return of 5 January 1621 has forty-four signatures witnessing the 'choyse' of Herbert. These include a number of aldermen and burgesses, but also two masons, two mercers, a 'vitler' and a blacksmith.[14] The Cowbridge return, meanwhile, has seventy-two signatures,

---

[11] NLW, Bute L3/84.
[12] Later that year William Herbert of Grey Friars wrote of his desire to secure local offices in order not to 'gaine anie thinge, but only to doe his honour [Pembroke] service': NLW, Bute L2/50.
[13] TNA, C219/37/352.
[14] TNA, C219/37/353.

sixty of them non-aldermen.[15] From these three surviving returns, a minimum of 216 individuals assented to the choice of the earl's nominee as their parliamentary representative. Pembroke's dominant influence in these towns was of paramount importance, but the fact that such a considerable number endorsed his choice reflects the reciprocal process of patronage in operation.[16] That this was not an unusual occurrence is suggested by a more complete survival of returns for the election of Matthew Davies for Cardiff in 1604. Although a number are damaged and many names obscured, the boroughs of Cardiff, Swansea, Aberavon and Loughor can be identified, the remaining return issuing from either Llantrisant or Neath or Cowbridge.[17] In all, the returns list some 320 individuals giving their assent to Davies's election. Interestingly, the return for Swansea possesses the signatures of some ninety-two 'freemen and burgesses within this towne', more than signed the return for Cardiff itself.[18] Swansea was held by the earls of Worcester, yet the Swansea electors concurred with the other boroughs as to who should represent them in parliament.[19]

This evidence for Cardiff points to a large borough electorate which was geographically dispersed and ranged over the estates of different territorial magnates. Such a situation could have led to confusion and rivalry if it was not handled carefully. The case of William Herbert in 1620/1 demonstrates how the politics of nomination by a leading peer such as Pembroke intermingled with the assent of men as lowly as a blacksmith in the small urban centre of Llantrisant. There

[15] TNA, C219/37/354.
[16] Pembroke's influence was significant in five of the seven contributory boroughs, Llantrisant, Cowbridge, Aberavon, Neath and Kenfig: R. Lewis, 'A Breviat of Glamorgan', ed. W. Rees, *South Wales and Monmouth Record Society*, 3 (1954), 96–110.
[17] TNA, C219/35, pt ii/195–201. Davies had close links with the Herbert family, acting as legal counsel to William Herbert of Cogan Pill: NLW, Bute L3/64. He was not, as is often believed, Pembroke's secretary who sat for Hindon, Wilts., in 1624.
[18] TNA, C219/35, pt ii/200.
[19] W. S. K. Thomas, 'Municipal government in Swansea, 1485–1640', *Glamorgan Historian*, 1 (1963), 27–31; Lewis, 'Breviat', 111. It is probably significant that Davies hailed from the Swansea area and held a bailiwick and other property in the town: G. T. Clark, *Limbus Patrum Morganiæ et Glamorganiæ* (1888), pp. 485–6, 527; TNA, PSO 5/2; C54/1791; West Glamorgan Archives Service, B/S Corp. B2, fos 107, 111, 151.

was little dispute as to whether Herbert would or would not have been chosen for the seat; the earl's interest was sure to prevail. But the very fact that the process acknowledged and accommodated the ideal of assent by the community at large demonstrates that such elections could be inclusive and affirm the social hierarchy. The electors from the contributory boroughs exercised their right of choice, a crucial element in contemporary views on the proper conduct of elections, but they cannot be said to have determined who was to be their candidate. Rather they concurred with the nomination of a leading peer, and affirmed their association with him.[20] The MP himself gained prestige, but also strengthened Pembroke's reputation with his assurances of thanks and service. As in the case of the county, the maintenance of good relations with the earl would hopefully bring tangible benefits in this community of political reciprocity. Some evidence of this can be found in the new charter which Cardiff secured in 1608 at the petition of the earl, whereby the town was authorized to carry out magisterial duties independently of the county in all but the most serious of cases.[21]

Although aristocratic patronage was a consideration in constituencies like Glamorgan and Cardiff, in other constituencies gentry families dominated the electoral scene with an economic power and social pre-eminence which effectively made them a kind of local aristocracy. There was thus a form of inter-gentry patronage operating in several constituencies which tended to be diffused horizontally through groups of family and kin. The Herbert families of Montgomery and Powis Castles, for example, controlled the shire and borough seats of Montgomery with little reference to outside interests. The return of Sir William Herbert of Powis Castle as knight in eight consecutive elections (1597–1628) is eloquent testimony of the family's influence. Similarly, the Vaughans of Golden Grove controlled elections in Carmarthenshire, while the Bulkeleys of Baron Hill were the dominant interest in Anglesey, even though

---

[20] For similar ideas on combining free choice by the electorate with pre-selection from above, see Atherton, *Scudamore*, pp. 261–2.

[21] W. Rees, *Cardiff: A History of the City* (Cardiff, 1962), 63–4; J. H. Mathews (ed.), *Records of the County Borough of Cardiff* (Cardiff, 1898–1911), i, pp. 7, 61–72.

internal family disputes threatened to undermine their control in the mid-1620s. A number of these families were soon to enter the realms of the peerage, but in terms of elections in their counties and shire towns, they already exerted a patronal influence which was akin to that of the nobility.

Perhaps because so many of these elections were mediated by fairly close family groups, and contests and contention were relatively rare, there is little surviving evidence regarding elections in these constituencies. What seems clear, however, is that generally they expressed the families' economic and social superiority in their locality.[22] There were occasional electoral challenges, although these were confrontations between the 'ins' and the 'outs' rather than contests between candidates espousing different political or religious attitudes. As we shall see, although constituencies like Carmarthenshire and Montgomeryshire were dominated socially and electorally by families like the Vaughans and Herberts, we cannot assume that these families operated without reference to wider social contexts. Ideas of accountability and service to the locality were commonplace discourses which shaped elections in these constituencies as elsewhere. In addition, we need to recognize that such elections were events situated within specific regional, social, cultural and economic contexts, and those elected needed to acknowledge the concerns of their electorates. Sir William Herbert and Hugh Myddleton may have been returned as members for Montgomeryshire and Denbigh boroughs, respectively, for all parliaments between 1604 and 1628, but both acknowledged obligations to their constituencies.[23]

Although it is difficult to recover evidence regarding the political assumptions underpinning elections in areas like Carmarthenshire and Montgomeryshire, material from constituencies where social structures were much more varied, with no dominant gentry family or families and where aristocratic involvement was absent, allows us to examine more closely what contemporaries considered to be at stake in parliamentary elections. Much of the surviving

[22] M. Kishlansky, *Parliamentary Selection: Social and Political Choice in Early Modern England* (Cambridge, 1986), pp. 12–14.
[23] See below, pp. 37, 60–1.

evidence is concerned with the pursuit of unanimity and order, commonplaces which shaped a good deal of the political discourse in early seventeenth-century England. The ideal of an election in which the hierarchical social relationships of the region were affirmed at the hustings may have been realized straightforwardly in constituencies like Montgomeryshire, but in those areas where no single family dominated local gentry society, this result had to be manufactured often by tortuous negotiation. In a gentry community obsessed with honour and reputation, a seat which was gained through a contest was of far less value than one secured with universal assent.[24] In December 1623, for example, Sir Richard Wynn wrote that his brother Henry's candidature for Merioneth's seat would bestow 'a great deale of honor, if it may be don without charge or competicion'.[25] In a constituency like Merioneth, where several potential candidates expressed an interest in securing the parliamentary seat, the potential for confrontation, defeat and dishonour was considerable, and much of the negotiation and politicking at election times was geared towards avoiding an election in which reputation and status were tested in the face of the community rather than simply affirmed. The ideal was achieved through mediation prior to the election, when Henry Wynn's candidacy was endorsed by most of the shire's leading gentlemen, and his return proclaimed this powerful discourse of unity in its declaration that Wynn was chosen with 'one assent & consent' of the Merioneth electorate.[26]

The construction of networks whose chief aim was consensus and settlement was a key element in the politics of parliamentary elections in many Welsh constituencies. Prospective candidates and their allies looked to build coalitions of support among prominent members of local gentry society, thereby creating a momentum which would dissuade

---

[24] On the role of honour in early Stuart political culture, see R. Cust, 'Honour, rhetoric and political culture: the earl of Huntington and his enemies', in S. Amussen and M. Kishalansky (eds), *Political Culture and Cultural Politics in Early Modern England* (Manchester, 1995), pp. 84–104.
[25] NLW, MS 9059E/1177.
[26] TNA, C219/38/292.

potential rivals from entering the fray. The bonds of family and kinship were those deployed most readily in the fabrication of such networks, drawing on ties of familial allegiance to build strong assemblages of electoral interests. Such affinities were perhaps particularly significant in Wales, where the historical development of kinship structures ensured that the bonds of family remained especially potent forces in the early modern period. In 1626, for example, Magdalen Bagenall, daughter of Sir Richard Trevor of Trevalyn, described the kinship group which was seeking to negotiate the Flintshire seat, mentioning the efforts of her father, uncle and three 'cousins' in managing a delicate situation where several candidates had declared an interest in the place.[27] Kinship affinities were also crucial in gathering information about potential rivals as well as the intentions of potential supporters. Andrew Brereton sent Thomas Myddleton of Chirk a detailed analysis of the emerging pattern of alliances in Denbighshire before the election of 1614, closing his letter as 'your ever assured kinsman to command'.[28] In the frantic preparations for the fractious Caernarfonshire election of 1620/1, Sir William Thomas assured Sir John Wynn that he was 'youre faithfull lovinge cosen that will not shrinke from yow'.[29] 'Friends' and associates were, of course, also central figures in the formation of support, as in the Merioneth election of 1624, when William Salusbury of Rûg commented how he had 'promised my voice and frends' to endorse the choice of his relations, Hugh Nanney of Nannau and William Vaughan of Corsygedol.[30]

Not surprisingly in a gentry society defined in large measure by prescriptive codes of honour, promises of support in these negotiations were seen as binding engagements; reneging on such assurances brought shame and disrepute. These undertakings promised stability at times of election, and their potency is conveyed in a good deal of

[27] East Sussex RO, GLY 559.
[28] NLW, Chirk Castle F10751. See also Chirk Castle E3399, where Brereton describes himself as 'your cousin and friend to use'.
[29] NLW, MS 9057E/925.
[30] NLW, MS 9060E/1312; C219/38/292. See also NLW, MS 9060E/1317.

Welsh election correspondence. Sir John Trevor, jun., of Trefalyn was daunted when his candidacy for the Flintshire place was challenged by Thomas Mostyn of Mostyn in 1625, but his cousin, Magdalen Bagenall, counselled Trevor that it was 'too late to recall yours and all your freinds ingagmentes ... you must now sticke unto it whatsoever comes of it', adding 'lett noe intereaty prevayle with you to parte with your interests in it howsoever it may prove'.[31] John Griffith of Cefnamwlch recognized the potency of such engagements in the bitter Caernarfonshire election of 1620/1. He asked for the support of a major figure in the county, Sir William Maurice of Clenennau, but learned that he had already promised to support Griffith's rival, Sir Richard Wynn of Gwydir. Griffith wrote back to Maurice acknowledging 'your promise is to[o] great a tie of yow, I acknowledge, to be recaled', but asked 'to grant me your favour in leaving your friends to their liberty [to vote as they chose] ... if without injury to yourself it may be so'.[32] Perhaps the most striking articulation of the strength of these pre-election pledges of support, however, comes from Sir Roger Mostyn, whose son, the aforementioned Thomas, also tried to obtain the Flintshire seat in 1624. Sir Roger had promised beforehand to give his support to Sir John Hanmer, however, and wrote 'I may not with my credit leave hym [Hanmer] thoe it were for the deerest I have, haveinge soe farre engadged my worde unto hyme longe since'.[33]

Although these negotiations were usually conducted on an interpersonal basis, on occasion more formal structures became involved in the delicate business of deciding on a parliamentary candidate. Perhaps the most significant of these was the county bench, the body which offered a model of local leaders working in harmony for the benefit of the community.[34] Anglesey's bench became an important arena

---

[31] East Sussex RO, GLY 559.
[32] NLW, Brogyntyn (Clenennau) 398, 400.
[33] NLW MS 9059E/1187. Mostyn was one of those entrusted with Hanmer's estate when he died in June 1624: East Sussex RO, GLY 554; TNA, PROB 11/145, fos. 240ᵛ–41ᵛ.
[34] V. J. Hodges, 'The electoral influence of the aristocracy, 1604–41' (Ph.D. thesis, Columbia University, 1977), 66–7.

for negotiating and arbitrating the county's parliamentary seat in the aftermath of Sir Richard Bulkeley's death in 1621, and the subsequent familial disorder which disrupted the electoral hold of the Baron Hill dynasty in the mid-1620s.[35] In the absence of concerted Bulkeley influence, there is much more surviving evidence in 1624 and 1625 than previously of gentlemen in surrounding shires manoeuvring to secure the seat. Owen Wynn described how the election of 1623–4 was discussed at the burial of David Owen Theodor of Penmynydd, 'wheere most of the gentlemen of the cowntrey' met. John Mostyn of Tregarnedd was supported by the influential Sir James Whitlocke, chief justice of Chester, and Wynn was informed that Mostyn's candidacy would be best served by Whitelocke's writing to the justices of the peace on his behalf, while Sir John Bodvel, a prominent local gentleman, would also endorse him at the next quarter sessions.[36] The county bench was thus viewed as a powerful legitimating body which could endorse and sanction the election in the absence of a strong lead from the Bulkeleys, and the Anglesey political community was later described as 'wholie bent' on supporting Mostyn's election.[37] Interestingly, reference was made to the fact that Mostyn was expected to 'give the gentlemen of that cowntrey thankes' for electing him at a later meeting of the great sessions in Beaumaris, and also to remit his parliamentary fees as a token of gratitude to the community.[38] Here, then, the exchange of honour and the responsibilities and engagements of the parliamentary election – what one contemporary described as the 'decorum to be used' in such instances – were to be acknowledged formally before one of the most significant assemblies of county authority. During Mostyn's return of 1624, local power and influence were marshalled in more formal settings and through more organized structures than the *ad hoc* coalitions discussed

---

[35] Bowen, thesis, 31–5.
[36] NLW, MS 9059E/1172. The under-age Bulkeley heir, Richard, also appears to have lent his support to Mostyn's candidacy: NLW, MS 9059E/1186; TNA, C219/38/310.
[37] NLW, MS 9060E/1276.
[38] NLW, MS 9060E/1242.

previously.[39] The bench of justices was a particularly influential body to help determine such candidacies because it was supposed to represent all county interests, and thus embodied the notion of unanimity and consensus which was so powerful in these election negotiations.

Institutional bodies like the quarter and great sessions could thus act as powerful agencies for constructing consent at times of parliamentary elections. The common councils of some Welsh boroughs presumably acted similarly in mediating the choice of parliamentary representatives, but the picture here is much less clear through lack of evidence and because of the involvement of contributory boroughs in many constituencies. Nevertheless, the electoral histories of towns such as Denbigh and Beaumaris indicate that their corporate bodies were the dominant factor in deciding on representatives, though such councils and corporations were, of course, often dominated by local gentry figures.[40]

The kinds of pre-election manœuvring and negotiation which have been discussed were geared less towards the accumulation of a greater number of 'voices' on election day than towards avoiding a choice between candidates altogether. In March 1614 Andrew Brereton wrote to Thomas Myddleton about the various constellations of support which were emerging behind two potential MPs for Denbighshire, Henry Salusbury of Lleweni and Simon Thelwall of Plas-y-Ward. Yet perhaps his most illuminating comment was that '*if yt come to allicion* there wilbe hard tongynge, but it is thoughte Mr Salusbury will carry yt away'.[41] Even where there was a surplus of candidates for the seat, Brereton believed that the divisive process of 'allicion' was not inevitably the result; rather negotiation, agreement and brinksmanship before the event would help a 'natural' choice to emerge who could receive the assent of the community without having to be tried by the poll.

The situation was even more delicate in the county's 1625

---

[39] The Anglesey bench was also prominent in determining the 1625 election: NLW, MS 9060E/1324; C219/39/252

[40] Bowen, thesis, 36–9, 54–5.

[41] NLW, Chirk Castle F10751 (my italics). In the event, Thelwall secured the Denbighshire place without any indication of a dispute entering the record.

election, when Sir Thomas Myddleton of Chirk Castle was challenged by the prominent lawyer with local roots, Sir Euble Thelwall. The lobbying for support was vigorous and occasionally bitter, yet shortly before election day Robert Wynn of Maes Mochnant could observe: 'I conceave the Theloals when all comes to all will not stand for the elleccon'.[42] In the event, neither man backed down and both appeared before the county court on 11 May 1625. Yet what is striking here is that even at this late stage the desire for accommodation rather than confrontation prevailed, and a compromise was reached 'by the mediacon' of the sheriff, Sir Richard Grosvenor. Myddleton was elected knight while he undertook to procure the burgess seat at Melcombe Regis (where he had already been elected) for Thelwall.[43] An analogy may be made with litigants attempting to dissuade the opposing party from ever bringing an action to trial, and then settling their case at the steps of the court.

Strategies of negotiation and the formulation of networks designed to secure a parliamentary place demonstrate that unanimity and unity at parliamentary elections were far from natural or inevitable: they had to be constructed with effort and deft management. However, the emphasis on avoiding contests and polling should not blind us to the fact that Welsh elections were aggressively political events in the sense that contests over the distribution and exercise of local power, and the pre-election tactics, were geared to one end: securing the parliamentary seat for one's own interest group. The rhetorics of consent and unity were powerful political languages in the conduct of early Stuart elections, but they were ultimately only rhetorics, and the naked pursuit of power, prestige and influence was present in every parliamentary election. The discussion of elections thus far has shown that powerful impulses towards accommodation rather than confrontation were often to the fore in early modern Welsh elections. Yet not infrequently the desire for compromise failed to defuse the very real social and political tensions present in several constituencies of early Stuart Wales, and electoral contests resulted. Such contests are

[42] NLW, Chirk Castle F12837.
[43] NLW, Lleweni 760.

particularly valuable for the historian because they generate a good deal more evidence than more 'straightforward' (s)elections, though this has meant that they have tended to dominate discussions of the early modern electoral process. Intrinsically fascinating as such contests are in their descriptions of communities torn apart and of desperate efforts by the participants to secure the parliamentary place, much of their interest lies in what they reveal of what contemporaries understood to be at stake in elections, of the underlying structure of political relationships and the issues on which local societies divided.

Most obviously, contested elections were struggles for power and prestige. A parliamentary seat was the highest office to which most Welsh gentlemen could aspire, and it offered the prospect of affirming (or enhancing) a family's position in county society as well as opportunities for influence and advancement at the political centre. A spectacular contest occurred in Radnorshire in 1621 between William Vaughan of Llowes and James Price of Mynachdy: freeholders were unlawfully created, votes were solicited in church and violence was threatened by partisan supporters.[44] Ultimately, this was a contest for social primacy in the region as Price's position in the county, which he had represented in parliament since 1593, crumbled on account of financial difficulties.[45] Vaughan, however, was the rising star in Radnorshire society, and the election of 1621 essentially revolved about his efforts to eclipse Price and establish himself prominently on the county stage. This contest brought an end to the electoral dominance of the Mynachdy Prices, while Vaughan assumed the leading position of *custos* on the county bench a year later.[46] Similarly, the

---

[44] TNA, STAC8/288/9. This election has been studied by Gruenfelder, who fails adequately to contextualize the election in the history of the Vaughan–Price struggle: J. K. Gruenfelder, 'Radnorshire's parliamentary elections, 1604–1640', *Transactions of the Radnorshire Society*, 47 (1977), 25–31.

[45] TNA, STAC8/15/9; 8/288/9. At the time of the election, Vaughan claimed Price was 'a man very much indebted unto many creditors in diverse greate somes of money', and was outlawed for debt.

[46] Bowen, thesis, 68–72. The Prices of Pilleth, who were related to the Vaughans as well as to the Mynachdy branch, were prominent in the county's electoral politics down to the Long Parliament.

Haverfordwest elections of the 1620s were characterized by the struggles between Sir Thomas Canon and Sir James Perrot, two local men who were prominent figures in both borough and county government. Their dispute arose from Perrot's belief that Canon had embezzled his father, Sir John Perrot, following the latter's attainder of 1592.[47] Their clashes over the representation of Haverfordwest thus became an element in a feud over power and influence in the region which lasted into the 1630s, and was conducted in particularly bitter terms, Perrot describing Canon as 'the only professed adversarie that I knowe I have in this world'.[48] The notorious election contests between the Wynns and their rivals in Caernarfonshire throughout the 1620s were also ultimately concerned with influence and authority in county society, and developed into a complex power struggle conducted in a variety of local, regional and indeed national contexts, with the election disputes as the most visible and acrimonious theatre of conflict.

The indivisibility of government and politics in this period ensured that, as has been noted, parliamentary elections were intimately bound up with discourses of honour and reputation. Prestige was not simply an abstract quality to be cultivated by a gentleman, but was an essential facet of his local authority and power. Consequently elections were viewed as opportunities to gain local (and indeed national) standing; they also ran the danger of losing face by defeat before the community. The extensive correspondence surrounding the Caernarfonshire elections of the 1620s enables a closer examination of the manner in which reputation and honour operated as central factors in elections of this period. Here the prominent (though by no means dominant) Wynns of Gwydir saw their electoral position in the county decimated by the challenge of the Griffiths of Cefnamwlch and their allies from the western part of the

---

[47] E. G. Jones (ed.), *Exchequer Proceedings (Equity) Concerning Wales, Henry VIII–Elizabeth* (Cardiff, 1939), p. 308. Perrot also attempted to implicate Canon in the Gunpower Plot, describing him as 'the cause of all enmitie that I have had almost with any other': Hatfield House, Cecil 113/89.

[48] TNA, SP16/67/107; 14/13/7; 16/18/63; 16/19/14; 16/234/2–2(i), 31, 41, 71; 63/242/227; Bowen, thesis, 79–81.

shire. A pervasive element in their correspondence is a concentration on the idea of an election as a trial of social standing, of 'credit'. In the first notice of the 1620 election, William Wynn directed his father, Sir John, to endeavour to make his brother, Richard, knight of the shire, noting 'it standeth uppon your and his reputacon'.[49] Thomas Powell similarly wrote that, Sir John's 'credit ... lyeth att the stake' in his endeavour to secure the county place.[50] The prospect of defeat was interpreted primarily in terms of social disgrace. One of Sir John's most ardent supporters, Sir William Thomas of Caernarfon, wrote that as John Griffith of Cefnamwlch was determined to stand against Richard Wynn, Sir John should consider whether he should attempt the election at all: 'will [you] put it to the tryall or hasard yor creditt theron?'[51] Thomas also noted that if Griffith took the seat 'the whole cuntrey would crye out upon us, and oure discreditt would oute live us all'.[52] After his family's eventual defeat in 1620, Sir John Wynn stated that the business of the election had 'drawne one mee the greatest publike disgrace that ever I had in my tyme'.[53] Sir Peter Mutton of Llannerch considered standing for the county seat in 1624, but commented that 'to stand for it and to lose it, weare such a disgrace as I could not forgett in hast'.[54]

These contests, then, revolved about reputation and honour being tested before the bar of county society. Desperate strategies, such as creating freeholders or bribing and coercing officials and voters, were employed by all parties as they strove to avoid disgrace and carry the election. Discourses of honour pervaded the election process, as supporters became 'as deeplye engaged in credict' as the candidates themselves.[55] The particular significance of the contest was that this credit was tested before the wider community, before those people whom the gentry had to govern and control, and in the eyes of whom gentry honour

---

[49] NLW, MS 9057E/915.
[50] NLW, MS 9057E/916.
[51] NLW, MS 9057E/921.
[52] NLW, MS 9057E/928.
[53] NLW, MS 9057E/942.
[54] Flintshire RO, D/GW/2106; NLW, MSS 9058E/1178, 1189.
[55] NLW, Chirk Castle F12837; also NLW, MS 9057E/921.

was ultimately constructed. In 1624, for example, Owen Wynn counselled his father not to contest the county election as the county would not support them, and therefore they should not 'put our selves into their hands for matter of creditt ane [any] more'.[56] The freeholders, therefore, had a real agency in election contests by means of this concept of honour flowing from the endorsement of the wider community, even if their choice was often conditioned by the attitudes of their landlords.

Important too is the evidence which these elections provide of gentry opinions of the political sophistication of these freeholders, who were marshalled by the rival camps on the county day. Owen Wynn was scornful of the voters who appeared at the initial, abortive, Caernarfonshire election in late 1620, informing his father

> [a]s for the meaner sorte of people, the more yow see them a reason of your actions, the further yow are off & better [it] would best please them, their toungs beeing ever subiect to ... base flatterie as their blynd fancie guydes them.[57]

Sir John Wynn's own contempt for the mass of freeholders who followed John Griffith was colourfully conveyed by his comment, 'if they gayne it by a company of barefoote beggers that must borrow clothes to come to the ellection & will sweare the value of the lands more then they are, I cannot healpe it'.[58] Although freeholders gained a vital importance at times of disputed elections, there is no evidence that the candidates considered them to be politically informed or sophisticated. They were feted by both sides, and men like Thomas Powell acknowledged a capacity for some individual action, counselling in 1620 that 'it will not ... be amiss to solicit those that are either neuters, or inclining to the adverse side'; but most of the electoral computations undertaken by the Wynns were based on the view that freeholders would follow the position of their landlords.[59] Despite the fact that the Wynns were disposed to

[56] NLW, MS 9058E/1172.
[57] NLW, MS 9057E/924.
[58] NLW, MS 9057E/996.
[59] NLW, MSS 9057E/916, 921.

disparage the community which had spurned them at the hustings, there is no evidence here, or indeed in election correspondence from elsewhere in Wales, that the candidates appealed to the freeholders in any terms other than by the most basic inducements of beer and food.[60] It must also be noted that reference to canvassing freeholders and organizing support appears only to have occurred with great determination when a contested election was in the offing.

The nature of early Stuart elections has been the subject of considerable historiographical debate in recent years, with Derek Hirst and Richard Cust, on the one hand, and Mark Kishlansky, on the other, questioning the degree to which the early Stuart process was one of election or selection. Hirst and Cust suggest that the increasing number of contested elections in the early Stuart parliamentary elections encouraged a growing participation by the 'middling sort', who were becoming increasingly concerned about the political and religious inclinations of those whom they elected. The concerns of electorates thus needed to be accommodated by candidates if they were to be successful at the hustings: elections and electorates became increasingly politicized. Kishlansky, however, suggests that early Stuart elections should more properly be understood as selections, wherein social considerations generally prevailed, and the election is rendered an essentially apolitical reflection of prevailing social hierarchies.[61]

Where is Wales to be located in this debate, which has rather neglected the Welsh constituencies? Contrary to the Hirst/Cust thesis, this overview suggests that little reference was made to matters of political or religious ideology in Welsh elections. It is striking, for example, that in the Caernarfonshire contests where records are fairly plentiful, there was no reference to wider political issues current in the country at this time, and questions of the religious proclivi-

---

[60] NLW, MS 9057E/921.
[61] D. Hirst, *The Representative of the People? Voters and Voting in England under the Early Stuarts* (Cambridge, 1975); R. Cust, 'Politics and the electorate in the 1620s', in idem and A. Hughes (eds), *Conflict in Early Stuart England* (Harlow, 1989), pp. 134–67; idem, 'Election and selection in Stuart England', *Parliamentary History*, 7 (1988), 344–50; Kishlansky, *Parliamentary Selection*.

ties of a candidate or his suitability for office were rarely raised as important determinants.[62] There is an absence of a language which may be considered truly political, that is to say, concerned with national issues informed by ideological choice, whether articulated in terms of 'Court' and 'Country' polarities, religious persuasion or the election of an individual who would prove a good servant of the state.[63] John Griffith of Cefnamwlch may have endeavoured to become a follower of the controversial royal favourite, Buckingham, while the Wynn faction followed their relative John Williams, lord keeper and bishop of Lincoln, yet there is little suggestion that such loyalties derived from ideological positions rather than from the use of patronage for purposes of local superiority, and there is hardly any indication that wider ideological debates filtered down the social scale to determine voting behaviour.

This is not to say, however, that issues which were recognizably ideological were absent from all elections of this period. Cust and others have identified the centrality of anti-popery as a remarkably powerful political discourse in this period, and there are indications that some elections in Monmouthshire were informed by such issues.[64] This is perhaps not surprising in a shire where Catholicism under the protection of the earls of Worcester was so pervasive. The return of Sir William Morgan of Tredegar, a leading figure of the Protestant interests in the county, as knight in 1624 and 1625 appears to have been related to the issue of anti-popery. Morgan had quarrelled violently with Catholic elements in the county, and it is probably not coincidental that his return occurred amidst the rising tide of anti-Spanish sentiment accompanying England's entry into the Thirty Years' War. Morgan used his election to present to parliament the 'infinite number' of dangerous recusants in

---

[62] J. K. Gruenfelder, 'The Wynns of Gwydir and parliamentary elections in Wales, 1604–1640', *WHR*, 9 (1978–9), 121.

[63] Cf. Cust, 'Electorate', pp. 138–58; idem and P. Lake, 'Sir Richard Grosvenor and the rhetoric of magistracy,' *Bulletin of the Institute of Historical Research*, 54 (1981), 48–50.

[64] Cust, 'Electorate'; P. Lake, 'Anti-popery: the structure of a prejudice', in Cust and Hughes, *Conflict*, pp. 72–106.

Monmouthshire.[65] The increasing religious and political tensions of the early 1640s also appear to have generated a more ideologically driven choice in the region's elections. The Long Parliament (1640) return of William Watkins for Monmouth boroughs appears to have been, in part, configured by a confrontation between the two most powerful magnates of the area, the Protestant Philip, fourth earl of Pembroke, and the Catholic Henry, fifth earl of Worcester. Lines of division were clearer at a by-election in the county in March 1642 caused by the death of the incumbent, Charles Williams of Llangibby. Henry Herbert of Coldbrook, a future parliamentarian and ally of Pembroke, was challenged by Sir Nicholas Kemeys, a future commissioner of array, at an election which took place in a period after the Irish Rebellion when the county began to divide along religious fault lines. Similarly, the intrusion of the Protestant Sir John Price of Newtown into the representation of Montgomeryshire in November 1640, after exclusion from the county's political community since 1629 by the crypto-Catholic Herberts of Powis, suggests an ideological edge to the electoral process.[66] The contest between Sir James Perrot and Sir Thomas Canon, meanwhile, was a confrontation between one of the most militant puritans in early Stuart Wales and a man alleged to have Catholic sympathies, though there is no direct evidence that this was ever an issue at the hustings.

Issues of principle and ideology could play a role at elections, then, but the striking aspect remains the remarkably small number of instances where such considerations can be identified. The lord president of the Council in the Marches of Wales, Ralph Eure, wrote of Monmouthshire in 1609 that 'few causes arise in the shire which are not made a question betwixt the Protestant and the recusant', yet what is surprising is that the confessional divide intruded so infrequently into electoral politics there.[67] Associates of the house

[65] TNA, STAC8/207/24, 28–32; J. Hawarde, *Les Reportes Del Cases in Camera Stellata, 1593–1609*, ed. W. P. Baildon (1894), pp. 312–15; NLW, Tredegar Park 93/51.
[66] Bowen, thesis, 16–18, 23–5, 481–93.
[67] TNA, SP14/48/121.

of Herbert such as Sir Edmund Morgan of Penhow and Nicholas Arnold of Llanthony were returned alongside Worcester nominees like Thomas Somerset. Indeed, it would appear that it was only under the pressures of civil war that electoral politics here genuinely came to display an ideological character. Moreover, although some historians have portrayed the elections to the Short and Long Parliaments of 1640 as a 'new world', characterized by the vigorous expression of anti-Court sentiment, the situation in Wales appears markedly different, with little evidence of such political engagement at the hustings. The electoral contest in Caernarfonshire in November 1640, for example, remained essentially a factional dispute with no discernible ideological flavour.[68] Such findings tend to support the Kishlansky thesis of elections being events principally concerned with issues of reputation rather than of political beliefs. Yet we must also acknowledge that normative discourses of Protestantism and service were probably in operation at many elections, and that their very commonplaceness meant that they did not find their way into the historical record. Very few potential recusant MPs can be identified, and it is likely that the Protestant credentials of candidates were important in seeing them returned. In the more than 250 elections held in Wales in this period, hardly any overt reference to such issues can be traced, which suggests that genuine ideological division rarely intruded into the Welsh election process.

In noting this relative absence of ideological conflict, it is inadequate to conclude that the country was simply uninformed about current political issues. This was patently not the case. Rather it would appear that the most divisive issues in the elections of the 1620s and 1640 in many parts of England simply were not experienced in Wales with the same vigour and immediacy, a theme pursued at greater length in Chapters 3–5. The burdens of war during the 1620s in Wales, though they were heavy, were not on the scale

---

[68] A. H. Dodd, 'Caernarvonshire elections to the Long Parliament', *BBCS*, 12 (1948), 44–6; idem, 'The Caernarvonshire election dispute and its sequel', *BBCS*, 14 (1950), 42–5.

experienced in most of England. Perhaps more importantly, the electoral patronage of the controversial duke of Buckingham was almost wholly absent from Wales, though it was an element which has been seen as important in generating political conflict in many parts of England. It is also difficult to detect an increase in the political temperature in Wales in reaction to the policies of Charles I's personal rule. Crucially, although Protestant, the Welsh possessed a rather conservative religious outlook, with puritanism making little headway before the 1640s. This meant that the vehement anti-popery which informed many elections in England during the 1620s and 1640 remained largely absent from the Welsh experience, with only the prominence of Catholic aristocrats in Montgomeryshire and Monmouthshire apparently generating confessional conflict in Welsh electoral politics. This is also significant for discussions of the nature of electorates in this period, for Richard Cust has argued that the stress on individual choice in elections and the ideologically motivated engagement of the freeholders were particularly associated with puritanism, a very weak force in early Stuart Wales.[69]

We should be wary, however, of concluding that Welsh elections were sub-political events without any broader meaning. Rather it may be argued that the insights of Cust and Hirst can be integrated with Kishlansky's emphasis on elections as primarily social events based on notions of honour and credit to form a more satisfying picture. Hirst's stress on the role of the electorate is a key in acknowledging the sense of duty and obligation which emerged in an election.[70] Although Hirst suggests that it was an expanding electorate which generated such obligations, this does not appear to have been as influential in Wales as elsewhere,[71] whilst acknowledging the centrality of gentry honour in the

[69] Cust, 'Electorate', pp. 137–9, 151–3, 161–2.
[70] Hirst, *Representative*. See also Russell, *Parliaments*, pp. 1–84; D. L. Smith, *The Stuart Parliaments, 1603–1689* (1999), pp. 26–31.
[71] This is not to deny that there were some large electorates, in excess of 800 in Radnorshire (1621) and 1,000 in Caernarfonshire (1621), yet there is little evidence that these acted independently of the gentry factions seeking election to parliament: TNA, STAC8/288/9; NLW, MS 9057E/921.

electoral process allows us to acknowledge this sense of accountability even when no reference is made to a large body of freeholders.[72] This is particularly the case when it is remembered that such discourses of honour were strongest among the political elite in Welsh constituencies. Indeed, where the election was determined among a small body of gentlemen who were usually the social equals and neighbours of a candidate, and to whom he was allied by bonds of kinship, it may be expected that the sense of obligation to represent this modest electorate was even greater than in an area where a wider franchise of lower social standing was involved. This was something reflected in contemporary bardic poetry addressed to gentry patrons, wherein the emphasis was placed on MPs as guardians of their constituency's interests.[73]

Such obligations to this relatively limited group emerge from the surviving Welsh election correspondence. In December 1639, Robert Ravenscroft wrote to Robert Davies requesting assistance for his friends at the Flintshire election, and promised 'you shall ever find me redy to doo you servis with my love'.[74] These were not mere platitudes, but genuine expressions of the ties to the small community which exercised effective political power. This idea of communality was a powerful one, and could even transcend the bitter disputes of the Caernarfonshire election in 1620. On that occasion Sir John Wynn could write to his son: 'tell the country when they are assembled that we are all countrymen & frends & soe must remayne. Though devided in this matter in oppinion, we ought not to give one another cause of offence or greivance.'[75]

The sense of obligation which was invested in the concept of community may also be seen in a candidate's expression of his desire to discharge a duty to the 'country'. In April 1625, Thomas Mostyn asked Robert Davies for his support in

---

[72] See the comments in D. M. Dean, *Law-Making and Society in Late Elizabethan England: The Parliament of England, 1584–1601* (Cambridge, 1996), pp. 14–15.
[73] J. G. Jones, *Concepts of Order and Gentility in Wales, 1540–1640* (Llandysul, 1992), pp. 178–9.
[74] Flintshire RO, D/GW/2119.
[75] NLW, MS 9057E/932.

gaining the Flintshire seat, and promised that he was 'ready to doe the office of an honest man for my country'.[76] In the same year, Sir Thomas Myddleton described his desire 'to doe my countrye a service' in standing for the Denbighshire place, while John Griffith was more expansive in a letter of November 1620 to Sir William Maurice, commenting 'you knowe best the experience yt is obtained by beeinge of a parliament & what every true lover of his countrie shold endeavoure to doe service ther'.[77] There was manifestly a sense of accountability to the 'country' inherent in an election, but there is no indication that the term was applied with the godly ideological implications it acquired in some other contexts during this period.[78] Rather did 'country' appear to refer to the locality, and more particularly to the political classes there and the honour which was to be gained by serving them faithfully.[79] In 1640/1, for example, Charles Price, MP for Radnorshire, refused to present a petition of grievances to the House of Commons because he claimed that it was subscribed by two men who were 'none of my country'. He did, however, promise to 'write to the justices & gentlemen of the countye by whom I was trusted, that they would certifye me from their next session whether or noe they desired that those articles should be presented'.[80] To suggest that such rhetoric was largely devoid of the ideological, confessional edge it acquired elsewhere is not to reduce Welsh elections to a kind of blind apolitical localism. Rather does such evidence suggest how service and obligations to electorates and localities constituted a central element in the political culture of Welsh elections and helped to influence the actions of the member at Westminster.

---

[76] Flintshire RO, D/GW/2109.
[77] NLW, MS 9060E/1315; NLW, Brogyntyn (Clenennau) 398. See also Griffith's comments in his petition to the king against the bishop of Bangor after the 1626 parliament, when he claimed to be acting 'in further dischardge of his duety to that county for which hee did serve': NA, SP16/30/8.
[78] For the use of 'country' as an ideological construct in opposition to 'court' values, see Cust and Hughes (eds), *Conflict*, pp. 19–21, 140–3, 145–59.
[79] For the use of 'country' rhetoric devoid of the overtones of godly Protestantism, see Atherton, *Scudamore*, pp. 262–4.
[80] BL, Add. 70,003, fos 132ᵛ–33. Price did not present the petition, claiming 'I sent into the county, but the country never certified me that I should proceede'.

Such notions of responsibility can also be discerned in elections for borough seats. Sir Hugh Myddleton, for example, though he was elected for Denbigh in every parliament between 1604 and 1628, took his responsibilities of representing the town's interests on a wider stage very seriously. A letter of 3 February 1614 relates to his election for the borough, and illustrates the bonds by which the election tied him to the town. He wrote to the corporation that

> noe burgis of Denbighe shalbe more forward & willinge then myselfe to further any good for the towne, and I take yt very frindlie that yow will imploye mee in any businesse that may tende to the publicke or privatt good of that towne.[81]

Such correspondence fits well with Hirst's analysis that the emphasis in many elections was to alight upon a man who would 'bring home the local goods'.[82] Revealingly, Myddleton also wrote to the town's authorities while attending this parliament, outlining the obligations he believed to have been placed upon him by his election. He assured them that he wished to use his office to 'doe the towne good in generall, or anie of yow in particuler', and protested 'yf I weare assured anie man ment as mutch good to the towne as I doe and would gaine noe more by the place, then I woulde upon the least request from yow surrender the place againe with thankes'.[83] Of course, a good deal of this was rhetorical nicety and convention, but the very fact that these letters were written using a language of service and community demonstrates the importance of such concepts in the relationship established between a representative and his constituency.

This does not mean that such members were to a man active agents for their constituents at Westminster. The obscurity and lassitude of the majority of Welsh MPs in the House are testimony to this, though perhaps their inaction is a reflection of the paucity of agenda requiring parliamentary action issuing from most Welsh constituencies. The available evidence indicates that the Welsh electorate did

---

[81] Denbighshire RO, BD/A/22.
[82] Hirst, *Representative*, p. 160.
[83] Denbighshire RO, BD/A/23.

not elect (or reject) their representatives on the basis of their connections with the Court or with favourites, or according to their ideological/religious predilections. There was something of a *via media* in Wales between the positions promoted by Hirst and Cust, on the one hand, and Kishlansky, on the other. Although it is likely that the Protestant credentials of a candidate were an essential element in most elections, there is very little evidence that the religious tensions of the early Stuart period became central issues at anything more than a handful of elections in Wales. The numbers which determined elections were (normally) relatively small and contests were rare, but nonetheless obligations were imposed upon a candidate by virtue of the social relationships which secured his election. There is little evidence to suggest that the larger numbers who participated in contested elections – as in Caernarfonshire – were truly independent or motivated by ideological concerns, but we should acknowledge their significance as the community which conferred that vital element of honour (or dishonour) upon candidates. This complex and multifaceted concept of honour was the essential component of all elections, and was articulated in the languages of reciprocity, service and obligation. These obligations will be considered more fully in the next chapter which explores the connection between electors and elected through an analysis of the business undertaken by Welsh MPs at Westminster.

2
WELSH PARLIAMENTARY BUSINESS, 1604–1629

Parliamentary elections established an important bond between electors and elected which was forged from notions of honour and obligation. 'Service' was a recurring theme in the correspondence of many Welsh parliamentary candidates, suggesting that elections could engender a sense of responsibility in the elected to represent their localities and interest groups in parliament. It is notable that in several elections preferences were expressed for the return of local men who knew the constituency and were felt to be able to represent its interests on the wider stage. At the meeting of the Anglesey justices to decide upon their choice of MP in December 1623, for example, it was noted that, although the candidacy of the Flintshire gentleman, John Mostyn, would be endorsed, Sir Sackvill Trevor's status as one 'dwelling in the cowntrey & one of them' meant that if he showed an interest in the place, he 'must be prefered before a stranger'.[1] As with the majority of English members, Welsh MPs were not particularly active in parliament, often on account of the lack of any legislative agenda emanating from their constituents. Additionally, 'accountability' in this period was understood to be an informal relationship based on honour, and not simply the mandating of a programme of action to be undertaken in parliament. Nevertheless, business which affected Wales and the Welsh did come before the parliaments of 1604–29, and this forms the focus of this chapter.[2] An examination of such business offers new perspectives on Welsh parliamentary activity under the early Stuarts, and further reveals the nature of the bonds which existed between a Welsh MP and his constituency. It

---

[1] NLW, MS 9059E/1172.
[2] This chapter is limited to the early Stuart parliaments before those which met in the markedly different political circumstances of 1640, when the pursuit of legislative business took on a rather different complexion.

acknowledges the Eltonian and Russellian emphasis on parliament as a legislative institution, and seeks to extend this by considering the motivations, contexts and ways in which legislation (both successful and unsuccessful) was initiated and prosecuted by Welsh members, and places parliament in a broader social context.

Unlike the work of A. H. Dodd, which concentrated largely on Welsh involvement in high politics and constitutional issues, the analysis offered here suggests that matters of a more parochial nature constituted a part of the parliamentary experience of Welsh MPs which was considered to be at least as important as questions of policy. Drawing on recent scholarship on the broader context of parliamentary business, this chapter also suggests that parliament in the early Stuart era provided a forum in which distinct Welsh interests, or 'lobbies', pursued their particular agendas.[3] Such groupings appear as much more ephemeral and of a quite different nature from Dodd's conception of a Welsh 'party' in the Commons. They differed considerably in their nature, scale and degree of organization, but all of them utilized parliament as one arena in which to promote or defend their interests. Within this framework the constituency can be considered as such a 'lobby', and this chapter examines some of the occasions when Welsh representatives promoted constituency concerns in parliament and which help to illustrate the nature of the ties between member and constituency, locality and centre. Closely related are issues which affected local economies, such as the disputes over Welsh cottons and Welsh butter in the 1620s, which prompted action at Westminster.

Other matters which demand attention in an examination of the nature of Welsh involvement in these parliaments

---

[3] D. M. Dean, 'Parliament and locality', in idem and N. L. Jones (eds), *The Parliaments of Elizabethan England* (1990), pp. 139–62; idem, 'Pressure groups and lobbies in the Elizabethan and early Jacobean parliaments', *Parliaments, Estates and Representation*, 11 (1991), 139–52. See also Russell, *Parliaments*; C. R. Kyle, '*Lex loquens*: legislation in the parliament of 1624' (Ph.D. thesis, Auckland University, 1994); idem, 'Parliament and the politics of carting in early Stuart London', *London Journal*, 27 (2002), 1–11; D. Scott, '"Particular businesses" in the Long Parliament: the Hull letters, 1644–1648', in C. R. Kyle (ed.), *Parliaments, Politics and Elections, 1604–1648* (Camden Soc., 5th series 17, 2001), pp. 272–341.

include those that promoted discussion of Wales's relationship with the wider British polity. Although the issues of the Anglo-Scottish union and the jurisdiction of the Council in the Marches did not have a specifically Welsh origin, they addressed fundamental questions about Wales's place in the 'Britain' which James I sought to create. These matters also stimulated debate on a provision of the union legislation which allowed the king to make laws for Wales without reference to parliament; there is some evidence of the construction of a Welsh 'lobby' in parliament to promote the repeal of this legislation. The British context, therefore, provided another dimension in which Welsh politics could operate at Westminster.

Thus, discrete interests from Wales could coexist in parliament and they attempted to use the institution in a variety of ways. It is important to note, however, that these interests were informal and transitory phenomena. Unlike the organized lobbies which promoted parliamentary business, such as the London companies, many of the interest groups envisaged here were the products of particular circumstances and in a sense were shaped by events. The issue of purveyance, for instance, produced an alliance of interest among the Welsh members in 1604 which promoted concerted action. However, it is difficult to believe that a formal organization against the levy could have been framed by Welsh members before their arrival in Westminster, simply because of the geography of the Welsh constituencies and the poor state of communications in Wales. Despite the limitations of grappling with often ephemeral groups which were the product of shifting contingencies, such an approach allows the politics of Welsh representation to be better understood.

Locality and legislation

One of the main contributions of the revisionist reassessment of early Stuart parliamentary politics has been to bring the role of the MP as an advocate for his constituency more sharply into focus. This contrasts with Dodd's highly influential thesis portraying the Welsh members as an ineffectual and inexperienced group serving a parliamentary 'apprenticeship' down to 1625.[4] Dodd's concentration on the high politics of Tudor and Stuart parliaments meant that his account gave such lesser local Welsh issues little importance. However, this and the following section illustrate how constituency interests in Wales were able to use parliament in order to address specific local grievances, demonstrating that Welsh members were apprised of the procedures and opportunities afforded by parliaments and could use them to advance the concerns of their constituents.

A particular local grievance concerned the bridge over the River Wye at Chepstow between Monmouthshire and Gloucestershire; in 1603 it collapsed. The bridge had been the subject of an Elizabethan act which made the two shires jointly responsible for its upkeep, and also provided for a fine on JPs if they defaulted in collecting assessments for the necessary repairs.[5] The measure was potentially divisive in that it made two separate county jurisdictions responsible for the bridge, and disagreement did indeed emerge after the collapse. In January 1604 the Gloucestershire hundred of Berkeley made a representation to the county bench in which it refused to contribute to the rebuilding of the bridge. It stated that the Gloucestershire half of the bridge was well maintained at the county's charge while Monmouthshire's side had been 'very weake & much decayed' and caused the collapse.[6] Such accusations and disputes across administrative boundaries were extremely difficult to resolve, especially when the levying of rates for reconstruction and maintenance was involved. Indeed, Sir Francis Bacon in 1604 wrote that the collapse occasioned 'great trowble & hindrance' in the country, and that the matter was being prosecuted at the Council in the Marches in an action of liability and recovery of the costs of repair.[7] The nature of this dispute made it particularly apt for

---

[4] Dodd, 'Apprenticeship'. This is perpetuated in G. R. Elton, 'Wales in parliament, 1542–1581', in his *Studies in Tudor and Stuart Politics and Government* (Cambridge, 1992), iv, pp. 91–108. However, see L. Bowen, 'Wales at Westminster: parliament, principality and pressure groups, 1542–1601', *Parliamentary History*, 22 (2003), 107–20.
[5] *SR*, iv, p. 629.
[6] Gloucester Public Library, MS 16,524, fo. 30.
[7] BL, Add. 64,934, fo. 22; also TNA, SP14/10A/86.

consideration by parliament since both interests could be represented and a decision could be made that would bind all concerned; it is perhaps not surprising, therefore, that the issue came before the Commons during the 1606 parliamentary session.

The initiative came from the Gloucestershire members, and a bill was introduced on 31 January 1606 whose purpose was the repeal of the Elizabethan act.[8] That this was a Gloucestershire initiative seems clear from the Berkeley representation of 1604 that rebuilding the bridge should be deferred until the next parliament, when 'by some good means order may be had that the inhabitantes of this countye shall be no otherwise charged to & with the same bridge then they were before the making of the said [Elizabethan] statute'.[9] The measure appears to have run into stiff opposition, however, probably from the Monmouthshire MPs, who would surely have wished Gloucestershire's contributions to continue; it was rejected at its second reading on 8 February.[10]

An altogether more constructive measure was introduced on 25 March 1606: a bill for the restoration and repair of Chepstow Bridge.[11] The final act indicates that it was a private bill, introduced in petitionary form from 'the inhabitants of the greatest parte of south Wales'.[12] It was committed after a second reading, but the debate in committee was far from straightforward as might be expected from a body which included the knights and burgesses of south Wales as well as the Gloucestershire MPs who were keen to avoid the costs of repair.[13] The lawyer, Mathew Davies, MP for Cardiff, who was probably the committee's chairman, reported the bill to the House on 11 April 1606.[14] There had been objections in committee to the bill's

[8] *CJ*, p. 262.
[9] Gloucester Public Library, MS 16,524, fo. 30.
[10] *CJ*, p. 265.
[11] Ibid., p. 288.
[12] *SR*, iv, p. 1098. The Elizabethan statute was similarly framed; see Elton, 'Wales in parliament', p. 97.
[13] *CJ*, p. 291. William Wiseman objected that the bill had been altered radically in committee: D. H. Willson (ed.), *The Parliamentary Diary of Robert Bowyer, 1606–1607* (Minneapolis, 1931), p. 117.
[14] *CJ*, p. 296.

original form for he noted amendments which had been offered there. The division of opinion now transferred to the floor of the House as the Monmouth member, Sir Robert Johnson, spoke against the revised bill and offered a proviso relating to Monmouth town. It seems clear that Johnson was attempting to obtain for his own constituency an exemption from the costs of making and repairing a new bridge.[15] Johnson's intervention is better understood in the light of a debate on the building and repairing of bridges during the 1614 parliament. Here again he moved for a proviso for Monmouth, asking that the town 'might be exempted from helping to maintain other bridges, since it maintained five at their own charge'.[16] A Welsh representative was advocating the interests of his constituents, and it is interesting that Johnson was actually a Buckinghamshire man, though he clearly felt obliged to defend the interests of those who had elected him. In the event, Johnson's proviso was defeated and Monmouth was made as accountable in the final statute as were all other parts of Monmouthshire.

The bill proceeded to the Lords, where it was closely associated with the earl of Worcester, who reported it from committee with some amendments. Worcester was lord of Chepstow, including the borough, and was evidently interested in a matter of local concern.[17] The bill returned to the Commons where it apparently had the support of a well-organized group since the Lords' amendments were considered on the very day of its transmission to the Lower House.[18] The parliamentary diarist, Robert Bowyer, noted that these were 'small amendements' concerning the courts in which fines for non-payment towards repair could be recovered.[19] However, this issue was seized on by Sir Roger

[15] Similarly, when a bill for the bridge at Newport, Monmouthshire, was presented to parliament in the 1590s, it ran into difficulties when a proviso was added which excluded contributions from other towns in the county: D. M. Dean, *Law-Making and Society in Late Elizabethan England: The Parliament of England, 1584–1601* (Cambridge, 1996), p. 240.

[16] M. Jansson, (ed.), *Proceedings in Parliament, 1614 (House of Commons)* (Philadelphia, 1989), p. 174.

[17] *LJ*, ii, pp. 424, 425; J. A. Bradney, *A History of Monmouthshire* (1904–33), iv, p. 12.

[18] *CJ*, p. 305.

[19] Willson, *Bowyer*, p. 149. The Lords' amendments were written on paper and

Owen, the member for Shropshire, who wished the phrasing in the bill 'or any court of equity' to have the additional phrase 'at Westminster' appended.[20] Owen was one of those who opposed the jurisdiction of the Council in the Marches over the four English border shires, and his objective was clearly understood by Bowyer, who noted that by this 'he would exclude the iurisdiction' of the Council.[21] The bill's sponsors in the Commons did not wish to lose the measure as a result of wrangling on this wider issue, and mustered enough support to reject Owen's suggestion and have the Lords' amendments inserted, thereby allowing the bill's progress into law.[22] The resulting statute noted the deficiencies of the Elizabethan act in providing for the upkeep of the bridge at the heart of this dispute, and established a more practicable system for maintaining the structure in future.[23]

This bill's passage reveals how Welsh constituencies could look to parliament to remedy difficulties and defend their interests. Significantly, it appears that, after presentation of the initial bill by the Gloucestershire representatives for repeal of the Elizabethan act, counter-measures were promoted by a group of south Wales MPs. This is perhaps not surprising when it is remembered that the bridge supported a crucial trade route to south Wales, described in the act's preamble as the 'meetest and moste necessary passage and highway leading into the parts of South wales and out of the same to London, Bristol and other parts of England'.[24] This suggests that distinct regional Welsh

are still attached to the body of the act: House of Lords RO, Original Acts, 3 James I, c. 23.

[20] Willson, *Bowyer*, p. 149.

[21] Ibid. The Elizabethan statute had made the Council in the Marches of Wales the only place where actions could be moved against JPs who defaulted on repair payments. Its substitution by the Court of Chancery 'or any other courte of equity' in the Jacobean act is indicative of how the Lords wished to avoid any potential dispute over the contentious issue of the Council's status.

[22] Ibid.; *CJ*, p. 305. There is no evidence to support Dodd's assertion that Owen was overruled by the speaker: Dodd, 'Apprenticeship', 34.

[23] *SR*, iv, pp. 1098–1100. An account of August 1608 shows a collection was made in several Monmouthshire hundreds towards the 'rebuilding of the Chepstowe Bridge': NLW, Badminton 959; see also Badminton 1230. Money was also evidently forthcoming from the Gloucestershire side: *CD1621*, iv, p. 307.

[24] For the importance of the bridges for trade in Monmouthshire, see also Huntington Library, Ellesmere 7420

coalitions could combine on such issues in parliament in order to defend the interests of their constituencies, particularly when their commercial welfare was threatened. Especially noteworthy is Johnson's advocacy of Monmouth's exemption from local taxation in 1604 and 1614, demonstrating that, even when members were not natives of their constituencies, they nevertheless might feel obligated to promote their constituents' interests in the Commons.

Such local business could be discharged more easily when a competent man was directing it, when the measure had broad support in both Houses or when there was a powerful lobbying force involved. The 1614 bill providing for twenty almshouses, a preacher and a schoolmaster in Monmouth out of the bequest of William Jones, a wealthy member of the London Haberdashers' Company, apparently possessed all these elements, but failed to become law along with all other measures in the abortive 'Addled Parliament'. William Jones bequeathed some £6,000 towards this charitable work (which was augmented by another £3,000 in his will), and the Haberdashers' Company, which was administering the donation, sought to ensure this bequest by legislation. The bill introduced into parliament in 1614 was principally designed to secure their purchase of the manor of Hatcham Barnes in Kent from Sir John Brooke, which was to generate funds for the upkeep of the school. The purchase was subject to mortmain legislation as it involved the alienation of property for establishing a charity, however, and it thus required a royal licence to complete; this explains why the cause in parliament was vigorously prosecuted by the vendor of Hatcham Barnes, Sir John Brooke.[25] The bill garnered support from Welsh members such as Mathew Davies, and recognition of its wider interest may be seen in the nomination of all the Welsh MPs to the committee considering it.[26] It also had an active sponsor in the Lords in the person of the earl of Worcester, steward of the manor of Monmouth,

---

[25] Guildhall Library, 15842/1, fos 181^v–88; 15874, fos 198–224; House of Lords RO, Main Papers, 23 May 1614; I. Archer, *The History of the Haberdashers' Company* (Chichester, 1991), pp. 72–82.
[26] *CJ*, pp. 478, 486, 492, 493.

who expedited its progress in the Upper House.[27] Despite this assemblage of impressive support and effort, the bill failed to become law because of the parliament's 'sudden dissolucon'.[28] The bill's fate demonstrates one of the difficulties in obtaining redress for local issues in early Stuart parliaments, namely, that the institution was very ineffective in actually passing such measures.[29] The number of private bills promoted was considerable, and unless an assiduous and well-connected promoter could be found, any prospective bill was likely to fall victim to delays and, ultimately, dissolution. Despite these difficulties, however, individuals in Wales and their MPs were evidently prepared to seek local redress in parliament when the opportunity presented itself.

An episode which reflects such hopes of parliamentary action and the pursuit of resolution in other arenas when frustrated at Westminster is provided by the representations made by the burgesses of Harlech, in Merioneth, to Sir William Maurice of Clenennau in 1604–6. Maurice was not the county's MP and sat for Caernarfonshire. He was, however, one of the most significant landowners in Merioneth and lived only a short distance from Harlech, whose burgesses addressed him when they wanted their case heard at Westminster.[30] In a letter of 12 March 1604, shortly before the parliament began, the burgesses wrote to Maurice 'concerneinge the buysynes to be done for them at the parliament'.[31] They asked him to 'make mocon that the sessions to be holden for the county of Merioneth may be, by act of parliament, kept allwayes at the sayd towne'.[32] If

[27] *LJ*, ii, pp. 711–12; HMC, *Hastings MSS*, iv, p. 273. Worcester's son was party to the sale of land upon which the almshouses and school were to be erected: Guildhall Library, 15874, fos 216–20.
[28] Guildhall Library, 15842/1, fo. 188. The exemption from mortmain legislation was secured by letters patent in November 1614: TNA, C66/2022/9.
[29] Russell, *Parliaments*, pp. 36–8.
[30] It may be significant that the county MP, Sir Edward Herbert, was a Montgomeryshire man who had fairly tenuous ties with the constituency.
[31] NLW, Brogyntyn (Clenennau) 205.
[32] A later petition revealed that the town had 'lately fallen into great decaye and povertye by reason that the great sessions holden for the ... county, which were usually heretofore kept within the sayd towne, be nowe of late yeres kept in other places of the ... shyre, to the greate and utter undoeinge of us': TNA, SP14/43/59; see also SP14/44/30, 30(i). Harlech had been lobbying for the sessions since at least 1592: HMC, *Salisbury MSS*, xiii, pp. 467–8.

Maurice were successful, the burgesses declared themselves 'contented to reward him for his paynes'. Written along the side of the letter was an additional request: 'that whereas there is noe burgise for the parliament for the townes in Merioneth, that you procure that for this shire as it is in all shires throwe Ingland & Wales'.

Evidently Maurice attempted to meet these requests, the Harlech burgesses writing to him in London on 6 June 1604 and entreating him to 'contynewe your suet for us', whilst offering a more tangible inducement of £100 'within one half a yere after the obteyninge of the saed Acte of Parliament'.[33] Despite the obvious preparation and the potential rewards, nothing was heard in either House of any measure approximating those outlined by the burgesses. It may well be that Maurice offered a bill to parliament but that it never reached a first reading. Maurice's commitment to the scheme, however, can be seen in his backing of new initiatives in 1609 to bring the sessions to Harlech by lobbying the lord president of the Council in the Marches (and new constable of Harlech), Ralph Eure, and other privy councillors on the town's behalf.[34] The town's petition for the great and quarter sessions to be brought to Harlech eventually was granted by signet letter in June 1609.[35] The Harlech case illustrates the important point that parliament was only one arena in which such business could be pursued. The law courts, the Privy Council and the Court were all potential sites of influence and action which could be approached in addition to, and often concurrently with, the periodic national parliaments. Given the obstacles to enacting a bill successfully and the presence of these other agencies, it is perhaps surprising that communities in Wales looked to parliament at all. Yet the particular attraction of legislation was its supremacy and its omnicompetence as the highest form of law against which there could be no appeal

---

[33] W. W. E. W[ynne], 'Documents relating to the town of Harlech', *Archaeologia Cambrensis*, 1 (1846), 254–5. They reminded him of their suit again shortly before he left for the third session of the parliament in November 1606: NLW, Brogyntyn (Clenennau) 224.

[34] NLW, Brogyntyn (Clenennau) 252–3, 465; TNA, SP14/43/58; Wynne 'Harlech', 259.

[35] TNA, SO3/4, unfol.

short of repeal, and which could override thorny legal issues whose resolution in the courts would be expensive and time-consuming.[36]

Rather different initiatives lay behind another local Welsh bill introduced in the last two parliaments of the 1620s, with an unusual blend of governmental and private interests seeking the ultimate sanction of statute. It concerned the lordship of Bromfield and Yale, a Crown possession in Denbighshire, and the concerns of its tenants about the security of their estates. After the lordship was granted to Prince Charles in 1617 and annexed to the principality of Wales, a survey by John Norden provided grounds for the prince's revenue commissioners to challenge the tenants' agreement with Elizabeth I on the status of their lands. The tenants claimed that the prince's commissioners had imposed 'arbitrarie' fines, and if an individual refused their terms, s/he would find his or her lands granted elsewhere.[37] Sensing the opportunity for profit, the Crown regranted the lordship in 1625 to commissioners who were empowered to take a composition from the tenants for the purchase of the fee farm, settling on a figure of twenty-five years' rent, or £10,000.[38] In the negotiations for this composition, the tenants agreed to compound 'upon promise of an act of parliament' to confirm the 1625 patent empowering the commissioners to grant the fee farm, thus enabling the tenants to acquire 'good and clear title' to the land.[39] The initiative for bills introduced in 1626 and 1628, therefore, came from the Denbighshire tenants, though the Crown was intimately involved, and the final act was framed 'at the humble suite and peticion of your ... subjects'. This is

[36] G. R. Elton, *The Parliament of England, 1559–1581* (Cambridge, 1986), pp. 32–9.

[37] TNA, LR2/60, fos 55, 60^{r-v}; C66/2099; E101/527/1; *SR*, v, pp. 31–2; Flintshire RO, D/G/3341, 3343; A. N. Palmer and E. Owen, *A History of Ancient Tenures of Land in Wales and the Marches* (2nd edn, Wrexham, 1910), pp. 211–12; J. Y. W. Lloyd (ed.), 'Survey of the lordship of Bromfield and Yale', *Original Documents (Archaeologia Cambrensis Supplement)* (1877).

[38] TNA, SP14/165/69; Flintshire RO, D/G/3344; NLW, Duchy of Cornwall D6; E. Curll, *The Life of ... Robert Price* (1734), pp. 24–5; R. W. Hoyle, '"Shearing the hog": the reform of the estates, *c*.1598–1640', in idem (ed.), *The Estates of the English Crown, 1558–1640* (Cambridge, 1992), p. 255.

[39] *CD1628*, ii, pp. 574, 577.

supported by a petition submitted by the tenants to parliament which stated that 'for the quietinge of their estates' they were 'humble suitors to this honourable house for an act of confirmacon'.[40]

The Crown's own interest in giving statutory authority to the 1625 grant probably gave the lordship's tenants a particular advantage in the parliamentary arena, and some official backing may be discerned in the fact that the bill of 1626 was introduced in the Lords rather than in the Commons.[41] Its promoter was probably a legal adviser to the Lords, Sir Thomas Trevor, scion of the leading Denbighshire house of Trevalyn, a member of Prince Charles's council and one of the commissioners entrusted with the conveyance of the Bromfield and Yale lands.[42] The bill's appearance in the Lords does not mean, however, that we should simply consider it to have become an 'official' measure, for it was viewed as a private bill and MPs supported it because it was desired so passionately by the lordship's tenantry.[43] Although the measure failed to become law because of an early dissolution, several local figures were associated with it, including Sir Euble Thelwall, MP for Denbighshire, and Sir Peter Mutton, a lawyer and native Denbighshire man, while all the knights and burgesses of Wales were nominated to the committee, as were two Welsh judges.[44] Despite its failure, the bill was reintroduced in 1628, probably by the earl of Bridgwater, steward of the lordship. After passing rapidly through the Lords, it was considered by a Commons committee which resembled closely that appointed in 1626, with the lawyer MP for Denbighshire, Sir Euble Thelwall, as its first-named member, possibly the chairman.[45] The bill ran into some difficulties, however, because objections were raised that it was improperly drafted and, more damagingly, that it alienated the king's lands when contemporary

---

[40] Flintshire RO, D/G/3343; see also NLW, Edward Owen Deeds 39.
[41] *LJ*, iii, p. 574.
[42] Dodd, 'Parliaments, 1625–1629', 31; *DWB*, p. 982; Flintshire RO, D/G/3345.
[43] *CD1628*, ii, pp. 567, 573–5, 576–7.
[44] *LJ*, iii, pp. 574–5, 631; *CJ*, pp. 861, 865; *PP1626*, iii, p. 346.
[45] *LJ*, iii, pp. 701, 703, 710; *CJ*, p. 880; *CD1628*, ii, p. 383; NLW, Duchy of Cornwall P10.

thought stressed that he should live off his own estates rather than tax the people to raise funds.[46] Thelwall defended the bill, as did Sir Edward Littleton, MP for Caernarfon and second justice of north Wales, and Sir Walter Pye, judge of the Brecon circuit. Although some difficulties necessitated the drafting of a new bill to assuage fears about changing the status of royal lands, it commanded enough support to pass into law.[47]

The Bromfield and Yale bill is especially interesting for its mixture of private and royal interest. It again demonstrates the willingness of a Welsh local interest group to obtain the security of statute law, although they were probably encouraged in this by the knowledge that powerful Court elements would support the measure in parliament. Especially noteworthy is the evidence of support in parliament from individuals – Thelwall, Trevor, Mutton and Bridgwater – who all had local associations and supported the bill. This provides convincing evidence, therefore, of how disparate members (in both Houses) could form something approaching an interest group when legislative initiatives affecting their regional/economic interests came before parliament. It should be stressed, however, that such groups might be transitory and informal with no coherent agenda for joint action beyond the issue of the moment. Nevertheless, far from these being businesses of little importance, historians are coming to recognize that such issues formed a significant part of parliament's work. Although the Welsh members did not proffer any notable legislative programme in these early Stuart assemblies, they cannot be dismissed as simply inexperienced or uninterested bystanders. The extent to which they might sponsor and support issues of concern to their constituents is further underlined by an examination of certain economic interests of the Welsh shires.

---

[46] This is much more complex than Dodd's erroneous belief that the Commons objected to a bill which furthered Thomas Trevor's interests: Dodd, 'Parliaments, 1625–1629', 31.

[47] *CD1628*, ii, pp. 573, 567, 570, 573–4, 576–7; iv, pp. 474–5; *CJ*, pp. 906, 913; *LJ*, iii, pp. 875–6, 878; *SR*, v, pp. 31–3. A memorandum of 1 July 1629 noted that the tenants had by now 'purchased their lands in fee farme': Flintshire RO, D/PT/869; BL, Add. 15,043, fo. 58ᵛ.

PARLIAMENT AND ECONOMIC INTERESTS

In addition to local legislation, matters affecting Wales's economy animated the principality's MPs in early Stuart parliaments. Although in some senses this constituted another aspect of local business, these economic issues often cut across boundaries and involved the representatives of several constituencies. Such matters were not necessarily moved by Welsh members, but their involvement in business which materially affected their constituents provides further evidence of the linkages between electors and elected.

The issue of purveyance early in the reign of James I gives an indication of how such matters engaged the interest of Welsh representatives. Purveyance was an ancient right of the monarch whereby his or her servants, the purveyors, could compel individuals throughout the country to sell them goods and services at prices fixed by the purveyors. In practice, counties frequently paid a 'composition' to the purveyor as a means of discharging their obligation. This practice was open to abuse and often created tensions, especially around the city of London where the purveyors were most active. Although an ancient levy, it was only late in the reign of Elizabeth I that purveyance was extended to Wales.[48]

The extension of this troublesome obligation to a distant royal court did not proceed smoothly, however, and there are indications that it encountered some resistance. In December 1600, shortly after Wales became subject to purveyance, the Privy Council wrote that the service was in some difficulties there, with many 'absolutelie' refusing to pay their levies. The following February, William Maurice, deputy lieutenant of Caernarfonshire, was asked to provide a list of those continuing to deny payment in the county.[49] The resistance in Wales provides the context for a petition submitted to parliament in 1604 by a number of Welsh MPs. The petition, now only surviving as a later copy, was submitted by 'the knights and burgesses for the counties of Wales attending in this present parliament', though only

---

[48] A. Woodworth, *Purveyance for the Royal Household in the Reign of Queen Elizabeth* (Philadelphia, 1945), pp. 41–2.
[49] NLW, Brogyntyn (Clenennau) 172, 177.

four representatives were named.[50] It appears to have been a product of popular constituency pressure, being presented 'in the name of the commons of those partes', although there was clearly an element of advantageous rhetoric in claiming wider backing. The petition described how Wales was 'never in former tymes charged with any manner of purveyance', and cited the problem of a poor Welsh economy being unable to provide the commodities required for the royal household. The petition continued that it was a grievance that 'those remote countyes should be newly charged'.

The petition is remarkable for its apparent unanimity, being presented in the name of all the Welsh MPs. This suggests that it was the product of a wide-ranging grievance felt throughout Wales, and that it was composed in London while the parliament was sitting and all Welsh members could be brought together. This may be an example of a genuinely Welsh interest group being constructed in response to a pressing and widespread complaint. Yet it was not a permanent interest in the Commons with a specifically Welsh agenda, but rather an ephemeral lobby, created by the nature of the grievance itself.

The time was propitious for addressing the matter because this parliament was deeply concerned with the abuses of purveyors. A petition against purveyance was presented to James I by the Commons during the first session, and this offers further evidence that at least some of the Welsh members were working on behalf of their constituencies. On 30 April 1604 the petition was read in the House, and it included a clause which stated that

> there is a new charge within these three or four years past, for the provision of sturks [young bullocks or heifers] for the household raised in all counties of Wales, never used before. And by colour thereof your Majesty's officers force them to a yearly composition, whereas in truth within most counties they have no sturks, and by such compulsory means almost all late compositions are grown.[51]

---

[50] BL, Add. 5,847, fos 163ᵛ–4. These were Sir Robert Knollys (Breconshire), Sir Richard Bulkeley (Anglesey), Roger Puleston (Flintshire) and Peter Mutton (Denbighshire).

[51] *CJ*, p. 191. The king's answer recorded that purveyance had been extended

This clause bears a close relationship to the earlier Welsh petition, and evidently Welsh MPs had managed to lobby the drafting committee and had their own grievance incorporated, giving it an extra weight and significance by its inclusion in a representation from the entire Commons.

Those Welsh members involved in promoting this clause did so from outside the drafting committee, since no Welsh MPs were named to it. An opportunity for more immediate influence came in May 1604 after a committee was assembled which called for members who, 'either by experience in their own particular, or by testimony of their country neighbours' could give 'more pregnant proof' on the matters contained in the petition.[52] Four Welsh members were named, and it is significant that they included Sir Robert Knollys, Roger Puleston and Peter Mutton, all named signatories to the original Welsh petition, along with the Monmouth member, Sir Robert Johnson, who was closely involved with the issue of purveyors, probably in concert with the secretary of state, Sir Robert Cecil.[53]

Although this session failed to resolve the question of purveyance, it is clear that some Welsh MPs had attempted to promote the interests of their localities on this issue. Significantly, no Welsh member spoke in favour of a proposed radical bill which would have offended the king, or the scheme for an annual composition of £50,000 to replace purveyance, which would have increased significantly the burdens on their constituents.[54] They had obtained an airing of their constituents' grievances, however, and in the delicate negotiations over the issue this was probably the best result for which they could have hoped.

Welsh complaints about purveyance continued after the session ended; Haverfordwest, for example, 'made refusall &

---

to Wales as it should not be privileged more than English shires, and maintained that the small annual composition from the twelve shires was 'very ... willingly embraced': ibid., p. 216.

[52] Ibid., p. 202.
[53] Bowen, thesis, 147–9.
[54] E. N. Lindquist, 'The king, the people and the House of Commons: the problem of early Jacobean purveyance', *Historical Journal*, 31 (1988), 560–1. Lindquist's observation that composition would have meant more remote shires significantly increasing their purveyance burden was particularly relevant to Wales.

denied' to pay its 20s. composition in August 1604.[55] The gesture towards reform in 1604 may have gone some way to placating constituents' fears about purveyance, but it had not removed them. A bill to abolish purveyance was reintroduced in the Commons during the 1605–6 session, and it has been suggested that this was a result of popular pressure in the counties.[56] As in 1604, most of the Welsh members appeared reluctant to be associated with a radical scheme for abolishing purveyance outright, but they continued to press the issue in the Commons. Significantly, Sir William Maurice, the member for Caernarfonshire who had corresponded with the Privy Council about resistance to purveyance in his county, spoke against the £50,000 annual composition for abolition on 6 and 11 March 1606, probably cognizant of the increased burden such a figure would represent for his comparatively undercharged constituents.[57] Another Welsh speaker on the matter was Sir James Perrot, the member for Haverfordwest, which had resisted paying its composition in 1604.[58] It is surely not coincidental that Welsh members representing the two areas which provide unmistakable evidence for resistance to purveyance compositions spoke out on this topic in parliament. It would seem that they were responding to concerns from the country over the recent imposition of purveyance in Wales, but that neither man demonstrated any inclination to offend James by proposing abolition of the levy without providing some kind of recompense. That the Welsh members did not speak out about purveyance during the 'Great Contract' debates in 1610 was probably because of the delicate negotiations then in train for the abolition of the so-called 'Henry VIII' clause, considered below.[59]

This resistance to purveyance in Wales appears to have been a reaction to a new levy for provisions (or sturks) which the country did not possess, rather than one which was

[55] Pembrokeshire RO, Haverfordwest Corporation 214; 129/2.
[56] Lindquist, 'Purveyance', 563–4. Cf. P. Croft, 'Parliament, purveyance and the City of London, 1589–1608', *Parliamentary History*, 4 (1985), 21–3.
[57] Willson, *Bowyer*, p. 61; *CJ*, pp. 282, 267.
[58] *CJ*, p. 282.
[59] TNA, SP14/55/59.

particularly burdensome, and this helped to configure the tactics of Welsh members.[60] All of them seemed wary of endorsing a high annual composition in return for abolition of the levy because they were aware that this would have meant significantly increased taxation in the Welsh counties. Additionally, the Welsh MPs were reluctant to endorse anything which savoured of challenging the king directly. Nevertheless, there appears to have been a genuine effort by MPs in parliament to represent the concerns and anxieties of the Welsh taxpayers, even engaging in collective lobbying to strengthen their cause. Purveyance, therefore, provides strong evidence of the contradictory forces operating on MPs in early Stuart parliaments, where they needed to balance maintenance of their stock among neighbours and constituents with advocating their interests in parliament, and at the same time ensure that favour at Court and the political centre was not lost by prejudicing the king's finances.[61]

Purveyance was unusual as an economic matter of concern to the whole of Wales, although the exemption of Wales from general taxation on account of a customary payment to the Crown known as the 'mise' offers some illuminating parallels. The mise was payable by Welsh counties on the accession of a new monarch or prince, and so mises were due at the accession of James I and at the creation of Princes Henry and Charles as prince of Wales in 1610 and 1616, respectively. There is evidence of Welsh lobbying in Tudor parliaments for exemption from subsidy payments while the mise was being collected.[62] Subsidy payments due from James's first parliament were also suspended in Wales because of the collection of mises for the king and Prince Henry. Although there is no direct evidence of a collective Welsh effort to secure exemption, it is likely that all Welsh

---

[60] The twelve counties of Wales only compounded for £360 per annum, with each county apparently paying £30. These were paltry sums in comparison with the £3,000 compositions of counties such as Kent and Sussex: G. E. Aylmer, 'The last years of purveyance, 1610–1660', *Economic History Review*, 2nd series, 10 (1957–8), 86; Flintshire RO, D/GW/1170; TNA, LS13/279, fo. 75^v.

[61] Russell, *Parliaments*, passim; Lindquist, 'Purveyance', 549–70.

[62] Bowen, 'Wales at Westminster', 114–15.

MPs supported the provisos moved for this purpose and which were sponsored by Sir Richard Bulkeley (Anglesey) in 1606 and Roger Puleston (Denbighshire) in 1610, possibly acting as spokesmen for a broader Welsh coalition.[63]

Similarly, in 1621 a Welshman sitting in an English seat, Sir Thomas Trevor, moved that Wales be exempted from subsidy payments, initially because of the mises being collected for Prince Charles, and when this failed to move the Commons, he lobbied for exemption because the 1610 subsidies had yet to be collected. On this occasion, he was supported by Sir James Perrot, MP for Haverfordwest. His proposal was defeated, however, and the Welsh counties were required to contribute.[64] Trevor's advocacy of Welsh exemption on both occasions is striking. A native of Denbighshire, he sat for Saltash but crucially was a prominent lawyer and solicitor-general for Prince Charles, for whom the mises were being collected. It was probably felt that Trevor could speak with authority in the House on this issue, and we may conjecture that he was operating as a spokesman for Welsh MPs in this matter. It is significant that King James later thanked 'those gentlemen that serve for the cuntry of Wales' for having dropped their claims for exemption.[65] The record that ninety-four individuals supported Trevor's motion for exemption in a Commons' division is also intriguing, the bald figure probably concealing a high level of Welsh interest. It seems likely that, as in the case of purveyance, general taxation affecting all Welsh counties engaged Welsh MPs collectively and encouraged a degree of cooperation in the Commons.

More usually, economic issues tended to affect particular regions rather than be of equal concern to all parts of Wales; this in turn affected activities in parliament when such matters were raised. This is so for an issue of particular concern in north and mid-Wales: the cloth trade. Welsh wool and cloth became a live issue in the early seventeenth century because of efforts to overthrow the monopoly on

---

[63] *CJ*, pp. 299, 449; *SR*, iv, pp. 1126, 1201.
[64] *CJ*, pp. 537, 544; *CD1621*, iv, p. 132, v, p. 279; TNA, SP46/65, fos 123–40. See below, pp. 87–9.
[65] *CD1621*, vii. 578, iv, p. 145; *CJ*, p. 549.

exporting Welsh cottons from the principality secured by the Shrewsbury Drapers' Company. These efforts were supported by London merchants who were anxious to buy directly from Welsh clothiers rather than having to deal with the Shrewsbury Drapers' representatives. Parliamentary initiatives were rare before the 1620s, but the Caernarfonshire member, Sir William Maurice, evidently took the opportunity of a debate on free trade in June 1604 to attack the Shrewsbury monopoly, whilst there were other rumblings of opposition from Welshmen in the 1614 parliament.[66] The Drapers' Company defended itself vigorously both inside and outside parliament, but the downturn of fortunes of the textile industry during the early 1620s focused attention on such monopolies and restrictions on trade, issues which were brought into question in the parliament of 1621.[67] Removing the Drapers' Company's monopoly would offer commercial opportunities for both the London merchants and the Welsh clothiers, and so both groups were active in lobbying their cause in the parliament, as too were the Shrewsbury drapers who desperately tried to shore up their position.

On 23 February 1621, the Drapers' Company agreed to send John Prowde to London with £10 'to solicit a cause in parlament wheare in the Welshe men woold have free libertie for all men to bie and transport [cloth]'.[68] It obviously knew that moves by the Welshmen and their London allies were afoot, and only three days after this entry was made in the Company's minute book, a bill 'for the free trade and traffick of Welch cloths' was introduced in the Commons.[69] It would appear that it was promoted by Welsh interests in the House, being referred to by Prowde as 'the Welch Bill for free trade'.[70] This assumption is strengthened by the fact that in its original form the bill promoted the interests of Welsh producers beyond those of other parties.[71]

[66] *CJ*, 987; NLW, MS 9055E/651.
[67] B. E. Supple, *Commercial Crisis and Change in England, 1600–1642* (Cambridge, 1964), pp. 52–72, esp. pp. 53–4.
[68] Shropshire Archives, 1831/6, fo. 35.
[69] *CJ*, p. 526.
[70] Shropshire Archives, 1831/20.
[71] House of Lords RO, Main Papers, 24 April 1621; T. C. Mendenhall, *The Shrewsbury Drapers and the Welsh Wool Trade in the XVI and XVII Centuries* (Oxford,

Perhaps the most persuasive evidence that this was a Welsh initiative comes from a report made by Attorney General Coventry to the Privy Council in June 1622. Relating the recent history of Welsh cottons, he recalled that

> upon complaint of the gentlemen & other inhabitants of Wales at the last convencon of parliament, a bill passed both houses where by that restraint was to have bene whollie taken awaie and trade left free without anie restriccon to persons or place.[72]

Coventry's report is also important in suggesting a link between the inhabitants of Wales and their representatives in parliament in the prosecution of this matter.

The bill for removing the Company's monopoly was subject to vigorous debate and negotiation in the Commons as the various parties pressed their cases.[73] It was also of great interest in Wales, for on the day of its commitment William Wynn wrote to his father in Caernarfonshire that 'the grevance towchinge the Welshe cottens hath beene alreadie moconed in the howse of parliament, and is like to overthrow the Shrewsburie men'.[74] However, although the bill was committed to a large group which included all representatives sitting in Welsh seats, the recorded debates on the measure show very little engagement by any of the Welsh representatives.[75] This might suggest that Welsh MPs had only a fleeting interest in the issue, but other evidence indicates that it illustrates rather the insufficiency of our parliamentary sources in revealing the full scope of political manœuvring at Westminster.

1953), pp. 171, 237–8. Mendenhall (p. 171) notes that the precise authors of the bill remain unknown. Cf. his comments, p. 187, and n. 2.

[72] TNA, SP14/131/37; *APC, 1621–3*, p. 264. See also the order of the Privy Council, based on Coventry's report, which mentioned the bill passing 'upon complaint of the gents. and other inhabitants of Wales', the Drapers' Company's memorandum that the bill passed 'by the importunat sute of the gent. of Wales', and the acknowledgement of Shrewsbury Corporation that liberty of trade was agreed 'by the generall consent of bothe the howses of parliamente uppon the sute of the gentlemen of Wales': TNA, SP14/131/77; Shropshire Archives, 1831/10; Oswestry Town Hall, A75/1/12.

[73] Mendenhall, *Shrewsbury Drapers*, pp. 170–9.

[74] NLW, MS 9057E/939.

[75] *CJ*, pp. 534, 564, 575, 588–9; *CD1621*, iii, p. 65; iv, pp. 119, 198, 252; v, pp. 93, 268; vi, p. 94. It is probably wrong to describe Sir James Perrot as the Welsh 'leader' on this matter simply on the basis of his moving for committal: Mendenhall, *Shrewsbury Drapers*, p. 172.

On 25 April 1621, Prowde informed the Drapers' Company that he had 'endeavoured by all the meanes I could make to stop the bill for the Welsh cottons that it could not passe the lower howse ... soe that it rests now that I doe my endeavoure to crosse it in the higher howse'. He added that this would be difficult as 'the Welshmen have solicited the Lordes to the uttermost. Sir William Herbert [MP for Montgomeryshire] & others of the Welsh gentellmen are discontented that wee bie not the cloth as accustomed'.[76] His comments indicate that, although the reports of debates on the floor of the House suggest little activity from Welsh MPs, men like Herbert were promoting their case vigorously behind the scenes and lobbying hard for the bill.

The suggestion that Welsh MPs like Herbert were actively furthering the bill outside the debating chamber is strengthened by Prowde's dispatch of 30 April. He wrote that the bill was likely to be passed by the Lords and observed 'this course is followed with more then ordinary ernestnesse by the Welshmen, especially Sir William Herbert'.[77] Herbert was the member for Montgomeryshire, the Welsh county closest to Shrewsbury, and which had a considerable economic interest in the clothing industry.[78] These comments indicate an active and effective interest furthering the bill's passage, and operating in a manner that has left no impression in the extant reports of this session. It is unclear to what extent this interest encompassed other MPs from the principality, but it does demonstrate that this measure was initiated and actively solicited by some Welsh members whose constituencies were intimately involved in cloth-making.

Further indication of lobbying can be found in a document which appears to have originated from the Welsh camp in parliament, and is endorsed 'reasons in maintenance of the Bill of free trade of Welsh Cottons'. It concentrated on the damage the Drapers' Company's monopoly was doing in the principality: 'By these meanes

---

[76] Shropshire Archives, 1831/20.
[77] Ibid.
[78] TNA, SP14/131/22(i); Shropshire Archives, 1831/10. In a petition from the clothiers of north Wales, the signatories of Montgomeryshire outnumbered those from all other counties: TNA, SP14/121/58.

the trade of cloathing in the parts of Wales remote from Oswestrie [where the cloth was sold] is utterly decayed, [and] many thowsands of people impoverished and become idle'.[79] The benefits of free trade were lauded in terms of allowing greater numbers of the Welsh to work to 'mainteyne the poorest sorte of people'. The concentration on the depredations suffered by Welshmen at the hands of the Shrewsbury drapers, suggests that it was an appeal to interested parties in the House by the Welsh interest which sought to further the bill for free trade.

The Drapers' Company fought back with similar methods. Prowde submitted a petition on behalf of the Company at the bill's second reading in the Lords, noting that 'the Welsh gentellmen are not a littell displeased with mee' for submitting the paper.[80] Prowde's cause was heard before the Lords committee on 8 May 1621, when he had some success in having the bill amended to defend the Company's charter.[81] He had occasion once more to note the Welshmen's vigorous defence of their interests,

> for [the provision in the bill concerning] transportation out of the creekes of north Wales, I could by noe meanes crosse that. It was soe much insisted upon by the Welshmen whose violence hath binn such in the prosecution of this businesse and theire behaviour give us iust cause to recompense them accordingly.[82]

Again, a coherent Welsh grouping was acting in an organized fashion. Such instances must raise questions about the extent to which debates in the House reflect Welsh activity in parliament. This kind of lobbying and negotiation did not take place on the floor of the Commons but in committee and, more probably, in the corridors of Westminster. Dodd's account of the bill in this exceptionally well-reported parliament makes little mention of Sir William Herbert, though Prowde's dispatches make it clear that he was a

---

[79] Flintshire RO, D/HE/733. A similar document is in the Wynn papers: NLW, MS 9059E/1182B (misdated in *CWP* as 1623).

[80] Shropshire Archives, 1831/20. The petition is reproduced in *CD1621*, vii, pp. 73–5, and discussed in Mendenhall, *Shrewsbury Drapers*, pp. 181–2.

[81] Shropshire Archives, 1831/20; 1831/6, fo. 37; *LJ*, iii, pp. 111, 117; *CD1621*, ii, p. 372; iii, p. 271; iv, p. 352.

[82] Shropshire Archives, 1831/20.

leading figure in the assault on the Shrewsbury Drapers' privileges.[83]

In addition to organized lobbying in parliament, there is evidence to suggest that the Welsh members received support within the principality itself. On 29 May 1621, a petition was sent from the clothiers of north Wales to the Privy Council complaining of the activities of the drapers at Shrewsbury, and calling for the market to be made free for all to buy and sell at Oswestry.[84] It is difficult to ascertain whether this was part of a concerted lobby because the petition was submitted after the bill had passed the Lords, but it may indicate an attempt to sway opinion in the Council and, thereafter, the king who could still have vetoed the measure. James I ended the session in the summer and the bill was not enacted in this parliament; the reaction in Wales is suggestive of the widespread support in the principality which provides a vital context for the parliamentary evidence, Owen Wynn commenting on 2 June 1621,

> the woorst newes I heare is that what hath bene done hitherto in parliament will not be enacted ... & then shall not the poore inhabitants of Wales enioy the benefitt of the libertie of the sale of their Welshe cottons. A miserable thinge; God amend it.[85]

That the efforts of interested parties both inside and outside parliament did indeed have some influence on the Privy Council may be seen in the fact that the councillors opened the trade in the manner desired in the bill by an order of 13 June 1621.[86] As in other instances already examined, parliament was being utilized as only one potential arena for determined lobbyists, and such instances underline the need to place Welsh parliamentary activity in a wider context of potential sites of influence in the country, Privy Council and Court.

The Council decree had the reverse effect to that which many in Wales had anticipated: the Drapers' Company now agreed not to buy any cloth except in Shrewsbury itself. This

---

[83] Dodd, 'Apprenticeship', 48–50.
[84] TNA, SP14/121/58. Nearly 200 Welsh clothiers signed this petition.
[85] NLW, MS 9057E/957.
[86] *APC, 1619–21*, pp. 396–7; Mendenhall, *Shrewsbury Drapers*, pp. 192–3.

move had disastrous consequences for Oswestry, where cloth had normally been sold, and for the Welsh wool trade in general.[87] The Welsh clothiers were now forced to travel to Shrewsbury where their largest buyer was located, the Drapers' Company. Shrewsbury had a monopoly conferred upon it by default, because the dream of increased markets did not materialize in a period of depression, and the Welsh clothiers were forced to look to the only body that would buy their goods. It was claimed that this 'enforced the poore Welch clothiers ... to begg for sale at theire [the Drapers' Company's] doores'.[88] This occasioned petitions to the Council from the counties of Merioneth, Denbigh and Montgomery, calling for the trade to be returned to Oswestry.[89] The petitions demonstrate the importance of the cloth trade to their economies by the large number of signatures from the justices and other leading gentlemen in these shires.[90] This evidence again indicates that the Welsh members who advanced the free trade case in parliament were responding to the desires of powerful interests in their local communities.

The period between the dissolution of the 1621 parliament and the sitting of the 1624 assembly witnessed confusion and experimentation in a Welsh cloth trade that was struggling to overcome the ravages of economic depression. The decision by the Council to free the trade ultimately proved definitive, however, and the legislative moves in the 1624 parliament concerning Welsh wool were much less controversial. As the Welsh had no solutions for the more intractable economic problems, they supported a free trade measure in 1624 that would allow them to sell their cloth on their own coasts and in their own market towns. Their opposition to the Drapers' Company's restraint of trade was enshrined in the final act, but the drapers had reaped such

[87] Shropshire Archives, 1831/6, fo. 38ᵛ; Mendenhall, *Shrewsbury Drapers*, pp. 192–3.
[88] TNA, SP14/131/21; STAC8/33/20; Oswestry Town Hall, A75/1/9; Longleat House, Whitelocke II, fo. 70.
[89] TNA, SP14/131/20, 22(i), 22(ii).
[90] One petition described the 'generall & universall consent of all the inhabitants of those partes whose names in respecte of the multitude could not be hereunto subscribed although their affections accord therewith': TNA, SP14/131/20.

unexpected benefits from the opening of trade that they offered no resistance. Consequently, the bill had a smooth passage through both Houses and onto the statute book.[91] The act made specific reference to the activity of the Welsh MPs in presenting their constituents' grievances before parliament, describing how the damage to local economies by the Shrewsbury drapers' restraint of trade 'was verefied by the generall voice of the knights and burgesses of the twelve shires of Wales and of the countie of Monmoth'.[92] This was a clear acknowledgement of the Welsh MPs' role as representatives of their communities and is again suggestive of the possibility of collective Welsh action. However, Sir William Herbert's prominence in Prowde's dispatches suggests that it was those representing the constituencies most involved with the cloth trade who were the most active on this issue. Analysis also reveals the danger of assessing Welsh activity at Westminster on the basis of parliamentary records alone, and of focusing solely on the activity of Welsh MPs and neglecting broader lobbying strategies undertaken in the constituencies and the Privy Council.

It is instructive to contrast the Welsh involvement with the Drapers' Company in 1621 and 1624 with another issue concerning the Welsh economy which came before these parliaments: the foreign export of Welsh butter. This trade was less extensive than that of cloth, being concentrated in Glamorgan and Monmouthshire.[93] As a consequence, it seems to have elicited less of a corporate response from Welsh MPs at Westminster, but nevertheless provides evidence of the interaction between local interests and their representatives in parliament. The foreign trade in butter from Wales, like that of Welsh cloth, came to the attention of the 1621 parliament because it was partly under the control of patentees, a favourite target of the Commons in

[91] *CJ*, pp. 686, 746, 757; *LJ*, iii, pp. 294, 303, 327–8.
[92] *SR*, iv, p. 1218. The act was evidently popular in Wales; Henry Wynn listed it as one of 'our billes', while his brother Owen numbered it among the 'many good actes' passed by the parliament: NLW, MSS 9059E/1220, 1228.
[93] F. V. Emery, 'The farming regions of Wales', in J. Thirsk (ed.), *The Agrarian History of England and Wales, IV, 1500–1640* (Cambridge, 1967), pp. 133–5; S. K. Roberts (ed.), *The Letter Book of John Byrd* (South Wales Record Society, 14, 1999), p. 57; TNA, PC2/50, p. 501; Huntington Library, Ellesmere 7420, 7517.

this assembly. The export of butter was regulated by statute, but patents were sometimes granted to allow its transportation from Wales.[94] On 20 February 1619, Richard Williams and David Lewis were granted a patent to export Welsh butter, apparently through the intercession of the duke of Buckingham. The patentees soon sold shares in the patent to Glamorgan gentlemen, London interests and the Bristol Merchant Venturers, and by 1619–20 the export of Welsh butter was largely in the hands of the Bristol and London merchants.[95] The Bristol interest is particularly noteworthy as the city relied heavily on imports of Welsh butter.[96]

This confinement of the trade to a limited group was detrimental to many merchants of south Wales who were barred from exploiting potentially lucrative foreign markets. The desire of some in south Wales to take advantage of these opportunities can be seen in the evidence of illicit trading between 1619 and 1621 in contravention of the patent.[97] This hunger for a more open market on the part of the inhabitants of south Wales, and of Glamorgan especially, coincided with the 1621 parliament's assault on patentees as scapegoats for recent economic difficulties.

A bill designed to open the foreign transport of Welsh butter to all subjects when prices were 3*d*. in the pound in summer and 4*d*. in the pound in winter was introduced in the Commons on 5 March 1621.[98] That this was a Welsh initiative is indicated by a proclamation of July 1621 suppressing the butter patent, wherein the king asserted that he was responding to 'the suit and desire of the inhabitants of the Dominion of Wales, expressed by a bill in parliament'.[99] It is possible to be even more precise about the person behind the bill, for a petition of October 1621 to the

---

[94] TNA, SP14/94/99.

[95] TNA, C66/2178; House of Lords RO, Parchment Collection, Box 1F; NLW, Bute L2/35–6, D77/2–5; M. E. Jones, 'Glamorgan, 1540–1640: aspects of social and economic history' (MA thesis, University of Wales, 1973), 267.

[96] P. MacGrath (ed.), *Records Relating to the Society of Merchant Venturers and the City of Bristol in the Seventeenth Century* (Bristol Record Society, 17, 1951), pp. 118–20.

[97] Ibid., pp. 121–2.

[98] *CJ*, p. 537.

[99] J. F. Larkin and P. L. Hughes (eds), *Stuart Royal Proclamations* (Oxford, 1973–83), i, p. 518. See also the draft bill: House of Lords RO, Main Papers, 26 May 1621.

lord treasurer from leading Glamorgan gentlemen about this grievance stated that 'wee did earnestlie recomend the care of that cause (among others) to ... William Price, knight of the parlament elected for this shier'.[100] This is important evidence of the manner in which the political élites in Welsh counties might charge their MPs with business to be undertaken in parliament for the benefit of the local economy. Price was visible on the floor of the Commons, for example, defending the bill he had tabled from the accusation that it set up a new monopoly by restricting butter exports solely to the Welsh ports. He also spoke at the bill's third reading.[101] Sir James Perrot, the member for Haverfordwest, also supported the measure, and was probably defending his constituents' interests because butter was a not insignificant export from Pembrokeshire.[102]

Although the bill proceeded to the Lords, its passage was hindered by pressure of business and then by the prorogation. However, William Price, working in conjunction with Sir Walter Pye, chief justice of the Brecon great sessions circuit (which included Glamorgan), continued to press the issue outside parliament, appealing to Lord Treasurer Cranfield for assistance. Cranfield interceded with the king on their behalf and had the patent suspended by proclamation during the recess, 'untill some acte of parliament shall passe' providing for the same effect.[103] The bill, however, was lost at the dissolution.

The 1621 bill, contrary to Dodd's assertion, was not partially realized by, or incorporated into, the 1624 act concerning the trade of butter, for this did not allow overseas trade, the main purpose of Glamorgan's 1621 bill.[104] That the 1624 bill did not strike directly at the provision for

[100] Centre for Kentish Studies, U269/1 OE126.
[101] *CJ*, p. 575; *CD1621*, iv, p. 198; v, p. 322; ii, p. 389; iii, p. 305
[102] *CJ*, p. 575.
[103] Centre for Kentish Studies, U269/1 OE126; Larkin and Hughes, *Proclamations*, i, p. 518; *CD1621*, vii, p. 469.
[104] *SR*, iv, p. 1231; Dodd, 'Apprenticeship', 59; idem, *Studies*, p. 24; House of Lords RO, Main Papers, 26 May 1621. Some contemporaries claimed that the patent was rendered void by the Monopolies Act of 1624, but it evidently remained in force: TNA, C2/ChasI/H53/62, fo. 5.

exporting Welsh butter is confirmed by the fact that Charles I reinstated the original patent shortly after he succeeded to the throne. In April 1625, Richard Williams, one of the original patentees, wrote joyfully to his fellow stakeholder, William Herbert of Cogan Pill, that 'our butter pattent is once more good'. He was clearly aware of the desire among Glamorgan's political community for opening the butter trade, writing 'I would you could get a certificatt from the countrey people and as many of the gentry as you could for the conveniency of it [the patent] rather then a generall transportation'. In this context, Williams also noted the calling of a new parliament, adding 'I wishe you weare a member of it', suggesting an awareness of the advantages of gaining a seat to defend private interests against an attack such as that of 1621.[105]

The parliamentary backlash against the patent did indeed materialize, but not until the 1626 assembly, when another bill, probably very similar to that of 1621, was introduced in the Commons, and significantly was submitted to a committee headed by the Glamorgan member, Sir John Stradling.[106] That it was designed to remedy the omissions of the 1624 act may be deduced from its title as related by one diarist: '[a] bill concerning the transportation of butter out of the dominion of Wales into foreign parts of our friends'.[107] This bill never emerged from the committee, however, probably because of deteriorating relations with France, the intended destination of much of the Welsh butter.

The issue of Welsh butter exports reveals a distinct geographical area – encompassing the southern maritime counties of the principality and especially Glamorgan – attempting to safeguard its economic interests through legislative action. The petition to Cranfield by the Glamorgan gentry is highly revealing in its depiction of the county's leading political figures 'recommending' the butter business (among other matters) to their knight for consideration in parliament. It demonstrates how election as an

[105] NLW, Bute L2/59.
[106] *CJ*, pp. 825, 831.
[107] *PP1626*, ii, p. 202.

MP imposed a responsibility to safeguard and promote the interests of the constituency. It may also be noted in this regard that the 'political community' here was represented by thirteen signatories, but that this in no way weakened the bonds between the constituency and its member.

The protection of Glamorgan's trading interests figured in the contributions of Cardiff's MP, Mathew Davies, in the debates on Minehead harbour during the first Jacobean parliament. The bill for repairing the harbour introduced in 1610 could not be seen in Wales as an innocuous local measure, because a draft indicates that it sought to place duties on imported commodities from Wales. This would have been particularly burdensome for Glamorgan because Minehead was one of the principal ports used by its traders.[108] It is not coincidental, therefore, that Davies opposed the bill at its second reading, the Commons clerk noting that he spoke 'for Glamorgan'. He later successfully moved to have all Welsh members added to the bill, and he offered a proviso at its third reading, probably exempting Welsh goods from the additional duties.[109] Fortunately for the Glamorgan coasting trade, the bill did not emerge from the Lords.

The impetus to protect regional economies in Wales can also be seen in the 1621 bill designed to prevent the importation of Irish cattle into mainland Britain. This was widely supported by the Welsh because Irish imports threatened the indigenous cattle trade which comprised a large part of the country's economy.[110] Sir William Herbert asserted in the Commons that 'Wales will be overthrown if ... Irish cattle be not prohibited'.[111] Sir James Perrot, a Pembrokeshire man whose county was deeply involved in the cattle trade, was also vocal in supporting the bill.[112] The general interest of the Welsh in the measure was acknowledged when

---

[108] Somerset RO, DD/L 1/55/1; Thomas, 'Glamorgan, 1540–1640', 260–8.
[109] *CJ*, pp. 398, 403, 416.
[110] In 1623 the Anglesey JPs complained of the difficulty of selling livestock and blamed the 'infinit stoare of cattle cominge from Ireland yeereli': NA, SP14/138/68(i).
[111] *CD1621*, ii, p. 357; v, pp. 157–8.
[112] *CJ*, p. 625; *CD1621*, ii, p. 382; iii, p. 290; iv, p. 363; v, p. 381.

the knights and burgesses of Wales were the first named members of the committee considering the bill.[113] Sir Richard Wynn's letter of 6 May to his father in Caernarfonshire reflects this Welsh interest: 'Thers this session of parlement ... [an] act for the barring of Eirish cattell which has bin comitted and wile undoubtedly passe the lower house, and I hope the hier, which concerns our country wonderfull much'.[114] He was to be disappointed, however, because the bill failed reach the statute book, though the issue continued to animate Welsh MPs beyond the Restoration.[115]

These legislative initiatives and debates on economic issues again reveal how distinct groups from Wales could utilize parliament as an assembly in which to promote and defend sectional interests. It is noteworthy that many of these initiatives cluster about the 1621 parliament, and to some degree represent the faltering and uncertain attempts of these Welsh economic interests to comprehend and respond to the difficulties of the severe depression which seized the country at this time. The analysis presented here shows that the lobbying tactics of Welsh MPs could be sophisticated, a conclusion which does not sit easily with the notion of the principality's members serving an 'apprenticeship' in Jacobean parliaments. It also illustrates how transitory parliaments provided only one arena for the advocacy of local and regional concerns, and were often integrated in a campaign of lobbying courtiers, the Privy Council, the lord president of the Council in the Marches and local assize judges, as well as in suits undertaken in local and national law courts. It offers concrete examples of the manner in which the honour and credit bestowed by the community at a parliamentary election could be reciprocated by concern shown for local issues in parliament. Nevertheless, far from all Welsh MPs were active on behalf of their constituencies or interests in their communities, but in this Welsh members did not differ from their English counterparts; parliamentary activity was often only undertaken when a legislative

---

[113] *CJ*, p. 615.
[114] NLW, MS 9058E/1096A (misdated in *CWP* as 1623).
[115] *CWP*, nos 2470, 2679.

agenda was formulated in the constituency, or when matters of immediate concern to a locality appeared in the Commons.

Welsh interests were also engaged by a quite different kind of parliamentary business. Matters occasionally came before parliament which touched on the relationship of the principality with the broader British polity, and the next section examines how Welsh representatives engaged with these issues.

WALES AND BRITAIN

James's accession to the English throne was interpreted by some contemporaries as the fulfilment of an ancient prophecy that the island of Britain would be politically as well as geographically and dynastically unified under one ruler. This powerful image of unity and mythic consummation was not lost on a number of Welshmen, who invoked their own history as ancient Britons to welcome James as one of their own.[116] Even accounting for the rhetoric of authors currying favour with the new monarch, the publications of Welsh writers like Robert Holland and George Owen Harry reflect the intimate associations of Wales with a notion of Anglo-Scottish union and the related matter of an united Britain.[117] Wales's status as the territory most recently and successfully united to England made it an obvious model for those who supported James's plans for uniting England with Scotland; among them was John Dodderidge, better known for his history of Wales.[118] This image also figured in the

[116] J. G. Jones, 'The Welsh poets and their patrons, c.1550–1640', *WHR*, 9 (1978–9), 248–9; idem, 'The Welsh gentry and the image of the "Cambro-Briton", c.1603–25', *WHR*, 20 (2000–1), 615–55.

[117] R. Holland, *Basilicon Doron ... Translated into the True British Tongue* (1604); G.O. Harry, *The Genealogy of the High and Most Mighty Monarch, James* (1604).

[118] B. R. Galloway and B. P. Levack (eds), *The Jacobean Union: Six Tracts of 1604* (Scottish History Society, 4th series, 21, 1985), p. 144. In his work on Wales composed around 1604, Dodderidge discussed the Anglo-Welsh union, in part 'because in some respect it may serve as a proiect and president of some other union and annexation by your maiestry of as much, or of more consequence and importance': John Dodderidge, *The History of the Ancient and Moderne Estate of the Principality of Wales* (1630), p. 40. For other examples citing Wales, see Galloway and Levack, *Union*, pp. 181–2, 213–14; J. Heyward, *A Treatise of Union* (1604), p. 3; J.

union debates in parliament, but it is surprising how little attention the union received from the majority of Welsh MPs, with the notable exception of Sir William Maurice of Clenennau, Caernarfonshire.

Maurice was a devotee of Welsh vaticinatory traditions and frequently echoed the rhetoric of fervent pro-unionists in emphasizing Wales's relevance to the construction of an united Britain. Maurice suggested that James take a new, more imperial title; as his sister wrote in February 1604, he was James's 'godfather, and intiteled his Highnes Kinge of Great Britaine'.[119] On 29 March 1604, a bill for the recognition of James's right to the Crown was delivered to the Commons; two days later it was supported by Maurice, who desired

> ther mighte be added to that bill the tytle of Emperore of Grate Brittayne, for that he did observe that an old provesee among the Welchmen was in the kinge in parte performed ... and wished that it might be fully fulfylled hearafter. The pr[o]phesee as he pronounced it was; A kinge of Brittishe bloude in cradle crowned with lyones marke shall joyne all brittyshe grounde.[120]

Maurice's prophetic allusion was later reproduced in a commonplace book, along with a note that he had invoked it 'when the treatie was of the union, to shewe by this prophesie that the same was unavoydable'.[121] Maurice clearly looked to myth and legend for his arguments concerning a union, and responded to the material produced by men like George Owen Harry rather than the more legalistic union debates which raged in parliament.[122] Among his papers is a damaged draft letter to a cousin regarding the union

Thornborough, *A Discourse Plainely Proving the Evident Utilitie and Urgent Necessitie of the Desired Happie Union* (1604), pp. 9–10; *The Miraculous and Happie Union of England and Scotland* (1604), p. 29; TNA, SP14/7/40; 14/10A/56.

[119] NLW, Brogyntyn (Clenennau) 204.

[120] C. Thompson, trans., *Obseruatyones of the Proceedinges in the Ple=mente held at Westeminster An° Primoe et Secundo Jacobi Regis* (Wivenhoe, 1990), pp. 10–11. See also HMC, *Buccleuch and Queensberry MSS*, iii, pp. 83–4.

[121] Bodleian Library, Tanner 169, fo. 62^v.

[122] For Maurice's other contributions to the union debates, see *CJ*, pp. 179, 327–8, 392, 952, 1002; Willson, *Bowyer*, p. 224; E. R. Foster (ed.), *Proceedings in Parliament, 1610* (New Haven, 1966), ii, pp. 4–5; HMC, *Downshire MSS*, ii, p. 240; TNA, SP14/26/48.

debates which testifies to Maurice's sincere belief in the prophecy that James was the fabled deliverer who would restore the kingdom of Britain 'to the pristine estate'.[123] It was for such reasons that a Welsh bard christened him the 'leader of the British party' ('penn plaid brytaniaid').[124]

Apart from Maurice, however, Welsh involvement in parliament was very thin on the ground.[125] Maurice continued to press the union issue throughout the 1604–10 parliament, even tabling a bill to entitle James 'Emperour of Great Brittaine'.[126] His was a lonely voice among Welsh MPs – indeed in the House more generally – where his preoccupation with prophecy was not considered germane in intricate legal debates addressing real fears of the implications of union for the English state. His continued advocacy exasperated many in the House, and his lengthy orations were dismissed as 'long, unnecessarie [and] weake'.[127] In part Maurice's enthusiasm fell victim to the latent ethnic tensions which undermined the entire union scheme, and they extended to anti-Welshness. For example, in 1610 Maurice 'prest hotly' for the title of 'King of Great Britain' to be confirmed by statute, but he was answered by Richard James, the member for Newport (IOW), who noted that the Welsh

> were first an ydolatrous nation, and worshipers of divels. In the beguinning of Christianity they were thrust owt into the mountaines, where they lived long like theefes and robbers, and are to this day the most base, pesantly perfidious people of the world.[128]

[123] NLW, Brogyntyn (Clenennau) 474.

[124] E. D. Jones, 'The Brogyntyn Welsh manuscripts', *NLWJ*, 6 (1949–50), 5.

[125] Bowen, thesis, 175. Cf. Peter Roberts, who states, without evidential support, that 'Welsh representatives, or a significant number of them, took a prominent part out of all proportion to their numbers in the exchanges and transactions over the question of a larger union with Scotland': 'The English crown, the principality of Wales and the Council in the Marches, 1534–1641', in J. Morrill and B. Bradshaw (eds), *The British Problem, c.1534–1707: State Formation in the Atlantic Archipelago* (1996), p. 139. Maurice aside, it is difficult to ascribe any real interest in the matter to other Welsh MPs.

[126] Willson, *Bowyer*, p. 189. Maurice sponsored a bill in 1610 to confirm statutorily James's earlier proclamation styling himself 'King of Great Britain': *CJ*, p. 394; TNA, SP14/24/23.

[127] Willson, *Bowyer*, p. 1 and n. 2. See also *CJ*, p. 392; R. Winwood, *Memorials of Affairs of State* (1725), iii, p. 119; HMC, *Downshire MSS*, ii, p. 240.

[128] TNA, SP14/24/23.

Although there are indications that the union excited an element of cultural nostalgia in Wales which was reflected in Maurice's speeches, this was a political discourse more suited to the bardic flurries which accompanied the accession of Henry VII than the hard-nosed politicking surrounding the union of the Crowns.

The issue of the jurisdiction of the Council in the Marches of Wales over the four English border shires provides some interesting parallels with the question of Anglo-Scottish union. The assault on the Council by border MPs has been considered at length elsewhere, but its relationship to the union issue has rarely been acknowledged.[129] Since the reign of Elizabeth, inhabitants of the four border counties of Gloucestershire, Herefordshire, Worcestershire and Shropshire had attempted to gain exemption from the jurisdiction of the Council in the Marches. The parliamentary attack was prosecuted by Westminster lawyers and MPs representing the border shires, especially the Herefordshire knight Sir Herbert Croft. Welsh interventions on the measure were not numerous, but it may be significant that Sir William Maurice again was the exception. A bill introduced in the 1606 session by two border MPs for the limitation of the Council's jurisdiction was opposed by Maurice at its third reading.[130] He stated that the four shires were 'specially added, that the president might have Englishmen to subdue the rudeness of the Walshmen if they rebelled'.[131] Alhough the bill was 'much disputed', Maurice is the only recorded Welsh speaker, and it may be noted that a passionate advocate of Anglo-Scottish union was prepared

---

[129] C. A. J. Skeel, *The Council in the Marches of Wales* (1904), pp. 130–45; P. Williams, 'The attack on the Council in the Marches, 1603–1642', *TCS*, (1961), 2–8; R. E. Ham, 'The four shires controversy', *WHR*, 8 (1976–7), 381–99; idem, *County and the Kingdom: Sir Herbert Croft and the Elizabethan State* (Washington, DC, 1977); G. D. Owen, *Wales in the Reign of James I* (Woodbridge, 1988), pp. 23–51.

[130] TNA, SP14/19/33, 34, 35; Bodleian Library, Tanner 91, fo. 139[r–v]; Skeel, *Council in the Marches*, pp. 134–7. At the committal stage the bill was referred to all the knights and burgesses of Wales, with Sir Richard Bulkeley, Sir Thomas Somerset and Sir Robert Mansell specifically named: *CJ*, p. 272; Willson, *Bowyer*, p. 49.

[131] *CJ*, p. 281. His comments have been interpreted as anti-Welsh, but they echo closely the arguments of many who believed the Council had been a pacifying force in Wales. See, for example, BL, Lansdowne 216, fo. 35[v]; TNA, SP14/31/36.

to oppose a bill which weakened the provisions of an earlier union.

The border shires' attack on prevailing constitutional ties in the western counties of the English state took place whilst James was attempting to strengthen legal bonds in the north, where a similar prerogative council existed.[132] The consequences for the northern council of a diminution of the authority of the Council in the Marches were clearly recognized by contemporaries.[133] The earl of Salisbury wrote that the challenge to the Council in the Marches of Wales meant that 'the counsell at Yorke wilbe allsoe over throwne by the same law, and other courtes & prerogatyves will in like sorte be examyned if this gapp be layed open'.[134] The moves against the Council in the Marches, therefore, had a direct relevance to the union project itself. This was stated plainly in an examination by the Lords of a bill introduced in the 1606 session attacking the Council's jurisdiction.

> Such exemption will prove but a deseigne for the Welshmen to free themselfes ... of the same government, and a manifest overture to abridge or dissolve the like aucthoritie of the Lord President & Councell in the North; especiallie now, when the happie union of England & Scotland maie happilie admitt more pretenses for the same then heretofore.[135]

That Maurice opposed the attack on the Council, should perhaps be viewed in a wider 'British', rather than merely a Welsh, context. Likewise, it is probably not coincidental that two of the most fervent proponents of the cause against the Council in the Marches, Sir Herbert Croft and Sir Roger Owen, were opponents of the union with Scotland.[136]

The examination of the constitutional relationship between England and Wales in the four shires case, combined with questions raised about the extent of Prince Henry's authority in his principality after 1610, encouraged

---

[132] R. Reid, *The King's Council in the North* (1921), p. 358; BL, Cotton Vitellius C.i, fo. 147; TNA, SP14/32/14.

[133] For example, Sheffield City Archives, Wentworth Woodhouse, Str.P. 13/125; TNA, SP14/31/36, 14/37/55.

[134] BL, Cotton Titus B.viii, fo. 51. See also J. Spedding (ed.), *The Life and Letters of Sir Francis Bacon* (1868), iii, pp. 380, 221, 229; TNA, SP14/77/15.

[135] TNA, SP14/19/35.

[136] Willson, *Bowyer*, pp. 248–9.

Welsh scrutiny of an anomalous provision in the Henrician union legislation. A clause in the act 34 & 35 Henry VIII, c. 26, drawing on precedents from the time of Edward I, allowed the monarch to make laws in Wales under the great seal which would be as valid as if they had been enacted by parliament.[137] This clause evidently unsettled a number of the Welsh gentry, who took steps to have it repealed in the 1610 parliament. Their initiative was distinct from the efforts to remove the four shires from the jurisdiction of the Council in the Marches, though in some respects it was a product of the debates on this matter.[138]

The bid to have the clause repealed became enmeshed in the attempts to achieve a financial settlement between king and Commons known as the 'Great Contract'. The Welsh initiative is to be found in a petitionary address to parliament, apparently composed during the session.[139] It is difficult to know exactly who was involved in the framing of the petition, though Peter Roberts considers it to read 'like the joint composition of the Welsh MPs' and it is hard to disagree.[140] Indeed, a petition of 1621 referred to 'the knights & burgesses [of Wales]' assembled in the 1604–10 and 1614 parliaments who made 'humble suite to yor majestie for a repeale & revocacon of that clause'.[141] This confirms that the earlier petition was a rare example of the Welsh MPs acting in concert on behalf of the principality and, as in the case of purveyance, that this issue saw the construction of what may legitimately be termed a Welsh interest group in the Commons. Again, however, we should be wary of characterizing this as a permanent or cohesive

---

[137] This section owes much to the penetrating essay by Peter Roberts: 'Wales and England after the Tudor "union": crown, principality and parliament, 1543–1624', in C. Cross et al. (eds), *Law and Government under the Tudors* (Cambridge, 1988), pp. 111–38. See also his 'The "Henry VIII clause", delegated legislation and the Tudor principality of Wales', in T. G. Watkin (ed.), *Legal Record and Historical Reality* (1989), pp. 37–50, and P. Croft, 'The parliamentary installation of Henry, Prince of Wales', *Historical Research*, 65 (1992), 179–84.

[138] Roberts, 'Wales and England', p. 129, notes that the Welsh petition concerning the clause in 1610 deliberately distanced itself from the complaints by the border MPs.

[139] TNA, SP14/55/59.

[140] Roberts, 'Wales and England', p. 129.

[141] TNA, SP14/119/138.

force in parliament, though admittedly it demonstrates how a matter affecting the whole of Wales could elicit a collective response from its representatives.

The Welsh petition of 1610 stated that the immediate circumstances for the legislative provision had long since passed, and claimed that the power to make discretionary law had only been given to Henry VIII and not to his successors. The Welsh MPs accordingly asked for repeal of the clause as part of the negotiations over the Great Contract from which otherwise they would receive 'litle benefytt'. These arguments evidently swayed the Commons, which included repeal of the clause as part of the Contract on 16 July 1610.[142] The next day a report was made to the House that the king had considered the grievances, and regarding the Welshmen's representation, 'he willingly yielded, it was a mark of conquest. He wished that England and Wales might be all alike. He would not that any law should be altered by his letters patents'.[143] From this point, removal of the 'grievance' had full royal backing, and it would appear that it was political circumstance rather than royal intransigence which prevented it from being enacted earlier.[144] Indeed, it was to be propounded by the king himself as a bargaining weapon, a 'bill of grace', offered to the Commons in this and subsequent parliaments.[145] The collapse of the Great Contract and the legislative nullity of the two succeeding parliaments, however, meant that the Henrician proviso remained on the statute book for another fourteen years.

The royal backing for repeal manifested itself in a bill, drafted by the king's 'learned counsell', and first read in the Commons on 13 April 1614.[146] Welsh interest was evident at

---

[142] Foster, *Proceedings, 1610*, i, p. 141; ii, pp. 278–9.

[143] Ibid., ii, p. 283; *LJ*, ii, p. 661; Winwood, *Memorials*, iii, p. 193; Dodd, 'Apprenticeship', 33. It is difficult to agree with Roberts that James's agreement was recompense for Welsh support for union with Scotland: Roberts, 'Wales and England', p. 130.

[144] Cf. Dodd, 'Apprenticeship', 56, who claimed the bill 'excited relatively little interest and no opposition, for it was in tune with the determination of the popular leaders to rid the country of the relics of Tudor dictatorship'.

[145] Foster, *Proceedings, 1610*, ii, p. 331, n.; *CJ*, p. 459; Jansson, *Proceedings, 1614*, p. 50.

[146] TNA, SP14/119/138; NLW, MS 9055E/651; HMC, *Hastings MSS*, iv, p. 241; *CJ*, p. 463.

its second reading on 18 April, when the lawyer Matthew Davies endorsed the bill which allowed full legal union with England to be finally realized, and thanked James personally 'for release of his power'.[147] Another Welsh lawyer, William Jones of Beaumaris, also supported the bill, which was committed to all the members for Wales and the four border shires, a provision suggestive of its general application and interest for the region under the jurisdiction of the Council in the Marches. The bill proceeded to the Lords where the Lord Chancellor endorsed it as a bill of grace 'offered . . . by his Majesty to his subjects for their good'.[148] Despite this favour, the bill proceeded no further in this parliament, but the Welshmen clearly did not wish to lose the measure and petitioned the king that they be allowed to reintroduce it in the next assembly.

The 1621 petition was more explicit about the Welsh impetus behind the bill, it being delivered in the name of 'the knights and burgesses assembled in parliament for the principality and dominion of Wales'.[149] They voiced their concerns that the power to alter law at pleasure 'might in succeedinge ages make them subiect to uncertainty both of lawes & goverment'. The Welsh MPs asked for the king's approval for their initiative, and were careful to make it clear that they wished in no way to 'restraine or abridge' the authority of the Council in the Marches. As in 1614, James was evidently supportive, and a bill, presumably identical or very similar to that submitted in the previous parliament, was introduced in the Commons on 6 March.[150] It followed the form and language of earlier entreaties, referring to the continued obedience of the Welsh nation and the redundancy of the powers given under the act, and called for the 'abolytion of distinction and difference betweene the subiects of England & Wales'.[151] Despite royal support and assurances from the petitioners themselves, the bill still

---

[147] *CJ*, p. 467; Roberts, 'Wales and England', p. 133. Davies reported the bill from committee: *CJ*, p. 490; Jansson, *Proceedings, 1614*, p. 302.
[148] *LJ*, ii, p. 708; HMC, *Hastings MSS*, iv, p. 264.
[149] TNA, SP14/119/138.
[150] *CJ*, p. 539; *CD1621*, ii, pp. 169–70; v, pp. 28, 273.
[151] House of Lords RO, Main Papers, 12 May 1621.

caused considerable disquiet among those most closely associated with the Council in the Marches. In late February the lord president of the Council, the earl of Northampton, wrote to one of the justices at Ludlow, Sir James Whitelocke, that 'the cheifest & onely busines that is moved in the parliament house concerning Wales is the generall desire of the knights & burgesses of the Principallity to repeal the clause of the act of 34th of Henry the 8'.[152] This was the most explicit reference yet that the measure had the full backing of all the Welsh members in the Commons. Northampton, however, had serious reservations, noting that he was 'not yet satisfied' of the extent to which the act would be 'prejudiciall to the kings power or government or validity of our instruccons'. He added that before the act passed he would confer with the king's counsel, and he asked for the opinion of the judges at Ludlow 'if you doubt any thing in it'.

Whitelocke and the other judges replied to Northampton in a letter dated the day after the bill's first reading in the Commons. They noted that they were 'no strangers ourselves to this business, for all of us have bin heretofore present at the debating thereof in former parliaments'. They were clearly alarmed that the proposed repeal could affect the powers of the Council in the Marches as well as the king's prerogative. The judges declared themselves

> all fully resolved, that if that clause be repealed, there must be a speciall saving & proviso for the fully upholding & maintaining of the kings power of altering, adding & diminishing the instruccons for this court & government otherwise there will ensue great danger thereby.[153]

Their concern that the bill could be used to prejudice the king's instructions which defined the Council's authority was shared by some members of the committee considering it, for on 27 April the civil lawyer Dr Barnaby Gooch reported the bill to the House with a proviso 'for the jurisdiccion of the counsell of the Marches'.[154] It is possible that

---

[152] NLW, Add. 339F, p. 119.
[153] Ibid., p. 120. The judges in question were Sir James Whitelocke, Sir Henry Townshend and Sir Francis Eure.
[154] *CD1621*, iv, p. 265.

Northampton had communicated his concerns and the opinion of the Ludlow judges to some of the committee members. This impression is strengthened by the terms of the proviso itself, which maintained that the bill would not 'extend to abridge the authoritie or jurisdiccon' of the Council.[155] It had an easy passage in the Commons thereafter, but appears to have run into some difficulties in the Lords. It was committed to a body of peers who had considerable local knowledge, with the earls of Worcester and Pembroke, the bishops of St Asaph and Bangor, and the lord president of the Council in the Marches, Northampton, all present.[156] Worcester reported the bill a week later with some minor amendments to the proviso from the Commons concerning the Council. The committee did not proceed any further until after the recess, when Worcester called for the bill to be considered again by the original committee.[157] They found it necessary to amend the proviso concerning the Council once more, probably at the insistence of Northampton.[158] It was reported back to the Commons, but fell victim to the paralysis of business over the question of parliamentary privilege.[159]

As with many other measures of the 1621 parliament, the bill was reintroduced in the Commons in the 1624 assembly, where it was committed to a body including Welsh lawyers such as Sir Euble Thelwall, Sir Peter Mutton and Sir Henry Williams, along with six other Welsh MPs.[160] After some difficulties over the exact wording of the original statute had been resolved, the bill passed the Commons, but encountered familiar problems in the Lords, where objections were made that it threatened the authority of the Council in the Marches. This occasioned a conference between committees

---

[155] House of Lords RO, Main Papers, 12 May 1621. The proviso is still attached to the main bill.

[156] *LJ*, iii, p. 130.

[157] Ibid., pp. 146, 172; S. R. Gardiner (ed.), *Notes of Debates in the House of Lords ... 1621* (Camden Soc., 103, 1870), p. 97.

[158] *LJ*, iii, pp. 186, 188; Roberts, 'England and Wales', p. 136. In the 1624 session, Thomas Powell alluded to Northampton's 'opposicion' to the bill: NLW, MS 9059E/1216.

[159] *CD1621*, ii, pp. 507–8; Russell, *Parliaments*, p. 141.

[160] *CJ*, p. 730; Roberts, 'Wales and England', 137.

of the Lords and Commons to try to resolve the difficulties, something encouraged by Prince Charles.[161] The opposition apparently stemmed from Lord President Northampton, but it was not sufficient to block the bill which duly passed on 4 May.[162] Henry Wynn noted this act particularly when he wrote from London to his father in Caernarfonshire, as did the Flint member, William Ravenscroft, who described how 'the bill of Wales is passed both howses, and many other good actes'.[163] Such dispatches demonstrate that the issue was of interest and importance to Welsh constituents as well as to MPs. The eventual statute was the same as the bill introduced in 1621, saving the much-contested proviso.[164] The act did not mention the Council in the Marches at all, but rather the force of the Henrician union legislation was generally affirmed.

The 'Henry VIII' clause provides a rare example of Welsh MPs working in concert in the Commons towards a single objective. It also demonstrates how the discussion of 'Britain' in the early Stuart parliaments stimulated an examination of Wales's relationship to a wider unity, and encouraged action over what was perceived to be a bar to that 'perfect' union envisaged by its Tudor architects. Although direct involvement on questions such as the Anglo-Scottish union was limited, the British framework nevertheless constituted another context within which Welsh politics operated in early Stuart parliaments.

The welsh 'party' and activity in parliament, 1604–1629

The issue of the 'Henry VIII' clause was rare among the measures involving Welsh MPs between 1604 and 1629, in that they promoted it *en bloc*. There were other instances, such as purveyance and the lobbying for exemptions from subsidy payments, when an argument can be made for collective

---

[161] *LJ*, iii, p. 314; Northampton RO, Finch-Hatton 50, fo. 74; Bodleian Library, Rawlinson D.1100, fos 22ᵛ, 40.
[162] *LJ*, iii, pp. 336, 339; NLW, MS 9059E/1216.
[163] NLW, MSS 9059E/1220; 1595E, fo. 159.
[164] *SR*, iv, p. 1219.

Welsh action in parliament, primarily because these were issues which affected the entire principality and might generate corporate action. Such responses had been envisaged by George Owen of Pembrokeshire in the late Elizabethan period; he believed that problems affecting the whole of Wales merited group action by all its MPs.[165] There is little concrete evidence from Tudor parliaments of Welsh members operating in this fashion, however, and the early seventeenth-century material suggests that this was a rare occurrence under James I and Charles I also.[166] One must remember that 'Wales' was a potent rhetorical symbol which was occasionally deployed to bestow legitimacy, even when only parts of the principality were concerned directly with an issue.[167] For the most part, however, Welsh MPs engaged with, or promoted, issues which were of interest to themselves or regional or economic interest groups within the principality. This calls into question some of the basic assumptions that underlie Dodd's assessment of Welsh parliamentary politics in this period, and consequently much of the subsequent historiography on early Stuart Welsh politics.

One of these assumptions is that there was a collegiality among Welsh members, that a Welsh 'interest' akin to a party existed in the early Stuart Commons. Dodd considered the commitment of bills to Welsh MPs to be a recognition of this 'interest'.[168] However, the committal of bills affecting certain constituencies to the representatives of those constituencies was common practice, and certainly did not mean that all members would be present at the committee. Indeed, the development of the naming of larger numbers of MPs from particular regions or professions to committees was partly a response to the small numbers who actually attended meetings.[169] This practice causes problems for

[165] G. Owen, *The Description of Pembrokeshire*, ed. H. Owen (1892–1936), iii, pp. 66–7, 69, 114–19.
[166] Bowen, 'Wales at Westminster'; Roberts, 'Principality of Wales', 131.
[167] See below, p. 264.
[168] Dodd, 'Apprenticeship', 12–14, 36; idem, 'Parliaments, 1625–1629', 47; idem, 'Wales under the early Stuarts', in A. J. Roderick (ed.), *Wales through the Ages* (Llandybie, 1960), ii, p. 56. He also wrote of the Welsh MPs 'embodying the political interests and traditions of a people': 'Pattern of politics', 70.
[169] C. R. Kyle, '"It will be a scandal to show what we have done with such a

Dodd's interpretation as fewer local Welsh bills came before the House. The lack of any reason for the committal to Welsh MPs led him to acknowledge that 'the cohesive bond between the Welsh members is visibly slackening as Welsh legislation in the House diminishes in volume and the number of topics on which they can speak with one voice and act together grows smaller'.[170] In fact, it is difficult to identify an issue where Welsh members spoke with 'one voice', and Dodd's conception of a Welsh 'interest', identified by the procedural conventions of committee nomination, breaks down.

Although cultural and linguistic factors probably cast the Welsh MPs as a distinct group at Westminster,[171] Dodd's characterization of them as a politically unified phalanx capable of possessing 'leaders' is highly problematic.[172] He considered that Welsh MPs' 'common interests often made them act as a group', and he discussed the Welsh members articulating 'collective views on questions of special moment to Wales'.[173] Although it has been shown that such a collective view could occasionally be formulated in response to certain issues, apart from the convention of committee nomination, such a coherent body of Welsh MPs is invisible in the available sources. Dodd also considered that the more prominent Welsh members constituted 'leaders' of the Welsh MPs, and he described Sir James Perrot in the 1621 parliament, for example, as a 'brilliant leader ... [of] the Welsh group'.[174] Not that Dodd viewed the Welsh MPs as a monolithic political bloc, but his assumption that they acted consistently and in concert appears to distort the evidence.

number"': House of Commons committee attendance lists', in idem, *Parliament, Politics and Elections*; idem, 'Attendance, apathy and order? Parliamentary committees in early Stuart England', in idem and J. T. Peacey (eds), *Parliament at Work: Parliamentary Committees, Political Power and Public Access in Early Modern England* (Woodbridge, 2002), pp. 49–58.

[170] Dodd, 'Parliaments, 1625–1629', 47.
[171] See, for example, the committal of the bill of grace for Wales in 1614 to 'all Welshmen of the house': *CJ*, p. 468.
[172] See Lloyd's criticism of Dodd in his examination of the MPs from south-west Wales, where he considers it a 'nonsense to attribute the virtues of individuals to the groups into which they may conveniently be categorized': Lloyd, *Gentry of South-West Wales*, p. 112.
[173] Dodd, 'Apprenticeship', 67; idem, 'Parliaments, 1625–1629', 16.
[174] Dodd, 'Apprenticeship', 48.

Dodd's thesis is also problematic in its treatment of the political outlook of Welsh MPs and his characterization of legislative activity. Dodd's work was a product of the Whiggish school associated with Wallace Notestein and Sir John Neale, and as such it implicitly accepted that politics from the accession of James I was characterized by an escalating dispute between king and parliament which resulted ultimately in civil war.[175] This led him to assess a number of Welsh MPs in the 1621 parliament on the basis of their civil war activities, and to describe Welsh MPs as 'loyalists', 'firmly schooled in monarchical sentiments' and 'rallying in a body to the crown'.[176] Few would now endorse such a polarized view of parliamentary politics between 1604 and 1629. Rather than being driven by a nascent royalism, most Welsh MPs in parliament were more concerned with maintaining a low profile and discharging local business. H. A. Lloyd has trenchantly described the torpor which characterized the political activity of the majority of MPs from south-west Wales during this period.[177] This relative anonymity describes most of the Welsh MPs who sat in parliament, yet it should not be exaggerated, for the majority of English MPs were similarly undistinguished. The impression given of lacklustre 'apprentices' failing to make use of parliament is compounded by the fact that we are dealing with only twenty-seven representatives in each parliament; starting from an expectation of 'Welsh' activity at Westminster, it is not surprising that the principality's members do not impress for there were few issues which generated collective action. We must also be sensitive to the nature of our sources, for, as has been shown, in the case of Sir William Herbert and the Shrewsbury drapers, intense lobbying at Westminster on matters of considerable local importance has often left almost no impression in parliamentary records. What evidence does exist suggests that, despite rare individuals like Sir James Perrot who contributed heavily to debate, the majority of Welsh members were moved by

[175] Elton, 'Wales', p. 92, n. 3.
[176] Dodd, 'Apprenticeship', 48, 67; idem, 'Parliaments, 1625–1629', 48; idem, 'Pattern of politics', 29.
[177] Lloyd, *Gentry of South-West Wales*, pp. 93–112.

matters of interest to their localities rather than by political ideologies.

Dodd's conception of the role of Welsh MPs in the business of parliament also needs some modification. He concentrated on the *causes célèbres* of these sessions, treating 'minor' measures cursorily and ignoring altogether other business that was clearly of importance to Welsh constituents. The examination of some of the business discharged by Welshmen in parliament demonstrates that it was frequently these 'minor' measures which agitated Welsh representatives most. In his examination of the legislative activity of Wales in the forty years after its enfranchisement, Geoffrey Elton concluded that Wales's tally was disappointing, 'and must call in doubt whether an entity to be called Wales had much reality'.[178] The legislative programme from Wales in the period 1604–29 is probably even less impressive, but it is misleading to attempt to construct the political validity of 'Wales' simply from the number of bills its representatives introduced in parliament. Welsh MPs did, nonetheless, engage in some legislative activity, and sought to promote and defend the interests of their constituencies in parliament. Ties to the constituency were one of the key influences exerted on a Welsh MP, and whether it was lobbying for an exemption from a tax to repair Chepstow bridge, or the repeal of the 'Henry VIII' clause, much of what happened at Westminster in these parliamentary sessions should be seen in the light of events in Wales. This is not to argue that Welsh MPs were simply apolitical localists or incapable of reconciling the needs of their constituents with a wider political perspective which was, in fact, one of the functions of parliament.[179] It is to this wider perspective that we now turn.

---

[178] Elton, 'Wales', p. 91.
[179] In his work on parliament in the 1620s, Conrad Russell concentrates overmuch on the negative nature of localist pressures on MPs: Russell, *Parliaments*, pp. 1–84, and passim.

3

THE BURDENS OF WAR: WALES IN THE 1620s

The outbreak of the Thirty Years' War in 1618 profoundly affected the internal politics of England. After James I's daughter, Elizabeth, and her husband lost the Palatinate to Catholic forces, England and Wales became increasingly involved in this confessional struggle which formed the backdrop to all parliaments of the 1620s. These developments also materially affected the localities through demands for money and men towards military involvement on the continent and in Ireland. Wales could not remain isolated from these wider events, though their impact on Welsh society has received little scholarly attention, and the work of A. H. Dodd remains the basis for modern evaluations of the Welsh reaction to the international tensions of the 1620s.[1]

The redirection of foreign policy in the 1620s as England became embroiled in a war with Spain and later France required considerable amounts of money which could not be provided by the traditional means of parliament alone, or at least could not be provided on terms which the government considered acceptable. As a consequence, a plethora of financial expedients was employed outside parliament throughout the 1620s to raise the necessary funds, culminating in the politically charged demand for a forced loan. This chapter will consider the success of these expedients in the shires of Wales, and also the closely related question of the political consequences of raising money without recourse to parliament. Intimately connected with these fiscal demands was the disruptive pressing of men to fight in the wars, which placed considerable strain on the Welsh lieutenancy and brought the realities of war to the remotest communities of the principality.

---

[1] For the cursory treatment of the 1620s in discussions of defence and security, see J. G. Jones *The Welsh Gentry, 1536–1640* (Cardiff, 1998), pp. 133–63; G. Williams, *Renewal and Reformation: Wales, c.1415–1642* (Oxford, 1993), pp. 358–80. Dodd's treatment can be found in 'Apprenticeship', 44–5, 54, 63–6; 'Parliaments, 1625–1629', 16–47; 'Pattern of politics', 29–34.

The war provided a backdrop for all the parliaments of the 1620s, and the discussion of foreign affairs formed an important context for Welsh MPs' activities. An attempt has been made to combine analysis of the impact of the continental conflict and a discussion of parliamentary action by Welsh representatives on the pressing issues of war, finance and counsel. This chapter offers a reassessment of the Welsh response to the European crisis of the 1620s by means of an integrated narrative wherein parliament and the locality are regarded as complementary sites of political experience and discussion.

The cause of the Palatinate and the parliament of 1621

Wales in the early seventeenth century was not the informational backwater it has sometimes been portrayed, and the deteriorating political situation on the continent after 1618 quickly became a regular topic of Welsh gentry correspondence.[2] Interest was also heightened by the participation in the fighting of prominent Welsh gentry such as John Salusbury of Lleweni and Sir Thomas Wynn of Melai.[3] The cause of Elizabeth and the Elector Palatine was soon pressed home to the wider population of Wales in a rather more direct way: by the request for a voluntary benevolence to assist them.

On 30 August 1620 the earl of Northampton, lord president of the Council in the Marches of Wales, wrote to the sheriff and justices of Flintshire about Baron von Dohna's request for financial assistance for the Palatinate. He noted that the Flintshire men had been 'desirous to know how the fruytes of these lettres have rypened in other shyres [of Wales]', informing them that 'divers have bine liberall already and noe lesse expectacon is had of others'.[4] The Flintshire deputy lieutenants replied in October that they had met several times

[2] Bowen, thesis, 118–33.
[3] *CWP*, no. 900; NLW, MSS 9060E/1340, 1345; 5390D, p. 155; Lleweni (Correspondence) 57; Brogyntyn (Clenennau) 391; R. Cust, 'News and politics in early seventeenth century England', *Past and Present*, 112 (1986), 69–70; N. Tucker, 'Volunteers in the Thirty Years' War', *NLWJ*, 16 (1969–70), 61–76.
[4] Cardiff Central Library, 5.50, fo. 86.

and found the county 'ready and willinge to further the said service to the uttermost of their abilities'. But, they continued, because of the low value of corn and cattle, they were 'altogether unable to yeeld to any contribution'. They did, however, have in their hands £100 which had been collected for the abortive mobilization of troops for Ireland in 1614, 'which some of the country are willing and desirous . . . [to] be imploied for the furtherance of the affairs of Bohemia'.[5] Northampton's letter and the reply of the Flintshire officials suggest that the Welsh response to the cause of the Palatinate, like that of many areas, was fairly generous.[6] Other evidence also suggests that there was a positive response to the request for this benevolence in Wales. Sir James Perrot, for example, complained in the 1621 parliament that Pembrokeshire's contribution had been retained in the sheriff's hands, while the sheriff of Carmarthenshire in 1620–1, Griffith Lloyd, at his death was found to have £91 'of the countreyes moneyes' levied for 'the distressed inhabitantes of the Pallattynate'.[7] Omissions like these underlined the fact that the benevolence was merely a request for money and not an enforceable tax. James could not rely on such voluntary contributions to support his diplomatic position towards Spain, and to bolster his position he resolved to call a parliament.

The 1621 assembly did not, as Dodd maintained, seek to take from the Crown 'the real work of government'.[8] There was, in fact, little real debate about the ideologies of confessional war, though the degree to which this bubbled under the surface is open to dispute.[9] James made it quite plain in his opening speech, however, that he believed parliament should grant supply to strengthen his negotiating position with Spain. The Welsh MPs responded to this request in a qualified manner. At the first reading of the subsidy bill, Sir Thomas Trevor asked for the Welsh counties to be excused from payment because they were concurrently collecting the

[5] NLW, MS 6285E, pp. 14–15.
[6] T. Cogswell, *Home Divisions: Aristocracy, The State and Provincial Conflict* (Manchester, 1998), 35–7.
[7] *CJ*, p. 594; *CD1621*, ii, p. 326; iii, p. 96; iv, p. 265; TNA, C205/14/11.
[8] Dodd, 'Apprenticeship', 54.
[9] See the essays by Russell and Cogswell in J. F. Merritt (ed.), *The Political World of Thomas Wentworth, Earl of Strafford, 1621–1641* (Cambridge, 1996), pp. 24–62.

mise, and repeated his request for a delay at the bill's second reading. Significantly, the Haverfordwest member, Sir James Perrot, although one of those most vocal in favour of an aggressive policy against Spain, supported Trevor's motion for a suspension. The proviso for Wales passed the House by 94 votes to 66, with the Welsh evidently being able to drum up considerable support outside the principality for what may have been seen as a traditional privilege.

Shortly afterwards, Welsh claims of exemption were dropped and James singled out the Welsh MPs for praise in a message to the House:

> especiallie he thanks those that had care to make it [the subsidy] as beneficiall to him as might bee by fewe exemptions, and perticulerly tooke notice of the good disposition of the gentlemen of Wales in relinquishinge that respite they were wont to have dureinge the payment of mises.[10]

What had happened in the interim? It is tempting to ascribe this *volte-face* to the Welsh members' desire to provide for the Palatinate, and make the grant as 'beneficiall' for James as possible. Yet the earlier endorsement of the proviso by Perrot, an enthusiastic supporter of the Palatinate cause, casts some doubt on this. A more plausible explanation lies in the fact that, immediately after James's message Solicitor-General Heath informed the House of the king's pleasure 'that the bills of grace showld be speeded, and that he wilbe as readie to take away the grievances as we to desire it'.[11] One of these was the bill for repealing the 'Henry VIII' clause which all Welsh members had petitioned James to allow in February.[12] The close proximity of this announcement to the Welsh abandonment of claims of exemption suggests the two were linked. It would appear that the Welsh MPs agreed to allow immediate collection of subsidies in return for expediting the Welsh bill of grace.[13] Although supply was not officially tied to

---

[10] *CD1621*, iv, p. 145.
[11] *CD1621*, iv, pp. 145–6.
[12] See above, pp. 77–9. The bill of grace for Wales had been entrusted to Sir Thomas Trevor on 27 February 1621: *CJ*, p. 529.
[13] The 1621 subsidies were indeed collected in Wales during 1621 and 1622, despite the fact that subsidies from 1606 and 1610 were still outstanding: TNA, C212/22/21–2; E401/2434, 2313; NLW, MSS 9061E/1412; 9062E/1517.

the redress of any grievances, it seems that the Welsh position on the subsidy was characterized by a more subtle approach directed towards the repeal of the Henrician clause. This challenges the idea that dropping claims of exemption simply reflected a 'sudden detonation of patriotic fervour', though several Welsh members were clearly sympathetic to the plight of the king's daughter.[14]

Foremost of these was Sir James Perrot of Haroldston, Pembrokeshire, and any discussion of the Welsh response to the continental crisis in the 1621 parliament runs the risk of being dominated by him.[15] He was by far the most active Welsh speaker on foreign affairs, but Perrot was an exceptional case and was not representative of Welsh MPs generally.[16] A fervent Protestant who held 'as good a claim to be called a puritan as anyone in the Commons',[17] he viewed the Palatinate crisis as part of a wider crusade against Catholics at home and abroad, a perspective which informed his contributions to public debate throughout the 1620s. Perrot obviously felt the plight of Elizabeth and her husband, the Elector Palatine, very keenly, and one copy of his *Invitation Unto Prayer* contains additional prayers and a dedication to the queen of Bohemia, handwritten by Perrot himself.[18]

Perrot is interesting for the manner in which he linked the international situation explicitly with religious conditions in Wales, providing some revealing evidence of how local contexts shaped the views of this forceful anti-papist. For example, in a debate on the bill against scandalous ministers on 23 November 1621, he took issue with Sir Dudley Digges, who had called it needless, stating that 'if the gentleman ... lived where I live, I think he would be of another mind, and whereas he thinks it a scandal to our ministry to punish scandalous ministers, I think ... it is a scandal to suffer them unpunished'.[19] This concern was again present in his speech

[14] G. D. Owen, *Wales in the Reign of James I* (Woodbridge, 1988), p. 159.
[15] Dodd, 'Apprenticeship', 43–6.
[16] H. A. Lloyd, *The Gentry of South-West Wales, 1540–1640* (Cardiff, 1968), pp. 104–7, esp. p. 107.
[17] Russell, *Parliaments*, p. 13.
[18] J. Perrot, *An Invitation Unto Prayer* (1624), MS dedicatory in volume at NLW.
[19] *CD1621*, ii, p. 439.

of 26 November, when Perrot declared himself firmly for 'a war of diversion' against Spain, but also pressed the need to 'settle a course at home for arms', because he claimed that there was but one barrel of powder in Wales. He also drew attention to the danger which could come from Ireland, which he described as 'the back door', an understandable fear for a Pembrokeshire man whose father had been lord deputy of Ireland.[20] The problem of recusancy animated him again in the subcommittee discussing religion on 29 November, when he described how, 'in a shire near him', a minister had preached against the Gunpowder Treason and had been beaten by papists who 'said they would teach him better doctrine'.[21] The impression given of Wales as a region dangerously infected with recusancy was strengthened in December with the submission to the Commons of a petition from Eleazer Jackson, a minister in Abergavenny, Monmouthshire, who had encountered violent opposition from the numerous recusants in the area.[22] Such apparent threats to the established religion in Wales helped to shape Perrot's concern with the religious situation on the continent. His famous 'declaration' of support for the Palatinate cause at the end of the first parliamentary session also reflected this yoking of foreign and domestic enemies; he called on members to 'provide for ... the mayntenance of true religion' as it 'was soe much distressed abroad in forraine partes & sought to be indamaged here att home'.[23] Perrot certainly did not conform to the Russellian model of a Commons man uninterested in war, but among the Welsh members of the 1621 parliament he was a lone voice advocating this kind of aggressive international Protestant vision.

The other Welsh MPs were almost invisible compared with Perrot. This does not necessarily mean that they were uninterested in the continental crisis, however, and we should

---

[20] *CJ*, p. 645; *CD1621*, iii, p. 449.
[21] *CD1621*, ii, p. 475. It is unclear whether this was a direct reference to the petition of Eleazer Jackson, to be discussed below, but Perrot was certainly concerned about communication between the recusants of Pembrokeshire and Monmouthshire: TNA, SP16/88/23.
[22] HMC, *Salisbury MSS*, xxiv, pp. 242–3; *CD1621*, ii, p. 544; v, pp. 245–6.
[23] TNA, SP14/121/79.

remember that most English as well as Welsh members were non-speakers.[24] The whole business of the Palatinate was very delicate, the question of foreign policy being considered part of the *arcana imperii* so that many felt uncertain about discussing it in the House. The earl of Pembroke's client, Sir Edmund Morgan of Penhow, for example, appeared very nervous about the Commons debating the question of ordnance lying in the Tower, reportedly ready for shipment to Spain. Export of ordnance could only proceed with a royal licence, so Morgan was quick to ask the House 'to tender his Majesty's honour', considering it 'not fit to press too far'.[25] This demonstrates how issues surrounding foreign affairs could easily lead into areas of the prerogative normally left well alone; thus, some of the Welsh reticence may be attributed to circumspection rather than a lack of interest.

The debate concerning the Catholic Edward Lloyd of Llwyn-y-Maen and his disparaging remarks about the Elector Palatine and his wife offered an opportunity for the Commons to demonstrate their concern about the cause of the Palatinate without offending James. It is accordingly interesting that a number of Welsh members spoke out as part of the violent backlash against him. William Ravenscroft, the member for Flint, was one of those who called for Lloyd to be 'fyned at 1,000^{li} towards the warrs of the Pallatinat'.[26] Similarly, one of the Welsh 'Prices' stated that Lloyd should wear a paper with his remarks on it, be placed in the pillory, fined £200 and made to ride backwards on a horse.[27] Sir William Herbert and William Salusbury also contributed to this debate. Lloyd's case was clearly of interest to Welshmen, Owen Wynn informing his father in Caernarfonshire that Lloyd had been 'censured grevouslie' by the Commons for his 'unreverent speeches'.[28]

The Welsh members, then, were not among those most

---

[24] Welsh reticence is not explained by a change of procedure in the House, as Dodd maintained: Dodd, 'Apprenticeship', 47–8. Cf. S. Lambert, 'Procedure in the House of Commons in the early Stuart period', *English Historical Review*, 95 (1980), 753–81.
[25] *CD1621*, ii, p. 70; *CJ*, p. 519.
[26] *CD1621*, vi, p. 120.
[27] *CJ*, p. 601; *CD1621*, iii, p. 125.
[28] NLW, MSS 9057E/954, 957.

forward in 1621 on the topic of the Palatinate, possibly through fear of royal disfavour.[29] Yet this did not mean that the Welsh were uninterested in the war. Shortly after the end of the first session, Richard Wynn criticized the official line of trying to bargain for peace with Spain. He described current policy as a 'great dishonor of our nacion', and commented that while the continental wars raged, 'we sleepe secure, seeing the fyre in our naibours houses'.[30] If there was a lack of contribution from Welsh MPs on the floor of the House concerning foreign affairs, it was not because of their ignorance of developments on the continent.

1621–1624: THE BENEVOLENCE AND THE SPANISH MATCH

The 1621 parliament had legislated for the collection of two subsidies as a free gift to the king in support of his foreign obligations. The demands for money in Wales came at a difficult time because a severe depression ravaged local economies. In August 1621, Sir John Wynn wrote of the general scarcity of money, noting that Wales was particularly affected.[31] With the depression biting hard, many Welsh shires found it difficult to contribute to James's foreign policy which was in desperate need of support.

In an effort to obtain more funds, on 31 March 1622 the Privy Council issued letters requesting a 'voluntary contribucion', or benevolence, for the Palatinate, claiming that the recent parliament had not granted James a 'lyberall and speedie supplie'.[32] The economic difficulties which north Wales was experiencing represented a major obstacle to such a demand, Sir John Wynn writing 'God help us, heere is much calling for money & the cuntrey have not it'.[33] Similarly, in May 1622, the JPs of Anglesey wrote to the Council about the

---

[29] On the restriction of public discussion of these matters, see the St Paul's lecture of Griffith Williams of Llanllechid on 5 December 1621: G. Williams, *The Delights of the Saints* (1622), p. 252.
[30] NLW, MS 9057E/959. See also NLW, MS 9057E/958; Carmarthenshire RO, Dynevor 154/1.
[31] *CWP*, no. 973.
[32] *APC, 1621–3*, pp. 176–8.
[33] NLW, MS 9062E/1517.

problems they were experiencing. They related how, after calling before them 'all the subsidie men, beinge all the men of abilitie' in the county, they

> tooke every one by himselfe alone, and used all the meanes and perswasions we coulde. But they alleadged theire povertie and wante of mony, being exceedinglie decaied in theire estate these foure laste yeares for wante of sale of cattle whereon theire whole estate dependeth. Some with much adoe have yealded to give one full entier subsidie ... The rest that would by noe meanes that we coulde use ... be drawen to give after that rate.[34]

They asserted that this was not special pleading, and the difficulties would continue to hamper collection until the Anglesey taxpayers could sell their cattle in August.

A schedule for the assessment of the benevolence in Anglesey survives; it indicates that the JPs did not exaggerate the problems the levy faced in this shire.[35] Some 143 individuals on the island paid at least one subsidy, but a further 105 were listed as subsidymen who 'could not be drawn to give after the rate [one subsidy]'. These did donate some money towards the benevolence, but another thirty-two 'refuced to contribute and did not appear uppon sumons', although two evidently 'after yealded'. The whole benevolence ultimately provided £86 5s. 4d., which amounted to around one and a half parliamentary subsidies. The yield, therefore, was quite high, differing markedly from that in many English counties, which simply went through the motions of levying the benevolence on a select few. Nevertheless, in Anglesey significant resistance was encountered, with a relatively large number refusing to contribute at the specified rate, and many more refusing to pay anything at all. The justices' letter indicates that we should be wary of attributing this resistance to constitutional qualms about extra-parliamentary taxation. The island was experiencing considerable hardship because of the decay in the cattle trade, and resistance was probably the

---

[34] TNA, SP14/130/100.
[35] TNA, E179/219/19A, 20A. The schedule is dated May 1622, the same month as the justices' letter. It is unclear whether this money was actually sent to the Exchequer as it does not appear in the accounts, but the schedule indicates that it was levied on the island's inhabitants: TNA, E401/2313, 2435; SP14/135/62; 14/156/15.

result of a simple lack of resources rather than ideological considerations.[36] Yet the presence among the refusers of Richard Owen of Gwenynog, son of the Catholic Hugh Owen, and Owen Wood, whose family had links with the Gwenynog clan, suggests that in some cases religious sympathies and recusancy may help to account for some refusals.[37] The denial of aid to the Protestant struggle against Spanish expansionism in these cases may have had a harder ideological edge.

Although the king had tried to raise funds by a benevolence in 1614, it remained an unusual and controversial way of obtaining money, and caused Sir William Thomas of Caernarfonshire considerable difficulties. He wrote a fascinatingly detailed letter to Sir John Wynn on 18 May 1622, asking what the counties of Flint, Denbigh and Merioneth

> are determined to doe concerneinge this matter of benevolence, what they meane to give the Kings majestie, and after what manner, and whether they give two entire subsidies or one, or otherwise every one his voluntarie gifte, not observinge any other certen rates or grounds, but yeeldinge and bestowinge as every man is inclynde, which cannot amounte to any great matter.[38]

His belief that a truly voluntary contribution would only yield a small amount suggests that there was little enthusiasm for the benevolence in the county, while his enquiry after the actions of other counties reveals a familiar desire among early modern taxpayers to follow rather than lead in responding to requests for money. Thomas stated that the justices, 'cominge together with much adoe', had rated the benevolence at two subsidies. However, in his commotes of Arllechwedd Uchaf and Is Gwyrfai, they had decided on one subsidy because of the 'greate scarsity and wante of money'. For those rated on their goods in the subsidy roll, he believed half that amount to be fair: 'to receave lesse of any man in this kind & nature we held it very unfittinge & in it self dishonorable, and no way aunswerable to his Majestys pleasure'. Clearly uncertain as to how the benevolence should be gathered, Thomas asked

---

[36] TNA, SP14/138/68(i).
[37] NLW, Carreglwyd I/2013; Bodewryd 971; TNA, SP16/11/37; E.G. Jones, *Cymru a'r Hen Ffydd* (Cardiff, 1951), p. 69. See p. 122.
[38] NLW, MS 9058E/1019.

Wynn if he knew of a better course. He added that if the Privy Council wished them to rate at the level of the subsidy roll, 'in generall for want of money we shall find somewhat to doe to pay that, and by alledginge the povertye of the cuntrey, we must crave longer tyme of the Lords for that money to be payed'.

The benevolence was evidently viewed as an innovatory means of gathering monies, and was hardly as 'voluntary' as James would have liked it to appear. In contrast to the more principled objections raised in some areas, Thomas's problems with the levy did not centre on resistance to its extra-parliamentary nature.[39] Rather he appears to have experienced difficulties with the mechanics of assessment and the problems of extracting money from a population experiencing economic depression. By 10 September Thomas was collecting the benevolence at the rate of one subsidy, a rate he understood to be followed in other counties. Arllechwedd Uchaf and Is Gwyrfai, however, were finding it difficult to achieve even this,

> by reason verie many weare cessed ... that weare poore men & complained much for the last payments they made, and where they then paid viiis., they will not pay iis., insomuch as I am driven to search oute some of the alder men that escaped the payment of the subsidie, to see if they may be drawen to give somewhat towards the increase and augmentacon of the summe to come as neare as we can ... to a subsidie.[40]

This confusion about rating and the poverty of the country seriously hindered payment.

By the end of 1622, hundreds within Carmarthenshire, Montgomeryshire and Monmouthshire had paid some money to the Exchequer.[41] The general economic difficulties were hampering collection in south Wales as well as in the north. The Carmarthenshire justices wrote in July that the amount collected was 'farr lesse then wee ... are willing or ought to

---

[39] Cust, *Forced Loan*, pp. 157–8; M. L. Schwarz, 'Lord Saye and Sele's objections to the Palatinate benevolence of 1622', *Albion*, 5 (1971), 12–22.

[40] NLW, MS 9058E/1034.

[41] Montgomeryshire (£34 2s. 0d.); Carmarthenshire (£31 0s. 4d.); Monmouthshire (£219 3s. 6d.): TNA, E401/2313, 2435; SP14/134/12; 14/156/15.

geve if the state of our countrey were better able then it is at this instant'.[42] The hundred of Derllys sent its contribution with an apology for the small amount, blaming the 'scarsity of money ... by the fall in the prise of wooll'.[43] Other Welsh shires were not so prompt. In a revealing memorandum of Michaelmas term 1622, one of the Wynn family noted, 'I have bene in the office in the Exchequer ... and I find that most of Wales are behind as well as wee' in the benevolence.[44] This lack of expedition moved the Council to write to the justices of Pembrokeshire, Cardiganshire, Carmarthenshire and Breconshire on 12 February 1623, accusing them of dilatoriness and enjoining greater effort, yet by April only Pembrokeshire had responded, paying £87 8s. 10d., a sum representing half its average subsidy yield, and considerably less than its 1614 benevolence contribution of £213.[45] In the absence of additional evidence, it is difficult to determine whether this low yield was attributable to economic distress or to a more principled resistance to an extra-parliamentary levy. Problems of a different kind were encountered in Flintshire, where £80 was raised, about the value of a single subsidy, but the money was retained in the hands of the county sheriff, Sir John Hanmer, and Edward Jones, high constable of Mold.[46]

The difficulties which the collectors faced are well illustrated by a letter Sir John Wynn and William Holland of Caernarfonshire wrote to the Privy Council in January 1623. They observed that, although the country was 'exceedinge poore past beleefe ... of that little they had, wee found them willinge past their abilitie to doe his Majesties service'.

---

[42] TNA, SP14/131/62. However, the leading gentleman of the county, Sir John Vaughan of Golden Grove, made a personal contribution of £100 towards the Palatinate cause earlier in the year: TNA, E401/2434.
[43] TNA, SP14/132/23, 75. Lloyd confuses the benevolence with a parliamentary subsidy: Lloyd, *Gentry of South-West Wales*, p. 120. It is difficult to see why Owen singles out Carmarthenshire as a county which resisted the benevolence: Owen, *Wales in the Reign of James I*, p. 186.
[44] NLW, MS 9058E/1043. Dodd confused this and other references to the benevolence with the subsidies voted in 1621: 'Apprenticeship', 55.
[45] *APC, 1621–3*, pp. 409–10; Centre for Kentish Studies, U269/1 OE1264, 1077; TNA, E401/2315, 2436; SP14/156/15; E351/1950. The Pembrokeshire justices noted that some money had been promised but was not yet collected, though no further contributions were forthcoming.
[46] *APC, 1627–8*, pp. 117–18.

However, they also described how 'some, knowinge wee had no authoritie to leavie yt, would yeeld to nothinge, and divers of them weare papists, which although they weare drawne to promise at first, in the end would paye nothinge'.[47] The belief that Wynn and Holland had no authority to levy the benevolence suggests a principled resistance by some of the inhabitants in Caernarfonshire. It may also reflect the fact that the inhabitants were aware that this was merely a request for money rather than a compulsory tax, and so could not be levied in the same way as a parliamentary subsidy. The resistance of the recusant community to a levy for combating Catholic forces is easier to explain, and perhaps supports the conjecture that religious imperatives lay behind some of the Anglesey refusals. Generally, however, the backwardness of the Welsh counties in collecting the benevolence appears to have stemmed from difficulties arising from the novelty of the levy and the general economic slump that Wales was experiencing at the time.

The small amounts the benevolence raised nationally helped to ensure that James's negotiation with Spain for a marriage for his son rather than military action remained at the heart of his foreign policy. The Welsh appeared interested but not especially disconcerted by the plans for a Spanish match, and there is little evidence of the large and vocal body of opinion found in many parts of England which criticized a policy that did little to address the Protestants' plight on the continent.[48] In sharp contrast to calls for an interventionist policy in the European war, Sir John Stradling of St Donat's in Glamorgan dedicated a lengthy poem to James I in 1623 which extolled the virtues of the king's pacific approach. He endorsed accommodation and understanding in foreign policy and turned his anger towards those at home who called for a war with Spain:

---

[47] NLW, Add. 466E/1064.
[48] T. Cogswell, 'England and the Spanish match', in R. Cust and A. Hughes (eds), *Conflict in Early Stuart England* (Harlow, 1989), pp. 115–19; idem, *The Blessed Revolution* (Cambridge, 1989), pp. 20–53; P. Lake, 'Constitutional consensus and puritan opposition in the 1620s: Thomas Scott and the Spanish match', *Historical Journal*, 25 (1982), 805–25; G. Redworth, *The Prince and the Infanta: The Cultural Politics of the Spanish Match* (New Haven and London, 2003).

> Strange it is to behold the vulgar sort
> And some of better ranke, borne with the tide
> Into this gaping gulfe: Nay, it's a sport
> To see them tickled with a foolish pride
> Of others acts: They, only full of words,
> When most of them scarce ever drew their swords.[49]

Stradling saw divisions in terms of policy rather than of faith, and, like James, viewed the increasing agitation for a confessional war as an invitation to destruction. Rather did he call on Christians to unite in battle against the Turk, the true enemy of Christendom. This was wholly different to the virulent anti-Spanish sentiment espoused by men like Thomas Scott. The gentlemen of Wales appeared to view the continental situation with concern, but considered James's judgement in foreign affairs to be sound, and so they did not criticize his policy, or at least did not do so openly.

The political situation was electrified by Prince Charles's decision to by-pass the laborious negotiations for the Spanish match and to woo the Infanta in person, leaving in disguise for Madrid together with the duke of Buckingham in February 1623. Charles's mission to Spain gripped the country as people waited to see if they were to acquire a future Catholic queen. There was also a burning desire in Wales to know more about what was happening in Spain. Manuscript tracts relating to the match were circulated, including Thomas Alured's lengthy letter to Buckingham counselling against the marriage.[50] Phillip Powell of Brecon, meanwhile, copied verses into his commonplace book relating to Charles's and Buckingham's Spanish adventure.[51]

For the most part, however, the Welsh do not seem to have been as wary of the prospective match as were more virulently anti-Spanish sections of English society. Nevertheless, there were many who expressed their relief when Charles returned to England in October 1623, safe and unmarried. Vicar Rhys Prichard of Llandovery composed forty-three free-metre

---

[49] J. Stradling, *Beati Pacifici: A Divine Poem Written to the Kings Most Excellent Maiestie* (1623), p. 11.
[50] Cardiff Central Library, 5.50, fos 41–3; 4.56, pp. 21–4; NLW, Peniarth 410 (ii).
[51] Cardiff Central Library, 3.42, pp. 43–4.

verses in Welsh on the prince's return, denouncing the cunning Spaniard who attempted to trick him, and calling for Christ to 'keep him from Papistry'.[52] Meanwhile, in Haverfordwest on 31 October, the mayor, Sir James Perrot, ordered the bells to be rung 'upon the returne of the prince from Spayne'.[53] There was a significant section of Welsh society which had misgivings about a Spanish match, and was deeply relieved to see Charles return home without a Catholic bride. This outpouring of relief was the prelude to a political realignment at Court which was to some extent reflected in the provinces, wherein Charles and Buckingham forged an alliance to engineer a declaration of war against the Spanish.

The breach with Spain and the 1624 parliament

The negotiations foundered on the terms of the marriage treaty, and when Charles and Buckingham returned to England they were determined to exact revenge on Spain. This meant the end of plans for a dynastic union as the prince and Buckingham resolved on constructing a pro-war alliance at Court. Their scheme revolved around the calling of a parliament to endorse a Spanish war and provide money for its prosecution. This parliament was invited by the king to offer advice on whether he should break the treaties of negotiation with the Spanish. Debate has raged among historians as to the strength of support for war among the Commons, and although the evidence is seriously limited, it is difficult to find in Wales the kind of aggressive calls for interventionism articulated in many parts of England.[54] This may help to account for the comparative silence of the majority of Welsh MPs on this pressing issue, beyond a group associated with the earl of Pembroke, who pushed for ending the marriage negotiations and voting money towards the war which was likely to follow. As in 1621, wariness of entering the perilous waters of the

---

[52] Jones, *Welsh Gentry*, p. 158.
[53] Pembrokeshire RO, Haverfordwest Corporation 31/2.
[54] On the strength of war feeling, contrast Russell, *Parliaments*, pp. 158–76, with Cogswell, *Blessed Revolution*, pp. 166–226, and M. E. Kennedy, 'Legislation, foreign policy, and the "proper business" of the parliament of 1624', *Albion*, 23 (1991), 44–60.

king's prerogative may also be important in explaining the reticence of many Welsh members. There is, however, some evidence that the changed political climate had made some impact in Wales. For example, in Monmouthshire, a county notorious for its recusant population, the staunch Protestant Sir William Morgan of Tredegar was elected, and he presented to parliament a damning list of papists in Monmouthshire, claiming that there was an 'infinite number of people of all sorts' who did not attend church there. He could be certain that such a claim would have a significant impact in the atmosphere of this virulently anti-Catholic assembly.[55]

In terms of Welsh involvement, the most significant aspect of the revolution in foreign policy after Charles's return was the tenuous alliance of interest forged between Buckingham and Pembroke.[56] Pembroke was vigorously anti-Spanish but personally disliked Buckingham. It was the coincidence of their interests with respect to the Spanish question that placed them on similar, though not identical, courses in 1624. This *rapprochement* encouraged some of Pembroke's electoral clients in Wales to speak rather more frequently on foreign matters in this parliament compared with that of 1621. It would be a mistake, however, to characterize Pembroke's clientage as a coherent group with regard to the question of Spain. The rabidly anti-Spanish views of someone like Sir James Perrot, for example, had little in common with the approach of a man like Sir John Stradling.

Perrot was associated with Pembroke, served as his deputy vice-admiral in south Wales from 1611, and shared the earl's anti-Spanish outlook.[57] In 1624 Perrot dedicated a book of prayers 'to my honourable and worthy friends in parliament'. The dedication dwelt on parliament's role as counsellor of the king in important decisions, and urged the MPs to seek guidance from God in their crucial deliberations, a clear reference to the treaties with Spain which were to be considered by this assembly. As in 1621, he continued to be a prominent anti-

---

[55] NLW, Tredegar Park 93/51; *CJ*, p. 776; BL, Add. 18,597, fo. 163ᵛ.
[56] R. E. Ruigh, *The Parliament of 1624* (Cambridge, MA, 1971), pp. 33–6.
[57] TNA, SP16/5/81; 16/91/57; 16/151/50; HCA14/43, pt 3, fos 402, 404; J. Perrot, *The Chronicle of Ireland, 1584–1608*, ed. H. Wood (Dublin, 1923), pp. 1–2.

Spanish advocate, and moved on the first day of the parliament for a communion expressing thanks for Charles's safe return.[58] The anti-Catholic proclivities of members associated with Pembroke were also shown early in the session, when Sir Robert Mansell, vice-admiral of the navy and the Glamorgan member, upbraided an MP who had opposed a motion to have a guard placed against papists, accusing him 'of great want of iudgement for not fearing what desperat papists mought attempt'.[59]

Sir William Herbert, Pembroke's first cousin who sat for Montgomeryshire, Mansell and Perrot were all supportive in the Commons of the breach of the treaties. Particularly belligerent interventions were made by Mansell, a naval officer who was presumably angling for a commission in any prospective military action, and who also needed to curry favour with his superior in the navy, Buckingham.[60] In the Commons, then, we find the animating force of patronage and clientage operating upon a small group of Welsh members, who pressed for the breach with Spain, and often supported comparatively heavy subsidies for the war which was 'likely to ensue'.

We must be wary, however, of reducing such men to mere ciphers of peers like Pembroke and Buckingham, for they were a diverse group who differed considerably in their approaches and positions. Patronage was a complex web of processes and negotiations, and was at its most potent and effective when the aspirations and attitudes of the client meshed with those of the patron. Both Perrot and Sir John Stradling enjoyed Pembroke's patronage but differed considerably in their political outlook. Throughout the 1620s Perrot pressed vigorously for the prosecution of the war against Spain. Stradling was much more circumspect, as we have seen from his book of 1623, and this impression is supported by

---

[58] Perrot, *Invitation Unto Prayer*, sigs. A3-A6; TNA, SP14/166, fo. 2; *CJ*, pp. 671, 715.

[59] C. Thompson (ed.), *The Holles Account of Proceedings in the House of Commons in 1624* (Wivenhoe, 1985), 5.

[60] N. E. McClure (ed.), *Chamberlain Letters* (Philadelphia, 1939), ii, p. 535; Bodleian Library, Tanner 392, fo. 61^{r-v}; BL, Add. 18,597, fos 94^v–95; TNA, SP14/166, fo. 91.

another tract which he dedicated to Pembroke in 1625. This meditated on the advice to break with Spain that was given to the king by the 1624 parliament; Stradling upbraided the more belligerent proponents of war, asserting his rather narrow interpretation that the Commons had simply advised breaking the treaties and supporting any possible subsequent military action rather than had voted for a war.[61] The point may have appeared a moot one to many, but it underlines how Pembroke's followers in the Commons who supported their patron's position were far from being a coherent group.

In addition, we should acknowledge the influence of constituency interests which entered into the equation of activity in parliament. Sir William Morgan's revelation of the state of Monmouthshire recusancy was, doubtless, partly fuelled by his feud with Catholic elements in the county and the opportunity presented to him by this anti-Catholic parliament.[62] Pembrokeshire was seen as particularly vulnerable to foreign invasion, and there were calls from the bishops of Bangor and St David's during the parliament for the potential landing site of Milford Haven to be 'blocked upp'.[63] As we shall see, one of Perrot's central concerns was the defence of his native county, and the increased religious tensions there led to the voicing of concerns that it was not safe for the recusant George Barlow to hold the lordship of Narberth on the Haven 'as the case now standeth betweene us and Spain', he 'beinge soe ill affected in religion'.[64] Perrot also combined his desire for a Spanish war with a concern for his constituents, and he made several speeches demanding that recusants in England and Wales be disarmed, Jesuits banished and the penal laws properly implemented.[65] He also showed concern for his constituents' pockets, arguing that James's demands for a large subsidy to support his foreign engagements were 'insupportable unless moderated by the time of levying', that

[61] NLW, MS 5666C.
[62] TNA, STAC8/207/24, 28–31.
[63] S. R. Gardiner (ed.), *Notes of Debates in the House of Lords . . . 1624 and 1626* (Camden Soc., NS, 24, 1879), p. 16.
[64] NLW, Duchy of Cornwall P3.
[65] *CJ*, pp. 732, 751, 756; Harvard University, Houghton Library, Eng. 980, p. 102; Northamptonshire RO, Finch-Hatton 50, fo. 44ᵛ.

is, spread over time to give the taxpayer some breathing space.[66]

From this complex mixture of ideological and professional imperatives, religious concerns, patronage and constituency interests, those Welsh members who did speak in debates on the foreign situation largely supported the breach with Spain and the war which would probably result.[67] These men helped to carry the position that the treaties should be ended and a supply of over three subsidies voted towards the so-called 'four propositions' of the defence of Ireland, the outfitting of the fleet, coastal defence and assisting English troops in Dutch service. Although most were pleased with this resolution, disagreements over the exact nature of the contract which had been made between monarch and parliament in the prosecution of foreign policy in 1624 were to blight the remaining parliaments of the decade.

DEMANDS FOR MEN AND MONEY, 1624–1626

The decisions taken in the 1624 parliament ensured that requests for men and money would soon be made in Wales, although the pace of military preparations had been quickening over the previous six years. The lord lieutenant of most Welsh shires was the earl of Northampton, while the earl of Worcester took responsibility for Glamorgan and Monmouthshire. Northampton was praised for his 'ardent zeale' for military discipline, but despite him touring his lieutenancy to inspect military preparedness shortly after his appointment in 1618, many areas of the principality remained in a poor state of readiness.[68] At a muster in Anglesey in August 1619, for example, the hundred of Dindaethwy was chided by its captain, Thomas Holland, because a significant number 'very obstinatlie and willfullie' refused to provide armour and weapons, while the trained band 'did most contemptuouslie make default of theire appearance at our musters to the great contempt of his Majestys service and to

---

[66] *CJ*, p. 741.
[67] For a more detailed discussion of these debates, see Bowen, thesis, 226–33.
[68] E. Davies, *Millitary Directions, or the Art of Trayning* (1618), sig. A2; Denbighshire RO, BD/A/1, fo. 83; BD/A/27.

evill example of others to comitt like defaults'.[69] The deputy lieutenants of Flintshire in 1620 found it difficult to raise the required numbers of horse for musters 'by reason of dearth and decayes of divers gentlemen of the country', while it transpired that the muster master there had not been paid for three years.[70] A return from Breconshire detailing the state of the weaponry noted that corselets were 'of an ould fashion and alltogether unserviceable', that the pikes were 'allsoe in decaie', and that there was 'noe shott'.[71] Deputy lieutenant Sir John Bodvel wrote in 1624 that he did not know how to make a return for Llŷn in Caernarfonshire, it being 'soe farre out of order, that at the last viewe fewe did shewe any armour, and that which came were not complete'.[72] This rather desperate situation was a product of a long period of peace and neglect, but it may also have something to do with Wales's geographical remoteness on the margins of the Privy Council's consciousness. Derek Hirst has noted that, because of the lack of compulsive conciliar power, there was a 'decline in musters efficiency in almost direct relation to distance from the metropolis', and this may help to explain the woeful ill-preparedness of Wales's lieutenancy on the eve of war.[73]

In November 1624, this feeble infrastructure was required to provide 1,000 men for service in Ireland, one of the four propositions specified in the 1624 subsidy act, yet only two weeks earlier Northampton had written to Secretary Conway asking for a £1,200 allowance, probably from the subsidies, 'for furnishing of the counties of Wales with armes'.[74] Almost immediately problems arose with the impressment as Anglesey's deputy lieutenants pleaded for exemption, claiming that the island was 'subiect to great danger if it shuld

[69] NLW, Carreglwyd I/142.
[70] Cardiff Central Library, 5.50, fos 87, 89. See also NLW, MS 6285E, p. 3.
[71] BL, Add. 10,609, fo. 37. For similar problems in Pembrokeshire, see NLW, Bronwydd 3360.
[72] NLW, MS 9060E/1278.
[73] D. Hirst, 'The Privy Council and problems of enforcement in early Stuart England', *Journal of British Studies*, 18 (1978), 58. See also Cogswell, *Home Divisions*, pp. 15–16, 42–9.
[74] TNA, SP14/174/28; *APC, 1623–5*, pp. 371–2, 472–5. Cf. Dodd, 'Parliaments, 1625–1629', 18, and Williams, *Renewal and Reformation*, p. 373, who mistakenly claim that 800 men were levied. In addition to this impressment, Monmouthshire had been asked on 31 October to provide 100 men for Mansfeldt's expedition.

Table 1. Levies of men in Wales for the Military Expeditions of the 1620s

	Mansfeldt (Oct. 1624)	Service in Ireland (Nov. 1624)	Cadiz expedition (May 1625)	Cadiz expedition (Sept. 1625)	Rhé expedition (July 1627)	Archers for Rhé (Aug. 1627)	Rhé expedition (Sept. 1627)[a]	Total[b]
Anglesey	–	50	–	–	–	–	–	50
Breconshire	–	100	100	–	50	12	50	262 (312)
Cardiganshire	–	50	50	–	50	12	50	162 (212)
Caernarfonshire	–	100	32	–	–	–	50	132 (182)
Carmarthenshire	–	100	100	–	50	12	50	262 (312)
Denbighshire	–	100	32	–	–	–	50	132 (182)
Flintshire	–	50	17	–	–	–	50	67 (117)
Glamorgan	–	150	150	–	100	24	50	424 (474)
Merioneth	–	50	18	–	–	–	50	68 (118)
Monmouthshire	100	–	150	100	100	24	50	474 (524)
Montgomeryshire	–	100	32	–	–	–	–	132
Pembrokeshire	–	100	100	–	50	12	50	262 (312)
Radnorshire	–	50	50	–	50	12	50	162 (212)
Total	100	1000	831	100	450	108	550	2589 (3139)

[a] It is unclear whether these men actually were levied and conducted.
[b] Totals in parentheses are the amounts including the second levy for the Rhé expedition.

be attempted by invasion of any enemy'.[75] Caernarfonshire was also found to be overcharged and its 100 impressed soldiers were reduced to fifty, which caused a confused process of reallocation of Wales's overall contribution by the Council of War.[76] The impressment in Caernarfonshire quickly became involved in the factional disputes which destabilized the county throughout the 1620s, while kinship ties with Lord Keeper Williams threatened to hinder further the impressment, as Sir William Thomas confessed that he would be 'shorte' of the thirteen men required from his allotted 'lymitte' because it consisted 'for the greater parte of my Lo: Keepers tenants'.[77] Sir John Wynn, meanwhile, appointed a muster at Trefriw to levy twelve men, but he confessed 'I cannot for my lief [know] what to doe with them' as the rest of the county was not ready to march.[78]

The levy was then thrown into confusion by a new directive from the Privy Council, requiring Caernarfonshire to furnish the original number of 100 men.[79] This caused consternation among the deputy lieutenants who were already struggling to make up their numbers, but Sir John Wynn commented ruefully that they had no reason to 'contest with them which have full authoritie in theire owne handes to alter and change the direccons as they please'.[80] However, even this modest impressment was causing the deputies to exceed the remit of their commissions. A delay forced them to impose a subsidy of twenty nobles on each 'lymitt' for the upkeep of the soldiers from the time of their impressment until their delivery to the conductor.[81] Sir John questioned what authority they had to do this, wishing that they would rather take the necessary

[75] TNA, SP14/175/50, 50(i). For Anglesey's earlier claims to exemption, see E. G. Jones, 'Anglesey and invasion', *Transactions of the Anglesey Antiquarian Society* (1947), 30–6.
[76] *CSPD, 1623–5*, p. 394; TNA, SP14/175/51; *APC, 1623–5*, p. 378.
[77] NLW, MSS 9060E/1268, 1290; *CWP*, nos 1288–9. It is unclear exactly how the deputy lieutenants divided Caernarfonshire into 'limits' for the impressment, but they probably allotted quotas by cantref. This suggests that Thomas was referring to the cantref of Arfon or Arllechwedd: see J. G. Jones, *Law, Order and Government in Caernarfonshire, 1558–1640* (Cardiff, 1996), p. 131.
[78] NLW, MS 9060E/1291.
[79] *CWP*, no. 1296; NLW, MS 9060E/1300.
[80] NLW, MS 9060E/1301.
[81] NLW, MS 9060E/1300.

funds out of the subsidy money 'and by no meanes any other imposition laid upon the countrey'.[82] The discharge of the impressment here was far from smooth as the deputy lieutenants attempted to mobilize a military machine which had lain effectively dormant since James's accession; the contradictory and confusing signals emerging from the Privy Council did not help. The sense of confusion in north-west Wales was heightened by the fact that ships carrying about 200 soldiers for Ireland were blown into Beaumaris by a storm, and the town had to provide £97 7s. 0d. for their upkeep.[83]

On 5 May 1625 new letters were issued by the Privy Council to the seven shires of south Wales to provide a further 700 men, this time for service on the continent, while a much more modest impressment of 131 men was instituted in north Wales.[84] The response of Sir William Thomas in Caernarfon to the rumours of a further levy illustrates the stresses which even these modest demands placed on local communities: referring to reports of the 'greate pressinge of men' in England, he confided, 'I pray God it come not to Wales'.[85] Further evidence of the burden of impressment can be seen in the 1625 Pembrokeshire election, when John Wogan threatened impressment against any who refused to support him.[86] Impressment also allowed scope for abuse and extortion, for example, in the case of Oliver David Lloyd of Montgomeryshire, who was fined £16 6s. 8d. by the Council in the Marches for the 'pressing of souldiers without warrant and exacting sevrall somes of money of them and releasing them of their appearance before the deputie liuetenaunt'.[87]

Impressment was also resented because it was a costly business which drained local resources. Clothing and conducting the 150 men which Glamorgan provided for the expedition to Cadiz came to £187 15s. 10d., including expenses such as for

[82] NLW, MS 9060E/1301.
[83] TNA, SP16/1/33(iii); *APC, 1625–6*, p. 20; House of Lords RO, Main Papers, 14 May 1625.
[84] *APC, 1625–6*, pp. 42–5, 75; NLW, MS 6285E, p. 26.
[85] NLW, MS 9060E/1341.
[86] *CJ*, p. 806. The clerk wrongly believed that this dispute applied to Monmouthshire.
[87] BL, Harleian 4220, fos 184ᵛ–185. Eight constables of towns in the county were fined along with him for the same offence.

buying stockings and shoes for the impoverished conscripts.[88] The 100 men demanded from Breconshire in 1625 required a levy on the county of £120. This was still not enough to meet the charge of impressment and coat and conduct money which the deputies were not authorized to take out of the subsidy money on this occasion, so a further £41 10s. 0d. had to be taken from the maimed soldiers' treasury.[89] Cardiganshire likewise could not provide the necessary coat and conduct money for their men which the Privy Council asked to be disbursed initially 'by the countrie'.[90] The demand for men here, as in the Irish impressment in Caernarfonshire, encouraged improvisation based on questionable authority. The Cardiganshire conductor happened to be the collector of the third subsidy voted in 1624, so the deputy lieutenants authorized him to defray the charge of the coat and conduct money from the subsidy which he had collected but not paid to the parliamentary treasurers.[91] The request for men in Wales was met with confusion and grumbling, but there was little sign that anyone raised objections that were more fundamental. There were indications, however, that the lieutenancy in several areas was not functioning smoothly, and the continued pressures of war would only expose these inadequacies further.

The parliament which was called in 1625 met in very different circumstances from its predecessor, the most notable change being Charles's accession to the throne in March. The king's and Buckingham's commitment to a continental war was quite different to the diversionary naval war which many in the Commons had seen as implicit in the four propositions agreed in 1624. This caused considerable disquiet among those who were summoned to Westminster in May 1625 when the government stated its need for extra monies for a war which had not yet actually materialized. For many of the MPs in plague-ridden London, the principal

[88] TNA, E112/275/3, fo. 5.
[89] TNA, SP16/61/27. The Pembrokeshire deputies similarly claimed that the levying and conveying of the 100 men had cost £180: SP16/22/70.
[90] *APC, 1625–6*, p. 43. Also ibid., p. 81. This money was sometimes later repaid, as in the case of Radnorshire, which received £36 17s. 4d. (almost certainly not the whole amount) of its coat and conduct money for transporting fifty men for Cadiz in October 1627: TNA, E403/2804, p. 18.
[91] TNA, SP16/3/92.

concern was how the 1624 subsidies had been spent, and what direction the war policy should take. Some felt that the subsidies had been misemployed by Buckingham towards unauthorized activities such as Count Mansfeldt's expedition against the Habsburgs on the continent, and they hoped to use this enquiry as a weapon against him. Once more, however, Welsh members on the whole were inconspicuous in this brief parliament, possibly as demands on the Welsh counties thus far had been comparatively light, but also because the position of the Pembroke interest was difficult to discern. Two notable exceptions, however, were Sir Robert Mansell and Sir John Stradling.

Mansell had been effectively ignored by Buckingham in the planning and prosecution of hostilities, despite his nomination to the Council of War. Personal and professional motives encouraged Mansell to utilize the 1625 parliament to attack his superior. He tried to steer the Commons to investigate Buckingham's war preparations and cast scorn on his intended naval mission against Cadiz. On the final day of the parliament, Mansell claimed that he 'neither desires the goodwill nor cares for the private hatred of that great Lord [Buckingham]', adding that an investigation of the military preparations in the light of the four propositions voted in 1624 should be undertaken, 'and where the fault lies, let him be punished accordingly'.[92] Although he was questioned before the Council for his outburst, friends such as the earl of Pembroke ensured that he was treated leniently.[93]

We have already seen how Sir John Stradling was unenthusiastic about war with Spain, but in the parliament he perhaps also responded to concerns over the comparatively heavy burdens already suffered by his native Glamorgan, which had been asked to provide 300 men for military service and which had paid over £650 towards the 1624 subsidies.[94] On 23 June, Stradling proposed that a committee be appointed 'to take examination of the bestowing of former monies given'.[95]

---

[92] *PP1625*, pp. 476–7.
[93] TNA, SP16/5/42; Yale University, Beineke Library, Osborn MS fb 155, fos 132–3; HMC, *Mar and Kellie MSS. (Supp.)*, iii, p. 233.
[94] TNA, E359/65–7.
[95] *PP1625*, p. 226. On the scrutiny of the 1624 monies, see M. B. Young,

Stradling was a deputy lieutenant in Glamorgan who was closely involved in the levy of men, and he may have proposed this course in order to open an investigation into how the 1624 subsidies had been spent. In addition, on 6 August he opposed the government's motion for further supply; again his motivation seems to have been a desire to protect his neighbours from having to pay further taxation.[96]

Although Buckingham's management and conduct of the war thus far had disappointed the earl of Pembroke, there is no clear evidence that the earl had broken with his former ally during this parliament. The negative tactics of Mansell and Stradling, therefore, appear to have arisen from personal and local grievances rather than from any grand conspiracy against the duke centred on Pembroke. This parliament, however, demonstrated plainly the disillusion of many people with Buckingham's management of the war effort. It voted a meagre two subsidies which left Charles and his favourite in an unenviable position. They had committed themselves to mounting a sea-borne attack on Spain and had been assembling the fleet at Plymouth, but they did not have sufficient funds to underwrite this and their other continental commitments. As a result, the king resolved to request additional support from the populace over and above the two subsidies authorized by parliament.

In their search for financial expedients, Charles and Buckingham turned to requesting loans by Privy Seal letters, a less controversial means of obtaining money than a benevolence. In September 1625 the country's deputy lieutenants were charged with determining the ability of those who could provide a loan and at what rate.[97] Although the Privy Seal itself assured individuals that the request was simply a loan which would not preclude the calling of a new parliament, many were becoming weary of the constant demands for money for a policy which had produced no concrete results. Henry Wynn of Gwydir, for example, warned that 'if thear come a parlament againe [the loans] will be theare questioned by

'Revisionism and the council of war, 1624–1626', *Parliamentary History*, 8 (1989), 1–27.
[96] *PP1625*, p. 417.
[97] *APC, 1625–6*, pp. 167–71.

what advise this comes to pass, that privie seales and subsidies come together'.[98]

The conjunction of levying the 1625 subsidies concurrently with the Privy Seal letters clearly impeded the collection of the latter in Wales because, in the face of yet another demand for money, some Welsh counties appear to have employed a kind of 'bureaucratic resistance', with prevarication and a minimum level of compliance. This tactic was, perhaps, particularly effective in Wales where the lord lieutenant had such an enormous jurisdiction and was physically distant from many of his agents in the localities. This was acknowledged by the earl of Northampton on 3 October in a letter to the deputy lieutenants of Flintshire asking for names of those able to lend; he remarked that he was wholly reliant on their efforts 'because I cannot conveniently come and conferre with yow'.[99]

The lack of progress on the loans in Wales led the Privy Council to write to the lords lieutenant of the Welsh shires on 28 December 1625, castigating them for their dilatoriness in returning certificates.[100] The earl of Worcester had sent letters concerning the loan to Glamorgan on 31 October 1625, but it seems that he received no response. The Council's rebuke appears to have prompted him to put pressure on the county, for the deputy lieutenants wrote a collective reply concerning the Privy Seals on 2 January 1626. Their response was, in effect, a straight refusal to contribute which was couched in the most apologetic terms. The deputies informed Worcester that whereas their 'principall care' was to satisfy the king, they also had a duty 'unto our countrie in delivering the true estate thereof'. They went on to detail the county's poverty which was 'more then heertofore wee have knowne it', and they singled out the 'extreame losses and miseries' sustained at the hands of Turkish pirates who had attacked their shipping. They acknowledged the 'urgencie of his Majestys affairs', but claimed, disingenuously, that they could only recall three or four substantial men in the county; although they had considered others who could contribute, the sums would be so

---

[98] NLW, MS 9060E/1371.
[99] Cardiff Central Library, 5.50, fo. 58.
[100] *APC, 1625–6*, p. 288.

meagre as 'his Majestys service will not thereby be so much advanced as the countrie greived and wee disreputed for returning of them'.[101] There was little enthusiasm apparent here for Buckingham's and Charles's foreign ventures, and counties like Glamorgan evidently exploited the possibility of evading this extra-parliamentary imposition; this contrasts markedly with the experience of the forced loan in 1626–7, when avenues for such evasion were closed down much more vigorously.

The lieutenant of the other eleven Welsh shires, the earl of Northampton, responded to the Council's charge of dilatoriness with his own letter of 11 January. He had attempted to implement the loan on Privy Seal letters at numerous meetings but, 'findeing my care fruitlesse and their refusalls constantly continued', outlined the causes of his delay. He maintained that the Welsh shires of his lieutenancy 'generally pretend poverty for their excuse, the late subsidies payd and yet to be payd, the chargeable leveyes of soldiers for sundry services; [and] the certainty of a parliament, with many others'. He informed the Council that the whole business 'must lye uppon my owne private labours', though he remained 'destitute of all hopes & finding it an infinite difficulty to perswade men to discover the state of their country'.[102] One indication of his labours can be seen in a letter which he had written to the deputy lieutenants of Denbighshire less than a week previously. He begged them to provide a certificate of those able to lend, adding that 'I should be loath to appear of so small credit & power with my d[eputy] lieutenants as not to prevayle in askinge soe reasonable a supply'; he also echoed the Council's original letters that it was 'the first triall of his subiectes affectiones, howsoever palliated by a plea of povertie'.[103] Northampton's reference to the prospect of a parliament suggests a widespread desire to have monies levied through traditional methods. Additionally, our ears should become attuned to the Welsh tactic of 'pretending' poverty which appears to have been an important weapon in

---

[101] TNA, SP16/18/5.
[102] TNA, SP16/18/33.
[103] NLW, MS 1575B, p. 20.

the armoury of local governors who looked to ease the burdens of taxation and impressment on their communities. Northampton's response highlights the main weakness of the loans by Privy Seal letters: they were not compulsory, they had little means of enforcement and they invited pleas of mitigation which were exploited fully by counties like Glamorgan.[104]

The Council's rebuke caused Northampton to redouble his efforts to obtain certificates of those capable of lending. On 15 January 1626, Sir Roger Mostyn wrote to Sir John Wynn that it had been 'ill taken whoe certified, as yow did, povertie, that nowe the reporte is that the lord president is quickened by another lettre to call the gent[lemen] to accompt'.[105] The multiplicity of taxes in recent times did not make payment straightforward for, as Sir John himself wrote to another deputy lieutenant of Caernarfonshire later that month, the county's deputy lieutenants needed to inform Northampton of the 'misery of the cuntry'; he added that 'it is harde to be believed what a masse of money the iii last deare yeres hath caried out of this countrey'.[106] Because of these difficulties and the general recalcitrance of the Welsh counties, by the end of January Northampton was able to send up certificates of those able to provide loans in only six shires.[107] He reminded the Council that this had been 'noe smale taske haveing had soe little assistance'. The effort required to produce even this meagre result suggests that Northampton faced serious logistical difficulties in his extensive lieutenancy. The reluctance of the deputies to comply was doubtless a result of the more general resistance to the mounting financial demands faced by the Welsh shires at this time. The degree to which this resistance was caused by ideological opposition to the nature of the Privy Seal loan, or to the foreign policy it was designed to support, is almost impossible to gauge. It is clear, however, that the burdens of war were quickly eroding whatever enthusiasm there had been in the Welsh counties for Charles's continental campaign.

[104] Cust, *Forced Loan*, pp. 35–6.
[105] Cardiff Central Library, 4.69, unfol.
[106] NLW, MS 9061E/1388.
[107] TNA, SP16/19/68. These were Denbighshire, Caernarfonshire, Carmarthenshire, Breconshire, Merioneth and Cardiganshire.

One Welsh shire, Monmouth, bucked this trend, and not only did it return its certificate of contributors, but it paid £300 in Privy Seal loans in February 1626.[108] This represented a complete payment by those who had been returned as able to contribute.[109] The county's diligence is probably attributable to the presence of the lord privy seal himself, the earl of Worcester. As a formidable influence in the shire, it would have reflected badly on him if his own county, of which he was also lord lieutenant, did not contribute to the loan quickly and in full. The stark contrast with other Welsh shires under the more distant Northampton reinforces Cogswell's conclusions in his study of Leicestershire, where a resident lord lieutenant, the earl of Huntington, had an important role in overseeing and expediting the military and fiscal demands of the 1620s.[110]

By April 1626, eight Welsh shires had returned certificates of those capable of lending. These assessments proved over-optimistic, however, as the concurrent levying of parliamentary subsidies and the voluntary nature of the loan meant that smaller amounts from each county actually found their way to the Exchequer.[111] The correspondence of the Wynn family provides the most compelling evidence of the tactics and negotiations which underlay the assessment and evasion of the loan. On 8 March 1626, Owen Wynn informed his father that the Privy Seal letters would shortly be arriving in Caernarfonshire, but he advised Sir John to 'be not hastie to pay; let yours come last in of anie others', and he added that the levy was refused in many places in England. He continued

> if yow did all ioyne in a peticon to the lord tresurer alleadginge the manie subsedies that weare latelie payd, the pryncess myze that is now a payinge & the generall povertie of Wales, I hope this with a litle other helpe would excuse the cowntrey.[112]

He told Sir John to join Anglesey and Merioneth in this business, and promised that 'I will doe my best endevour to follow it'. If a petition were unsuccessful, however, all was not lost,

---

[108] TNA, E401/2320, 2441. A further £10 was paid on 22 May 1626.
[109] TNA, E401/2586, pp. 253–4.
[110] Cogswell, *Home Divisions*, pp. 5–6.
[111] *APC, 1625–6*, p. 419.
[112] NLW, MS 9061E/1395.

and Owen continued: 'I will doe what I can for yow & then let everie man shifte for himselfe'. This provides a fascinating insight into the methods by which such financial demands could be frustrated, impeded or avoided altogether, without challenging their validity directly. Although there is no evidence of resistance to this levy on grounds of its extra-parliamentary nature, it nevertheless reveals a sophisticated appreciation of the means and languages that local governors could adopt in order to frustrate the loan.

The collector of the Privy Seal loan in Caernarfonshire, Sir William Thomas, was a kinsman of Wynn who had been made collector through the efforts of Sir John's sons in London, apparently because he was 'the weakest of our side', and being made collector spared him from contributing.[113] Thomas sought Sir John's advice on the levying of the loan and indicated that those assessed would meet at Pwllheli to agree their position.[114] This advice came from London on 26 May, when Owen Wynn told his father 'yow need not pay your privie seale before yow heare from mee agayne'. He asked that Thomas be informed that Owen was working on the lord treasurer to have the Caernarfonshire loans remitted, and added that he would 'dyrecte my course as I see the parliament goe on'. He expressed his belief that Denbighshire would pay nothing, and he informed his father: 'I know noe reason whie wee should be soe forward in theise remote partes whence litle is expected except wee desire to be more officious then others'. The grounds of Owen's hopes for exemption were the other taxes that were shortly to be imposed on the shire, namely, four subsidies which had not been paid from 1606 and 1610: 'these with the generall povertie of the cowntrey may well acquite us of this great burthen for the present'.[115]

After the dissolution of the 1626 parliament, Owen Wynn wrote that the lordship of Ruthin, Denbighshire, had successfully petitioned the lord treasurer to be discharged of its Privy

---

[113] There were precedents from the 1605 Privy Seal loan for sparing collectors' contributions: NLW, MS 9052E/336.

[114] NLW, MSS 9061E/1395, 1403. Professor Jones confuses the Privy Seal loan with the forced loan of 1626–7: Jones, *Law, Order and Government*, pp. 115–17.

[115] NLW, MS 9061E/1412. These subsidy arrears were indeed levied in Anglesey, Caernarfonshire, Denbighshire, Glamorgan, Pembrokeshire and Radnorshire in 1626–8: TNA, E179/224/598; E401/2322–5.

Seal loans. In what amounted to an indictment of the loan's effectiveness, he wondered 'that they had not authorised mee or some other to have done the like in the name of the whole cowntie', and he added that the same could be done for Merioneth.[116] He noted that 'delayes in remote partes in this busynes cannot be dangerous for money is not to be had with us, [and] most partes of the kingdome doe refuse to pay at all'. In June 1626, Sir William Thomas composed a memorandum listing eleven men in Caernarfonshire who had paid a total of £145 toward the Privy Seal loans, while twenty-seven others had, as yet, paid nothing.[117] A number of the latter were labouring to procure discharges and many of them claimed to have already been successful in having their loans remitted but had not yet produced the necessary documentation.[118] In the event, the money which had been collected never found its way to the Exchequer; Owen Wynn's advice was followed and a petition was sent to the Privy Council asking for the payment to be remitted. The Council agreed and ordered Thomas to cease the collection.[119]

As may be seen in Table 2, as far as the government was concerned the Privy Seal loan was a complete failure in Caernarfonshire. A centrally placed ally – Owen Wynn – kept the local gentry informed of the loan's poor progress elsewhere, manœuvred in London to have it remitted, and supplied advice on how payment could be avoided. Elsewhere in Wales the loan was not a total failure, but of the nine counties to which Privy Seals had been directed, only Monmouthshire contributed the full amount. In Breconshire, for example, the collector, Thomas Price, received £105 from seven individuals, some way short of the £255 which the deputies had assessed on nineteen men.[120] The defaulters' reasons for non-payment were communicated to the Privy Council, and the excuses included impoverishment at having

[116] NLW, MS 9061E/1417; Dodd, 'Parliaments, 1625–1629', 23. Again Dodd's analysis of this loan is marred by confusion with other forms of taxation.
[117] NLW, MS 9061E/1421.
[118] NLW, MS 9061E/1422.
[119] *APC, 1626*, p. 95.
[120] TNA, SP16/30/85, dated June 1626 in the calendar (*CSPD, 1625–6*, p. 364), but more probably written in May when the loan was paid in: TNA, E401/2321, 2442.

Table 2. Payment of Loans on Privy Seals, 1626[a]

County	No. of contributors	Total assessment	Date paid	Amount paid	% of assessment	1604 Privy Seal payments[b]
Breconshire	19	£255	19 May 1626	£105	41	£185
Caernarfonshire	38	£540	–	£0	0	£235
Cardiganshire	22	£250	–	£0	0	£315
Carmarthenshire	31	£445	28 June 1626	£160[c]	36	£150
Denbighshire	44	£605	13 July 1626	£85[d]	14	£210
Flintshire	15	£260	6 June 1626	£110	42	£485
Merioneth	20	£315	8 July 1626	£135	43	£120
Monmouthshire	29	£310	3 Feb./22 May 1626	£300/£10	100	£400
Radnorshire	57	£570	27 May/1 July 1626	£300/£80	66	£100

[a] TNA, E401/2586, pp. 253–4, 337–8, 341–4, 365–7, 369–72, 375–6, 379–80, 383–4; E401/2320–1, 2441–2; E403/2803, p. 132; E401/2590.
[b] TNA, E401/2585, pp. 45–7, 57, 63, 67, 70–2.
[c] The sheriff, Sir Henry Jones, retained £90 of the shire's Privy Seal loan: TNA, C205/14/11.
[d] The lordship of Ruthin in the county was discharged of payment after petitioning the lord treasurer: NLW, MS 9061E/1417.

recently been appointed sheriff, debts on land, the expenses of supporting children and general poverty. Two brothers, Morgan and Griffith Llewellyn, charged at £10 each, claimed that they were 'never valued to be worth ... in subsidie above xxs a peace', adding that they hoped 'it was never intended to make use of subiects so meane in quality in this nature of service'.[121] In Carmarthenshire, a later commission discovered that £90 of Privy Seal loan collected by Sir Henry Jones of Abermarlais had not been paid to the Exchequer and remained in his hands.[122] This sum would have considerably boosted Carmarthenshire's returns; in the absence of further evidence, it is difficult to say how far such practices affected the collection in other shires.

Poverty, evasion and corruption meant that the nine Welsh counties listed in Table 2 managed to provide only part of what had been anticipated. The remaining shires had manœuvred successfully to avoid contributing. Glamorgan pleaded the depredations of pirates and so apparently avoided the levy, while Sir William Thomas believed that Anglesey was not called upon as it had 'no relateinge atturney to present names'.[123] The loan's overall failure is particularly noticeable when compared with an earlier Privy Seal loan requested by James in 1604, as can be seen in Table 2.[124] The failure of the Caroline loan seems largely attributable to the accumulation of taxes imposed since 1621, which, along with the stresses of providing men and equipment, helped to erode any enthusiasm.

FEAR OF INVASION AND BUCKINGHAM'S IMPEACHMENT

As the Privy Seal loan was being collected, the expedition to Cadiz mounted by Charles and Buckingham ended in ignominious failure and retreat, leaving many to wonder at the

---

[121] TNA, E401/2586, pp. 383–4; TNA, SP16/30/85.
[122] TNA, C205/14/11; SP16/312/6, 6(i); SP38/17 (18 May 1638); Bodleian Library, Bankes 43, fos 112–13. Dodd confuses this with a refusal to pay ship money: see below, p. 170.
[123] NLW, MS 9061E/1403.
[124] Difficulties of non-payment and evasion on that earlier occasion were experienced in some Welsh shires, however: NLW, MSS 1600E, fo. 352; 9052E/320, 335; Add. 465E/322.

tactics adopted against one of the most powerful countries in Europe. The deputy lieutenants of Pembrokeshire witnessed at first hand the results of the disaster when one of the ships returning from Spain, *The South Phoenix*, was blown into Milford Haven in December 1625. The soldiers were billeted in the towns of Pembroke and Haverfordwest, and many were in an appalling condition, 'most of them wantinge shirts, stockings, shooes and some clothes, whereby they become uncleane, feoble and fall sicke'.[125] The plight of the soldiers is conveyed graphically in Haverfordwest's corporation records; 17s. 6d. was spent on the 'shrowdes of fyve soldiers which dyed in this towne'.[126]

The cost of supporting the 108 soldiers billeted from 11 January to 21 February was a heavy £161 6s. 10d.[127] Although the Privy Council agreed to the request that this be defrayed from the county's first subsidy voted in 1625, the deputies also asked that the £180 coat and conduct money disbursed in May 1625 for dispatching Pembrokeshire's contingent of 100 men for Cadiz should be repaid.[128] In December 1626 the county justices alluded to the fact that they still had not been paid for victualling the Cadiz soldiers, and they informed the Council that the collector of the 1625 subsidy, George Owen, had been questioned for not paying the money.[129] Owen was subsequently issued with a process out of the Court of Exchequer for non-payment of the £148 subsidy money. However, on petition in February 1627, the Council agreed to allow him the £161 for the billeting, but ordered that the money be defrayed from the county's forced loan which was then being levied, demanding that the £148 subsidy money be paid as normal.[130] It would appear that the cash-starved government would not, or could not, pay Owen from central funds, and so prevaricated until taxes raised locally could be used as a means of discharging its debt in Pembrokeshire. After the

[125] TNA, SP16/18/50.
[126] Pembrokeshire RO, Haverfordwest Corporation 2052/3. See also TNA, SP16/18/63; 16/19/14.
[127] TNA, SP16/22/70.
[128] *APC, 1625–6*, p. 330.
[129] TNA, SP16/42/87. Owen paid the second subsidy of 1625 on 11 May 1626; the first subsidy of £148 was, of course, still outstanding: TNA, E401/2321, 2442.
[130] *APC, 1627*, p. 88.

collection of the forced loan, Owen duly paid the county's first subsidy of 1625 into the Exchequer on 11 April 1627.[131] Thus, the whole affair bred confusion and diverted funds which should have been directed to the prosecution of the war. Such occurrences can have done little to encourage zeal for the war, or those who were directing it, among the people of Pembrokeshire.

The opening of hostilities with Spain affected Welsh maritime shires like Pembrokeshire in another way, as the fear of invasion grew. On 28 August 1625, the Privy Council informed Northampton of measures which should be taken in Pembrokeshire to secure the most vulnerable parts of the realm.[132] Coastal areas like Pembrokeshire were obviously most at risk, and he was required to see that effectual musters were provided in the county, the beacons kept in good repair, sufficient watches kept, key points fortified, and an adequate supply of gunpowder maintained. In addition, in those places 'lykest to invite an enemy to land in', a regiment of 1,000 men from the trained bands was to be put in readiness. This was a timely intervention, for only three days previously Sir James Perrot, deputy vice-admiral of south Wales, had written to his superior, the earl of Pembroke, about the safety of the Pembrokeshire coastline and his desire to have Milford Haven fortified to protect the county from invasion.[133]

The Council letter prompted Northampton to visit Pembrokeshire in September 1625 to view the defences there, Haverfordwest spending 13s. 0d. on gunpowder for the trained band 'to receave my lord president'.[134] Although he encountered some difficulties in making up the requisite numbers of men in the county on account of the fact that the Privy Council was misinformed about the size of the trained bands, Northampton wrote to Secretary Conway on 15 September that he intended to 'arme and trayne the soldiers to my best endevor', admitting that 'I myself out of my dutie

---

[131] TNA, E401/2323.
[132] *APC, 1625–6*, pp. 141–2.
[133] TNA, SP16/5/81, 81(i). In another letter Perrot warned that 'at all times when forrayne invasion hath byn intended agaynst England, this hath byn a place [e]spetilly designed by the enimie': SP16/5/82.
[134] Pembrokeshire RO, Haverfordwest Corporation 63/1.

unto his Majestie and the service came hether, feareing it would not have been soe well without me'.[135] Once more the problems of a distant lord lieutenant appear significant in understanding the response of the Welsh counties to the financial and military impositions of the 1620s. During his stay, Northampton was approached by Sir James Perrot about the exposed state of the county. He requested that Haverfordwest be fortified, but added: 'I finde the countrey but poore and lesse able in regard at the last leavyes to Plymouth and by the releeving of those which were driven in there by foule weather and layed upon the countreys charge'.[136] The exactions arising from the decision to take part in the continental wars which Perrot had advocated so forcefully were having a significant impact on his county and his neighbours.

Perrot's concerns about Pembrokeshire's defences found their way into Northampton's report to the Council. He noted that the fortification of Milford would 'assure the countrey and put many out of feare whoe nowe lye naked and exposed to the iniury and violence of any pirate', but, echoing Perrot, he cautioned that the county

> in regard of diverse leavyes for the releeving of such as were ... by tempest driven into Milford, and the late provision of armes, are nowe so unable, that if the charge of fortifieing in places convenient should be imposed on them, I cannot see howe they can beare yt.[137]

In other respects Northampton was satisfied with Pembrokeshire's readiness. He had raised 500 armed men to supplement the existing trained bands (though they needed more arms), and in the event of an emergency he arranged that the bands of neighbouring Cardiganshire and Carmarthenshire should augment Pembrokeshire's forces. The beacons were repaired and sufficiently guarded, and the coast was well watched.[138] These measures did not remove Perrot's fears of invasion or the vulnerability of Milford

---

[135] TNA, SP16/6/65.
[136] TNA, SP16/6/85.
[137] TNA, SP16/6/86.
[138] Probably as a result of Northampton's attention, the town of Tenby strengthened its defences in 1626, as it had done during the invasion scare of 1588: Tenby Museum, TEM/Box 16.

Haven, however, and he implemented a scheme for raising money throughout Wales to fortify the haven, though it met with little success at a time of repeated requests for cash from the central government.[139]

Pembrokeshire was not the only Welsh county which feared that the opening of hostilities would bring dire consequences at home. Perrot's fear of a papist fifth column assisting a Spanish invasion gained new currency in many areas, and elicited a directive for recusants to be disarmed throughout the kingdom.[140] Such threats were considered particularly dangerous on the exposed island of Anglesey which had resisted levying troops because of the possibility of an invasion.[141] In December 1625 the worried bishop of Bangor, Lewis Bayly, wrote to Charles I about a ship which had been seen off Anglesey and was of particular concern because of the suspicious activities of a returned Catholic exile, Hugh Owen of Gwenynog. Bayly claimed that 'all the popish crewe flocked about him', and he detailed his fears as to what these actions presaged:

> The rest of that faction are heere so audacious that they never durst be so bold if they knew not of some invasion or conspiracie intended ... These partes are very weake & unfurnished, 100 armed men would surprise the Ile of Anglisey and possesse Carnarvonshire, for heere no man hath either shott or powder or knowes how to handel a peece ... the armor which they have in Bewmaris Castle is rustie & unserviceable, theyr pickes so olde that they are worme eaten, the powder for the moste parte through age & worse keeping turnd to dyrte.[142]

There was little evidence of an efficient lieutenancy here. Even more worrying, Bayly went on to describe the deliberate misinformation about the county's military capacity offered by its deputies:

> If the cuntrey should be putt to a sudden neede your Majestie should finde that the generall certificates made to the Lord President of Wales

---

[139] BL, Add. 64,891, fo. 14[r–v]; *APC, 1626*, pp. 113–14, 144–5; *APC, 1627*, pp. 181–2; *APC, 1627–8*, pp. 114–18, 123–4, 312–13; *APC, 1628–9*, p. 312; TNA, SP16/61/27; 16/92/31, 74.

[140] *APC, 1625–6*, pp. 188–90; Cardiff Central Library, 5.50, fos 92–3; TNA, SP16/11/60, 61; 16/12/74; 16/18/5, 5(i); NLW, MSS 6285E, p. 34; 9061E/1388.

[141] Around this time one correspondent wrote that Anglesey was 'the second place of most dainger in all Wales' after Milford Haven: TNA, SP16/89/33.

[142] TNA, SP16/11/37.

would but deceave both your Majestie and the cuntrey. We have but to many deputy lieutenants in these litle counties ... now we are growen to have 6 ... whose cheefe care is to favor their nearest frindes & to powle the poore cuntrey in generall.

He called for a commission to inquire into the true state of armour and men in Caernarfonshire and Anglesey, 'who bordering on Ireland stand in the neerest danger'. This remarkable letter illustrates the deep unease at the Catholic threat in Wales at this time; it also reveals the institutional weakness of the lieutenancy in the northern counties. It highlights once more the problems of the Welsh lieutenancies, which were so far removed from the lord lieutenant himself, who was unable to provide close supervision of local militias from Ludlow. This situation allowed deputy lieutenants to neglect their duties and the local forces to fall into disrepair. In such circumstances an invasion in such an exposed and ill-equipped area must have appeared wholly plausible. Anglesey's perilous condition was confirmed in a letter from the island's deputy lieutenants to Northampton of January 1626; it may have been composed as a response to Bayly's earlier allegations of their deceptions. The Anglesey deputy lieutenants communicated their fears of how the island was open 'to the spoile and over runninge of ane enimie', claiming that it had been depopulated by the recent dearth, and that their best defence lay in the fortifications made in 1588 which were now 'leveled with the grownd'. They also confirmed Bayly's observation that they were 'utterly disfurnisht of ordinance'; what they did possess was 'in great decaie & out of order'.[143]

It was in this uneasy atmosphere, and after the cumulative burdens of war taxation, that Charles decided to call another parliament in the hope that it would grant him more funds for a foreign policy which was becoming increasingly discredited. The failure of the war effort was attributed by many to the influence of the king's closest adviser, the duke of Buckingham. Charles I called the 1626 parliament because he was desperate for money to discharge obligations to his continental allies and to meet the costs of actions already taken.

[143] TNA, SP16/19/60.

The period between the 1625 and 1626 parliaments had witnessed a rapidly deteriorating relationship between England and France, despite the fact that the French king's daughter was now Charles's bride. The deplorable conduct of the war effort meant that those who had begun an attack on the duke in the 1625 parliament now had even stronger reason to seek his removal from the 'most important offices of trust and honour by sea and land'.[144]

Once more the stance of the earl of Pembroke is important in understanding the actions of members such as Sir Robert Mansell, although the extensive patronage of Buckingham garnered him some Welsh allies in the Commons. It was Buckingham's monopoly of offices and counsel that caused Pembroke to assemble a group in the Commons which would support an attack on the duke. The duke's client, Sir James Bagg, wrote to Buckingham that Pembroke had placed Sir Robert Mansell in Lostwithiel on a blank indenture, and he also mentioned Sir William Herbert of Powis Castle as one of Pembroke's dependants 'and therefore yor knowne enymies'.[145] The parliament of 1626 was to be a judgement on the duke and his war policy, to be prosecuted for the most part by Pembroke in concert with his allies in the Commons.[146]

Mansell was among the duke's most prominent critics. As in 1625, the examination of how the 1624 subsidies were spent provided an opportunity for him to denounce the favourite and his conduct of the war. He was scathing about Buckingham's role and the tactics which had been adopted, but most of this appeared to be personal animus, unrelated to any discontent in his native Wales. In addition to being a naval expert, however, Mansell was also the king's servant on whom heavy pressure was brought to bear by the king and Privy Council to end his attacks. When asked to choose between his hatred of Buckingham and his duty to the monarch, the latter won without question and Mansell was silenced.[147]

[144] J. Hacket, *Scrinia Reserata* (1693), ii, p. 15.
[145] TNA, SP16/523/77.
[146] Russell's view that the Commons was opposed to war has been revised by a more convincing model which demonstrates that many in the Commons were opposed rather to the war policy which Buckingham advocated and the manner in which he prosecuted it: M. B. Young, 'Buckingham, war and parliament: revisionism gone too far?', *Parliamentary History*, 4 (1985), 45–69.
[147] Bowen, thesis, 255–9.

Pembroke's other Welsh allies were surprisingly reticent in the attacks on Buckingham, although none rose to defend the favourite. One contribution worthy of note came after a report of 16 February 1626 concerning the restraint of sea trade because of infestation by pirates. In a clear case of a man representing his community's interests in the Commons, Sir John Stradling informed the House:

> Glamorganshire [is] ransacked by the pirates of Sallee and they dare not pass from thence over to Somersetshire by water for fear of them, neither dare to pass over into Ireland for a bark lately coming from Ireland. They have lost 2 or £3,000 in that shire.[148]

Stradling's speech recalled the letter of the Glamorgan deputy lieutenants (of whom he was one) to Worcester on 2 January 1626; it had cited the ravages of pirates as a reason for refusing to pay Privy Seal loans.[149] There may also have been a more political motive for Stradling's contribution, however. The guard of the coasts was the responsibility of the admiral, Buckingham, and his neglect became the basis of one of the impeachment charges against him. It is perhaps more than coincidence that Stradling, a Pembroke client who sat for Glamorgan by the grace of the earl, raised this issue, which was later used by Mansell, the previous incumbent of the seat, as a way of attacking the duke.

The other Welsh members in Pembroke's orbit were inactive on the issue of Buckingham's impeachment. Stradling's only other contribution was late in the session, during the debate on the remonstrance which was proposed after impeachment proceedings had stalled.[150] The other Welsh MP who contributed actively to the attacks on the duke was the lawyer, Charles Jones of Castellmarch, who assisted Selden in the presentation of charges against Buckingham.[151] There were other signs, however, that Buckingham's dominance of court patronage had garnered some allies among the Welsh members.

The most visible of these was John Griffith of Cefnamwlch,

---

[148] *PP1626*, ii, pp. 56–7.
[149] See above, pp. 111–12.
[150] *PP1626*, iii, p. 434.
[151] *CJ*, p. 854.

Caernarfonshire, who had sought Buckingham's patronage since at least 1621.[152] His contributions on the impeachment sought to defend the favourite. For example, in a debate of 2 May which questioned whether the Commons' charges against Buckingham should be transmitted to the Lords, as a prelude to impeachment, or to the king, who would be more lenient with the favourite, Griffith advocated the latter course, claiming that Charles would not 'respect a private man more than the kingdom'.[153] About this time, Owen Wynn wrote:

> John Griffith seekes to currie favour with the duke & to that end hath made manie motions in the house of parliament for him, in soe muche as he hath gotten himselfe the reputation of a [blank] and made his cowntrie men in generall rydiculous to such as heard him.[154]

Griffith was clearly a vocal advocate for the duke, though probably for his personal ends more than out of any commitment to Buckingham's war policy. He may have supported Buckingham with an eye to the impending retirement of his own father-in-law, Sir Richard Trevor, as deputy vice-admiral of north Wales, and in December 1626 Trevor recommended Griffith to Buckingham, describing him as 'made faythfull to yor grace ... by particular obligacons'.[155]

The duke's other Welsh ally was Charles Price of Pilleth, Radnorshire, a military man who had been captain of a company of Welsh soldiers in Ireland in 1625.[156] He attempted to persuade the Commons to 'fall to other business' when attacks against Buckingham's detention of a French vessel were in train, and on 20 March he moved that impeachment proceedings be discontinued and attention turned to the king's needs.[157] There had been earlier indications of Price's

---

[152] NLW, MSS 9057E/988; 9058E/1013.
[153] *PP1626*, iii, p. 130.
[154] NLW, MS 9061E/1406.
[155] TNA, SP16/35/15; HCA30/820/33. While the parliament sat, Griffith informed the secretary of the admiralty, Edward Nicholas, that he would approach Buckingham for support in an unspecified matter relating to north Wales, possibly referring to the vice-admiralty. He was appointed to the position by Buckingham in February 1627: TNA, SP16/23/110; BL, Add. 37,817, fo. 17.
[156] *APC, 1623–5*, p. 441; TNA, SP14/184/2.
[157] *PP1626*, ii, pp. 260, 322. Contrast Williams's assessment that Price was an agent of Pembroke, 'eager enough to voice' opposition to the duke in the Commons: Williams, *Renewal and Reformation*, p. 479.

pro-Buckingham stance when, in 1625, he supported the duke's plea for further supply for the Cadiz fleet. His position was probably shaped largely by his employment as a military man who risked losing all hope of a commission if he opposed the duke. Indeed, Price was to be found in Buckingham's company at Portsmouth in 1628, when he was the first man to inform Charles of the duke's assassination.[158]

Examples such as these suggest that, for the most part, the position of the Welsh MPs regarding the impeachment was based more on personal ambition than on opposition to, or support for, the war effort. However, Mansell was the only member of Pembroke's Welsh clientage to engage actively in the impeachment, and the lack of aristocratic patronage in many areas of Wales may in part explain the comparative silence of Welsh MPs during the proceedings against the duke. The impeachment was as much a revolt against Buckingham within the Privy Council as it was an attack by the Commons, and the comparative absence of a powerful aristocratic presence in most of Wales may have contributed to the general quiescence of the principality's representatives during the furore over the duke.[159] The impeachment failed to overcome Charles's loyalty to Buckingham, and the parliament was dissolved on 15 June without granting any further subsidies towards the war. The king desperately needed money for his foreign designs and was forced to improvise with schemes of doubtful legitimacy in an attempt to recoup the subsidies lost at the dissolution.

THE SEARCH FOR MONEY: THE FORCED LOAN AND FINANCIAL EXPEDIENTS, 1626–1628

After the dissolution of the 1626 parliament, the king removed from their county commissions a number of individuals who had opposed Buckingham in the Commons. It is indicative of the passive role of most Welsh MPs that none of

---

[158] J. Jacobs (ed.), *Epistolae Ho-Elianae: The Familiar Letters of James Howell* (1892), i, p. 254.
[159] K. Sharpe, 'The earl of Arundel and the opposition to the duke of Buckingham, 1618–1628', in idem (ed.), *Faction and Parliament* (Oxford, 1978), pp. 230–3.

the principality's county benches was affected; Mansell was displaced from the commissions in Kent and Norfolk.[160] This purge of Buckingham's most visible opponents was part of a reorientation of policy at Court centred on Buckingham and Charles's desire to govern without parliament. This would require new sources of finance as both remained committed to the war, and a new demand for a benevolence assessed at four subsidies was forthcoming in July. Nationally this was a disaster, with less than £1,000 finding its way to the Exchequer.[161] Owen Wynn, a well-placed Welshman in London, outlined to his father in Caernarfonshire how he should respond to the request; in doing so, he provided valuable insight into the means by which Charles's exactions could be evaded and their effects mitigated in Wales. He wrote that

> delay can breed us noe danger (as the case stands) & let our poore cowntrey rather follow & that a great way of them give presidents in these tumultuous tymes. Our ould generall plea must be stood upon now of anie other, which is the extreame povertie of those remote partes, & this plea will free us if the cowntrey fynd out a sufficient sollicitor to follow their busynes.[162]

Although the claims of poverty may have had some basis in fact, Wynn's advice appears to have been concerned with avoiding the burden by tried and tested tactics which fell short of direct resistance. It is also clear that he had little sympathy with Charles's claims that the money was essential because the country faced a national emergency.

In Flintshire, Sir Roger Mostyn believed that little would be done regarding the benevolence because the county had recently resolved to pay the subsidies which were still outstanding from the 1610 parliament and were delayed on account of payment of the mise due after Prince Henry's investiture as prince of Wales.[163] In a letter of 8 August, Mostyn expanded on this position, noting that Flintshire and Denbighshire had agreed to pay the 1610 subsidies, but that

---

[160] BL, Harleian 286, fo. 297. Cf. Dodd, 'Pattern of politics', 33, who stated that Mansell was removed from the Glamorgan bench, though he was never actually a member of that commission.
[161] Cust, *Forced Loan*, p. 91.
[162] NLW, MS 9061E/1424.
[163] NLW, MS 9061E/1431. For the prince's mise, see above, pp. 56–7.

as for the benevolence, 'I finde both counties unwillinge thereto'.[164] This indicates that the gentlemen of these counties discriminated between the two levies, deciding to reject the demand not sanctioned by parliament. He added that the counties would demonstrate a willingness to comply, but allege their poverty as the reason for non-payment, 'which I thought good to give yow notice, which I praie yow make use to yor selfe, and burne this lettre'.[165] This illustrates that the leading Welsh gentry in adjoining counties could devise a joint strategy for non-payment of such taxes. The pleas of poverty appear to have been at least partly genuine, however, and Mostyn ended his letter with the rumour that the unpaid subsidies of 1606 were also to be collected, 'and howe able poore Wales is to meete that charge with other levies that daiely come upon us iudge yow yorself'. The cumulative demands of the war were clearly taking their toll and encouraged systematic and organized evasion in the face of Charles's demands.

On 18 September 1626, Sir John Wynn remarked on the difficulties the benevolence was facing in Caernarfonshire. He noted its fatal weakness, namely, that in cases of refusal 'wee are not to use any coertion, but perswasion'. Wynn had some misplaced confidence that this would achieve results: 'I think I shalbe able to perswade most of them . . . though they grumble ageinst [it]'.[166] The lack of coercive power meant that those who wished to avoid payment were given the opportunity to prevaricate and refuse without fear of reprisal. Ultimately, Caernarfonshire paid nothing towards the benevolence.

This negative response was repeated throughout Wales, with some counties giving more overtly political reasons for their resistance. On 29 July the Pembrokeshire justices informed the Privy Council that they had convened a meeting of the county's 'gentry and comons' and had enjoined them to contribute 'in the effectuallest manner wee could', but that the people desired some further time to consider the request, 'which in regard of their backewardnes wee yealded unto,

---

[164] Flintshire paid £33 18s. 4d. towards the 1610 subsidies on 15 November 1626: TNA, E401/2322.
[165] NLW, MS 9061E/1434.
[166] NLW, MS 9060E/1369.

earnestly perswadinge them in the meane tyme rightly to weigh and consider the urgent and important occasions of his Majesties affaures'.[167] The Council encouraged the justices with a letter of support which enjoined them to give a good example 'by your owne forwardnes'.[168] This did not have the desired effect, however, and in an arresting example of principled resistance to the benevolence, the gentry and subsidymen excused themselves from presenting a voluntary payment on account of the extraordinary burdens on the shire:

> it had ministered noe small comfort to theire hearts and alacrity in susteyninge this heavy chardge lyinge already uppon them, if by course of parliament this supply had ben added to theire former burden, althoughe thereby they had ever soe much wanted.[169]

Similar sentiments were voiced by the taxpayers of Monmouthshire about a month later, when nineteen justices of the county informed the king that they had encouraged payment, yet the subsidymen

> resolutly answered us that they are ready and willinge to spend their bloodes and dispend their estates in the defence of yor royall persons and noble kingdom. But to condiscend to performe the tenor of the said lettres or to pay the said subsidyes they utterly refused, except the same be graunted by act of parliament.[170]

Their use of the term 'subsidies' is significant, suggesting that one difficulty which the benevolence encountered here was that it was interpreted as a direct attempt by Charles to raise taxation without reference to parliament. This was seen as distinct from the request for a loan, which produced a quite different effect in the county in 1627. These are vitally important indications that the poor performance of the benevolence in Wales was not merely attributable to its inherent weaknesses. The men of Pembrokeshire and Monmouthshire demonstrated a devotion to the ideal of taxation with consent of parliament, and this also appears to have influenced reactions in Flintshire and Denbighshire. It is diffi-

---

[167] TNA, SP16/32/66.
[168] *APC, 1626*, p. 175.
[169] TNA, SP16/33/57.
[170] TNA, SP16/34/30.

cult to estimate the degree to which such ideological considerations hampered collection of the benevolence in the other counties of Wales, but some Welsh taxpayers were evidently fundamentally opposed to a benevolence no matter what emergencies were allegedly threatening the country.

The sole contributor in Wales was John, Lord Vaughan of Golden Grove, Carmarthenshire, a man who had lost his position as comptroller of Prince Charles's household at the accession and was probably angling for renewed favour: he contributed £100.[171] This derisory sum from the thirteen shires of Wales was of a pattern repeated throughout the rest of the kingdom. Charles would have to turn to other mechanisms for raising funds if his war policy was to continue.

In the summer of 1626 there was an abortive attempt made to levy a new Privy Seal loan, as well as a demand for maritime counties to provide ships for the war effort, a move that prefigured the levying of ship money in the 1630s. These requests were almost total failures in Wales as they were in other parts of the realm and engendered more confusion than money.[172] In the wake of these failures, the government organized its available resources in a more determined manner and embarked on the most effective and contentious of the financial expedients adopted before the personal rule: the forced loan. The new loan was to be levied on all taxpayers at the heavy rate of five subsidies. The Privy Council selected commissioners for the loan in each county, and in Wales, as in other shires, these were modelled closely, but not always exactly, on the judicial bench.[173] The first response from the principality came on 30 December 1626, when Worcester's son, Lord Herbert of Raglan, gave Buckingham an account of the collection in Monmouthshire. He assured the duke that the proceedings 'goeth on with the wished success, cheerfully and not withowt some repining against them that fayled in their promises and deceaved his Majesties expectation in not geving the supply necessarie to a busines of soe high consequence'.[174] The county's compliance and Herbert's reference

[171] BL, Add. 64,897, fo. 127; TNA, E401/2442, 2321.
[172] Bowen, thesis, 267–8.
[173] Cust, *Forced Loan*, pp. 52–4; TNA, C193/12/2, fos 65–79ᵛ.
[174] TNA, SP16/42/114.

to criticism within the shire of the 1626 parliament for not voting subsidies was in stark contrast to Monmouthshire's opposition to the extra-parliamentary benevolence four months earlier. This contrast is even more striking when it is considered that eighteen of the nineteen justices subscribing to the earlier letter opposing the benevolence were now loan commissioners.[175] It is possible that Lord Herbert, who was not a JP but had been included as a loan commissioner, wished to portray his efforts in the best possible light. However, the performance of the county would seem to indicate that Herbert was speaking with good reason, because Monmouthshire paid £800 to the Exchequer on 14 February 1627, with further payments amounting to £512 in May.[176] The total represented about 84 per cent of the five subsidies which the king hoped to raise by the loan.[177]

A possible explanation of Monmouthshire's positive response lies in a Privy Council letter sent to the commissioners shortly after the initial payment had been made. The councillors thanked the Monmouthshire men for their diligence, and significantly added that the earl of Worcester and his son had been 'earnest suitors' that the coat and conduct money which the county had paid for the Cadiz soldiers should be reimbursed from the Exchequer.[178] This represented a considerable concession and indicates a major departure from earlier levies: the Crown was willing to bargain rather than exact the loan without benefit to the locality.[179] The presence of Worcester and Lord Herbert was doubtless also an incentive for the county to pay; it is clear that they advocated the Crown's cause forcefully and their industry was probably important in gaining subscriptions. Sir Thomas Aubrey in Glamorgan, the other county of which Worcester was lord lieutenant, recorded that he attended a meeting

---

[175] TNA, C193/12/2, fos 36–7.

[176] TNA, E401/2322–3.

[177] The government quotas for the loan at a rate of five times the payments on the second subsidy voted by the 1625 parliament can be found in TNA, SP16/84/89.

[178] *APC, 1627*, pp. 65, 127–8. In May 1627, the Council ordered repayment of Monmouthshire's coat and conduct money for 250 men, rather than for the 150 initially allowed: ibid., p. 267.

[179] Cust, *Forced Loan*, pp. 118–35, 322. A similar concession was made in Radnorshire: *APC, 1627–8*, p. 94; TNA, E403/2804, p. 18.

'touchinge [the] loanes' with the earl in Cardiff in January 1627, again suggesting Worcester's galvanizing influence on this issue.[180] The tenor of the king's declaration launching the loan may have given the Monmouthshire justices some reason to support this financial innovation, because he announced that it would not be made a precedent or hinder the calling of a parliament.[181] Unlike the benevolence, which the Monmouthshire justices considered to be simply the levying of subsidies without reference to parliament, the use of a loan appears to have helped allay their fears about extra-parliamentary taxation.

The commissioners of the other county mentioned in Herbert's letter, Glamorgan, made specific reference to this provision as the basis for the payment of the forced loan in the shire. They claimed to have found

> noe opposition but a generall conformitie and willingnes (many even beyond their abilities) to geve full satisfaction to his Majesty. They resting on his Majestys gracious intention to maintaine them in their aunciont imunities and privileges, and that this course nowe enforced by pressing necessitie, shall not be drawen into example or president.[182]

Similar sentiments were expressed by the Cardiganshire commissioners.[183] The king, therefore, had taken some of the constitutional 'sting' out of the levy, while making it a test of obedience and conformity in a time of emergency.[184] This potent combination apparently allowed counties such as Monmouthshire to overcome their qualms regarding extra-parliamentary taxation.

The loan was well received in Carmarthenshire, whose commissioners reported that 'we finde the most parte of the inhabitants poore and wonderfull decayed in their estates, yet we found them all with all cheerefull and dutifull hearts most

---

[180] L. Bowen (ed.), *Family and Society in Early Stuart Glamorgan: The Household Accounts of Sir Thomas Aubrey of Llantrithyd, c.1565–1641* (Llandybïe, 2006), p. 81. Worcester's effort to prosecute the loan contrasts with his personal position: he was upbraided by the Council in July 1627 for not having paid his own loan: *APC, 1627*, pp. 419–20.

[181] J. F. Larkin and P. L. Hughes (eds), *Stuart Royal Proclamations* (Oxford, 1973–83), ii, p. 111.

[182] TNA, SP16/53/84.

[183] TNA, SP16/54/74.

[184] Cust, *Forced Loan*, pp. 48–9, 62–7.

willing... to lend'.[185] The Pembrokeshire commissioners, in a similar reversal to that seen in Monmouthshire over extra-parliamentary taxation, wrote that after 'many meetings, expence and travell' the county's subsidy payers yielded willingly to the loan.[186] Eventually the loan yielded £717 in the county, representing about 86 per cent of that expected by the government. The commissioners' efforts elicited a letter of thanks from the Council in April 1627.[187]

In financial terms the loan may be considered a success in Wales. Most counties came close to achieving the required sum of five subsidies, as may be seen in Table 3. A number of shires had paid the majority of their loans to the Exchequer by May 1627, but there was some delay in full payment in certain areas, and a number of people were returned as defaulters. Despite the supposed 'cheerefull and dutifull hearts' of the Carmarthenshire subsidymen, the commissioners could return a certificate of thirty-eight names of those who 'refused to pay the moyety of the loane'.[188] Not all were refusals or motivated by ideological concerns, however: some were living outside the county or were under age and hence not liable to pay. Another return submitted by the Pembrokeshire collector, Thomas Price, enumerated twenty-three defaulters and Price provided reasons for non-payment.[189] Death accounted for ten individuals, residence outside the county for five, two others were in gaol, and another pleaded poverty.

On 12 May the Council wrote to eight Welsh counties thanking them for their cooperation thus far, and requesting further effort to achieve full payment.[190] This demand for further contributions perplexed the commissioners of

---

[185] TNA, SP16/54/54.
[186] TNA, SP16/57/3. See also Pembrokeshire RO, Haverfordwest Corporation 228, 2054/5. Howells overstates resistance to the loan in Pembrokeshire: B. Howells, 'Government and politics, 1536–1642', in idem (ed.), *Early Modern Pembrokeshire, 1536–1815* (Aberystwyth, 1987), p. 154.
[187] *APC, 1627*, p. 203.
[188] TNA, SP16/55/85.
[189] TNA, SP16/58/112. See also SP16/83/56.
[190] *APC, 1627*, pp. 272–3. These were Cardiganshire, Caernarfonshire, Carmarthenshire, Flintshire, Merioneth, Pembrokeshire and Radnorshire. A letter was also directed to the county borough of Carmarthen.

Radnorshire who had paid close to five subsidies in April.[191] They informed the Council that the county was 'one of the least and the poorest within the kingdome, yet notwithstanding most willing to yeld the kings Majestie all service and supplies of us required according to our abillitie'. They reminded the Council that a large sum of £380 (equivalent to four subsidies) had previously been lent on the basis of Privy Seals, and that the inhabitants of the county 'did willinglie and freely without negatyve voyce lend the somes required' of the forced loan.[192] To push for extra money after such compliance would seriously damage the commissioners' political capital in the county. Nevertheless, a further letter demanding full payment came in August as the Council scrambled to finance a relief campaign to save Buckingham at the Ile de Rhé. This caused the commissioners to reiterate wearily the county's general acquiescence, though they managed to return the names of potential contributors in the form of four men and one widow who 'refuse (and as yet doe refuse) to pay'.[193] They were each rated at only £1. The ceiling for the loan had been reached in Radnorshire, and it sent no further money to the Exchequer.

The Council's letter in May appears to have prompted Caernarfonshire to make its first payment of the loan. It had possibly been hoping that its traditional tactics of delay and prevarication would yield results, but the resolute stance of the king and the Council did not allow such methods to prevail.[194] The Council's directive also jolted the Cardiganshire collector, John Jenkins, into further action: a month later he made a large payment to the Exchequer. Jenkins, however,

[191] TNA, SP16/58/13; E179/224/589A.

[192] TNA, SP16/66/73. The Council's letter elicited a similar response from the Pembrokeshire commissioners, who asserted that their county 'did as generally & readily contribute to that service as any wee knowe or can conceave to have done in any countie within the realme of England or the Principality of Wales': SP16/73/6.

[193] TNA, SP16/79/71. For the purposes of taxation, women usually only featured as widows, as the legal personalities of married women were understood as being incorporated with those of their husbands. Wealthy spinsters did, however, occasionally appear in tax documents: R. Schofield, *Taxation under the Early Tudors, 1485–1547* (Oxford, 2004), p. 108; A. Laurence, *Women in England, 1500–1760* (London, 1994), p. 241.

[194] TNA, SP16/67/70.

Table 3. Payment of the forced loan, 1626–1627

County	Dates of payment	Amounts paid	Total	% of 5 subsidies
Anglesey	1. 17 April 1627 2. 29 May 1627	1. £253 6s. 8d. 2. £100	£353 6s. 8d.	63
Breconshire	1. 25 April 1627 2. 9 June 1627	1. £571 16s. 9d. 2. £243 3s. 3d.	£814 19s. 0d.	87
Cardiganshire	1. 14 April 1627 2. 16 April 1627 3. 11 June 1627	1. £323 14s. 0d. 2. £10 16s. 0d. 3. £221 10s. 0d.	£556 0s. 0d.	81
Carmarthenshire	1. 12 April 1627 2. 14 April 1627 3. 17 April 1627 4. 28 June 1627	1. £302 17s. 4d. 2. £1 19s. 0d. 3. £7 17s. 0d. 4. £287 15s. 0d.	£600 8s. 4d. (£653 8s. 4d. with Carmarthen borough)	78*
Caernarfonshire	1. 20 July 1627 2. 1 Sept. 1627	1. £150 0s. 0d. 2. £70 13s. 4d.	£220 13s. 4d.	72
Denbighshire	1. (hundred of Chirk): 2 July 1627 2. (Lordship of Denbigh): 12 Nov. 1627 3. (Lordship of Bromfield): 14 Nov. 1627 4. (hundred of Ruthin): 29 November 1627	1. £75 15s. 0d. 2. £186 9s. 4d. 3. £140 4s. 2d. 4. £109 0s. 0d.	£511 8s. 6d.	84
Flintshire	1. 1 May 1627 2. 4 May 1627	1. £400 2. £18 15s. 4d.	£418 15s. 4d.	84

Glamorgan	1. 31 January 1627	1. £30	
	2. 21 March 1627	2. £800	
	3. 9 Nov. 1627	3. £200	
	4. 10 Nov. 1627	4. £97	£1127	92
Merioneth	1. 18 October 1626	1. £6	£6	2
Monmouthshire	1. 14 February 1627	1. £800		
	2. 8 May 1627	2. £340		
	3. 11 May 1627	3. £172 3s. 9d.	£1312 3s. 9d.	84
Montgomeryshire	1. 11 January 1628	1. £290 1s. 10d.		
	2. 30 April 1628	2. £250	£540 1s. 10d.	61
Pembrokeshire	1. 6 April 1627	1. £644 19s. 6d.	£666 0s. 0d.	
	2. 18 April 1627	2. £21 0s. 6d.	(£717 3s. 4d. with Haverfordwest)	86*
Radnorshire	1. 16 April 1627	1. 363 6s. 8d.	£363 6s. 8d.	85
Carmarthen Town	1. 12 April 1627	1. £25 17s. 0d.		
	2. 17 April 1627	2. £0 13s. 0d.		
	3. 26 June 1627	3. £26 10s. 0d.	£53	*
Haverfordwest	1. 7 April 1627	1. £49 17s. 10d.		
	2. 19 April 1627	2. £1 5s. 6d.	£51 3s. 4d.	*

Source: TNA, E401/1914–15; E401/2322–4; E401/2442–3; SP16/84/89, 16/85/77.
* Figures calculated along with the county boroughs of Carmarthen and Haverfordwest, which the Exchequer included in the county totals.

informed the Council that the commissioners had faced some difficulties in the shire.[195] He sent the board a return of 194 individuals who had not contributed. This was a considerable show of defiance, perhaps fomented by the prominent Price family of Gogerddan, among whom John, Thomas and Dame Gwen Price were the highest rated refusers.[196] It is possible that the powerful Prices discouraged payment of the loan among subsidymen lower down the social order. There is room for ambiguity here, however, because Jenkins singled out James Thomas of Dyffryn Clydach, the petty collector for Llanbadarn Fawr, as the principal cause of disruption to the collection. Gogerddan was situated in this hundred, so it is difficult to tell whether the Prices were returned because of Thomas's non-compliance or whether they encouraged his refractoriness. Thomas Price had been accused in Star Chamber of removing the names of a number of his tenants in this hundred from the subsidy roll in 1624 and of securing 'such assesors as were at his appointment and devotion' in Llanbadarn Fawr.[197] Recalcitrance over the forced loan, therefore, may simply represent another form of tax evasion, with the Prices exploiting their local dominance in order to protect the pockets of their neighbours. Even in such a case, we must also acknowledge that this was hardly fulsome support for the loan as an emergency war measure.

Although generally a success in Wales, there are indications that the loan met with significant resistance in Denbighshire. A surviving schedule of those charged with the loan in the hundreds of Is Aled and Is Dulas reveals that one of the most prominent men in the shire, Sir Henry Salusbury of Lleweni, a loan commissioner, did not pay the £10 rated on him, but unfortunately the schedule does not expand on the reasons for his non-payment. The presence on this schedule of two other Salusburies who refused to pay suggests that non-compliance may have been coordinated at a familial level.[198]

---

[195] TNA, SP16/68/47, 47(i).
[196] S. R. Meyrick, *History and Antiquities of the County of Cardigan* (Brecon, 1907), p. 309; P. W. Hasler (ed.), *The House of Commons, 1558–1603* (1981), iii, p. 250; T. I. Jeffreys Jones (ed.), *Exchequer Proceedings Concerning Wales in Tempore James I* (Cardiff, 1955), pp. 104, 112–13.
[197] TNA, STAC8/234/9. See also BL, Harleian 4220, fo. 184; TNA, E179/274/28.
[198] TNA, E179/221/204A.

Even more damaging, however, was the refusal of recusants to contribute. This compounded Salusbury's non-payment in the commote of Henllan, a centre of recusant activity where nine recusants refused to subscribe to the loan.[199] As with non-payment of the Palatinate benevolence in Anglesey, the fact that the loan was intended to support a campaign against Catholics on the continent may help to account for the comparatively high representation of recusant non-payment in these Denbighshire hundreds. The amount given by the county was, however, more than respectable, approaching 85 per cent of five subsidies, but Salusbury's case and the recusant refusals suggest that the collection was not straightforward.

Three Welsh counties performed particularly badly in the collection of the loan. According to the receipts, Merioneth's only contribution came from Sir John Lloyd, who paid £6, presumably when he was in London. The Privy Council dispatched letters to the county in May and August 1627 requesting it to expedite the business, but they do not appear to have had any success. Unfortunately, no direct evidence survives to explain why the county paid nothing further. It may be that this especially impoverished shire's comparatively large payment on the Privy Seal loan the year before discouraged payment of further loans. It is possible that the money collected for the loan was used to offset recent military payments such as the coat and conduct money. It is even possible that Merioneth escaped payment because of the small sum involved, only £250.

Both Montgomeryshire and Anglesey performed poorly in their loan payments, bringing in about 60 per cent of the reckoned five subsidies. In October 1627, the Council wrote to Montgomeryshire's commissioners that they 'cannot but marvell and construe it as a neglect of his Majesty's service' that no return had been forthcoming.[200] However, the letter acknowledged that some commissioners had assured the Privy Council of their efforts to pay their own money and to secure loans from the populace. It was reported that the money was

---

[199] For recusancy in Henllan, see E. G. Jones, 'Catholic recusancy in the counties of Denbigh, Flint and Montgomery, 1581–1625', *TCS* (1945), 119, 126–7; TNA, E134/8JasI/Easter 11.

[200] *APC, 1627–8*, p. 77.

'for the moste parte ... alreadie paid in to the collectors, however detayned in theire hands'. The commissioners were enjoined to redouble their efforts and press 'such as are yet behynd in theire loanes'. However, the payments were received at the Exchequer at a very late stage in January 1628 and again as late as 30 April when a new parliament which denounced the forced loan had assembled.[201] Anglesey paid its contributions fairly promptly and, although these were comparatively small, its commissioners were not censured. This may suggest that monies were defrayed from the loan locally, perhaps towards the dilapidated defences detailed in 1626.

The forced loan brought about £7,500 into the Exchequer from Wales. In a rather crude comparison with the subsidies voted in 1625, this represented about 85 per cent of the desired payment. It was, therefore, a considerable financial success and we cannot be certain how much of the shortfall was distributed locally towards military costs. For all its financial success, however, there are indications that collection was not straightforward in some counties. Delays, negotiation and prevarication appear to have been factors as in the case of other levies, but there is little sign that the forced loan represented any kind of ideological or political watershed for the people of Wales. Whereas some counties had expressed concern about the unparliamentary nature of the 1626 benevolence, no such voices were raised about the loan. This is not to say that such concerns had evaporated. Rather the king's assertion that this was merely an emergency measure which was not to be repeated and would not inhibit the calling of a parliament seems to have allayed fears and facilitated payment. In addition, the opportunity to use some of the money towards outstanding local charges, such as the coat and conduct levy, speeded collection. It must be noted too that, even allowing for the poverty of the region, the counties of Wales seem to have been taxed at low, manageable levels. The assessment of the loan for the thirteen counties was around £9,150, a figure which pales beside the demands from English counties; for example, the four English shires under the jurisdiction of the Council in the Marches were asked to supply a total in the region of £20,000. Even allowing for their

---

[201] TNA, E401/2324–5.

impecuniosity, Welsh taxpayers seem to have been under-assessed compared with their English counterparts, and this probably made the exactions somewhat easier to bear. Unfortunately, in those areas where the loan failed most conspicuously, the evidence for understanding the circumstances and the motives of failure is lacking. The most that can be said is that resistance was not so great as to leave a significant mark in the extant sources. An indication of the relatively uncontentious nature of the loan in the principality may be inferred from the absence of any Welshmen among the refusers released from prison by the Privy Council in an amnesty of 1628.[202] The loan produced no martyrs from Wales like John Hampden, and there is little indication that it became a contentious topic in the elections to the parliament convened in 1628.[203]

The fiscal expedients of 1626–8 had been adopted in order to allow Charles and Buckingham to continue with their foreign engagements without recourse to parliament. Through poor judgement and bad luck, their foreign policy had come to include armed conflict with France as well as with Spain. However, the effort to liberate the Huguenots of La Rochelle by means of an expeditionary force ended in an even more humiliating failure than that to Cadiz. Charles and Buckingham had hoped that such action would ingratiate them with pro-Protestant opinion in England which looked with despair on the recent direction in foreign policy. There had been further impressment of men in Wales for this new expedition, which produced familiar complaints of poverty and vulnerability from counties like Pembrokeshire, but there was no sign of the bitter and violent resistance which flared up in some English shires.[204] The military failures, combined with the repeated demands for men and money, meant that there would be a reckoning, and after considerable debate in the Privy Council which overcame Charles's resistance, the decision was taken to summon a parliament. This parliament

---

[202] *APC, 1627–8*, pp. 217–18.
[203] See Dodd's comments, 'Parliaments, 1625–1629', 36–7, and 'Pattern of politics', 34. This contrasts sharply with the ideological resistance described in many parts of the country in Cust, *Forced Loan*.
[204] TNA, SO 1/1, fos 55, 70ᵛ; SP16/75/37; *APC, 1627*, pp. 455–7, 500–1.

amounted to an inquisition into financial and military innovations of the previous two years, and the way in which the fundamental liberties of the subject had been placed second to the requirements of a disastrous war policy. The Commons sought to create safeguards for these liberties which ultimately found their expression in the Petition of Right.

In a parliament dominated by the exchanges of lawyers, it is not surprising to find much of the Welsh contribution coming from men who were representatives of this profession more than their constituencies. Individuals like Edward Littleton, who was prominent in the debates on the liberties of the subject, represented the position of the Inner Temple rather than opinion in north Wales, where he sat for Caernarfon. The Welsh gentlemen sitting in parliament were, for the most part, silent in the great debates on liberty and the law. One of the reasons for this may lie in the fact that, for all the impositions placed on it, Wales did not suffer the billeting of soldiers which blighted the shires of the southern coasts of England, or the use of martial law. It is also important to note that the demands made on Wales in the 1620s, though substantial (at least 2,500 men were required from the thirteen shires), were not of the same magnitude as the levies for the wars of the late Elizabethan period when some 9,400 Welshmen had been pressed into service.[205] It must also have helped that the largest initial levy in Wales shipped men to Ireland rather than to face action on the continent. The threat to personal liberties, therefore, may have appeared to many Welsh MPs as a rather more remote matter, in contrast to its immediate relevance in the south of England.

It is noteworthy that the sole Welsh MP who called for an inquiry into the state of the constitution at home was Sir James Perrot of Pembrokeshire, a county which had experienced billeting and had voiced concerns about non-parliamentary taxation. He yoked together his usual concern for defence of the coasts with the papist presence at home in a speech on 2 April 1628 which demanded remedy against these 'vipers in our bosoms' before consideration of the king's requests for more money.[206] He later asserted that the correct course of

[205] G. C. Cruickshank, *Elizabeth's Army* (Oxford, 2nd edn, 1966), p. 290.
[206] *CD1628*, ii, p. 246.

taxation should be 'by parliament', echoing Pembrokeshire's response to the 1626 benevolence. He also advocated that monies should be directed towards the defence of Milford Haven, which remained unfortified and open to attack.[207]

Familiar patterns of patronal ties and vested interests were again in evidence among the Welsh members during the parliament. There had been a reconciliation between Pembroke and Buckingham after the dissolution of 1626, and this probably helped to delay attacks on the favourite by men like Mansell while the investigation into the liberties of the subject was being conducted. However, Mansell continued to snipe at the foreign policy from which he had been excluded, and once a new front opened up against the duke late in the session, Mansell once more fell eagerly upon his superior.[208] By contrast, Buckingham and his foreign policy continued to enjoy the support of John Griffith of Cefnamlwch and Captain Charles Price of Pilleth, members for Caernarfonshire and New Radnor respectively. Both were involved in the military and both had probably witnessed the consequences of inadequate funding. Griffith certainly served as a volunteer and participated in the offensive at the Ile de Rhé outside La Rochelle, while it is highly likely that Price was also in the duke's company.[209] Price and Griffith supported large subsidies for the war effort and defended the duke against renewed attacks piloted by Sir John Eliot.[210] Griffith in particular was active in defending his patron from accusations of Arminian tendencies, asserting on 5 June that he had witnessed his 'duty of service to God daily' at Rhé.[211] Price, meanwhile, asserted that 'I cannot with conscience and by an implicit faith condemn a man I know not guilty. And I shall clear him to see the contrary.'[212]

Perrot was more cautious towards Buckingham, informing

---

[207] *CD1628*, ii, pp. 298, 304. Rumours of attacks on Milford were circulating in the summer of 1628: HMC, *Fourth Report*, p. 290; T. Birch, *Court and Times of Charles I* (1848), i, pp. 376, 380.
[208] Bowen, thesis, 281–5.
[209] *CSPD,1627–8*, pp. 373, 391; *CD1628*, iv, p. 127. Cf. Dodd, 'Parliaments, 1625–1629', 46.
[210] *CD1628*, ii, p. 318; iii, pp. 155–6, 161; iv, pp. 127–8, 160.
[211] *CD1628*, iv, p. 127.
[212] Ibid., p. 277.

the House that he desired the favourite's 'reformation rather than his ruin', and asking only that he be relieved of his 'chief and almost sole command of sea and land'.[213] His experiences in Pembrokeshire caused him to doubt Buckingham's military capacities, though it would appear that he did not view him as a fundamental threat in the same way as did Eliot.[214]

Again, patronage and service appear to have been important factors in configuring the attitudes of those Welsh members in the Commons who publicly spoke about the duke and the war. In more general terms, there appears to have been hardly any impetus from Wales for an inquiry into the war and the liberties which had been overridden in its prosecution. The reason for this probably lies in the fact that the principality, for the most part, avoided the more immediate and damaging effects of war, and no Welsh person was imprisoned without cause shown for refusing the forced loan. This may account for Dodd's perceptive characterization of the Welsh members in 1628 as providing no suggestion of 'the evolution of local factions into anything like a coherent opposition to the court'.[215] The burden of the war in most areas of Wales, though substantial, was simply insufficient to create concerted opposition among its parliamentary representatives to the direction of foreign policy and the breach of personal liberties.

The parliament voted a large supply of five subsidies and passed the Petition of Right, but it did not manage to topple Buckingham. Popular feeling against the favourite and the war continued to run high, however, and the duke was assassinated in August 1628 as he prepared to sail with another fleet to La Rochelle. His death was reported to 'much perplex' John Griffith, who was said to have 'spent most of his substance to serve the duke and had nothinge but faine promises and hopes of preferment which with the duke are now

---

[213] Ibid., p. 248.

[214] In January 1628, Perrot wrote to the secretary of the Admiralty, Edward Nicholas, about his efforts to defend Buckingham's rights as admiral in south Wales: TNA, SP16/91/57; SP14/215, pp. 71–2. The stance of Perrot's patron, the earl of Pembroke, may also have informed his position on this issue: Russell, *Parliaments*, p. 384.

[215] Dodd, 'Parliaments, 1625–1629', 37. See also idem, 'Pattern of politics', 34.

fallen to the ground'.[216] Buckingham's death and the subsequent defeat of the expedition helped to convince Charles of the necessity of inclining towards peace.

Conclusion

Negotiations to end the war were doubtless welcomed in Wales as elsewhere. The war's impact on the principality was substantial and has not received the historical attention it deserves. The demands for men and money were a regular feature of life in the 1620s, and the burdens were not inconsiderable, especially in a county like Pembrokeshire which also experienced billeting, or Anglesey where, like Pembrokeshire, the threat of invasion hung over the populace like a cloud. Parliamentary subsidies, benevolences and forced loans jolted Welsh taxpayers out of the ease they had enjoyed for most of the reign of 'Rex Pacificus', and during the 1620s about £30,000 from these sources was raised for the war effort in the thirteen shires. However, even these figures are incomplete because they do not account for monies disbursed locally on equipping troops and replenishing county armour and magazines. In 1619 alone, for example, the corporation of Haverfordwest had to spend £26 9s. 6d. – in excess of two parliamentary subsidies – on purchasing new weaponry in accordance with government directives.[217] Replayed on a larger scale, such expenses in the Welsh shires must have been considerable. An Exchequer case against the deputy lieutenants of Glamorgan provides evidence of this: the defendants enumerated how £310 had to be levied on the county in order to provide for the magazine in accordance with a Council directive of 10 July 1626, while a further £300 was required for the provision of the county's levies and their conduct towards Cadiz and Rhé. Over and above this were the costs of equipping and drilling the trained militia, who were exercised 'almost weekelie' in this period.[218] This represented a substantial addition to the c. £3,600 which the county paid in subsidies and loans in the 1620s.

[216] NLW, MS 9062E/1533.
[217] Pembrokeshire RO, D/RTP/HAM/96.
[218] TNA, E112/275/3; SP16/18/46; 16/66/27; 16/116/9. On the significance of such costs, see Cogswell, *Home Divisions*, passim.

There is clear evidence of an attachment to taxation through parliament, while the financial expedients designed to support the war effort met with grumbling and evasion in many Welsh counties. However, in comparison with many areas of England, Wales was spared the worst excesses of billeting and martial law, a fact which helps to account for the general compliance.[219] Wales also appears to have been relatively under-taxed, with the rating on prosperous shires such as Glamorgan bearing little comparison with that even on the less affluent and populous English counties. Wales's relative isolation from the political centre appears to be a key to understanding its experience in the 1620s. The Privy Council was poorly informed of conditions in Wales and its potential revenue. In 1626 it enquired of the Flintshire subsidy commissioners why their assessments had fallen so dramatically since Elizabeth's reign, from £623 to £85. The commissioners patiently replied that the Council had been looking at the revenue from mises rather than the subsidy, and claimed that its ratepayers actually were improving on the Elizabethan subsidy.[220] However, when one compares the subsidy collection of this relatively prosperous border county of around £85 with that of over £600 from neighbouring Cheshire, one must be drawn to wonder at the magnitude of the discrepancies.[221] Such contrasts are underlined when it is noted that the tiny county of Rutland contributed more in subsidies and loans during the 1620s than every Welsh county except Monmouthshire, and the combined average subsidy yield from all thirteen Welsh shires was about the same as that received from Lincolnshire.[222] This region, which supported around 8 per cent of the nation's population, contributed only 3 per cent of the nation's parliamentary subsidies. We should also

[219] In this respect, Wales demonstrates an interesting parallel with the experiences of a county like Lancashire: B. W. Quintrell, 'Government in perspective: Lancashire and the privy council, 1570–1640', *Transactions of the Historic Society of Lancashire and Cheshire*, 131 (1981), 52.

[220] TNA, SP16/24/58.

[221] M. J. Braddick, *Parliamentary Taxation in 17th Century England* (Woodbridge, 1994), 309–11. See Cogswell's comment that Leicestershire's parliamentary subsidy netted '*only* £750': *Home Divisions*, 17 (my emphasis).

[222] For these figures, see S. Healy, 'Oh, what a lovely war? War, taxation and public opinion in England, 1624–29', *Canadian Journal of History*, 38 (2003), 452–5.

remember that the Welsh counties were exempted from fifteenths and tenths, which were a significant component of the parliamentary grants of 1624, and that there is very little evidence of what may be described as 'popular' protest against even the more controversial levies in Wales in the 1620s.

Distance and remoteness meant that Wales was insulated from the close scrutiny by officials at the political centre: there were no peers riding the fastnesses of Caernarfonshire (for example) to enjoin compliance with the forced loan.[223] Sir James Perrot in Pembrokeshire, occupying what he described as one of 'these remote angles of the realme', was moved to inform the Privy Council that its directives 'come hither soe slowly and soe incertayne' that administrative performance was disrupted.[224] In September 1627, the mayor of Monmouth queried why the Council had demanded the remainder of the forced loan from his town when it had been joined with the county for payment and had fully satisfied its quota.[225] It emerged in the mid-1620s that the Council did not know the strength of the trained bands in the counties of Wales.[226] A commission of the 1630s in south-west Wales revealed that some of the monies levied in the 1620s had been retained by local officials and never reached the Exchequer.[227] Brian Quintrell's observation that the Council saw the northern county of Lancashire 'through a glass, darkly' is just as applicable to Wales, if not more so.[228] The presence of the lord president and the Council in the Marches did not seem to alleviate this problem. The earl of Northampton voiced concerns about his own capacity to compel administrative performance in his extensive lieutenancy. He remarked that he had tried to coordinate the collection of the Privy Seal loans in 1625–6, but after 'sundry sollicitations and meetings ... in severall places far remote', he found it almost

---

[223] Some revealing observations on the relationship between distance from London and expected payment of the forced loan can be found in the dispatches of the Tuscan ambassador: HMC, *Skrine MSS*, pp. 98–9, 102, 105.
[224] TNA, SP16/19/14; 16/5/81.
[225] TNA, SP16/77/13.
[226] TNA, SP16/6/65.
[227] TNA, C205/14/11; for earlier complaints of officials retaining public monies in Wales, see NLW, MS 9055E/871; 9060E/1268, 1289.
[228] Quintrell, 'Government in perspective', 37.

impossible to obtain accurate assessments from his deputy lieutenants of those able to lend.[229] In 1626, the bishop of Bangor warned that deputy lieutenants in north-west Wales actively deceived Northampton about the true state of the region. Although one of the Council in the Marches' main roles was the supervision of the Welsh shires, the lord president often seems to have been as much in the dark as the Privy Council. As Lord President Bridgwater wrote despairingly to Secretary Windebank in 1640, 'partes of my lieutenancy are farre remote from the place of my aboade at Ludlow ... to speake the truth I live here with suche intelligence that I do not knowe what to thinke'.[230] Significantly, Penry Williams's research has revealed that the Council's authority was greater in shires which were physically close to Ludlow than in those along the coast.[231] The striking speed and efficiency with which the demands for men and money were met in Glamorgan and Monmouthshire, then, appear to reinforce Cogswell's observations regarding the importance of a diligent and resident lord lieutenant – in this case the earl of Worcester (in concert with his son) – in meeting the requirements of the central authorities.[232]

The situation offered scope for the foot-dragging and prevarication which characterized the response of north Wales to levies such as the Privy Seal loan. The evidence from the Wynn correspondence suggests the use of sophisticated and well-established tactics for avoiding or impeding the collection of money, by collusion, central lobbying and exploitation of the region's geographical and informational remoteness. When Owen Wynn advised his father to rely on 'our ould generall plea ... [of] the extreame povertie of those remote partes' in avoiding payment, he offered an insight into how the Privy Council's perception of Wales allowed its local governors effectively to deploy languages and discourses of inability which would not have been so readily believed or so effective in other regions.[233] Claims of 'the generall povertie of

[229] TNA, SP16/18/33.
[230] TNA, SP16/466/55.
[231] P. Williams, 'The activity of the Council in the Marches under the early Stuarts', *WHR*, 1 (1960–3), 140.
[232] See, for example, TNA, SP16/66/27; 16/74/79; 16/116/9, 31.
[233] NLW, MS 9061E/1424.

Wales' appear throughout gentry correspondence with the authorities in the 1620s, though their ubiquity may raise some doubts as to their validity.[234] Owen Wynn's allusion, in a letter to his father, to 'theise remote partes whence litle is expected' reveals how these common discourses could work to the advantage of Welsh county governors in their transactions with the political centre.[235] The earl of Northampton appears to have been aware of such tactics in his report on the dilatory payment of the Privy Seal loans, observing that 'they generally *pretend* poverty for their excuse'.[236] Counties jostled with one another to present themselves as 'the least & poorest' in the kingdom, with Flintshire, Anglesey, Breconshire and Pembrokeshire all claiming this distinction in their communications with the Privy Council.[237] Doubtless there was more than a grain of truth in the description of the hardships that communities claimed to face, particularly during the depression of the early 1620s; nevertheless, there is strong evidence that the kinds of languages formed part of a tried and tested strategy for shielding communities from the demands of central government.

From the partial evidence available, it would appear that the forced loan proceeded smoothly in most areas, and resistance, where it can be located, does not seem to have been organized on ideological lines. Perhaps a religious element should be noted in explaining such compliance, for, as Richard Cust has shown, opposition to the loan was often most significant in areas where puritan tendencies were pronounced. As is discussed in Chapter 5, the puritan presence in Wales before the civil wars was modest indeed, and in the 1620s hardly registered on the scale. We should reflect on the possible connections between the lack of aggressive

---

[234] NLW, MS 9061E/1395.
[235] NLW, MS 9061E/1412.
[236] TNA, SP16/18/33 (my emphasis). This chimes well with the observations of an earlier lord president, Edward, Lord Zouche, when discussing the 1605 Privy Seal loan in Wales. He observed of Sir John Wynn, the collector of the loan in Caernarfonshire, that he 'would be a good common weale man, weare yt not that he affecteth his neighbors and cuntry menn to much, for he is very loath to certifie who ys able to send the kinge any money', and argued 'that wee might have lent well more then our privie seales come to': NLW, 9052E/335.
[237] TNA, SP16/24/58; 16/25/37; 16/30/85; 16/32/66; Cardiff Central Library, 5.50, fo. 100.

puritan commentators in Wales during the 1620s and the comparative absence of ideological dissent from the policies of Charles and Buckingham. There were critical voices raised in Wales because of an unpopular war, such as that of John Harry of Monmouthshire who wished the king and Buckingham dead because one of his impressed friends had died in the war, but the evidence suggests that his case was exceptional.[238]

If we look to the Welsh members of the parliaments of the 1620s, the local burdens of the war did make some impression, for example, in speeches by Stradling and Perrot. Yet the political attitudes of the principality's MPs in general appears to have been conditioned more by patronage networks or personal interests than by grievances emanating from their constituencies. In the balance against Sir Robert Mansell and Sir William Herbert who looked to Pembroke, we may place John Griffith and Charles Price as acolytes of Buckingham. Perrot emerges as a passionate advocate of an anti-Spanish war, a position derived from his own fervent Protestantism and fears about Catholicism at home. Yet what is striking about Perrot is his uniqueness among Welsh members: as a puritan advocating an aggressive anti-Catholic foreign policy, among the Welsh members – indeed in the country at large – he was a rare breed.

It also appears that these patronal links, and the experience of war in the 1620s in Wales, did not politicize local politics to the extent which can be discerned in counties such as Leicestershire or Cornwall. There were tensions, of course, as may be seen in Caernarfonshire where the Wynn/Griffith feud was given an added dimension by the fact that the Wynns looked to Lord Keeper Williams while the Griffiths courted Buckingham. However, there is little evidence that such ties assumed an ideological significance in relation to war, taxation or the militia in Caernarfonshire itself. For the most part, factional disputes at Court failed to translate into gentry divisions in Wales. The comparatively weak presence of aristocratic patronage may help to explain this, alongside the political significance of Wales's comparative isolation from the disputes at the centre.

[238] TNA, SP16/527/59.

An examination of fragmentary evidence from the Welsh counties as well as from Westminster, then, reveals that the wars of the 1620s certainly raised the political temperature in Wales after the pacific years of James I's reign. However, the exactions of war do not appear to have been sufficiently burdensome to alienate the local communities from the rule of Charles I to the extent that they did in other parts of the kingdom.

4
WALES AND THE PERSONAL RULE (I): SHIP MONEY

The personal rule, 1629–40, was a decade characterized by fiscal and religious innovation, coupled with peace abroad and an increasing emphasis placed on order and obedience by the Court and the Privy Council. It was also, of course, a period when Charles I called no parliaments, and this significantly affected the manner in which the provinces articulated their responses to government policies; Wales was no exception in this respect. Analysis of the impact of the personal rule on the principality to date has been meagre, and for the most part assessments rest almost entirely on some brief comments in articles published by Dodd in the late 1940s.[1] As Glanmor Williams has noted, 'we know far too little as yet to be able to generalize with confidence about the reactions of the Welsh shires to the years of personal rule'.[2] Dodd's evaluation, however, was located within a 'Whiggish' paradigm which stressed isolated cases of resistance and examined the 1630s very much with the constitutional conflicts of the 1640s in mind. In addition, his analysis was based on limited source material and made several serious factual errors. Reliance on Dodd's account has perpetuated the impression of the 1630s in Wales as simply a curtain-raiser to the Civil War years, and there has been little attempt to examine the reception of contentious Caroline policies in their own terms.[3] In addition, this approach has influenced the manner in which the troubled years 1640–2 in Wales have been interpreted, as the perceived growing resistance to ship money and religious innovations play into an account of Welsh opposition to Charles's government in 1640, an opposition which is required to evaporate

---

[1] Dodd, 'Pattern of Politics', 34–47; idem, 'Parliaments, 1640-42', 59–61.
[2] G. Williams, *Renewal and Reformation: Wales, c.1415–1642* (Oxford, 1993), pp. 480–1.
[3] See, for example, J. G. Jones, *Early Modern Wales, c.1525–1640* (Basingstoke, 1994), pp. 119–20, 200–6.

with unseemly haste by 1642 to allow for the country's dominant royalism. The rather limited nature of the historiography is compounded by the manner in which the recent revisions and reinterpretations of national politics and religion in this period have almost completely avoided discussing the Welsh experience. In many ways this in itself reflects the thin Welsh historiography, but it also indicates a wariness and a reluctance to engage with a region which is seen as different and unfamiliar. It is intended that the following discussion of financial and religious policy in Wales during the 1630s should allow Wales to be connected with current debates and historiographical trends, and that the separateness or similarity of the experience of the principality be tested on a more solid evidential basis.

The analysis offered in this and the following chapter examines the impact of Charles's main financial and religious policies in Wales during the 1630s detached from Dodd's teleological schema, and it deploys new sources and approaches in assessing the responses of the Welsh counties to Charles's contentious initiatives. In so doing, the analysis offers the first detailed study of the implementation of ship money and Laudian policy in Wales, and attempts to integrate this with an evaluation of Welsh political culture that helps to explain the principality's stance in the early 1640s in a more satisfactory way than existing accounts allow.

Evidential problems have bedevilled assessments of the 1630s in Wales as elsewhere, largely because the nature of dissent and disaffection is particularly hard to assess in the absence of a parliament and because of the generally cautious nature of political debate. These problems are compounded in Wales by a lack of personal correspondence surviving from the 1630s which might have provided a more intimate view of local responses to government policy. Consequently, any evaluation has to be reconstituted mainly from official sources, in which dissent or opposition is unlikely to have been prominent. It has been argued that the response to the financial demands of the 1630s provides the best basis for an examination of the relations between government and locality, and this chapter follows such an approach in an analysis of the levying of ship money in the

Welsh counties.[4] Although it has often been cited as a major element in the growing dissatisfaction among the Welsh towards the personal government of Charles I, no detailed investigation of Welsh responses to the financial innovations has yet been attempted. This chapter seeks to address this historiographical lacuna, and the subsequent chapter considers the reaction in Wales to the controversial religious innovations associated primarily with Archbishop William Laud.

The origins of ship money and the execution of the first writ, 1634–1635

Despite Charles I's withdrawal from the European conflict, the decision to govern without parliament left his administration in dire need of money. As a result, in 1630 he resorted to an antiquated expedient of fining individuals worth £40 per annum or more who did not attend his coronation to be knighted.[5] In Wales, these demands once more prompted the deployment of the language of poverty, remoteness and inability, with shires like Anglesey, Pembrokeshire and Merioneth again vying for the title of poorest county in the principality.[6] There is also evidence of considerable foot-dragging and even examples of gentlemen in Merioneth, Radnorshire and Anglesey suggesting that their Privy Seal loans of 1625 had yet to be repaid as had been promised, and that this should cover their obligation to pay a composition fine.[7] This reaction suggests some principled resistance to this extra-parliamentary levy, but for the most part pressure by the Privy Council brought grudging payment from Welsh counties and there is little evidence of concerted or principled opposition. In total, the four commissions for knighthood composition issued between 1630 and 1632 brought in approximately £5,600, or the equivalent of about three parliamentary subsidies, from the

---

[4] A. Hughes, *Politics, Society and Civil War in Warwickshire, 1620–1660* (Cambridge, 1987), pp. 100–1.
[5] For a full discussion of knighthood composition in Wales, see Bowen, thesis, 315–25.
[6] TNA, E178/5943; E178/5887; E178/7154, pt ii, fo. 135.
[7] TNA, E178/7154, pt ii, fos 122, 125, 133; E178/5943; E178/5887.

shires of Wales, a figure in line with receipts elsewhere in the country.[8]

Although this expedient raised a considerable amount of money, it could not be extended into a recurrent levy and went only part of the way towards providing for the king in the absence of parliament. Charles was forced, therefore, to consider other methods of raising funds such as forest fines, while in north Wales another project was in the form of a commission of March 1633 'for the better answearing and preservacon of his Majestys revenewes'. Here leading gentlemen were appointed to examine the accounts of receivers, sheriffs and other officials and to uncover any arrears in rentals or fines due to the Crown.[9] Such stop-gap measures could not address the king's need for money to defend his coasts adequately, especially when this need became more pressing in the early 1630s as the build-up of foreign navies and an increase in piracy threatened security.

The king and his advisers therefore resolved in 1634 to resurrect another antiquated levy, ship money, schemes for which had been mooted earlier in the century.[10] This was promulgated to the people as an emergency service, not a tax, the service rendered to the Crown in the shape of each county being required to provide a ship as part of a fleet designed to defend the realm. Initially it was levied only on the maritime shires, which meant ten out of the thirteen Welsh counties received a writ in late 1634. The writ's stated purpose was to combat pirates and provide for the navy in a period when religious conflict continued to rage in continental Europe. Such aims probably had a particular resonance in the Welsh coastal shires which were being pestered by pirates.[11] In 1633, John Griffith, vice-admiral of

[8] TNA, E401/1917–1921; K. Sharpe, *The Personal Rule of Charles I* (New Haven and London, 1992), p. 116; T. Cogswell, *Home Divisions: Aristocracy, the State and Provincial Conflict* (Manchester, 1998), p. 195; B. W. Quintrell, 'Government in perspective: Lancashire and the Privy Council, 1570–1640', *Transactions of the Historic Society of Lancashire and Cheshire*, 131 (1981), 55.

[9] TNA, E178/7322.

[10] A. Thrush, 'Naval finance and the origins and development of ship money', in M. C. Fissel (ed.), *War and Government in Britain, 1598–1650* (Manchester, 1991), pp. 137–50; Bowen, thesis, 268.

[11] C. E. Hughes, 'Wales and piracy: a study in Tudor administration, 1500–1640' (MA thesis, University of Wales, 1937), 209–12.

north Wales, had written to the lords of the Admiralty concerning 'those losses & verie great prejudice which the mutuall comerce betwixt theese partes of Wales and the kingdom of Ireland doth suffer by reason of certaine piratts', and he repeated his concerns the following year.[12] This problem also affected shipping in south Wales, and on 7 July 1634 the deputy lieutenants of Pembrokeshire informed the Privy Council that their coastline had been infested with pirates for the last five years, and that currently there were two or three rovers about Milford Haven.[13] This fear of pirates along the Welsh coasts probably ensured that these areas would welcome the ship writs and their stated aim of securing the seas, and this doubtless helped to facilitate the levying of ship money.[14]

Ship money reinvigorated the role of the sheriff in local government; he became solely responsible for the execution of the writs and for any failures associated with them. Even before the administrative duties of levying ship money burdened the sheriff, his had been considered an expensive and onerous position. It is not surprising, therefore, that there is evidence of men attempting to avoid the office in Wales even prior to the first writ. Avoidance was usually achieved by means of a third party petitioning the lord president of the Council in the Marches or another influential agent to omit a name from the list of candidates.[15] Owen Wood, for example, was exempted from the Anglesey shrievalty in 1634 through the influence of Archbishop Laud.[16] Faction could also play a role in the choice of sheriff, as in the case of Anglesey in 1633, when the Bulkeleys of Beaumaris pleaded with the lord president of the Council in

---

[12] TNA, SP16/240/14; 16/228, fo. 68^{r-v}; 16/262/8; 16/264, fo. 11^v; 16/275/56.
[13] TNA, HCA30/853, fos 114–24. I am grateful to Dr Andrew Thrush for this reference. On the problem of piracy in this area, see also TNA, SP16/264, fo. 32; 16/271/73; 16/272/51, 76; 16/273/40; 16/274/3; 16/275/16; SP63/254/12; PC2/44, p. 94.
[14] Dodd, 'Pattern of politics', 36; idem, 'Parliaments, 1640–42', 59. A similar explanation has been posited for the relative ease of ship money collection in Sussex: A. Fletcher, *A County Community in Peace and War: Sussex, 1600–1660* (1975), p. 208.
[15] Pleas were also made to the justices of the local circuits to stop names being presented to the lord president in the first place: NLW, Bute L2/86.
[16] Huntington Library, Ellesmere 7130.

the Marches, John Egerton, first earl of Bridgwater, to stop any nominee of their rival, Thomas Cheadle, being made sheriff.[17] The levying of ship money, however, vastly increased the prominence and importance of the sheriff's office in local government, and after 1634 made the choice of sheriff a vital political as well as administrative decision.

The first ship writ appears to have been executed in Wales without any serious resistance. Probably highly significant in explaining this compliance among the Welsh counties was the fact that the Privy Council had woefully under-assessed them. Notes by the clerk of the Council, Edward Nicholas, on 'some considerable mistakings' in this first writ, indicated that

> whereas his Majesties writt requires of the maritime places in Wales a shipp of 400 tons mann'd with 160 men for 26 weeks, I finde upon the list in the councell booke but 2204^{li} set downe for the charge ... which is 2000^{li} lesse then will doe that worke.[18]

In fact, the Welsh counties were even more lightly burdened than Nicholas's note suggests, for they had been associated with Cheshire, Lancashire and Cumberland in this payment and had to contribute only half the £2,204 assessed (see Table 4). This was equivalent to less than a single Welsh parliamentary subsidy and only 1 per cent of the national ship money total. Despite this, the first writ in the Welsh shires did not proceed completely without incident, largely because of confusion over the mechanics of implementing this novel demand. Joining Cheshire, Lancashire and Cumberland with the Welsh shires created an unwieldy and untried bloc of disparate counties, and the large distances involved between them made it difficult for the respective sheriffs to apportion the money required accurately or equitably. Sir John Bridgeman, chief justice of Chester, wrote to Lord President Bridgwater on 4 January 1635 that the sheriffs of Glamorgan and Monmouthshire, along with the mayor of Newport and the bailiff and aldermen of Cardiff, had arranged a meeting at Ludlow on 29 December regarding the levy. Having only received the writ on 1

---

[17] Huntington Library, Ellesmere 7110, 7118, 7137, 7175, 7177.
[18] TNA, SP16/276/7; PC2/44, p. 265; Dodd, 'Pattern of politics', 36.

December 1634, these officials had sent to the sheriffs of Carmarthenshire and Carmarthen town to arrange this meeting to discuss the apportionment of the ship money among the various jurisdictions involved. Bridgeman noted that each county was to inform its neighbour of the need to attend so 'all concerned might have notice thereof'. Ludlow had been chosen as a 'place most indifferent for all of them', but also because 'if any difference should fall betweene them att theire meetinge they might have the assistance of this councell for reconciliacon'. However, only the sheriffs and officials from Glamorgan, Monmouthshire, Newport and Cardiff had attended, and the authorities of Chester offered a new meeting in their town, which caused consternation among those who had gone to Ludlow,

> not only for haveinge made a longe and troublesome journey in vaine, but especially for that before the tyme of meeting propounded att Chester, the 30 daies after theire receipt of the writte wilbe expired and thereby the power of taxacon [assessments] wholly devolved to the sheriffs insomuch as they were in purpose to leave the whole busines to the sheriffs of Wales, they makeinge up the number aucthorised by the writte and more for taxinge Wales.[19]

Fearing that this would 'breede a hindrance to the service', Bridgeman advised the officials to attend the Chester meeting because the presence of other officials 'would be very needfull there to give informacon of the abilities of the places within theire sevrall lymitts to the end the charge may be equally layed'.

This meeting did indeed take place in Chester on 12 January, when apportionments were agreed, but the lengthy trek caused the Haverfordwest representatives to claim 10*s*. from the corporation 'towards theire chardges in goeinge to Chester about the shipp'.[20] This phrasing indicates one of the other confusions surrounding this first levy in Wales:

---

[19] BL, Add. 64,909, fo. 25. Under the 1634 writ, town officials were allowed to assess themselves. However, after a thirty-day period had elapsed, this right fell to the sheriff. From the second writ onwards the towns, like the counties, were rated by the Privy Council: M. D. Gordon, 'The collection of ship money in the reign of Charles I', *Transactions of the Royal Historical Society*, 3rd series, 4 (1910), 146–7.

[20] Pembrokeshire RO, Haverfordwest Corporation 2058/3; Cheshire and Chester Archives, ZM/L/2/277.

most read the demands of the writ literally, believing they had to provide a ship rather than the money for a ship. Bridgeman wrote that the levy was 'much incouraged' after he had indicated to the sheriffs that Charles would indeed accept money instead of a ship, for the Welsh officials had maintained that they could not otherwise discharge their duties, 'there beinge noe seasoned tymber fitt for that purpose'.[21]

This episode demonstrates the administrative difficulties involved in levying ship money over such a wide area. The practice of joining such diverse counties together in an unwieldy association which cut across traditional boundaries and jurisdictions proved impractical. The potential for disagreement in such an arrangement was reflected in the desire to hold the meeting at Ludlow so that the Council in the Marches could arbitrate in any dispute. The government learned from its mistakes on this occasion, however, and divided Wales into northern and southern divisions of six counties each (Monmouthshire remaining separate), and gave each county an individual assessment when the demand for ship money was renewed in 1635.[22]

Despite these problems, the first writ was very successfully implemented in the principality, and represented a light tax burden. Indeed, in Arllechwedd Isaf, Caernarfonshire, it actually generated a surplus, which the inhabitants later asked should be spent on repairing a local bridge.[23] On 7 March 1635 Bridgwater wrote to Sir John Coke about the collection in Wales, remarking 'considering the unseasonablenesse of the weather & the difficulty & danger in travelling there, I coulde not have thought they coulde have beene so forwarde in those partes'.[24] He alluded, however, to one problem which was to bedevil subsequent levies: the transportation to London of money raised in Wales.

[21] BL, Add. 64,909, fo. 25.
[22] Bridgeman's letter was forwarded to Secretary Coke by Bridgwater 'to doe with it what you please'. Such representations doubtless helped to shape the decision to alter the arrangements for Wales in 1635: BL, Add. 64,909, fo. 27; A. A. M. Gill, 'Ship money during the personal rule of Charles I: politics, ideology and the law, 1634 to 1640' (Ph.D. thesis, University of Sheffield, 1990), 85.
[23] Caernarfonshire RO, XQS/1638.
[24] BL, Add. 64,909, fo. 45.

Bridgwater believed that the hiring of individuals to guard it on its journey would be 'both chargeable & dangerous', and dismissed transportation by carriers. He thereupon suggested a means, later employed by some Welsh counties, of using 'hable & honest traders'. Given Bridgwater's ringing endorsement of the collection in Wales, it was probably these transportation difficulties rather than tardiness that led to the Privy Council sending a letter to eight Welsh shires on 14 March 1635, to chide them for not having shown more promptness.[25] This appears to be confirmed by the fact that Bridgwater received the outstanding ship money in mid-April. The Welsh counties' assessment of £1,111 was paid in one lump sum, suggesting coordination in the principality and possibly even its transportation by a single hand.[26] It may also testify to the comparatively short supply of cash and credit facilities in Wales, and the principality's reliance on seasonal sales of cattle to inject ready money into the regional economy. The shortage of money and use of drovers who would have credit in the capital were features of ship money collection in several counties in later writs, and they may help to explain the patterns of payment in this and subsequent levies.[27]

The first writ had encountered problems in Wales which stemmed almost exclusively from difficulties associated with the novelty of the levy. The assessment, collection and transportation of ship money were undertaken on an *ad hoc* basis, with confusion and improvisation prejudicing its efficient collection. The administrative structure employed by the government was also unsatisfactory, and it was reformed when the levy was repeated in 1635.

---

[25] TNA, PC2/44, pp. 470–1. These were Anglesey, Caernarfonshire, Cardiganshire, Carmarthenshire, Denbighshire, Flintshire, Glamorgan and Monmouthshire.

[26] TNA, PC2/44, p. 528; SP16/287/5, 53; *CSPD, 1635*, p. 484; Cheshire and Chester Archives, ZM/L/2/277.

[27] See, for example, TNA, SP16/420/68, and below, p. 178, n. 90.

NEGOTIATION AND COMPLIANCE:
SHIP MONEY, 1635–1636

In mid-1635, the king and his councillors determined to renew the supposed emergency demand for ship money, extending it to all counties and corporations throughout England and Wales. Consequently, Breconshire, Montgomeryshire and Radnorshire received their first demands by the writ issued in August. The sheriffs who had collected the 1634 writ remained in office, and were now made responsible for assessing and levying the new demand after their term was extended until January 1636.[28]

In an effort to avoid the declining yields associated with the local assessment of the subsidy, the Council designated a lump sum to be levied on each shire.[29] By this writ, Wales had to contribute £10,500, a ten-fold increase on the previous assessment. The northern bloc of Welsh counties had to find £4,000, the southern bloc £5,000, while Monmouthshire, which had to provide £1,500, was assessed separately. However, despite this huge jump in the assessment, comparatively speaking the country continued to be treated fairly leniently, for although £10,500 represented nearly six parliamentary subsidies, the whole of Wales was asked to provide a sum comparable only with individual counties like Devon, Lincolnshire and Somerset.[30] It is difficult to be confident when assessing Wales's economic potential in this period because we lack adequate quantitative studies, but it is hard not to believe that the 'ould generall plea' of Welsh poverty had a role in determining the view of those at the political centre of Wales's ability to pay. In many respects the government's perceptions of the relative prosperity of England and Wales were based upon outdated comparisons from the early Tudor era, when Wales's economy was emerging from a difficult period in which war, partible inheritance and political separation from England had suppressed growth. The political and economic developments of the sixteenth century

[28] *CWP*, no. 1588; *CSPD, 1635–6*, p. 160.
[29] M. J. Braddick, *Parliamentary Taxation in 17th Century England* (Woodbridge, 1994), pp. 78–117.
[30] Gill, 'Ship money', 119–20.

allowed the local Welsh economies to improve markedly, however, rendering these old assessments of ability to pay increasingly anachronistic, while widespread under-assessment and evasion of the subsidy further eroded the possibilities for exploiting the true wealth of Welsh communities.[31] Yet it seems that these antiquated assessments continued to shape central attitudes to Wales and also to provide a vocabulary of penury which the Welsh taxpayers could draw upon usefully in their negotiations with the centre.[32] The contrasts in assessment between individual Welsh counties and those in England reveal some of these disparities. Monmouthshire's total charge was £1,500, the highest of all Welsh counties, but that of neighbouring Herefordshire, which was seen as a poor English shire, was £4,000. Although there is no doubt that Wales was poorer than most parts of England, one wonders to what extent its contemporary reputation for poverty was based on economic realities or old prejudices and a lack of accurate information at the centre. The total requirement for £10,500 was certainly considerable in relation to governmental demands within living memory, but there is a suggestion that Wales's relatively light burden helps to account for the general picture of compliance found in the collection of ship money on the writs of 1635 and 1636.

Alison Gill has pointed out the need to chart the dynamics of ship money payments in order to construct a picture of how each assessment was received on the ground.[33] This offers a more satisfactory means of understanding the impact of each writ than the usual emphasis on the final declared accounts, sometimes composed years after the issue of a writ, because we can then gauge the alacrity or slowness with which communities responded to the demands placed on them. This has previously not been attempted for the Welsh counties. Using the accounts of navy treasurer Sir William Russell, figures have been provided in Tables 5–9

[31] See below, pp. 268–9.
[32] See, for example, the continued difference in minimum property qualifications for Welsh and English JPs (as established by the Acts of Union) which proved a useful bargaining counter for some Welsh counties when the knighthood composition scheme demanded a minimum £25 payment from English and Welsh justices: TNA, E178/5943; Bowen, thesis, 317.
[33] Gill, 'Ship money', 335–72.

later in this chapter which record each county's payment at regular intervals until eighteen months after the issue of the writs.[34] This provides a better understanding of the internal dynamics of ship money collection in Wales, although it must be remembered that reliance on cattle sales in many counties depressed payment before early summer when the livestock was sold and ready money became available.[35]

The sheriff was the key official in levying ship money, and he was made solely responsible for apportioning his county's assessment among its administrative subdivisions of commotes and hundreds. He also decided the basis of this apportionment. The sheriff was thus dependent to a large degree on the diligence of the lower officials who implemented the levy.[36] In October 1635, for example, the sheriff of Flintshire, Peter Griffith, issued orders to the constables of Prestatyn hundred to call before them two or three of the 'best freehoulders' in their constabulary, and to divide and assess the sum of £68 2s. 4d. rated upon the hundred.[37] The sheriffs could not make the collection personally throughout their jurisdictions, and had to rely to a considerable degree on the industry and assiduousness of such lower officials. We must acknowledge, therefore, that a good deal of the information regarding the implementation of the levy 'on the ground' has been lost to us. In the Prestatyn case, we know that only £40 8s. 10d. had been collected by early January 1636, but did this shortfall represent resistance or simply administrative delay?[38] All we can say for certain is that Flintshire paid its full quota on this writ on 11 March 1636, before most counties in England.

Sheriffs' instructions were also unclear as to the form the rating should follow, providing only that the 'most usual common payments' in county rates (such as those for poor relief) should be applied. However, the sheriff was also given latitude to modify rates according to his own discretion, and

---

[34] These accounts are in TNA, SP16/386–16/473.
[35] TNA, SP16/347/60; 16/385/59; 16/448/13.
[36] Gill, 'Ship money', 278–82; H. A. Langelüddeke, 'Secular policy enforcement during the personal rule of Charles I' (D.Phil. thesis, University of Oxford, 1995), 131–251.
[37] NLW, Peniarth Estate CA/52.
[38] NLW, Peniarth Estate CA/53.

whereas one sheriff might apportion his county's quota according to payments towards the repair of bridges (for example), his successor could implement a completely different basis of assessment based on purveyance assessments.[39] This gave considerable scope for challenges to be made against the levy on the basis of an inequitable or unfair apportionment by the sheriff, the rate employed to derive an assessment, or of the total county assessment departing from previous payments relative to those of neighbouring shires.[40] Outright opposition to the levy was difficult for contemporaries to pursue, especially as the demand for ship money was framed in terms of obligation to the king, making payment ultimately a test of loyalty. As a consequence, some of the 'traditional' pleas of poverty used by many areas of Wales in the face of demands for money were rendered unacceptable to the government, although, as has been mentioned, these may already have had some influence in establishing the ceiling of Wales's apportionment in the first instance. This necessitated subtler forms of evasion or resistance couched in deferential language and transmitted in terms acceptable to the Privy Council. Much of the available evidence comes from the State Papers and Privy Council registers which are, perhaps, not the best places in which to find opposition to the levies.[41] Nevertheless, a sensitive approach to the evidence, while not seeing all evasion or negotiation as an indication of resistance, provides information about the response to ship money in the Welsh shires.

A letter from the sheriff of Radnorshire, Morgan Vaughan, illustrates the processes by which rates were agreed in his county. Although the sheriff was ultimately responsible for apportionment, lack of consent and unity over the division of assessment could seriously impede collection. Vaughan stated that he had 'called an assembly of all the justices of peace, constables and the better sorte of all

[39] See below, pp. 187–8, 192–3.
[40] For a penetrating analysis of rating disputes and the forms of opposition to ship money, see Gill, 'Ship money', chs 3–4.
[41] P. Lake, 'The collection of ship money in Cheshire during the sixteen-thirties: a case study of relations between central and local government', *Northern History*, 17 (1981), 71; S. P. Salt, 'Sir Simonds D'Ewes and the levying of ship money, 1635–1640', *Historical Journal*, 37 (1994), 253–87.

the inhabitants ... which I rather did in respect of the service was soe unusuall'.[42] The novelty of ship money in a county experiencing it for the first time indicated the desirability of consensus, which was given here when rating was confirmed 'with one mutuall assent and consent'. He described a situation of consultation and consent which allowed a relatively trouble-free collection; Radnor was one of the most responsive counties in the entire kingdom, sending most of its money to London a mere three months after the writ was issued.[43] Things were not necessarily as straightforward elsewhere in Wales.

A month after the writs had been sent out, eleven prominent inhabitants of Cardiganshire, most of them JPs, wrote to the Privy Council about the rate at which the county had been assessed. They professed themselves ready to bear a share of the burden, but claimed a 'just exception against the proportion of charge'. They maintained that they had been overrated by being placed on a par with neighbouring Pembrokeshire and Carmarthenshire, claiming that traditionally they were assessed 'both in our subsidies, leavies of men & charges of conduction and all other publick taxes [at] but halfe the rate ... those counties were assessed unto'.[44] The petitioners feared that this would create a damaging precedent; they added that 'wee are like in the future to the great damage of our poore countrey to rise much higher in our rates then formerly', and they reminded the Council that the amount demanded was 'above six entire subsidies'. They asked, therefore, that their proportion be reduced in line with other 'publick charges'. The Cardiganshire justices had voiced the same concerns in 1626, when an earlier, abortive, attempt was made to levy ship money; on that occasion they offered to contribute only if Pembrokeshire bore two-thirds of the costs.[45] This, together with the references to traditional rates of 'publick charges', is a reminder that ship money did not always create

---

[42] TNA, SP16/315/6.
[43] There was some delay in transporting the monies collected from the corporation of New Radnor, however: TNA, SP16/302/45; 16/315/6–7.
[44] TNA, SP16/298/32.
[45] TNA, SP16/32/66, 66(i); 16/36/19; *APC, 1626*, p. 175.

rating disputes, but frequently exacerbated existing tensions over public contributions. It is also tempting to see this as an early attempt to deploy the language of poverty and inability to pay by the Cardiganshire petitioners (a practice which was itself perhaps viewed as 'traditional') in establishing its position in relation to the Council and its neighbours. However, such tactics were less effective in the levying of ship money than with previous taxes, because non-negotiable targets had been set by the central government rather than by locally based assessment, as was the case with the parliamentary subsidy.

The response from the Council demonstrated how the unusual arrangements for levying ship money, particularly in dividing Wales into two distinct blocs, allowed disputes to be transferred back to the local arena and helped to neutralize the potential for resistance. The Council acknowledged that if traditional rates had been ignored, a remedy should be available, but it did this very subtly, allowing Cardiganshire to 'abate or increase the proporcons ... as you should find cause' as long as the £5,000 charged on the six counties of south Wales was ultimately 'made upp amongst you'.[46] In making the six counties jointly responsible for the charge, the only recourse the Cardiganshire men had was to negotiate with neighbouring shires for them to increase their rates and allow the Cardiganshire levy to be lowered – hardly a likely prospect! The Council effectively evaded responsibility for arbitrating between shires by their inclusion in a larger administrative bloc which possessed no effective mouthpiece or administrative structure by which it could communicate its interests to the centre. The potential for dispute and resistance was thus translated into purely local terms, whilst the government appeared to offer latitude and reasonableness.

This was not always the response to representations, as may be seen in the case of Flintshire. The sheriff, justices and 'principall inhabitants' of the shire petitioned the Council in late 1635 that the rate of £738 4s. 8d. imposed upon them was too high; after all, the county had 'of long tyme beene

---

[46] TNA, PC2/45, p. 162.

taxed and assessed but in halfe so much as ... Denbigh and Mountgomery by speciall order and direccons from the Board in the tyme of the late Queene Elizabeth'.[47] The inhabitants had paid at this proportion according to the 1634 writ (the apportionments which had been agreed by the respective sheriffs at Chester) and so they requested a return to the 'ancient rule and order'. The Council stated that the rate should stand for the present lest the collection be disturbed, but it added that the position would be reconsidered in any 'farther occasion of publique charge'.[48] This was a quite different response to that given to Cardiganshire, probably because the Flintshire men could cite a conciliar directive in support of their case.

Indeed, when a third ship money writ was issued in 1636, the Privy Council informed Chief Justice John Bridgeman of Flintshire's complaint, requesting that he, 'by reason of your knowledge of yt place, may best discerne the true state thereof'.[49] This reminds us of the Privy Council's lack of detailed knowledge of distant regions like Wales, and the scope this gave for manipulation or exploitation of central directives. Bridgeman held a meeting at Ludlow in early February 1637 with the sheriffs (or their deputies) of Flintshire, Denbighshire and Montgomeryshire, to which Denbighshire's representative, William Wynne, had come prepared, having arranged a prior meeting with several of the county's most prominent gentlemen to agree their position.[50] After this conference, Bridgeman agreed that Flintshire was overcharged and recommended a reapportionment, but he added that the collection based on the third writ was far advanced in all these shires.[51] The Council, aware that a reassessment in the middle of the collection could prove disastrously disruptive, held that the current

---

[47] TNA, PC2/45, pp. 238–9; NLW, MS 6285E, p. 43. For the Elizabethan precedent, see *APC, 1589–90*, pp. 383–4; *1598–9*, pp. 597–8.

[48] Notes taken at the Council record the decision 'that the ... rate shalbee noe president to the prejudice of that county and that upon further occasion the particulars by them alleaged shalbee taken into consideracon and care had for their ease accordingly': TNA, SP16/342/73.

[49] TNA, PC2/46, pp. 460–1.

[50] NLW, Chirk Castle E6102.

[51] TNA, SP16/346/24.

rates should continue for the present. They betrayed the fact that the 'emergency' ship money was to be renewed by asking Bridgeman 'out of your experience and knowledge of the state and condicon of those partes' to apportion sums 'to be hereafter assessed' on all counties of Wales according to traditional rates.[52]

Bridgeman's attempts at 'indifferent' rating, however, were still not to the liking of the Flintshire men, who claimed that it was 'otherwise then was heretofore observed'. They requested, accordingly, that Lord President Bridgwater, in concert with Bridgeman, settle an 'equall & indifferent rate ... according to the aunciente custome', not only for the three shires, but for all north and south Wales.[53] This request appears to have been granted because the rates imposed by the 1637 writ do not correlate with Bridgeman's original estimates. The Flintshire rate was reduced further than Bridgeman offered, and that of Caernarfonshire increased, suggesting that it had been under-assessed previously. There was also some tinkering with the rates for the counties of south Wales, while the total for both parts of the principality remained the same.[54] The further reduction of the Flintshire rate in comparison with Bridgeman's estimates suggests that the county's petitioners were influential in the 1637 reassessments. The whole episode further testifies to the willingness of the government to countenance adjustment of rates if these were shown to be contrary to tradition, but not their overall reduction. It also betrays the Privy Council's reliance on local knowledge in a remote part of its jurisdiction where its coercive power was attenuated by distance and a lack of representation, and by the necessity of relying on officers of the Council in the Marches who, as we shall see, were themselves not always best informed about conditions in the principality.

In the execution of the 1635 writ, Wales's distance from London added a further layer of administrative difficulty to the levying of ship money in the case of Denbighshire. Here the collection of money proceeded smoothly but the sheriff,

[52] TNA, PC2/47, pp. 149–50.
[53] TNA, SP16/376/135.
[54] Gordon, 'Ship money', 162; TNA, SP16/346/24.

Hugh Lloyd of Rossindale, died before it could be sent to London.[55] His son professed to be too young to send the money in person, but Lloyd's successor as sheriff, Hugh Lloyd of Foxhall, claimed that this was 'meerely an evacon to ridd himselfe from the care & charges of the . . . moneyes & expences in convoyinge the same . . . & soe (as it seemes) to fixe the same upon the succeedinge sheriffe'. This dispute seriously impeded the receipt of money in London, for in August 1636, some eight months after the first Welsh county had paid, the Council was still pressing the Denbighshire sheriff for the outstanding monies.[56] This illustrates too how Welsh sheriffs saw the transportation of collected money to London as a particularly onerous part of their responsibility. The sheriffs of Anglesey and Cardiganshire petitioned the Council to be freed from the expense of conveying money to London, but both were rebuffed on the grounds that this could set an expensive precedent if other shires demanded similar concessions.[57] Sympathy must also lie with John Herbert, sheriff of Brecon, who had collected all the money from his county by 3 December 1635, but requested exemption from the charge of transportation, he 'being above 80 yeares olde'.[58]

In all, the Welsh counties performed remarkably well in securing payment on the 1635 writ. As can be seen in Table 5, they were very prompt in returning money to London, and led even English counties which were much closer to the capital. Almost all Welsh shires made full and quick payment; those problems which were encountered can be attributed to factors other than outright refusal or resistance. It must be remembered, however, that many of the negotiations and disputes which occurred were resolved at the local level and consequently leave no trace in the official sources. In Eifionydd, Caernarfonshire, for example, Richard Coytmor appealed to the county bench that the constables had imposed a charge of 26s. on the town of

[55] Huntington Library, Ellesmere 7061B, 7195; TNA, SP16/312/49.
[56] TNA, SP16/312/50; 16/317/62, 71; 16/330/57; PC2/46, p. 336. Denbighshire's assessment was not paid in full until November: SP16/336/48.
[57] TNA, PC2/45, pp. 352–3; SP16/314/46.
[58] TNA, SP16/303/19, 33; 16/314/46; PC2/45, p. 266.

Cricieth 'for their owne use and benefite over and above the principall charge ... to the greate wronge of the parishioners'.[59] The constables claimed to have been acting appropriately, however, and the justices apparently arbitrated the assessments locally because nothing further was heard of the matter.

Collection in other areas also appears to have been more complex than the final accounts suggest. The sheriff of Glamorgan, William Lougher, was one of the first to pay the money demanded by the 1635 writ, receiving thanks from the king for his efforts.[60] Even here, however, Lougher informed the Council that he had executed the writ 'with no small labour and paines in the indifferent and equall assessing, levying and gathering' of money.[61] Rating was the most contentious aspect of ship money, because conventions of assessment could be upset through the actions of a single Crown representative, the sheriff, who could readily be accused of partiality and unfairness. Although the disputes which did materialize in the principality over this writ were essentially localized, they reflected a more general dislike of rating and the novelty of ship money. As elsewhere, resistance was not articulated in overtly ideological terms, but the stresses this levy placed on local communities can be seen even at this early stage.[62] Dodd is mistaken, however, in claiming that Sir Henry Jones of Abermarlais and David Lloyd of Forest, Carmarthenshire, were prominent resisters against the 1635 writ who 'infected [the] ... whole county by ... example'.[63] In fact, the £90 for which Jones was cited before the Council was not for his ship money assessment, but rather an amount levied on Privy Seal letters in 1625 which he, as the collector, had not paid to the Exchequer. The £91 which Lloyd was said to have refused was, in fact, the amount collected towards the Palatinate benevolence by his relative, Griffith Lloyd.[64]

[59] Caernarfonshire RO, XQS/1636/28.
[60] TNA, SP16/305/15; PC2/45, p. 302.
[61] TNA, SP16/302/85.
[62] On the lack of overt ideological resistance, see Gill, 'Ship money', 304–17, 405–16.
[63] Dodd, 'Pattern of politics', 37–8.
[64] TNA, C205/14/11; SP16/312/6, 6(i); SP38/17 (18 May 1638).

The other arrears can also be explained other than by ideological resistance. The largest anomaly was that of Carmarthenshire, which was apparently £160 in arrears according to the 1635 writ. The money in fact was raised by the county, as appears from a letter of the sheriff, Rowland Lewis, of January 1638. Lewis informed the Council that the 1635 sheriff, Thomas Vaughan, had £110 remaining in his hands, and Richard Thomas, mayor of the county borough of Carmarthen, retained £50.[65] Neither had paid these sums to the treasurer of the navy, but the arrears noted in the final account should not obscure the fact that the whole of the sum was collected. The arrears of Pembrokeshire, meanwhile, arose from the fact that the sheriff, John Scurfield, drowned in February 1636 while taking the money to London. His successor, John Wogan, explained that the £43 arrears had been paid by the county but were lost with the sheriff.[66]

'THE DISEASE OF RATEINGE': THE SHIP WRITS OF 1636 AND 1637

The issue of another writ in 1636 indicated that ship money was becoming, as some had feared, an institutionalized tax rather than an emergency response to extraordinary conditions. The difficulties associated with assessment, collection and responsibility for arrears clearly reduced the number of men who were willing to take the office of sheriff. This problem was recognized by the Privy Council, which, in anticipation of another levy, informed Bridgwater on 12 September 1636 that King Charles, 'for some especiall reasons', required a list of five or more of the most able and 'well affected' men in each county who could serve as sheriffs in Wales.[67] Nominations were not usually given until shortly before the pricking took place, but the government evidently wanted extra time to consider who should implement the forthcoming writ. The early request surprised Bridgwater, then residing on his Hertfordshire estate, and

[65] TNA, SP16/379/50.
[66] *CSPD, 1636–7*, pp. 153, 218.
[67] TNA, SP16/331/46; PC2/46, p. 346.

on 17 September he drafted a letter to Lord Keeper Coventry to the effect that it would not be possible to provide the names in time, 'my notes & papers being at London & the sicknesse encreasinge about my house there that I can not goe thether for them'.[68] He assured Coventry, however, that he would attempt to gather names 'with all the speede I can'.

Three days later Bridgwater wrote to Coventry again, expressing the hope that the difficulties he was experiencing in sending the names of candidates would 'not be any prejudice in these partes to his Majestyes service, to which I hartely wishe good successe'.[69] He continued that letters had been sent to the Welsh judges for a speedy return of worthy candidates within their circuits, but in the event of difficulties he would undertake to make the returns himself. On the same day, he informed the judges that they were to 'sett apart' all other business, and provide the names of four or six of the 'hablest, most serviceable & well affected persons ... though perhapps you thinke it some what before the ordinary time'.[70]

Despite his best efforts to expedite the matter, by 30 September Bridgwater had only received a return from Sir John Bridgeman, and he informed Coventry that he was 'almost in despaire of hearing from the rest of the justices of the Welche circuits'.[71] He had, therefore, compiled the return himself, with a copy of the previous year's shrieval roll, a book of Welsh JPs and his own 'weake memory & the best information I could possibly gett in these partes'.[72] Bridgwater added that he 'presumed well of their affections & readynesse to the service, but God (not myself) knoweth mens hartes ... I shall praye that they may be sedulous &

---

[68] Huntington Library, Ellesmere 7232.
[69] Huntington Library, Ellesmere 7233.
[70] Huntington Library, Ellesmere 7234, 7236.
[71] Huntington Library, Ellesmere 7427.
[72] Bridgwater thanked Thomas Alured, auditor of fines at Ludlow, for sending him a book containing the names of the JPs, 'by which I founde some light in the darke streets whereof I was'. He added, however, 'I should have beene more confident in the perusall thereof but yt I mett the names of some ... therein without note or marke which of my owne knowledge be deade': Huntington Library, Ellesmere 7241.

industrious in the performance of their dutyes'. He then offered an illuminating discussion of the ship levy in Wales during the previous year, and his fears for the execution of the current writ. He maintained that his choice of candidates was the best possible under the circumstances, but

> unlesse some course may be taken for even & equall proportionable assessments, I feare some difficulty. For your Lordship may remember howe many complaintes were presented the last time upon that occasion, & though some weere relieved by the Borde, yet diverse founde no ease; whereof I can remember ... the county of Flynte ... Anglesey was taking the like course to have enformed your Lordships of their complainte, had not I prevented it by telling those that weere to sollicite in that behalfe that it woulde be fruitlesse for the time passed, so that they weere best to looke forwarde & not to give any impediment to the then present service or to trouble the Borde with a fruitlesse bemoaning of themselves.[73]

This indicates that rating disputes were an even greater problem in Wales during 1635–6 than is revealed by the extant communications between the Welsh sheriffs and the Council. It is noticeable, however, that Bridgwater did not locate any more fundamental opposition to ship money than disputes over apportionment, and the lord president presented diligence in executing the writ as the best avenue to royal favour, thereby frustrating obstruction or opposition.[74]

Bridgwater's return of potential shrieval candidates is also revealing of the problems ship money faced in his large and diverse jurisdiction: he added a number of comments about the choice of this most important officer during the collection of ship money.[75] Sir Henry Jones of Abermarlais (Dodd's putative refuser of the 1635 writ) was included as a possible sheriff, but Bridgwater added that he 'may be too oulde or infirme' to serve. This suggestion that the pool of potential candidates in Wales may have been limited is strengthened by Bridgwater's inclusion of Evan Gwyn in the Cardiganshire return; he found Gwyn 'strooke out of the booke of the peace, which made me scrupulous to sett

---

[73] Huntington Library, Ellesmere 7239.
[74] For the relationship between collection and favour, see Lake, 'Ship money in Cheshire', 44–71.
[75] Huntington Library, Ellesmere 7240.

downe his name, but I coulde not make up the number by any supply that I know'.[76] The return was compiled in haste in order to comply with the Council's directions, and this meant that he was not well apprised of the suitability of candidates. Concerning Radnorshire, Bridgwater commented, 'I professe I dare not deliver my opinion, but all the names in the liste are suche as have beene formerly certefied unto me, or suche as I founde in the booke of the peace'. The Council order, which was probably designed to give the government time to select the most reliable candidates, merely succeeded in engendering haste, confusion and a list of potentials based on rudimentary and defective assessments of their capabilities. This was not the best way to launch the third writ of ship money.

The Council proceeded in a more determined manner in the supervision of this writ, directing (for example) Sir Lewis Mansell, sheriff of Glamorgan, to return the names and assessments of all those who refused to pay their ship money by 24 January 1637.[77] Outright refusal was rare, however, and a more intractable problem in Wales as elsewhere was the disputes over rating. For example, the inability to find a quick solution to Flintshire's rating grievances hindered the execution of this writ. On 20 February 1637, the sheriff, Thomas Mostyn, informed the Council that his work had 'beene much hindered, trusting to have an abatement of the charge'.[78] Difficulties over rating were also experienced in Montgomeryshire, where the sheriff, Lloyd Pierce, commented that he had made his assessments according to an 'ordinary division', but admitted that this method was 'no equall way to followe' because these rates had been laid down thirty years previously and 'many parishes are decayed & others impaired'.[79] Indeed, in March 1637 the hundred of Llanidloes complained that this 'partiallity & ... inequallity' of rating was 'retarding ... the service'.[80]

[76] Gwyn was omitted from the county bench in 1627–8, but was included in all commissions from at least 14 December 1628: J. R. S. Phillips (ed.), *The Justices of the Peace in Wales and Monmouthshire, 1541 to 1689* (Cardiff, 1975), p. 194.
[77] TNA, C231/5, p. 223.
[78] TNA, SP16/347/57.
[79] TNA, SP16/355/69.
[80] TNA, PC2/47, pp. 281–2. This hundred's assessment was a significant shift in

The case of Carmarthenshire offers some evidence of how the process of rating could promote local inequalities and tensions. The sheriff's schedule of assessments survives and may be compared with the apportionment of one of the recent parliamentary subsidies. The required sum of £760 represented about five parliamentary subsidies as levied in the 1620s. However, considerable variations emerge in the internal distribution of this amount when the subsidy assessments are compared with the ship money rating. The town and parish of Laugharne, for example, was rated at 16s. in the 1628 subsidy, but in 1636 was assessed at £20, which represented an enormous increase of twenty-five fold.[81] However, a parish like Bettws in the hundred of Kidwelly paid £6 10s. 0d., only three times its 1628 subsidy. It is noteworthy that the parish of Llangathen, the home of the sheriff, Rice Rudd, paid £5 in the subsidy and only £9 in ship money, less than twice its subsidy assessment. It would appear, then, that Rudd may have attempted to shield his neighbours in his apportionment of the overall sum. Such wide variations help to explain the considerable passions which rating could provoke.

Indications survive from this levy of the role of lower officials in levying ship money, something which remains obscure because of the poor survival of evidence relating to this subordinate echelon of administrative performance in Wales. These survivals highlight the manner in which ship money became the concern of officials beneath the sheriff himself. Ship money mobilized a constituency of officials, including constables and overseers of the poor, in a manner not found in previous levies such as the benevolences, forced loans or subsidies of the 1620s, which had largely been implemented by the higher ranking deputy lieutenants, justices of the peace or subsidy commissioners and collectors.[82] The scope of ship money meant its administrative

---

its proportional charge in the county compared with earlier arrangements for the subsidy: SP16/355/69(i); E179/222/395; 179/223/402.

[81] TNA, E179/220/123; SP16/345/26(i).

[82] Parish assessors and sub-collectors did work under the subsidy commissioners, but Braddick indicates the 'key positions in the subsidy administration were those of commissioner and of collector': Braddick, *Taxation*, p. 66.

machinery needed to be more extensive, and was modelled on the assessment and collection of local taxes like those for poor relief or church rates. In contrast to the comparatively prosperous constituency which paid parliamentary subsidies, such local rates reached much further down the social scale, meaning that many more people were paying ship money compared with the taxes, loans and benevolences discussed in Chapter 3. William Wynn of Llanfair, the sheriff of Denbighshire, referred to his reliance on this lower order of officialdom when he informed Edward Nicholas in March 1637

> that where the high constables and such other persons . . . were bothe litterate, discreete & of the better quallitie, the assessments went facile on without any great complaint of partiall dealing . . . But that in other limitts as well the ignorance of those under officers as the parciallitie of some others . . . did infinitely distract and retarde the service.[83]

This meant that Wynn was not able to finalize his assessments until early February 1637, four months after the writ was issued, and it illustrates the extent to which the sheriff relied on compliance by the lower orders in effecting collection. The hundred of Edeirnion in Merioneth provides another valuable insight into the labours of these local officials. Two constables wrote to the sheriff concerning their rating in the hundred, 'which hath beene our whole labor and imploymente this fortnight'. They described the process by which the assessments were made; this closely reflected the sheriff's own task but on a smaller scale. They gathered the 'prime men' of the hundred together to see the assessment imposed by the sheriff 'equally distributed accordinge to the aunciente custome'. The oversight of this procedure they described as 'a dayly toile to us & some expence', and so they requested the sheriff 'to be soe favorable as to ease us from further doeings therein and appoint some other collectors'.[84] One of the constables, Harry Jones, wrote to the sheriff on 27 January 1637 that Thomas ap Humffrey, a collector, considered himself affected 'of the new disease of

---

[83] TNA, SP16/349/51.
[84] NLW, Brogyntyn (Clenennau) 497.

rateinge', by reason of which he encountered much neglect.[85] Jones himself, who was evidently not discharged of the burden of collecting despite his best efforts, required directions from the sheriff 'touchinge those that will not pay their moneye upon demaunde'. The experience of ship money, then, was not an administrative burden only for the sheriff, but was transmitted down the social scale, and was perhaps felt most keenly by those lower officials who had to extract the money from the inhabitants. These instances also indicate the degree to which the collection relied upon the diligence of these men; despite the Council's official stance that the sheriff was solely responsible for the implementation of ship money, the latter needed to secure the consent and cooperation of a network of lower officials to make the levy viable. There is a suggestion here of the resistance and reluctance encountered lower in the social order, but the evidence is regrettably incomplete and fails to indicate the nature and motivation of any lack of cooperation. All we can say is that at this time there is little evidence of widespread, concerted opposition in Wales, but it is suggestive of the degree to which the business of ship money reached down the social scale of early modern Wales and presented hundredal and parish officials as well as sheriffs with unpalatable choices of rating and collection when dealing with their neighbours and friends. The disruptive potentialities of ship money at such parochial levels are glimpsed in the brief survivals.

In 1636–7, ship money certainly encountered a number of other obstacles, one of the most notable being a severe outbreak of plague which was particularly prevalent in Radnorshire. Although evidence of the plague's impact is most complete for this county, it is likely that it also disrupted collection elsewhere in Wales.[86] The parish register of Presteigne records the first death from plague on 20 June 1636 with a 'p', while new sheets of parchment had to be added in subsequent months to record all the town's victims.[87] The plague also raged in New Radnor throughout

---

[85] NLW, Brogyntyn (Clenennau) 498.
[86] Huntington Library, Ellesmere 7233, 7418, 7420.
[87] Herefordshire RO, AE62/1, p. 364.

1636, and seriously hindered collection in the county: the sheriff noted that he could not gather ship money from these two towns, and an account of October 1637 shows that £198 remained outstanding on this writ.[88]

Recurrences of the plague continued to disrupt the collection demanded by subsequent writs. It is an indication of the tenacity of the Privy Council that it persisted in harrying the blighted inhabitants for relatively meagre sums. Despite the plague, there was no remission granted by the Council, which demanded the arrears due from Presteigne on the 1636 writ, and it expected a similar payment in accordance with a new writ issued in 1637. The sheriff, the town's inhabitants and the county's justices all petitioned the Council, and even the king, in 1638 to look favourably on Presteigne's inhabitants who were 'scarce able as yett to subsist'. However, the government's unflinching stance on the necessity of collection meant that the pressure to comply continued. What is remarkable about this level of central pressure and intransigence is that Prestigne's two assessments totalled a mere £24 16s. 0d.[89] The episode demonstrates how insensitive the Council could be to local exigencies, and such a hardline position on paltry sums could not but fail to alienate local communities faced with inflexible demands for money.

It is also noticeable that money from Wales came in more slowly than on previous occasions, and defaulting and arrears appear to have increased (see Table 6). This, however, may have been a result of factors other than resistance and disease, such as the difficulty of conveying the money to London. The sheriff of Denbighshire complained that he had 'noe secure way by returne to pay the money ... unlesse in somer time by drovers'.[90] In Caernarfonshire, meanwhile, William Lewis Anwyll experienced difficulties in collecting the money 'by reason many divitions are in many parishes and that it would require tyme to conferre with the

[88] BL, Add. 70,002, fos 122–4, 127, 135; TNA, SP16/348/46; PC2/48, pp. 333–4
[89] TNA, SP16/385/83; 16/386/25–7; 16/401/72; PC2/49, p. 584
[90] TNA, SP16/349/51. He entrusted £400 he had collected to a drover in July 1637, but was informed that the man had 'disappoynted him', although he was able to settle most of his arrears by September: SP16/366/51; PC2/48, pp. 136–7; *CSPD, 1637*, p. 532.

counstables about it'. He maintained, however, that 'I doe as yett finde noe opposicion'.[91]

The situation in Pembrokeshire merits special comment. The sheriff was Sir John Stepney of Prendergast. His mother, Jane, had refused to pay the 10s. ship money imposed on her in Haverfordwest by the 1635 writ, and the borough's mayoral accounts for 1637 reveal that she also refused to pay the 5s. levied on her on this occasion.[92] Even more striking on the latter writ was the refusal of her son, the sheriff, to contribute the 12s. for which he was liable in the town.[93] This anomalous situation may have been the product of Haverfordwest's special status as a county borough which possessed its own sheriff and borough officials, who may have apportioned the town's quota of £40 in a manner which displeased Stepney and his mother.[94] Whatever the explanation, Sir John does not appear to have provided the best model for levying ship money in Pembrokeshire, suggesting perhaps that Bridgwater's haste in choosing sheriffs precluded his conferring with the circuit judges as to who might experience difficulties. No such problems are recorded from elsewhere in Pembrokeshire, but Stepney did not levy the money with great alacrity.[95] He did, however, collect all the shire's assessment, although only 86 per cent found its way to London, and he expressed his wish that 'the next sheriffe should nott be troubled' with outstanding arrears.[96]

The accounts of the Haverfordwest mayor, William Bowen, for 1636–7 also reveal his request for an allowance of £2 for going with Rice Vaughan and Sir John Stepney 'to

[91] TNA, SP16/349/64.
[92] Pembrokeshire RO, Haverfordwest Corporation 2059/3. Dame Jane Stepney was a widow who held property in Haverfordwest under the terms of her father-in-law's will; she also resided there: F. Green, 'The Stepneys of Prendergast', *West Wales Historical Records*, 7 (1917–18), 122–4, 129; NLW, Edwinsford 2366.
[93] Pembrokeshire RO, Haverfordwest Corporation 2060/6. He also defaulted on his payment in the borough in 1638–9: ibid. 2062/6.
[94] There had been earlier difficulties between the county and Haverfordwest sheriffs in agreeing the town's contribution: TNA, PC2/45, p. 295.
[95] TNA, SP16/366/45; 16/369/43; PC2/48, pp. 333–4; PC2/51, p. 103.
[96] TNA, SP16/369/43. Sir William Russell's accounts as treasurer of the navy of November 1637 noted that the outstanding £100 from the county had been collected but remained in the sheriff's hands: SP16/371/71, 126; 16/372/48.

meete with the sheriffes of south Wales to confirre conserninge the rate of the shippe'.[97] This suggests that the sheriffs of the southern division in Wales acted in concert over rating, possibly as part of the reassessment process which followed from the Flintshire representations of 1635 discussed earlier. This meeting probably allowed the sheriffs to compare assessments and to agree on whether any representations should be made to the Council about inequalities, and possibly to allow tactics of complaint to be discussed.

Another writ for ship money was issued in 1637; it has been associated with the greatest demonstration of reluctance to pay before the collapse of the final two demands. Rating disputes had become endemic, and Hampden's test case caused delays and refractoriness while people waited to see whether ship money would be declared illegal.[98] As arrears were still being collected in some Welsh counties from the previous writs and the sheriffs were harried by the Council, the shrievalty appeared more onerous than ever. In his return nominating candidates to be Welsh sheriffs, Bridgwater confessed that he had 'mett with more difficultyes in three of the circuits then I coulde have wished or thought of'. In Montgomeryshire the Powis Castle interest had protected a number of potential candidates from serving, while Flintshire and Denbighshire were so poorly furnished with 'fitt men' that Bridgwater had been forced to include the names of some of his cousins.[99] Bridgwater's marginal notes such as '*quarae*, if [he] come to church', or 'suites in lawe' against some names on the list which he compiled for Lord Keeper Coventry again reveal the relatively low stock of willing men from the county elites in the principality.[100] Referring to the choice of sheriffs, Marmaduke Lloyd, justice of the Brecon circuit, wrote that 'not one that I returned was prickt in any county, but meane men were prickt, whose estates were not able to bear the charge of that office'.[101]

[97] Pembrokeshire RO, Haverfordwest Corporation 2060/3.
[98] Gill, 'Ship money', 202–11, 443–70.
[99] Huntington Library, Ellesmere 7238.
[100] Huntington Library, Ellesmere 7246.
[101] Shropshire RO, 212/364/17.

Rating disputes were the most impeditive aspect of ship money, and the execution of the 1637 writ in Cardiganshire was disrupted by the most protracted dispute experienced in Wales. It revolved around the variance between Uwch Aeron and Is Aeron, traditional units of administration dating from the medieval period by which the county was split into northern and southern divisions, respectively. The antagonism between these units recalls how the need to settle on some form of equitable distribution of assessments within counties sometimes reawakened what John Morrill has described as 'dormant but profound jurisdictional conflicts'.[102] Previous writs had evidently engendered friction because the first indication of a problem came in a petition of the southern division of Is Aeron to the Privy Council in June 1637. Its complaint about the inequity in the rating compared with Uwch Aeron was referred by the Council to the court of great sessions, which possessed the local knowledge and representation to make a binding judgement.[103]

However, local knowledge could also mean local influence, and on 18 September 1637 the court ordered that Uwch Aeron pay two-thirds of all rates, while Is Aeron was only burdened with one-third.[104] Although Uwch Aeron was indeed the larger of the two, this decision flew in the face of traditional apportionments and prompted a counter-petition whereby the northern division claimed that taxes had usually been split equally. They also claimed that the great sessions' order had been read 'when none of the parties concerned were there to make opposicion'.[105] The matter was referred once more to the great sessions, with the Council adding rather unrealistically that this dispute should not hinder collection.

The disruption caused by the disagreement is clear in a letter of 10 February 1638 written by the county's unfortunate sheriff, John Steadman of Strata Florida. He maintained that the adjustment of the 'ancient course' of taxation by the

---

[102] J.S. Morrill, *Revolt in the Provinces: The People of England and the Tragedies of War, 1630–1648* (Harlow, 1999), p. 42.
[103] TNA, PC2/48, pp. 11–12.
[104] TNA, SP16/370/84(i); PC2/48, pp. 449–50.
[105] TNA, PC2/48, p. 548; SP16/380/1.

great sessions 'hath begotten much unreadines both of assessinge and payinge in the persons greived with that alteracon'. The decision meant that the rates used by former sheriffs had been rendered useless, and this caused him enormous difficulties: 'noe man concerned by this alteration assistinge the service with the same willingnes of payment as formerly'.[106] The reassessment had sabotaged the collection rather than expedited it, and part of the reason probably lay in the fact that the order had been made by the great sessions court, an itinerant body with little compulsive authority to back decisions in such jurisdictional disputes. It was possibly for this reason that the Privy Council, in a directive of 16 June 1638, referred the matter to the Council in the Marches, ordering Bridgwater to 'imediately settle and sett downe the rates' and communicate his decision to Steadman.[107]

An authoritative decision was certainly required because the sheriff informed the Council that he had been able to raise about half the money due in the county; 'partly in respect of certaine differences and varience' between the two divisions, however, he was unable to make present payment.[108] One of the judges at Ludlow, Marmaduke Lloyd, informed Bridgwater that he and his fellow judges had arranged to consult with 'some of the cheifest persons in each division', and had ordered the original rates be employed for assessment so that 'the kings service may not be neglected by the opposicion of the inhabitants in those severall devisions'.[109] These disagreements had a severely detrimental effect on the collection of ship money, and full payment was not secured until mid-December 1639.[110] The Council's agreement to reform Cardiganshire's rates should probably be placed in the context of the government's drive in 1637 to address such disputes by settling rates on the authority of assize judges and JPs.[111] It was believed that this

[106] TNA, SP16/381/70.
[107] TNA, PC2/49, p. 278.
[108] TNA, SP16/381/70.
[109] BL, Add. 64,916, fo. 103.
[110] TNA, SP16/435/78.
[111] Gill, 'Ship money', 202–9; T. G. Barnes, *Somerset, 1625–1640* (Cambridge, MA, 1961), pp. 220–1.

would remove the grounds upon which most disputes were based, but without local knowledge this still had to be undertaken by local bodies whose decisions did not possess the force of a Council directive. It is difficult to know whether the episode in Cardiganshire represents a tactic to oppose and evade the levy, or whether real grievances over systems of rating were involved. It is certain, however, that the various moves and counter-moves on the part of the two divisions allowed them to delay and prevaricate for a considerable period without opposing the ship money directly.

The execution of this writ in other parts of Wales provides further evidence of widespread delay in payment, though few signs of outright resistance (see Table 7). In late April 1638 nine Welsh counties were castigated by the Privy Council for having paid nothing whatsoever.[112] Increasingly the Council came to see the responsibility for such laxity as resting solely with the sheriff, and this was especially so after the verdict in Hampden's case. In their letter to the defaulting Welsh sheriffs, the Council asserted that they could 'make noe better interpretacon of this your supine neglect then that it proceeds from some disaffeccon in yow, the sheriff'.

This verdict was harsh. Many sheriffs were doing their utmost to implement the collection, but they were hampered by a number of factors. Thomas Whitley of Aston, Flintshire, maintained that the constables had laboured 'very earnestly', but noted that they had met with 'some rubbs' in collecting the money.[113] In Merioneth, Hugh Nanney averred that all the 'abler sorte ... doe pay with all alacritie, but that the scarsitie of money among the meaner sorte causeth some delay'.[114] Nanney expressed his belief that Charles wanted all his subjects 'mildly' dealt with, 'which makes me presume to leavie the mize more leasurely

---

[112] TNA, PC2/49, pp. 123–4. These were Breconshire, Cardiganshire, Caernarfonshire, Carmarthenshire, Denbighshire, Flintshire, Merioneth, Pembrokeshire and Radnorshire.

[113] TNA, SP16/385/88. See also SP16/389/70; 16/390/45; 16/392/55. There is evidence that Whitley had to resort to distraint in order to obtain money: Flintshire RO, D/G/3275/22.

[114] TNA, SP16/386/54.

of the poorer sorte'. This is eloquent testimony as to how delicate was the sheriff's task: he had to extract money for the central government without alienating his local community. Significantly, Nanney also added: 'I cann heare of none that is refractorie and unwilling to pay'. The collection of ship money may have been onerous and burdensome, placing significant stresses on local communities, but there is no evidence to support the proposition that it was generating widespread and politicized disaffection in Wales.

There were indications of severe delay and backwardness in many areas of Wales in relation to this writ, but more concerted resistance is very difficult to locate. There may be some support for the claim that the collection of money was delayed while Hampden's case was proceeding, as men waited to see whether the levy would be declared illegal.[115] The rate of payment was extremely slow while the case was being heard in mid-1638, but the eventual judgment, bullishly publicized by the government, removed many of the reasons for prevarication or opposition. It is striking that by February 1639 the vast majority of money from the Welsh counties had been paid, except in Cardiganshire which was blighted by the protracted rating dispute.[116] In Wales there seems to have been no stiffening of opposition after the verdict, but rather a resignation that ship money had been declared legal and the king's right affirmed. The outstanding arrears started coming in soon after the judgement was given.

Breakdown and collapse? Ship money, 1638–1640

The writ issued in 1638 was executed in quite different circumstances to those of earlier demands, most notably because Charles was preparing to go to war with his rebellious northern kingdom which had risen against Laudian innovations in the Church. These circumstances included numerous additional charges on the populace, and it was probably for this reason that the amounts required by this

---

[115] Sharpe, *Personal Rule*, pp. 728–9.
[116] TNA, PC2/51, p. 103.

writ were set at around a third of previous rates.[117] This reduced burden probably helped to facilitate collection, though its impact was compounded by the other charges required for raising a force to oppose the Scots. The multiplicity of demands was reflected in a petition of a husbandman, John Williams, to the Caernarfonshire quarter sessions. Having lands in two different parishes, he complained that he 'was cessed of the pouder mise in the sume of 12d, of the shipp mise ... 11d, of the coate & conduct mise ... 12d' on both of these holdings, and he requested relief.[118] Although the amounts were small, this accumulation of charges represented a real burden for such ratepayers lower down the social order. It is also noticeable that ship money represented only one-third of the public monies which Williams had to find.

Bridgwater moved early to ensure the return of sufficient men to execute the writ in Wales, recalling how previously he had been called on 'very unexpectedly' to provide names.[119] In his return of potential candidates, Marmaduke Lloyd, a justice on the Brecon circuit, maintained that he had sent the names of the 'best men of estate & quality', adding that 'the greatest men are fittest to serve the kynge in these tymes'.[120] This careful choice of men appears to have produced good results; Michael Evans informed William Wynn of Merioneth that the pricking had chosen in almost all the shires of north Wales 'men of very greate sufficiencie'.[121]

For the most part, however, the reduced sums failed to induce prompt payment (see Table 8). There were exceptions, such as Glamorgan, which quickly paid £524 towards its £547, Edward Nicholas noting that this was the first money collected on this writ.[122] Elsewhere there was consid-

---

[117] TNA, SP16/538/8.
[118] Caernarfonshire RO, XQS/1639.
[119] Huntington Library, Ellesmere 7258–61.
[120] Shropshire RO, 212/364/17.
[121] NLW, Brogyntyn (Clenennau) 518.
[122] TNA, SP16/413/10. Although only £23 short of Glamorgan's total, the sheriff still received a rebuke from the Council for his 'neglect'! The remainder was, in fact, the amount due from Cardiff, the responsibility of the bailiff rather than the sheriff; it was paid on 21 September 1639: PC2/50, pp. 457, 597; *CSPD, 1639*, p. 516.

erable delay while charges for the Scottish wars began to accumulate, and eight Welsh counties had paid nothing at all by June 1639.[123] Sir Thomas Powell wrote from Denbighshire in April 1639 that he had not as yet received any considerable sum, 'notwithstandinge my often callinge upon the constables and collectors for more speedie payment with intimacon of my intent to proceede ... against their wilfull delayes'.[124] The use of 'wilful' here may indicate something more determined than simple neglect or indolence on the part of the lesser officers. There is also the possibility, however, that Powell was merely echoing the forceful rhetoric employed by the Privy Council regarding laxity in collecting money in an attempt to portray his own efforts in the best possible light. A month later he sent £100, still complaining that the money came in 'very slowlye'. Illustrating the problems caused by the concurrent military levies, he noted that part of the money

> before it was or could be payed to mee, hath bene invaded and use made of it to pay conduct money for soldiers; which in regard of the present necessitye to have that service dispatcht, the deputy lieutennants here it seemes deemed to bee a tolerable incroachment.[125]

Although a greater reluctance may be observed in the payment of ship money on this writ, concerted resistance on more ideological grounds is again difficult to locate. Richard Bulkeley in Anglesey, for example, averred that he knew of 'noe lett or impediment I ame like to meete ... save the poverty of the inhabitants'.[126] In Merioneth, Griffith Lloyd informed the Council that he had heard of 'little or noe complaint of any unequalitie or any deniall or refusall, onlye the rawnesse & slownesse of some of the cessors, collectors & others'.[127] In Flintshire, John Eyton of Leeswood did not contact the Council until 16 October 1639, nearly a year after the writ had been issued. Yet this did not necessarily indicate growing resistance, for he claimed that he had expe-

[123] TNA, PC2/50, p. 457. These were Anglesey, Breconshire, Caernarfonshire, Carmarthenshire, Flintshire, Merioneth, Montgomeryshire and Pembrokeshire.
[124] TNA, SP16/417/38.
[125] TNA, SP16/420/33.
[126] TNA, SP16/418/64.
[127] TNA, SP16/418/84.

rienced no impediment in executing the writ apart from 'slownes of payment for want of meanes more then will'.[128] Again there is a lack of expedition, doubtless compounded by wider economic problems, but little indication of outright resistance.

A survival from this county shows that disputes over ship money, even in local contexts, were still articulated primarily in terms of difficulties with rating. David Lloyd Thomas, one of the constables of Rhuddlan hundred, appealed to the great sessions on behalf of a number of townships there. He claimed that payments on the 1635 and 1636 ship money writs had been assessed on the basis of the 'princes mize and other mizes for bridges & such necessary occacons'. Assessments for the 1637 and 1638 writs, however, had been altered by one of the hundred's most powerful inhabitants, Sir John Conway, who ordered that the rate for purveyance be used instead. The townships believed themselves to be overcharged under this latter assessment, and asked the sheriff to reinstitute the old system. This caused Conway to use

> many threateninge speeches against yor petitioner, and [he] much opposed the paymente ... by causeinge distresses taken for the said mize to be *replevined*, to the retarding of his Majesties service, which caused ... great trouble and hinderance with distraccon & unsetled course of assessmente.[129]

Two local justices supported the petition, asking that it be referred to some of the county's most prominent figures, including Sheriff Eyton and John Owen, bishop of St Asaph, 'to sett some order for the levyinge of all mizes'. These figures found that the 'constant course [for] ... publique imposicons' was indeed the prince's mise, and recommended that the great sessions produce an order to that effect.[130] On 24 October 1639, the justices duly followed the recommendation 'for the avoyding of all future distraccons and differences which may retard any publicke services for

---

[128] TNA, SP16/431/32. He also informed the Council that he had not written before as he did not wish to interfere with 'your more important affaires' until he had completely discharged his service.
[129] NLW, Great Sessions 4/982/7/15.
[130] NLW, Great Sessions 4/982/7/16.

the comon wealth'.[131] Such disagreements might retard the collection, but they suggest that, even after five burdensome demands, when disputes arose they revolved principally around the way in which ship money was imposed, not because it was imposed in the first place.

According to Gordon's figures, based on the final declared accounts, two Welsh counties defaulted completely on this writ: Montgomeryshire and Carmarthenshire. However, other evidence demonstrates that this was not the case, and Gordon's figures, though widely accepted, are incorrect. The accounts of the treasurer of the navy, Sir William Russell, reveal that Carmarthenshire in fact paid £300, just £1 short of its full requirement, on 14 December 1639.[132] Similarly, although collection in Montgomeryshire was seriously delayed, possibly because of an outbreak of the plague in late 1638, it too had provided full payment by March 1640.[133] Thus, although payment was long overdue in these counties, ship money was a considerable success rather than the total failure indicated by the declared account. That these totals do not appear in the final accounts may be attributable to a clerical error, or perhaps the government improperly diverted the money to other uses, such as the mobilization against Scotland. Taking account of these figures, therefore, 97 per cent of the money demanded in the principality by this writ eventually was collected, a remarkable pattern of compliance across thirteen diverse counties.[134]

It was not, then, until the final writ that ship money experienced a general breakdown in Wales. A number of factors combined to make this later demand a comprehensive failure. The decision to increase ship money to its previous levels after the reductions of 1638–9 must have been most unwelcome. The Council's gaze was directed elsewhere, and

---

[131] NLW, Great Sessions 4/982/7/17.
[132] TNA, SP16/435/78.
[133] TNA, SP16/448/7; 16/400/94; 16/410/149; 16/444/37; PC2/51, pp. 314–15, 349, 370.
[134] Gordon, 'Ship money', 159, 162. This indicates that Wales performed considerably better than the country as a whole, which averaged around 80% payment, although this figure may also ignore monies raised which were never paid in: Sharpe, *Personal Rule*, p. 589. Cf. Dodd, 'Pattern of politics', 37–8, who asserts that the breakdown of ship money began with the 1638 writ.

its supervision of ship money could not be as comprehensive as in the past. In addition, the multitude of other charges contributed to a general reluctance to pay, as did the widespread belief that a parliament would be called imminently, thereby removing the necessity for prerogative financing. Many at the centre recognized that there would be considerable resistance to these writs yet decided to issue them nonetheless.[135]

The many financial charges, the prospect of a parliament and general poverty meant that reaction to this writ in Wales was qualitatively different from that to earlier levies. The impression is of a population which was unwilling to yield monies in the absence of concerted and consistent pressure. Monmouthshire had been one of the most reliable counties in the country, having no arrears outstanding from any of the previous demands. However, in early February 1640, the sheriff, John Milborne, informed the Privy Council that he found 'soe many complaints ... of pressures and wrong dealing in the particuler ratements by constables' that he could not effect the business as quickly as he would have liked, 'unlesse I shall give the county just cause to exclayme upon mee'.[136] Again the conflicting demands of centre and locality are clearly evident, and it is also noteworthy that initial resistance was in terms of disputes over rating, though this would harden into more threatening forms of resistance as Milborne and his officials tried to extricate more money from the county. By July 1640 the more diligent Monmouthshire officers had lawsuits begun against them by disgruntled individuals, 'that it doth not onely somewhat daunt them but gives very ill example and doth discurrage many of the rest'.[137] This resistance to ship money was understandable when the county was simultaneously providing £600 to supply soldiers raised for action against Scotland and who had been delayed in the county, and was expected to pay a further £400 towards their upkeep in the immediate future.[138]

[135] BL., Add. 11,045, fo. 43.
[136] TNA, SP16/444/70.
[137] TNA, SP16/459/39.
[138] TNA, PC2/52, p. 551.

Defiance hardened as the year wore on. In September, Milborne wrote that many distresses had been taken but they could not find anyone willing to appraise them, and that there were 'noe buyers at all to be had'. He painted a picture of communities determinedly resisting the levy:

> in divers towns of this county when they perceyve those officers to come into the towns for execucon of that service, divers of the inhabitants thereof that are charged with payments to that service shutt and make fast theire dores, that as yet distresse cannot be had without breaking open theire houses.[139]

This graphically illustrates the difficulties faced by the sheriff and his officers, and the extent to which ship money, compounded by other impositions, had alienated local communities from these representatives of authority, and, by extension, the central government itself. It is important to note, however, that there is an almost complete absence of evidence for a cumulative estrangement from ship money in the county during the later 1630s; this was the first sign of intransigence from this previously compliant area, and points to particular circumstances in 1639–40 which galvanized resistance.

Similar difficulties were noted in Cardiganshire, where Richard Price of Gogerddan was the sheriff. His delays on the 1639 writ did not receive a favourable response from the Council, which demanded in early March 1640 that he pay his assessment. In April Price wrote that his difficulties stemmed from the 'povertie & the scarcitie of money in the countrey at this time of the yeare', and he requested more time.[140] After further pressure from the Council, Price submitted a petition in which he maintained that he had attempted to effect payment 'by all faire and gentle meanes he could', but that he could not receive 'one pennie thereof'.[141] He further reported that he had made a number of distraints, but that he could 'gett noe money for anie man to offer for them anie one pennie, though often sett at sale'.

---

[139] TNA, SP16/467/57.
[140] TNA, SP16/450/33; 16/455/5.
[141] TNA, SP16/376/141. Misdated in calendar (*CSPD, 1637–8*, p. 141), leading to the erroneous statement in Williams, *Renewal and Reformation*, p. 481.

He therefore intimated that there was now a more general and fundamental resistance than his earlier assertions of mere poverty. The Council's response revealed a singular detachment from the reality of implementing ship money in the provinces; it suggested that he send the distrained goods to market, 'promiscuously, without proclayming them to bee distresses [so] they may be asoone bought as the cattell of other men'.[142]

In an attempt to provide closer supervision of the collection, in July 1640 the Council ordered the escheators – as men with local knowledge – to 'advise' the sheriff, in effect directing them to be instruments of central supervision. The escheators' reports are important because they provide a more impartial account of the proceedings on ship money than that of the sheriff himself. In Cardiganshire, the escheator, Thomas Parry, reported on Richard Price's efforts. Unlike Price, he did not concentrate on poverty or distresses, but rather noted a resumption of the difficulties concerning apportionments between Uwch Aeron and Is Aeron, suggesting that in his assessments Price had favoured Uwch Aeron, where he lived. Parry asserted that this was 'the onely occacon which I finde that the shipp moneys is not paied in yt lower division of Isayron'.[143] Thus, the best approximation of an impartial observer at this time viewed the resistance in Cardiganshire primarily in terms of a rating dispute and favouritism by the sheriff.

Perhaps the best description of the difficulties faced by a sheriff in Wales in the execution of the 1639 writ comes from a series of letters written by the sheriff of Flintshire, Ralph Hughes of Diserth. His dispatches to Edward Nicholas, clerk of the Privy Council and conciliar overseer of ship money, are less restrained than many letters sent to the Council, evidently because he was acquainted with his correspondent (he described himself as 'a man sometymes well knowne to you and your good father'). Though official in nature, the letters are rather personal in tone, and provide valuable evidence from a sheriff, freed, in part at least, from the

---

[142] TNA, PC2/52, p. 643.
[143] TNA, SP16/464/6.

obfuscation discernible in many of the reports to the Council.

In late February 1640, Hughes wrote a long letter to Nicholas describing his efforts in the execution of the writ and complaining of the 'difficulties and distraccon which I dayly meete withall'. He maintained that after he had issued warrants for the division of assessments, 'I found the countrey not to agree upon any constant rule to make theire subdivisions', adding that some wished to use the prince's mise, while others favoured the rate for purveyance.[144] The problem was evidently the same as that described by the inhabitants of Rhuddlan in 1639, and the great sessions order of September 1639 had clearly not settled the matter conclusively. This is confirmed by the representation of the townships of Tre'r Castell and Llewerllyd in the parish of Diserth, which petitioned the great sessions court in 1640 that it make an order concerning assessments.[145] In a valuable indication of how the use of traditional rates could lead to inequality and dispute, the inhabitants claimed that

> in fomer tymes the leyes [levies] being small and therefore little heede & respect being taken of every particular assessment, and the high constables continuing many yeares in theire offices and haveing liberty without contradictions to make assessments as they pleased, the divisions upon the towneshipps of Trer Castell and Llewerllyd have beene unequally made, and nowe the leys [levies] being raysed to greate somes, this inequality growes heavie & burdensome to such as suffer thereby, especially the poorer sort.[146]

The inhabitants claimed that whereas Tre'r Castell contained three times as much land as Llewerllyd, it was charged at a quarter of the latter's rate. In September 1640, the court ordered a meeting between the sheriff and Sir John Conway, the principal disputants.[147] On the basis of the order given for Rhuddlan in the previous sessions, the court ordered that the prince's mise be used as the basis of all assessments. Even at this late stage, then, disputes were still very much concerned with inequality in assessment and

---

[144] TNA, SP16/446/36.
[145] NLW, Great Sessions 4/982/8/2.
[146] NLW, Great Sessions 4/982/8/5.
[147] NLW, Great Sessions 4/982/8/4.

there is little suggestion that they concealed a wider body of more principled discontent.

Hughes informed Nicholas that after the earlier dispute regarding Rhuddlan had been settled by the great sessions, many of the assessors favoured themselves and their friends, and placed the burden on the poorer sort. He noted that 'in this case the sheriffe must either stopp his eares against all complaints, or in admittinge all, spend moste of his tyme in disputes'.[148] He also mentioned that bad harvests in 1636 and 1637 meant that the county was 'lately growne exceeding poore, especially the ordinary freehoulders & tenants'. Significantly, Hughes commented that although such conditions hindered payment, 'the whole cuntrey generally be moste willing to paye this mize as they can'. Even at this stage, he could not locate principled opposition to the levy itself, but rather emphasized the stresses it placed on the bonds within local communities.

At the end of March, Hughes wrote to Nicholas again, having received a rebuke from the Council for his neglect, a charge which was clearly misplaced. He had managed to collect £300 of the required £575, but again expressed his fears that the shire's poverty would impede collection. Once more he maintained that people were not opposed to the levy *per se*. 'I must confesse, I never found any unwillingnes in any for to paye this mize as theire abilities serves, soe I found moste that were able now quicke to doe theire duties and paye their moneyes then before.'[149]

There had been something of a change by the time Hughes next wrote to Nicholas in June 1640. He noted that he had received further letters from the Council demanding payment and had done his best to clear his arrears, and 'after much threatning and many distresses made, I have gott in a matter of 150^{li}'. His measures suggest that resistance was becoming more concerted; he was also less certain of the mood of his county, informing Nicholas

> whether povertye (the comon disease which hath bin too long in this countrey . . . & still increaseth), or the multiplicitye of newe charges &

---

[148] TNA, SP16/446/36.
[149] TNA, SP16/449/33.

supplies for maintenance of souldiers, or the late discomfortable newes of the parliaments dissolucon, or what other or more causes there are of these cloudes, I knowe not ... yet (god be thanked) I fynde none here possessed with the spiritt of opposicon but, where abilitye serves, all comands are executed with dutie.[150]

His mention of the Short Parliament is interesting, because many in the assembly had condemned ship money and there were prospects of a bargain being struck to remove it in return for supply.[151] Apparently some of the Flintshire men hoped that the parliament would remove the need to pay their ship money. This may account for some of the difficulties which Hughes had experienced earlier, when rumours of a parliament may have engendered similar hopes to those at the time when Hampden's case was being heard. Yet for all this, Hughes still declined to find any 'spiritt of opposicon' in his shire, despite the fact that he would have been the focus for such resistance.

As in Cardiganshire, Hughes obtained his own centrally appointed monitor in the form of the escheator, John Wynn. In his report to Lord Treasurer Juxon, Wynn identified 'abuses comitted concerning the assesments' as the main cause of 'reluctancie' to pay, but he did not mention any more fundamental reason for the delays.[152] In his final extant letter Hughes wrote to Nicholas on 23 November 1640 and again ruminated on the difficulties he faced in extracting the last of the outstanding money, once more citing the general plea of poverty, and adding 'I beleeve many of them had just cause'. He admitted having 'small hopes ... of ever being able to levye the whole'.[153]

This series of letters offers a fascinating insight into the execution of the final writ in Flintshire. Hughes's obstacles were considerable, but the letters are testimony to his industry in cajoling and coercing money from an obdurate body of ratepayers in increasingly difficult circumstances. It is clear that there was substantial resistance, though Hughes

---

[150] TNA, SP16/457/78.
[151] C. Russell, *The Fall of the British Monarchies, 1637–1642* (Oxford, 1991), pp. 93–4.
[152] TNA, SP16/467/10.
[153] TNA, SP16/472/15.

attributed this more to poverty, the multiplicity of charges, and the hopes of a parliament, rather than to any deep-seated opposition in the county. The true extent of opposition to ship money is perhaps impossible to assess accurately, but Hughes's correspondence suggests that, in Flintshire at least, it was more a product of particular circumstances of the period than the culmination of antipathy towards ship money that grew steadily during the 1630s.

It should also be noted that Hughes's correspondence, corroborated by the reports of the escheator, shows that Gordon's figures for arrears in Flintshire, as in Carmarthenshire and Montgomeryshire in 1638–9, are not wholly reliable. According to the declared accounts, Flintshire was in final arrears of £275 on this writ, having collected £300 out of a demand for £575 (or 52 per cent). In fact, Hughes collected a further £160 which he conveyed to London, and he and the escheator agreed that he had collected an additional £50 by November.[154] This means that in total £460 (or 80 per cent) was paid to London, and £510 (or 88 per cent) was actually collected in the shire. As has been noted previously, the fact that the £160 sent to London does not appear in the final accounts can probably be attributed to its meeting expenses such as those for the Scottish war. That the declared accounts may not reveal the whole truth concerning the final levy is also suggested by the case of Caernarfonshire. The accounts reveal payments identical with Flintshire's: £300 paid out of a demand of £575. However, a presentment of the grand jury at the county's quarter sessions in October 1642 shows that the shire was more compliant than this. The jury noted that

> the shippe moneys were paid to William Hookes, as he was high sheriffe ... but he did not pay them over as was required, and afterward theire was an order made that the said moneys should be paid to the countie backe againe or to the use of the countie (which are not).[155]

Evidently more money was collected here than found its way to London. This is supported by the report of the escheator, Robert Davies, who informed Juxon in September 1640 that

---

[154] TNA, SP16/450/115; 16/457/78; 16/459/70; 16/467/10; 16/472/15.
[155] Caernarfonshire RO, XQS/1642; *LJ*, iv, p. 418.

'most parte of the shipping money ... is alreadie collected and paied in, the rest is in hande agatheringe'.[156] Similarly in Carmarthenshire, the declared accounts indicate that the county performed badly on this writ, paying in only £100 out of £790. However, the escheator, Howell Howell, informed the treasurer on 3 September 1640 that the 'slacknes of some few' had impeded the collection, but added that 'the most part' had already paid. He further expressed his conviction that 'the residue wilbe upon the haveinge in of this harvest, soe that by Michaellmas all wilbe in a readines'.[157] Indeed, a later account testified that Carmarthenshire's sheriff, John Harris Davies, had collected £700 in ship money (88 per cent) which had not been accounted for.[158] The Council was apparently aware that Flintshire, Carmarthenshire and Monmouthshire had collected 'much more money' than had been transported to London, and in October 1640 called on them to pay this in, but the directive had little effect.[159] Meanwhile, in Montgomeryshire, where a shortfall of £564 was recorded, in a letter of 15 November 1640 the escheator maintained that the ship money was 'all paied unto the sheriffe & his officers'.[160] It is not surprising that this was never sent to London because the Long Parliament was already in session and was vocal in its condemnation of ship money as an illegal tax, yet this does not alter the fact that apparently all the money actually was levied in the county. One historian has recently suggested that the success of the levy cannot be measured solely in terms of the money it generated; the political capital the government sacrificed in obtaining it needs also to be taken into account.[161] In counties such as Flintshire, this cost was considerable, but the fact that so much of the money was eventually levied must modify the judgement of the final demand for ship money in Wales.

---

[156] TNA, SP16/466/18.
[157] TNA, SP16/466/33.
[158] TNA, SP28/251, unfol.
[159] TNA, PC2/53, pp. 33–4.
[160] TNA, SP16/471/74.
[161] Gill, 'Ship money', p. 341.

Conclusion

Despite difficulties with the nature of the sources for an assessment of ship money, a striking pattern emerges in Wales of relatively trouble-free compliance and prompt payment compared with many regions in England. Difficulties with ship money were articulated in Wales, as elsewhere, primarily in terms of disputes over assessments. Whereas patterns of resistance in counties like Somerset appear to have developed into a kind of institutionalized form of opposition, there is little indication that the problems in Wales represented anything more than jurisdictional or administrative disputes of a sort found earlier. Those Welshmen who spoke out against the levy were lawyers in the Short Parliament rather than people in the principality. Although there was dilatoriness and individual cases of resistance and distraint, an underlying pattern of compliance is revealed. Even during the breakdown associated with the final writ, it appears that its failure was not as complete as has previously been assumed. The most detailed studies of ship money yet produced have been sensitive to the 'post-revisionist' emphasis on division and political conflict in pre-Civil War Britain, and yet acknowledge the counties of Wales to be among the 'most diligent and consistent' in their payments, and fail to find any convincing evidence for 'outright disaffection' there.[162]

It is difficult to explain this pattern because few people made explicit statements as to why they paid or refused to pay. It is clear that ship money in Wales, as elsewhere, penetrated the social bedrock more deeply than had previous taxes. In Merioneth, Hugh Nanney's collection of assessments cover over seventy close-written pages, while in Caernarfonshire William Thomas informed the Council that a schedule of all those assessed would include 'many thousands' of individuals.[163] Although there is no doubt that payment became more grudging and communities were placed under severe stress by the government's demands,

---

[162] Ibid., 483, 533; Langelüddeke, 'Secular policy enforcement', 185–6.
[163] NLW, Peniarth 430E; TNA, SP16/380/98.

payment from these many thousands was comparatively unproblematic. It seems likely that concern about security along Wales's coastline made ship money more palatable there, but this falls short of explaining fully the reception described above. It may be significant that the overall burden on Wales remained relatively light, despite the fact that ship money affected layers of society not normally troubled by central taxation. It has been suggested that, although payments represented an often enormous increase compared with subsidy assessments, in real terms the Welsh counties were under-assessed compared with their English counterparts. For example, the fact that Breconshire was asked to pay the equivalent of five subsidies on most writs was perhaps less significant than the fact that it was paying only a quarter of that expected from neighbouring Herefordshire. That this burden was spread more widely may have helped to 'share the burden' as much as to engender local hostility. The fact that the better sort could transfer a good deal of the payment to those beneath them may have helped to isolate it somewhat from the political elites, and perhaps moderated the vocal backlash against ship money that is noticed elsewhere. This is not to rule out the possibility that such sentiments were expressed in local communities, but we must acknowledge that they have, for the most part, failed to register in the extant sources.

Even allowing for this, it is noticeable that wider debates about arbitrary government and non-parliamentary finance are almost completely absent from the Welsh evidence. We cannot say that the Welsh were ignorant of the issues involved because contemporary correspondence shows that discussion of Hampden's case and ship money was being conducted among elites.[164] In a primarily monoglot Welsh oral culture the extent to which this occurred at lower levels is unclear, but with an increased number of ratepayers, and evidence of parochial discussion of rating issues, we may assume a concomitant expansion of debate and dialogue about the collection of ship money. If this were so, it does not appear to have engendered a great deal of ideologically

---

[164] For example, NLW, MS 17012D; Brogyntyn (Clenennau) 514, 518.

informed opposition. The political culture in Wales during the period of ship money appears to have revolved more around issues of local rather than national significance. It is possible that bodies such as the great sessions or the Council in the Marches helped to earth such concerns, acting as agencies for arbitration before matters reached the Privy Council. Yet we have seen that such interventions could foment as often as mollify local disputes, and Bridgwater's confusion over the 1637 shrieval selection suggests the perceptual distance as much as the physical proximity of the Council in the Marches for the Welsh shires. This is not to say that ideological issues were wholly absent, or that they did not contribute to some responses, particularly in the case of the 1639 writ. Rather it is to acknowledge that these issues did not coalesce into a determined, vocal and intransigent body of opinion of the sort that could be found in many parts of England. Ship money was burdensome, and the performance of the 1639 writ showed how weak were the supports on which it rested in Wales. It is difficult to reconcile the analysis presented above with the traditional picture of rising tensions and opposition in Wales leading to its alienation from Charles's government by 1640; in most accounts, this alienation is then converted, by some half-explained alchemy, into the Welsh royalism of 1642. It may be that there are some more convincing connections to be made between the payment of ship money and Wales's political allegiances in 1642.

The close rhetorical association between the Welsh and the monarchy, reinforced by the accession of the Tudors, may help to explain this pattern of compliance as ship money was particularly framed around ideas of service, loyalty and deference to royal authority. However, it is difficult to see this rather nebulous and abstract ideal translating itself directly into the conformity which seems to characterize payments in the 1630s. Another element in the complex notion of royal authority which may have had greater weight is religion. Alison Gill's comprehensive study of ship money has argued convincingly that the greatest resistance to ship money can be associated with those areas where a more radical Protestant tradition held sway.

Conversely, the ritualized nature of Church of England Protestantism, closely associated as it was with secular authority and hierarchy, helped to inculcate an obedience and deference that militated against such opposition. This may be an important component of the 'underlying attitudes of conformity and obedience' which Gill sees in Wales's ship money record.[165] As has been suggested with the forced loan and other levies of the 1620s, the comparative absence of puritan influence in Wales, and an attachment to the Established Church, may help to interpret Welsh responses in the 1630s. Hardly any attempt has been made to uncover the nature of religious conformity in Wales during this decade, however, and the next chapter will examine the responses in the principality to the religious policies of personal rule.

---

[165] Gill, 'Ship money', 294–6, 484–9, 362.

Table 4. Payment of the 1634 ship money writ (issued 20 October 1634)

County	Assessment (£)
Anglesey	70
Beaumaris	10
Breconshire	n/a
Caernarfonshire	100
Caernarfon	6
Cardiganshire	54
Cardigan	4
Carmarthenshire	100
Carmarthen	15
Denbighshire	160
Denbigh	10
Flintshire	85
Flint	2
Glamorgan	200
Cardiff	15
Merioneth	n/a
Monmouthshire	170
Newport	8
Montgomeryshire	n/a
Pembrokeshire	100
St David's	2
Radnorshire	n/a
Total	1111[a]

Sources: For 1634–5 writ, Cheshire and Chester Archives, ZM/L/2/277; TNA, SP16/286/8; 16/286/8; 16/287/5. For subsequent writs the accounts of the treasurer of the navy, Sir William Russell, have been used: SP16/302/45–16/473/103.

[a] The £1,111 from these counties was paid in a single bloc received by the earl of Bridgwater on 25 April 1635.

Table 5. Payment of the 1635 ship money writ (issued 4 August 1635)

County	Assessment	Paid by 1 Jan. 1636	Paid by 1 April 1636	Paid by 1 July 1636	Paid by 1 Oct. 1636	Paid after 1 Oct. 1636	Arrears by 1 Jan. 1638	Final arrears[a]
Anglesey	448	–	448 (100%)					
Breconshire	933	–	933 (100%)					
Caernarfonshire	447	–	447 (100%)					
Cardiganshire	654	10 (1.5%)	654 (100%)					
Carmarthenshire	760	–	600 (78.9%)				–160	–160
Denbighshire	1117	–	–	32 (2.8%)		1117 (100%)		
Flintshire	738	–	738 (100%)					
Glamorgan	1449	60 (4.1%)	1449 (100%)					
Merioneth	416	–	416 (100%)					
Monmouthshire	1500	1500 (100%)						
Montgomeryshire	833	–	833 (100%)					
Pembrokeshire	713	–	670 (93.9%)				–43	–43
Radnorshire	490	448 (90%)				490 (100%)		
[North Wales]	4000						0	0
[South Wales excl. Mon.]	5000						–203 (4%)	–203 (4%)

[a] These are the final totals as found in the declared accounts used by M. D. Gordon in 'The collection of ship money in the reign of Charles I', *Transactions of the Royal Historical Society*, 3rd series, 4 (1910), 162.

Table 6. Payment of the 1636 ship money writ (issued 12 September 1636)

	Assessment	Paid by 1 Jan. 1637	Paid by 1 April 1637	Paid by 1 July 1637	Paid by 1 Oct. 1637	Paid after 1 Oct. 1637	Arrears by 24 Mar. 1638	Arrears by 1 June 1639	Final arrears[a]
Anglesey	448	–	–	200 (44.6%)	448 (100%)			0 (0%)	
Breconshire	933	–	–	500 (53.5%)		900 (96.4%)		−33 (3.6%)	−33
Caernarfonshire	447	–	–	404 (90%)		447 (100%)		0 (0%)	
Cardiganshire	654	–	–	10 (1.5%)	654 (100%)			0 (0%)	
Carmarthenshire	760	–	360 (47.3%)	760 (100%)				0 (0%)	
Denbighshire	1117	–	–	550 (49.2%)	1048 (93.8%)	1088 (97.4%)		−29 (2.6%)	−29
Flintshire	738	–	–	734 (99.5%)				−4 (0.5%)	
Glamorgan	1449	–	1449 (100%)					0 (0%)	
Merioneth	416	–	–	400 (96.1%)		416 (100%)		0 (0%)	
Monmouthshire	1500	–	1500 (100%)					0 (0%)	
Montgomeryshire	833	–	–	–	833 (100%)			0 (0%)	
Pembrokeshire	713	–	–	–	390 (54.6%)	613 (86%)		−100 (14%)	−90
Radnorshire	490	–	–	142 (29%)	292 (58.8%)	490 (100%)		0 (0%)	
[North Wales]	4000						−33 (0.8%)	−33 (0.8%)	−29 (0.7%)
[South Wales excl. Mon.]	5000						−133 (2.6%)	−133 (2.6%)	−123 (2.4%)

Table 7. Payment of the 1637 ship money writ (issued 9 October 1637)

County	Assessment	Paid by 17 Mar. 1638	Paid by 16 June 1638	Paid by 1 Sept. 1638	Paid by 22 Feb. 1639	Arrears by 27 April 1639	Arrears by 26 Oct. 1639	Final arrears
Anglesey	448	–	448 (100%)			0 (0%)	0 (0%)	
Breconshire	933	–	280 (30%)	400 (42.8%)	819 (87.7%)	−54 (5.7%)	−54 (5.7%)	−54
Caernarfonshire	575	–	270 (46.9%)		517 (89.9%)	−58 (10%)	−18 (3.1%)	
Cardiganshire	654	–	–	–	360 (55%)	−294 (44.9%)	−294 (44.9%)	
Carmarthenshire	790	–	–	400 (50.6%)	790 (100%)	0 (0%)	0 (0%)	
Denbighshire	1122	–	505 (45.2%)		854 (76.1%)	−72 (6.4%)	−72 (6.4%)	−67
Flintshire	575	–	150 (26%)	350 (60.8%)	550 (95.6%)	−25 (4.3%)	−25 (4.3%)	−25
Glamorgan	1449	1389 (95.8%)	1449 (100%)			0 (0%)	0 (0%)	
Merioneth	416	–	100 (24%)		416 (100%)	0 (0%)	0 (0%)	
Monmouthshire	1500	1400 (93.3%)	–	1470 (98%)		−30 (2%)	0 (0%)	
Montgomeryshire	864	–	200 (23.1%)	400 (46.2%)	800 (92.5%)	−64 (7.5%)	−64 (7.5%)	−64
Pembrokeshire	683	–	600 (87.8%)		683 (100%)	0 (0%)	0 (0%)	
Radnorshire	490	–	–	100 (20.4%)	490 (100%)	0 (0%)	0 (0%)	
[North Wales]	4000					−219 (5.4%)	−179 (4.4%)	−156 (3.9%)
[South Wales excl. Mon.]	5000					−348 (6.9%)	−348 (6.9%)	−54 (1%)

Table 8. Payment of the 1638 ship money writ (issued 5 November 1638)

County	Assessment	Paid by 1 Jan. 1639	Paid by 18 May 1639	Paid by 28 Sept. 1639	Paid by 14 Dec. 1639	Paid after 14 March 1640	Arrears by 16 May 1640	Final arrears
Anglesey	168	–	–	168 (100%)			0 (0%)	
Breconshire	361	–	–	100 (27.7%)	341 (94.4%)		−20 (5.6%)	−20
Caernarfonshire	216	–	–	211 (97.6%)			−5 (2.4%)	−5
Cardiganshire	248	–	–	100 (40.3%)	124 (50%)	144 (58%)	−13 (5.2%)	
Carmarthenshire	301	–	–	–	300 (99.6%)		−1 (0.4%)	−300 (error)
Denbighshire	424	–	100 (23.5%)	399 (94.1%)			−25 (5.9%)	−25
Flintshire	216	–	–	100 (46.2%)	156 (72.2%)		0 (0%)	
Glamorgan	547	–	524 (95.8%)	547 (100%)			0 (0%)	
Merioneth	154	–	–	100 (64.9%)	154 (100%)		0 (0%)	
Monmouthshire	650	–	393 (60.4%)	649 (99.8%)			−1 (0.2%)	
Montgomeryshire	322	–	–	–		322 (100%)	0 (0%)	−322 (error)
Pembrokeshire	260	–	–	140 (53.8%)	260 (100%)		0 (0%)	
Radnorshire	183	–	–	50 (27.3%)	183 (100%)		0 (0%)	
[North Wales]	1500						−30 (2%)	
[South Wales excl. Mon.]	1900						−34 (1.7%)	

Table 9. Payment of the 1639 ship money writ (issued 18 November 1639)

County	Assessment	Paid by 14 March 1640	Paid by 20 June 1640	Paid by 9 Oct. 1640	Paid by 1 Dec. 1640	Arrears by 31 Dec. 1640	Final arrears
Anglesey	448	–	436 (97.3%)			–12 (2.7%)	–12 (2.7%)
Breconshire	933	–	–			–933 (100%)	–933 (100%)
Caernarfonshire	575	–	300 (52.1%)	–	–	–275 (47.9%)	–275 (47.9%)
Cardiganshire	654	–	–	–	–	–654 (100%)	–654 (100%)
Carmarthenshire	790	–	–	100 (12.6%)		–690 (87.4%)	–690 (87.4%)
Denbighshire	1122	100 (8.9%)	600 (53.4%)	720 (64.1%)		–402 (35.9%)	–402 (35.9%)
Flintshire	575	–	–	300 (52.1%)		–275 (47.9%)	–275 (47.9%)
Glamorgan	1449	–	1354 (93.4%)			–95 (6.5%)	–95 (6.5%)
Merioneth	416	–	405 (97.3%)			–11 (2.7%)	–11 (2.7%)
Monmouthshire	1500	–	400 (26.6%)			–700 (46.7%)	–700 (46.7%)
Montgomeryshire	864	–	–	80 (9.2%)	300 (34.7%)	–564 (65.3%)	–564 (65.3%)
Pembrokeshire	683	–	450 (65.8%)			–233 (34.2%)	–233 (34.2%)
Radnorshire	490	–	80 (16.3%)	300 (61.2%)		–190 (38.8%)	–190 (38.8%)
[North Wales]	4000					–1539 (38.4%)	–1539 (38.4%)
[South Wales excl. Mon.]	5000					–2795 (55.9%)	–2795 (55.9%)

5

WALES AND THE PERSONAL RULE (II): RELIGION

The 1630s witnessed an attempt by the archbishop of Canterbury, William Laud, in concert with Charles I, to promote a particular conception of the 'Anglican Church' in England and Wales.[1] This concentrated on the sacramental aspects of worship and the physical body of the Church and proved contentious in many areas, yet there has been little examination of its implementation in Wales and the reaction it elicited. Indeed, historians have been more disposed to deny that Laudian[2] reforms had any impact in Wales before the Restoration.[3] This is hard to reconcile with another dominant strand in Welsh historiography which emphasizes the Laudian persecution of Wales's first nonconformists in the 1630s. Indeed, the hunt for nonconformity and the beginnings of dissent dominate the historiographical landscape of pre-Civil War Wales in a manner which seriously distorts our understanding of early Stuart religion and society. The

---

[1] I use 'Anglican' somewhat anachronistically as a convenient shorthand for the complex constellation of conformist impulses towards the Church of England and its canons and constitutions as developed since 1559. Although I am aware of the problems in such usage, there seems no better alternative: J. Morrill, 'The Church in England, 1642–9', in idem (ed.), *Reactions to the English Civil War, 1642–1649* (Basingstoke, 1982), p. 231, n. 2; J. Spurr, *The Restoration Church of England, 1646–1689* (New Haven and London, 1991), p. xiii; A. Walsham. 'The parochial roots of Laudianism revisited: Catholics, anti-Calvinists and "parish Anglicans" in early Stuart England', *Journal of Ecclesiastical History*, 49 (1998), 620–51. Cf. J. Maltby, '"The good old way": prayer book Protestantism in 1640s and 1650s', *Studies in Church History*, 38 (2004), 235.

[2] 'Laudian' is used in this chapter to describe the corpus of Church policies in the 1630s, regardless of whether it was Charles I or Laud who was the driving force behind them. Doctrinal debates over matters such as Arminianism and predestination which attended the Laudian programme aroused hardly any comment in Wales, but our evidence can reveal something about the more contentious emphasis on the physical institution of the Church and its priesthood in the 1630s. For this interpretation, see P. Lake, 'The Laudian style', in K. Fincham (ed.), *The Early Stuart Church, 1603–1642* (1993), 161–85; K. Fincham, 'The restoration of altars in the 1630s', *Historical Journal*, 44 (2001), 919–40.

[3] H. O. Wakeman, 'The Laudian movement in Wales', *Cymru Fydd*, 3 (1890), 275–85; B. Williams, 'The Welsh clergy, 1558–1642' (Ph.D. thesis, Open University, 1998), 84, 359.

reasons for this excessive concentration on a few isolated dissenters can be traced to the prevailing Welsh nonconformist tradition of the later nineteenth and early twentieth centuries, within which influential Welsh religious historians such as Thomas Rees and Thomas Richards operated.[4] The search for the heroic forebears of a national dissenting tradition shines through their work and pervades much of what has come after. Their influence has been enormous in establishing the framework within which pre-1640s religion in Wales has been studied, and the topics and personalities on which it has concentrated.[5]

Yet these narratives are built around a tiny constituency of radicals whose contemporary influence was minor, yet whose nonconformity ensured they left a disproportionately large mark in the historical record. It should also be mentioned that there are serious problems with the reconstruction of any 'Puritan movement' in Wales during the 1630s, because much of the source material derives from the writings of the protagonists themselves during the radically different circumstances of the 1640s and 1650s. As a result of such factors, the response in Wales to the religious developments of the 1630s has been told in polarized terms, with little mention made of the conforming majority and the projects of Charles I and Laud to build a reinvigorated and decorous Church of England centred on ceremonialism, hierarchy and order.

This chapter seeks to revise the prevailing notion that the Laudian programme effectively by-passed Wales and had no impact there beyond persecuting a few radicals. We should note, for example, that the Welsh episcopate of the 1630s, particularly those bishops appointed during Laud's archiepiscopate, reflected his patronage and ceremonial predilections. Men such as Roger Mainwaring (St David's), William Roberts

---

[4] T. Rees, *History of Protestant Nonconformity in Wales* (1861); T. Richards, *The Puritan Movement in Wales, 1639–53* (1920), and many other works.

[5] The list of such works is extensive, but a representative modern sample includes R. G. Gruffydd, *'In That Gentile Country ...': The Beginnings of Puritan Nonconformity in Wales* (Bridgend, 1975); G. H. Jenkins, *Protestant Dissenters in Wales, 1639–1689* (Cardiff, 1992); J. G. Jones, 'Some puritan influences on the Anglican Church in Wales in the early seventeenth century', *Journal of Welsh Religious History*, NS, 2 (2002), 19–50.

(Bangor) and Morgan Owen (Llandaff) were closely associated with Laud and his ideas on the Church and its ecclesiology. Their promotion reminds us of the importance which the ecclesiastical establishment in London placed on reform in the principality as well as in England.[6] This chapter offers evidence that policies such as the turning of communion tables into altars were implemented by these bishops in the principality, and what was striking was the limited and isolated nature of the protest which materialized. In seeking to contextualize and enrich this analysis, the chapter also uses the discussion of religion during the 1630s to offer conclusions on the nature of Welsh 'Anglicanism' in the pre-war period; it suggests that it was a more vital and vigorous force than traditional accounts have presented, and was less undermined by puritanism than is often believed. Although the chapter does not seek to conflate the problematic categories of 'Laudianism' and 'Anglicanism', the crippling poverty of Welsh source material creates a serious problem in establishing a distinction between the two.[7] Rather does the analysis suggest ways in which the religious history of the 1630s can be read in terms of conformity and adaptation to prevailing cultural norms; this tells us something about the nature of Welsh religion and ecclesiology before the outbreak of war. It will be suggested that considerations of language and economy made it difficult for a more radical strain of churchmanship to prevail in Wales, and that such conditions encouraged a greater attachment to the liturgy of the Church of England, itself an important part of the Laudian conception of worship. It is hard to distinguish between 'Prayer Book Protestants' and Laudian enthusiasts because of the nature of the sources, but this chapter suggests that comprehending both categories under a workable, if not entirely adequate, penumbra of 'conservative conformism' allows a more fruitful interpretation of this period, and helps

---

[6] K. Fincham, 'William Laud and the exercise of Caroline ecclesiastical patronage', *Journal of Ecclesiastical History*, 51 (2000), 80.

[7] The paucity of the Welsh ecclesiastical archive for this period is not paralleled in any English diocese, except possibly Carlisle. The almost complete loss of visitation records, office and instance books creates a particular barrier in assessing the impact of Laudianism.

us to understand some of the religious underpinnings of the Welsh royalism that emerged in the early 1640s.

THE WELSH CHURCH IN THE 1630s

The nature of religion in Wales was to a large degree conditioned by the country's linguistic distinctiveness and the poverty of the Church, which hindered the establishment of an effective preaching ministry along the lines desired by puritan reformers. These factors helped to foster a spirituality among the Welsh which was conservative in nature, a religion of the liturgy rather than of the puritan sermon, and a religion that in important respects was more inclined to be receptive to aspects of Laud's particular vision of worship than was the case in most dioceses in England. Brendan Bradshaw has identified such impulses in the Reformation settlement in Wales, noting how the inhabitants' 'conservative predilections' and their 'traditionalist cultural environment' allowed Catholic survivals such as altars and crucifixes to continue in a society which nevertheless possessed a confessional commitment to Protestantism and the Church of England.[8]

The overwhelming preponderance of monoglot Welsh speakers meant that the nature of spirituality in Wales reflected those religious values which were most effectively expressed in the vernacular. In pre-Civil War Wales these centred on a moderate Church of England Protestantism based on translations of the Scriptures and the Prayer Book, and texts such as Edward James's Welsh edition of the homilies.[9] Conversely, it is important to note that this linguistic division meant that much of the message in the writings of puritans in England remained inaccessible to the vast majority of Welsh men and women, and no radical message was effectively and systematically promulgated in the native language until the 1650s.

William Morgan produced a Welsh translation of the Bible

---

[8] B. Bradshaw, 'The English Reformation and identity formation in Wales and Ireland', in idem and P. R. Roberts (eds), *British Consciousness and Identity* (Cambridge, 1998), pp. 72–83.

[9] G. Williams, *The Welsh and their Religion* (Cardiff, 1991), pp. 155–60.

in 1588, but it was intended primarily for use in church and was prohibitively expensive for most individuals.[10] It was not, therefore, until Sir Thomas Myddleton and Rowland Heylin sponsored the publication of *Y Beibl Bach*, priced at 5*s*., in 1630 that more than a small minority in Wales could afford the Scriptures in the vernacular, yet even afterwards many complained of the shortage of Bibles in the principality.[11] This meant that there was little scope in Wales for the kind of individual scriptural piety associated with the growth of puritan beliefs elsewhere.[12] Rather was access to the Bible through the Church, and this meant the interpretation and dissemination of the Scriptures remained largely in the hands of the clergy rather than the laity.

In addition, the Book of Common Prayer had been rendered into Welsh in 1567, receiving important revisions in 1599 and 1621, when Edmwnd Prys's metrical version of the psalms was included. This book achieved a formidable popularity in Wales, where there was a more powerful attachment to this basic text of Anglican worship than to any radical religious work.[13] The Welsh liturgy became inextricably bound up with the rhythms of parish life and an important component in Welsh popular culture. Welsh attachment to the Prayer Book was highly visible during the Civil Wars, and became a subject for parliamentary satirists such as the pamphleteer who attributed the country's royalism to the fact that 'they have scarce had any more Reformation then the Common Prayer Book, a Masse-booke junior; they have scarce heard anything beyond the letany or absolution'.[14] It is important to recall that Laud sought to elevate the liturgical aspects of church service in his reforms, and in many ways this appealed to that element of worship most familiar to, and cherished by, Welsh congregations.

---

[10] G. H. Hughes (ed.), *Rhagymadroddion, 1547–1659* (Cardiff, 1951), p. 123. The Bible for St Mary's, Swansea, cost 22*s*. 8*d*. in 1622, for example: West Glamorgan Archive Service, Swansea Corporation D2, fo. 83ᵛ.

[11] J. Ballinger, *The Bible in Wales* (1906), pp. 26–30; NLW, Great Sessions 4/16/3/7, dorse; BL, Add. 70,106, fo. 156.

[12] C. Durston and J. Eales, 'Introduction', in eadem (eds), *The Culture of English Puritanism, 1560–1700* (1996), p. 16.

[13] G. Williams, *Wales and the Reformation* (Cardiff, 1997), pp. 384–5; idem, *The Welsh and their Religion* p. 159; Dodd, *Studies*, p. 43.

[14] *Mercurius Britanicus*, 26 (5–12 March 1645), 202.

The Church of England received little challenge in Wales during the 1630s, and the puritans who emerged faced enormous difficulties. As has been seen, the religious texts which were available in the Welsh language did not deal with matters of controversy or reform but rather were concerned with 'raising the day-to-day level of belief and conduct'.[15] This militated against a wider participation in the more radical puritan culture found in areas of England. Indeed, the areas where some Welsh radicalism can be detected in the 1630s were located on the English border where interaction was frequent, or in towns like Wrexham and Cardiff which possessed trading contacts with the English cities of Chester and Bristol.[16] The poverty of the Church in Wales also represented a barrier to the easy dissemination of radical religious ideas; it could not support anything approaching the preaching pastorate considered so central to the dissemination and nourishment of puritan ideals. Before the 1640s there was remarkably little call for religious reform from within the principality, despite the chronic problems of impropriation, non-residence and pluralism stemming from the Church's poverty. The reformers themselves recognized that puritan values had made little headway in Wales, bewailing the 'want of vision & teaching of Gods word' there.[17] This was demonstrated graphically in the move of the celebrated radical William Prynne to the gaol at Caernarfon in 1637. On his way, Prynne was enthusiastically supported by the people of St Albans who prayed for him as he passed, and was met with cheers of support and donations of furniture and bedding from the godly citizens of Chester. A correspondent noted significantly that there was 'no resort to Prynne at Carnarvon': there was simply no godly community to welcome him there.[18]

---

[15] G. Williams, 'Unity of religion or unity of language? Protestants, Catholics and the Welsh language, 1536–1660', in G. H. Jenkins (ed.), *The Welsh Language Before the Industrial Revolution* (Cardiff, 1997), p. 220.

[16] C. Hill, 'Puritans and the dark corners of the land', in his *Change and Continuity in Seventeenth Century England* (1974), p. 12; G. H. Jenkins, R. Suggett and E. M. White, 'The Welsh language in early modern Wales', in Jenkins (ed.), *Welsh Language*, p. 84.

[17] BL, Add. 70,109, no. 69; Add. 70,002, fo. 367.

[18] *CSPD, 1637*, p. 433.

The linguistic distinctiveness of Wales and the barrier this presented to the Word-based piety of the puritans were thus allied to an affection for the Prayer Book and liturgy which allowed a conservative form of 'Prayer Book Protestantism' to prevail. The impression gained of the religious complexion of pre-Civil War Wales suggests that it would have been more receptive to the sacramental piety associated with Laudianism than were most other regions of the kingdom. Laudianism's emphasis on symbolism, ceremony and the liturgy, rather than on the sermon, meshed more readily with the conservative predilections of post-Reformation Wales compared with the (predominantly Anglophone) spirituality of the puritans. Nevertheless, the impact of the Laudian Church in Wales is difficult to reconstruct, primarily because of the paucity of available sources, but some tentative conclusions are possible which indicate that the Laudian programme did not by-pass Wales in the 1630s, and suggest that its reception helps us to understand the true nature of Welsh religion and spirituality in the decade before the Civil War.

THE CLERICAL ESTATE AND THE FABRIC OF THE CHURCH

For Charles and Laud, the poverty of the Church weakened its parochial structure and challenged their elevated conception of its status and authority. Poverty was a particular problem for the Church in Wales, and there are some indications that the king and his archbishop attempted to safeguard the revenues and buildings of the Church there. Bishops such as Theophilus Field of Llandaff, and later of St David's, were vocal in their complaints about the poverty which they encountered in their dioceses.[19] On one occasion, he petitioned the king that he be allowed the temporalities from his last translation, 'in regard the revenues of the ... bishoprick are small'. In addition, 'for the better supportacon of hospitalitie and other incident charges', he asked that he be allowed to hold 'some spirituall livings not exceeding 100^{li} *p. ann.* in the first fruits'.[20] A day

---

[19] TNA, SP16/75/84; 16/150/110; BL, Add. 34,274, fo. 158.
[20] TNA, SP16/74/42.

after this letter was written, Laud wrote to Secretary of State Conway that he had moved Charles to allow Field to hold one benefice and one dignity *in commendam* with his bishopric, adding that the king had agreed.[21] Charles also attempted to 'augment' the bishopric in the early 1630s by negotiating for the lease of the rectory of Abergwili to be acquired by the bishop.[22]

It was a similar story in north Wales. Dr John Owen, though elevated to St Asaph in 1629 in preference to Laud's nominee, complained to the archbishop that he held no livings *in commendam*, except the archdeaconry, and requested 'that he may have the corn now upon the ground ... without which he shall not be able the next year to keep house there'.[23] There are indications that Charles and Laud responded positively to these pleas of poverty, Owen receiving two livings *in commendam* in 1633 'for the better enabling of you to keepe hospitality & support the charge belonging unto you as bishop'.[24] Field's successor at St David's, and Laud's associate, Roger Mainwaring, received a similar grant from the king in 1637, to avoid the 'greate incoveniences' that would affect both Church and State 'if the authoritie of bishops bee not supported as it ought'.[25]

In other moves directed to safeguard the clerical estate, the bishops of Llandaff, St Asaph and St David's received letters from Charles I, ordering them not to negotiate leases for a term of lives instead of the specified twenty-one years.[26] William Murray of Llandaff was subsequently reported to have 'been very careful for the settling of the rights and profits' of the bishopric.[27] Edmund Griffith, bishop of Bangor, received a similar letter from Laud in August 1634.

[21] J. Bliss and W. Scott (eds), *The Works of William Laud* (Oxford, 1847–60), vii, p. 8.
[22] TNA, SO1/2, fo. 137.
[23] Bliss and Scott, *Works of Laud*, vii, p. 23; Fincham, 'Caroline ecclesiastical patronage', 80–1.
[24] TNA, SO1/2, fo. 139; SP16/237/38.
[25] TNA, SP16/363/80.
[26] NLW, SD/Ch/B/4, p. 63; LL/Ch/4, pp. 126–8; 'Llanllyfni papers', *Archaeologia Cambrensis*, 3rd series, 6 (1863), 282; E. Yardley, *Menevia Sacra*, ed. F. Green (1927), pp. 322–3.
[27] Bliss and Scott, *Works of Laud*, v, p. 354.

In addition, Laud stated 'in yt diocesse I hold it requisit you enlarg your care concerning the landes of your bishopricke already demised'. He therefore placed a formidable task on Griffith, requiring him to have every tenant holding lands in the bishopric make a survey thereof and declare all his interests to the bishop. Laud indicated that the reason for this undertaking was 'to prevent the concealment of the churches land, and to discover such as goe about to conceale the same'.[28] This drive to find revenues in the diocese was an important factor in the elevation of Griffith's successor, William Roberts, in 1637. He was reported to have been promoted by Laud after he discovered, presumably in discharge of the archbishop's orders, £1,000 of concealed Church lands in the diocese.[29] It is important to note that such concern with revenue and the clerical estate was central to the Laudian conception of the Church; alienation of ecclesiastical land and revenues by lay impropriators was considered by Laud to be sacrilegious.[30]

The Laudian view of religious uniformity focused on the sanctity of the parish church and cathedrals, a strikingly different emphasis to the 'community of believers' at the heart of more puritan conceptions of spirituality. As Julian Davies has written, 'the patristic emphasis on the visibility of the church and the inherent holiness of the church fabric necessarily led to a concern for the restoration of churches [under Laud]'.[31] The impoverished state of Welsh dioceses meant that many churches were ruinous rather than beautiful, and there is some evidence that more concerted steps were taken under Laud to remedy these defects, and that these were of a different tenor to earlier types of parochial maintenance. Shortly after his nomination to St David's, Laud had sought an estimate for the repair of residences

[28] Lambeth Palace Library, Misc. 943, fos 337–8.
[29] D. Lloyd, *Memoires* (1662), p. 599; J. Walker, *An Attempt Towards Recovering an Account of the Numbers and Sufferings of the Clergy* (1714), ii, p. 2.
[30] A. Foster, 'Church policies of the 1630s', in R. Cust and A. Hughes (eds), *Conflict in Early Stuart England* (Harlow, 1989), 198–201; I. Atherton, 'Viscount Scudamore's "Laudianism": the religious practices of the first Viscount Scudamore', *Historical Journal*, 34 (1991), 571–4, 593–4.
[31] J. Davies, *The Caroline Captivity of the Church: Charles I and the Remoulding of Anglicanism* (Oxford, 1992), p. 73.

there, and in 1625 a resolution was passed that members of the chapter elected to the position of 'Master of the Fabric' had to enter into a bond to safeguard the fabric of the cathedral.[32] Although he rarely visited his diocese, Laud soon set about building and adorning a chapel at the episcopal residence at Abergwili.[33] Laud's successor in the see, Theophilus Field, also showed an interest in the physical state of parish churches, informing Laud in his report of 1634 that impropriators had pulled down chancels of local churches or 'suffered them to fall'.[34] Such concerns reflected the priorities of royal policy, as in October 1629 the king had issued a proclamation to prevent the decay of churches. This called on all clerical personnel to enquire into the state of their local churches, 'and where they find ought amisse, to cause the same to be speedily and carefully amended'.[35] Of course, the repair of churches did not begin with Charles and Laud, but the nature and theological underpinnings of the Caroline concern for church fabric were very different from earlier *ad hoc* repairs, and there is evidence that this novel programme elicited a response in some Welsh parishes.[36]

In the parish of Chirk, Denbighshire, in June 1630, the churchwardens drew up plans for re-edifying the parish church. They declared that the church was 'ruinous and decayed both in the glasse windowes, roofe, steeple and bells', and that 'the roofe letts in raine at every shoure'. They noted that work had already begun to prevent further decay, but added that the body and roof of the church remained unrepaired because of the poor example of Sir Thomas

---

[32] J. W. Evans, 'The Reformation and St David's Cathedral', *Journal of Welsh Ecclesiastical History*, 7 (1990), 10; Yardley, *Menevia Sacra*, p. 325.

[33] W. Prynne, *Canterburies Doome* (1644), p. 120; Bliss and Scott, *Works of Laud*, iii, pp. 170–1; J. S. McGee, 'William Laud and the outward face of religion', in R. L. DeMachen (ed.), *Leaders of the Reformation* (Susquehanna Univ. Press, 1984), pp. 327–8.

[34] Bliss and Scott, *Works of Laud*, v, p. 329.

[35] J. F. Larkin and P. L. Hughes (eds), *Stuart Royal Proclamations* (Oxford, 1973–83), ii, pp. 248–50.

[36] Foster, 'Church policies', 202; G. Yule, 'James VI and I: furnishing the churches in his two kingdoms', in A. Fletcher and P. Roberts (eds), *Religion, Culture and Society in Early Modern Britain* (Cambridge, 1994), pp. 188–204; J. F. Merritt, 'Puritans, Laudians and the phenomenon of church-building in Jacobean London', *Historical Journal*, 41 (1998), 935–60; C. Marsh, 'Sacred space in England, 1560–1640: the view from the pew', *Journal of Ecclesiastical History*, 53 (2002), 297–8.

Myddleton, who refused to pay towards the restoration and 'diswaded others also from the paymente of the loans'.[37] Probably bolstered by the proclamation, the churchwardens moved against Myddleton by submitting a petition to the Privy Council in May 1632. They maintained that Sir Thomas and his tenants had refused to contribute to the repair of the 'mother church of Chirck', and that consequently suits had been brought against him in the diocese of St Asaph and the Court of Arches.[38] In his defence, Myddleton claimed that Chirk enjoyed immunity from any assessment because it was a marcher lordship.[39] The Council ordered that all suits be stayed, and that Myddleton contribute towards the reparation of the church 'out of his owne free guift . . . according to his owne offer'. Myddleton paid his 10$s.$, but approached the Council himself in December 1632 to claim that the churchwardens were continuing their suits against him.[40] This may indicate that the churchwardens were operating from motives which were more personal than pastoral, but it does not alter the fact that there was a drive in Denbighshire to repair parish churches, and that considerable efforts were taken by the churchwardens to secure payment from the most prominent squire in the area.

Evidence of this determination to repair and maintain parish churches can be found elsewhere in Denbighshire. At Gresford, for example, Anthony Lewis of Burton bequeathed £300 to the parish church in his will of 1634, to be spent on the repair of windows, paving the floor and making new pews.[41] In October 1635, John Salusbury was keen to build a new church in the town of Denbigh to replace the current dilapidated building.[42] In January 1635, Bishop John Owen

[37] NLW, Chirk Castle F12894.
[38] NLW, Carreglwyd I/241; TNA, PC2/42, p. 38.
[39] It is possible that this episode was related to Myddleton's efforts to consolidate and strengthen his authority and independence in the lordship of Chirk, something which been resisted by local gentry: Flintshire RO, D/G 642; NLW, Chirk Castle, F6684, F7205, F9895, F12764. F13624; TNA, C66/2593/2.
[40] NLW, Chirk Castle F6503, F9545.
[41] D. R. Thomas, *The History of the Diocese of St Asaph* (Oswestry, 1908–13), iii, p. 248.
[42] He commented on the drive to repair churches elsewhere in the country, 'whereby works of as great a burthen as this is have ben brought to, both in repairinge & building of churches': TNA, SP16/300/64.

of St Asaph made a detailed report to Sir John Lambe, dean of the Court of Arches, of a case concerning the repair of the large but decayed church at Wrexham.[43] The parishioners maintained the church with a weekly collection, but because this was insufficient to stave off further decay Owen's predecessor, John Hanmer, had instituted a collection of £100 on the entire parish. Owen stated that one half of those assessed had contributed while others had refused, including those now before Lambe; they also refused to contribute to a second collection for the church's repair. Owen maintained that their excuses for non-payment were 'frivolous', hiding 'baser intentions in them, that they would avoyd a leavy to spare their purses'. Despite his assertions, however, the ideological motive in this drive can perhaps be detected in the presence of Sir Thomas Myddleton among the names of those possessing property in the parish who refused to contribute to the repair; this may suggest that his opposition to the repair of Chirk rested on similar considerations.[44]

The repair of churches in this diocese was given greater emphasis after the metropolitical visitation of 1636. A certificate has survived from the parish church of Aberhafesb, dated 28 August 1636, which indicates that the churchwardens received directions after the visitation 'to repayer & redresse all defects in & aboute the church & church yard'.[45] Bishop Owen himself gave priority to the repair and maintenance of church buildings, as may be seen in his visitation articles of 1637.[46] Similar concern with the church fabric and church yards was also present in the articles issued by successive bishops of Bangor in 1634 and 1640.[47] The churchwardens' accounts for St Mary's in Haverfordwest, in the diocese of St David's, show a large amount of repair work and renovation on the fabric of the church in 1635.[48]

The repair and support of cathedral churches as exem-

[43] TNA, SP16/282/84.
[44] NLW, Chirk Castle F11472.
[45] NLW, SA/Misc./1775.
[46] Fincham, *Visitation Articles*, ii, p 173.
[47] Ibid., pp. 119, 123.
[48] This included 'drawinge the kinges armes' in the church which were framed and finished in gold: Pembrokeshire RO, Haverfordwest Corporation 2033/1-3, 2059/3.

plars for parishes was one of the central aspects of this policy, and some evidence survives to suggest that this drive had an impact in the Welsh dioceses. In a letter of June 1637, Laud indicated that the deceased bishop of Bangor, Edmund Griffith, had 'beene at great chardge in paving the chauncell and crosse isle ... with good free stone'. He also noted that the clergy of the diocese at convocation had granted Griffith a tenth toward repairs 'by way of benevolence'. The archbishop maintained that this benevolence should continue to be collected by his successor, William Roberts, 'considering the necessitie of the worke and the meanesse of my lords estate, deceased'.[49] This benevolence seems to have caused some resentment in the diocese, where the inhabitants of one parish petitioned Laud about the matter in January 1637. They maintained that no such levy towards the repair of the church had been made before; they claimed that Bishop Griffith had (as an innovation which was clearly disliked) chosen churchwardens in the parish who, on the bishop's directions, 'ceased and chardged the peticoners for the repaire or provision of ornaments in the said churche'.[50] And, further, 'they alleadged their former exemptions and the insupportability of the burthen to lay the charge of the repair of the cathedrall upon the poore inhabitants', but they were nonetheless called before the chancellor of the cathedral and excommunicated. This indicates that the bishop was implementing the directions of the 1629 proclamation, and that this drive was of a quite different tenor to the normal contribution to repairs.

Restoration was also being undertaken at St Asaph Cathedral in the 1630s, and a good deal of work was recorded by the proctor of the bishop's court, Peter Roberts. In June 1638, a new pavement was finished between the parish church and the cathedral, and 'great timber trees' were brought into the cathedral yard for the 'making of a newe steeple loft bellphrie there'. During October and November 1638, the steeple and belfry of the cathedral were

[49] NLW, Carreglwyd II/229.
[50] TNA, SP16/344/47. Unfortunately the name of the parish is obscured in the original.

'repayred and boorded, and the frame of iii bells there reedified'.[51] Thus, the Laudian drive to repair and maintain churches did have some impact in Wales, though it is not possible to be certain of the regional variations in the implementation of the policy.

Charles's and Laud's concern with church fabric, and with the state of cathedrals in particular, reached its height in their plan to re-edify the dilapidated St Paul's Cathedral as the 'mother church' of the realm.[52] After appealing to the corporation of London to provide money for this project, commissions were issued to the counties requesting contributions towards the repair. Individual clergymen gave personal donations towards the work, and these included several of Laud's former colleagues in Wales.[53] On 30 June 1634, the chapter of Llandaff Cathedral gave twenty marks 'towards the reparacon of the cathedrall church of Powlls', and provided that the same amount should be given out of the half-yearly rents paid to the chapter by the earl of Worcester.[54] At a less exalted level, the Bulkeley diarist of Dronwy, Anglesey, recorded that on 20 October 1634 he paid '6d benevolence towards St Pauls Church', as part of the county's initial payment of £20.[55]

The government attempted to obtain commitments from individuals for annual contributions, but this met with little success in Wales. In Cardiganshire, the commissioners for St Paul's managed to collect £39 18s. 4d. from the 'persons of abilitie', and though they provided a schedule of those who had defaulted or who could increase their donations, they admitted 'wee could obteyne no promises for annuall contributions of any'.[56] A similar refusal to pay annual contributions

---

[51] D. R. Thomas (ed.), *Y Cwtta Cyfarwydd* (1883), pp. 180–2.
[52] K. Sharpe, *The Personal Rule of Charles I* (New Haven, 1992), pp. 322–8.
[53] These were Morgan Owen, Laud's chaplain who became bishop of Llandaff in 1640, Thomas Howell, brother of author John and later bishop of Bristol, and Archdeacon Brand of Cardigan: Davies, *Caroline Captivity*, p. 77; *DWB*, pp. 368–9; A. Wood, *Athenae Oxoniensis*, ed. P. Bliss (Oxford, 1813–20), iv, col. 804.
[54] NLW, LL/Ch/4, p. 123.
[55] H. Owen (ed.), 'The diary of Bulkeley of Dronwy, Anglesey, 1630–1636', *Transactions of the Anglesey Antiquarian Society*, (1937), 130; Guildhall Library, 25475/1, fo. 46ᵛ.
[56] TNA, SP16/298/38; Guildhall Library, 25475/1, fo. 43.

came from Wentloog hundred in Monmouthshire, although an initial payment of £21 was raised and another £10 was provided in May 1638.[57] In some instances administrative performance was impressive, however. In the commote of Ardudwy, Merioneth, for example, although only £12 2s. 2d. was raised in 1637, this represented payments by 321 parishioners, while the £27 6s. 5d. from the hundreds of Skenfrith, Raglan and Trellech in Monmouthshire was raised by 519 individuals.[58] Ensuing commissions elicited similar responses, and although individuals throughout Wales contributed in some numbers on the understanding that it would not become an annual charge, the service managed to generate only about £1,800 in Wales, roughly equivalent to a single parliamentary subsidy.[59]

These and other returns indicate that the levy for St Paul's had to contend with many other charges that were occupying the minds of Welsh people at this time, and the repair of a distant cathedral would probably have been low on their list of priorities.[60] There was little sign, however, that the dilatoriness or lack of enthusiasm was based on religious opposition to the Laudian predilection for the externals of worship. Although the evidence is partial, it seems that the emphasis on the clerical estate and the fabric of the Church which formed an important component of the Laudian programme had some resonance in Wales which previously has been ignored. The concentration on the physical church was also seen – more contentiously – in the decoration of church interiors and the emphasis placed on the ceremony and paraphernalia associated with the sacraments.

---

[57] Guildhall Library, 25475/1, fos 58ᵛ, 104. The commissioners claimed that an annual contribution was not practical because of the charge of repairing sea walls after a severe flood: TNA, SP16/291/105.

[58] Huntington Library, Ellesmere 7419, 7422.

[59] Guildhall Library, 25475/1; Huntington Library, Ellesmere 7409, 7417, 7420, 7422, 7517; Gwent RO, Misc. MS 648, pp. 13–14; NLW, Tredegar Park 64/6–7, 105/145.

[60] Further material on the collection in Wales can be found in TNA, SP16/288/87, 103–4; 16/368/68; PC2/44, pp. 238, 533; PC2/45, p. 419; PC2/46, p. 36; PC2/48, pp. 117–18; Huntington Library, Ellesmere 7400, 7411, 7412, 7417–18, 7421, 7512.

Adornment and altars

In close alliance with the king, William Laud attempted to remodel the Church of England according to ideals of order and aesthetic beauty. An insistence on strict canonical observance meant priority was given to the ceremonial and liturgical aspects of church services, especially the eucharist. In addition, his conception of the visible Church as one filled with an immanent holiness requiring respect, even veneration, led to an emphasis on the adornment and beautification of church interiors. This was one of the most contentious aspects of ecclesiastical policy in the 1630s, bringing accusations of ceremonial innovation and cryptopopery. Alhough the sources do not exist to make a detailed study of the impact of the new ceremonialism in Wales, some suggestions can be made about this facet of Laudianism in the principality. It cannot be said that a Laudian programme was coherently implemented, but the concentration in most Welsh historiography on the few nonconforming individuals of the 1630s has failed to acknowledge that these innovations were experienced in the Welsh dioceses.

William Laud was bishop of St David's from 1621 to 1626, and it is often stated that he made no impact on the diocese because of his absence from the see for most of his incumbency.[61] This may be an over-simplification. It has already been mentioned that Laud built a chapel at the episcopal palace of Abergwili; he also lavishly adorned it and turned it into a model of his ecclesiological and aesthetic tastes. At his trial, the chapel dedicated to St John the Baptist was one of the pieces of evidence presented against him. The pattern and arrangement of furniture in the chapel followed the example of Lancelot Andrewes, an *avant-garde* churchman who stressed the liturgical aspects of worship and was a major influence on Laud.[62] The puritan lawyer William

---

[61] G. Williams, *Renewal and Reformation Wales, c.1415–1642* (Oxford, 1993), p. 481; D. G. Walker, 'The Reformation in Wales', in idem (ed.), *A History of the Church in Wales* (Bridgend, 1976), p. 73.
[62] W. Prynne, *Canterburies Doome* (1644), pp. 120–4; P. Lake, 'Lancelot Andrewes, John Buckeridge and *avant-garde* conformity at the court of James I', in L. L. Peck (ed.), *The Mental World of the Jacobean Court* (Cambridge, 1991), pp. 113–

Prynne indicated that the communion table had been set up at the east end of the chapel and was railed in, which was a crypto-Catholic practice condemned by many as turning the table into an altar. In addition, the lavish adornments of the chapel were described: two candlesticks on the altar, a chalice with a gilt cover engraved with a star, a silk-covered cloth to lay over the chalice, two cloths for the altar, and so on.[63] The archbishop denied that this was how the chapel had been set up, maintaining that it was the 'patterne of Bishop Andrews chappell and furniture'. However, his sympathetic biographer noted that Laud provided the chapel with 'rich furniture and costly utensils and what soever else was necessary or convenient for the service of God'.[64] The chapel of the diocesan would have exerted a considerable influence on the churches of the see, and there is further evidence to suggest that Laud did indeed promote the adornment of churches during his time at St David's.

In the 1630s, Thomas Jones of Hereford dedicated a poem to Herbert Price of The Priory, Brecon, which alluded to Jones's spiritual awakening on being thrown from his horse after profaning the Sabbath. After his experience, he became a painter and recalled,

> Doctor Laud, the Lord Archbishops grace
> Of Canterbury, being Bishop of this place
> Saint Davies call'd, his Lordship [Herbert Price] promise made
> That by commission I should use that trade,
> Throughout his dioces to beautifie
> The House of God, by his authoritie.[65]

In short, Laud, as bishop of St David's in the 1620s, sponsored the painting and adornment of parish churches. Jones continued that after the translation of Bishop Field to the see, Herbert Price requested the painter's commission be

33; N. Tyacke, 'Lancelot Andrewes and the myth of Anglicanism', in P. Lake and M. Questier (eds), *Conformity and Orthodoxy in the English Church, c.1560–1660* (Woodbridge, 2000), pp. 5–33.

[63] An account of these popish accoutrements was published at length in the parliamentary press: *Mercurius Civicus*, 55 (6–13 June 1644), 527–26 (irregular pagination).

[64] P. Heylyn, *Cyprianus Anglicus* (1671), i, pp. 88, 133.

[65] T. Jones, *Mercy Triumphing Over Judgement, or a Warning for Sabbath-Breakers* (1640), sig. C3.

renewed, which was duly granted. Jones then related that 'with my men Gods house I did adorne'. He later took on a bilingual apprentice (Jones himself did not speak Welsh) and they both beautified the churches of the locality. Towards the end of the poem Jones asserted that he had 'painted most of the churches' in Breconshire.[66] Adornment of churches was disliked by the more radical Protestants, who believed that such augmentation smacked of popery; they wished to worship in plainly decorated churches. It is surely significant that Jones made no mention of any resistance to his efforts from the Breconshire parishioners.

Another indication of Laudian tendencies in the period whilst Laud was bishop of St David's may be seen in his attitude towards the communion table. In his visitation articles of 1622, Laud used the uncontroversial set of the Calvinist Archbishop Abbot, but he modified the article concerning the communion table in a small but significant manner. He altered Abbot's question as to whether the table was in the 'chancell or church' at communion time, so as to enquire whether it was in the 'chancell'. As Fincham has written, this was 'early and important evidence of Laud's view of the correct location of the communion table in parish churches'.[67] It is possible, then, to see early indications of Laud's concern with liturgical practice and the adornment of churches in his time at St David's. This concentration on liturgy and ceremonial became more pronounced during the 1630s, and this 'Laudian style' had some impact in the Welsh dioceses.

The removal of the communion table to the east end of the church and its railing in were widely enforced only after the metropolitical visitation of the Welsh sees in 1636.[68] The parish register of Trefeglwys noted that the visitation met at

[66] Ibid., sigs C3ᵛ, C6ᵛ.
[67] Fincham, *Visitation Articles*, i, pp. xxi, 110. Cf. Davies, *Caroline Captivity*, p. 216. Laud's concern with the position of the communion table and the utensils of the eucharist while he was bishop of St David's is also apparent in his correspondence with Sir John Scudamore of Herefordshire: TNA, C115/102/7760, 7765.
[68] In some areas, however, a concern with the sanctity of the holy table can be found before this time. This may be seen in Bishop Griffith of Bangor's enquiry in his 1634 visitation articles as to whether the table was 'so used out of divine service or in it, as it is not agreeable to the holy use of it, by sitting, throwing hats on it,

Dolgellau on 1 June 1636, 'wherein excellent decrees were acted ... speaciallie the rayling about the altar, the rayling & paving of the seaven foote ... with bricke from wall to wall within the chancell [and] the removing of all seats impinging thereon'.[69] In his visitation articles of 1637, Bishop Owen of St Asaph attempted to ensure that the orders of the metropolitical visitation were enforced. He enquired 'is your communion table fairely railed about with joyners worke, your chancell and church paved, all seats within the seven foot within your chancell removed?'[70] There are indications that these directions were carried out in St Asaph and the other Welsh dioceses. At the parish church of Llanynys, Denbighshire, in 1637, the clerk was paid £2 for 'a new alter, and rayles about the same', and a further 1s. 6d. was paid for 'barres and glewe for the railes and the alter'.[71] In St David's in the same year, the churchwardens of St Mary's, Haverfordwest, paid 35s. 'for the makinge of the rayles & the communion table', while Richard Tomme was given £2 to place rails across the chancel.[72] At Gresford in Denbighshire, the galleries at the east end of the church were removed and the communion table was placed altarwise and railed in compliance with the visitation orders.[73] Problems arose over the new altarwise placement of the table at Llansilin in Denbighshire. The table has one end carved, suggesting that it stood tablewise before the 1630s, with the carved end facing down the nave. However, a petition was directed to Laud from the parish authorities in July 1637; it accused Edward Morris of setting a seat in the chancel which

---

writing on it, or is it abased to other prophane uses?': Fincham, *Visitation Articles*, ii, p. 119.

[69] 'D.R.T.', 'The registers of Trefeglwys', *Montgomeryshire Collections*, 32 (1902), 206.

[70] Fincham, *Visitation Articles*, ii, p. 174. This refutes Davies's conjecture that Owen did not enforce the rail in his diocese: Davies, *Caroline Captivity*, p. 239, n. 175.

[71] Denbighshire RO, PD/78/1/39, fo. 11. The communion table bears the date '1637', and appears to have been donated by William Salesbury of Rûg: M. E. S. Speight, 'The forgotten church of Llanynys', *Denbighshire Historical Society Transactions*, 11 (1962), 114.

[72] Pembrokeshire RO, Haverfordwest Corporation 2038/3.

[73] Thomas, *St Asaph*, iii, p. 248; D. L. Davies, 'The historical development of Gresford church', *Denbighshire Historical Society Transactions*, 7 (1958), 111–12.

had been earlier removed by the churchwardens in compliance with the metropolitical visitation. Morris appealed to the archbishop that his seat 'was noe way prejudiciall to the standing of the comunion table alter wayes', and claimed the churchwardens had exceeded their commissions in this respect.[74]

In eastern Caernarfonshire, the parish church of Llanrhychwyn possesses communion rails dated 1636, and similar ones are to be found at Llangelynin in the same county.[75] At Hawarden and Wrexham, later reports indicate that their churches possessed altar rails, and that the communion table was placed in the east end of the church.[76] In south Wales, the parish church of Cwmcarfan, Monmouthshire, received a new altar table in 1637, while 'Laudian' rails were introduced at Cadoxton-juxta-Barry, Glamorgan, along with a raising of the sanctuary floor.[77] Altar rails were enforced in Breconshire by Bishop Mainwaring, who had shown a considerable attachment to the veneration and adornment of the altar before his elevation to St David's in 1636.[78] The articles issued by Bishop Roberts of Bangor in 1640 appear to accept that there were rails about the communion tables in his diocese. He enquired about the practice of churching women, asking whether they 'come and kneele at a side neere the communion table without the rayle, being vayled.'[79]

The contentious word 'altar' appears to have become

---

[74] NLW, Carreglwyd I/994. See also SA/Misc./547.

[75] *Royal Commission on Ancient and Historical Monuments in Wales and Monmouthshire (Caernarfonshire)* (1956), i, pp. 128, 158. Addleshaw and Etchells indicate that altarwise communion tables were to be found in numerous churches of Caernarfonshire and Anglesey prior to the mid-nineteenth century: G. W. O. Addleshaw and F. Etchells, *The Architectural Setting of Anglican Worship* (1948), p. 125, n. 2.

[76] T. Carte (ed.), *A Collection of Original Letters and Papers . . . Found Among the Duke of Ormonde's Papers* (1739), i, pp. 32–3.

[77] M. Salter, *The Old Parish Churches of Gwent, Glamorgan and Gower* (Malvern, 1991), p. 17; G. R. Orrin, *Medieval Churches of the Vale of Glamorgan* (Cowbridge, 1988), p. 116.

[78] Davies, *Caroline Captivity*, p. 225; *CSPD, 1635*, pp. 394–5.

[79] Fincham, *Visitation Articles*, ii, p. 123. Insistence on the use of the veil in churching was also characteristic of Laudian practice: D. Cressy, 'Purification, thanksgiving and the churching of women in post-Reformation England', *Past and Present*, 141 (1993), 135–9.

more common among Welsh people in referring to the communion table at about this time. In 1640, William Vaughan of Llangyndeyrn, Carmarthenshire, wrote against those who 'startle at the altars ancient name'.[80] Earlier in the decade, the incumbent of Llanrhaeader, Denbighshire, made a representation to Laud, describing himself on one occasion as 'beinge in his vestments at the high altar'.[81] Thomas John ap Hugh of Talley, Carmarthenshire, meanwhile, bequeathed 4*d.* in his will of January 1638 'unto the high aulter of St Davids'.[82] Such usage suggests that the Laudian vocabulary, so hated by more reformed elements, was infiltrating the social order beyond the clergy.

It seems significant that the only instance of obviously principled resistance to the policy in Wales comes from Montgomery town, close to the border with England, and in the diocese of Hereford. In 1631, the puritan gentleman Sir Robert Harley of Brampton Bryan professed an interest in who was to assume the living after the death of the incumbent, 'Mr Thomas', who was dangerously sick. On 8 December 1631, Harley wrote to the radical minister John Brinsley of Great Yarmouth, indicating his hope that Brinsley would be placed in the living. He stated that, although the place was in the gift of the lord keeper, he would present whomsoever the local magnate, Lord Herbert of Chirbury, recommended. Harley continued that Chirbury 'sayes he loves a puritan but not a predestinator'.[83] Richard Griffiths of Sutton, an alderman of the town, also showed concern as to who was to be presented to the living after Thomas's death. In January 1632, Chirbury assured Griffiths, 'as one whom I cheefly desier might have satisfaction therin', that the new incumbent, Mr Coote, was a 'sincere minister of Gods worde'.[84] The presentation was, therefore, of interest to the leading puritan gentleman of the area, who hoped that a radical minister would be instituted, and to one of the town's

---

[80] W. Vaughan, *The Church Militant* (1640), p. 304.
[81] TNA, SP16/383/24. See also SP16/371/68.
[82] NLW, SD/1638/87.
[83] HMC, *Portland MSS*, iii, pp. 29–30; G. F. Nuttall, *The Welsh Saints, 1640–1660* (Cardiff, 1957), p. 6.
[84] TNA, 30/53/7/13.

aldermen who demonstrated a similar wish for a 'sincere minister'. On Easter Day 1637, Richard Griffiths went to the town's church to receive communion. He and his family went to 'the usuall place in the chancell which ever before tymes it [communion] was given usually to the whole parish'. They remained there while communion was administered to the rest of the congregation at the new altar rails. Coote came to Griffiths's family and 'used some perswasive reasons to them to come up to the railes wherwith the comunion table is altarwise newly ingirt'. Griffiths refused, so Coote told him that he would pray for him, which he did '3 severall tymes with 18 low prostrate bows to the alter'. Griffiths demanded that he be allowed to take communion 'in the ancient usuall place', and asked Coote why he made him 'a gazing stocke to the congregation'. Coote relented and administered communion to Griffiths and his family in the chancel, but asked the congregation to bear witness to Griffiths's 'hardnesse of heart, pride & rebellion.'[85]

Griffiths's opposition was directed against the new altar policy and its tendency towards 'idolatry', as was illustrated by Coote's bowing to the altar, something which puritans particularly despised. It is significant that the account of this incident is to be found among the papers of Sir Robert Harley, whose religious proclivities were shared by Griffiths.[86] The proximity of Montgomery to the border suggests a correlation between this more principled kind of resistance and influences from England such as Harley's puritan household at Brampton Bryan, where plans for evangelizing Wales had their seed in the late 1630s and early 1640s.[87] The kind of resistance found in Montgomery appears to have been almost completely absent from other parts of the principality, and the altar policy seems otherwise to have been adopted with little comment.

This emphasis on the communion table as an altar was one manifestation of the Laudian stress on rites and ceremonies in the Church. The visitation articles issued by Owen

[85] BL., Add. 70,002, fo. 138.
[86] For their association, see Huntington Library, Ellesmere 7352; BL, Add. 70,106, fo. 155.
[87] Hereford Cathedral Library, 6450/3, p. 32; Bowen, thesis, 440–54.

at St Asaph in 1637 illustrate the centrality of these decorous rites in the churchmanship he was attempting to foster. He asked whether the minister

> doth administer the holy communion every moneth, or thrice in the yeare at least ... Doth he use and never omit the signe of the crosse in baptisme: or doth he ever baptize in any bason or other thing but the usuall font? Doth he mary without a ring ...?[88]

This emphasis on rites displaced the puritan priority of preaching as the means whereby religious knowledge should be inculcated, and it is noteworthy that in the articles which Owen issued in the altered circumstances of 1642, the passage was omitted completely.[89] The Laudian stress on the sacraments also entailed a new concentration on the eucharist. It is probably not coincidental, therefore, that many Welsh churches received benefactions of church plate and communion artefacts during the 1630s. Fourteen communion cups have survived which were donated to churches in the diocese of St Asaph during that decade, a significant increase on survivals from the 1620s.[90] An elaborate cup decorated with a representation of the crucifixion – which was at variance with the plain aesthetic tastes preferred by those with puritan inclinations – was donated by William Bold of Anglesey to the church at Llechcynfarwy in 1632.[91] In 1637, Sir Thomas Aubrey of Llantrithyd, Glamorgan, gave his parish church a 'silver standing cupp' inscribed with the words 'drinke ye my bluid'.[92] In October 1639, the bishop of Bangor, William Roberts, informed Laud that some of his parishioners had lately given 'testimony of their piety' by 'bestowing a couple of faire chalices of good valew upon the poore cathedrall'.[93] Importantly, he added that the cathe-

---

[88] Fincham, *Visitation Articles*, ii, p. 175.
[89] Ibid., p. 181.
[90] M. H. Ridgeway, *Church Plate of the Diocese of St Asaph* (Denbigh, 1997), pp. 284–5.
[91] *Royal Commission on Ancient and Historical Monuments in Wales and Monmouthshire (Anglesey)* (1937), p. 116, and plate 66.
[92] Glamorgan RO, P/38/CW/1, fo. 54. Aubrey's family was connected with the 'high church' group at Oxford which included men like Gilbert Sheldon: P. Jenkins, 'Welsh Anglicans and the Interregnum', *Journal of the Historical Society of the Church in Wales*, 32 (1990), 51–3.
[93] TNA, SP16/431/69. Roberts himself had given a 'fine service of plate' to the

dral 'shall not bee much behind our neighbors either in necessaryes or beauty'. Roberts himself clearly felt the augmentation of the cathedral to be important, and in his will he left £100 for adorning the choir of 'the poore cathedral church of Bangor'.[94]

In 1639, it was reported that the church of Llanfihangel Esceifiog, Anglesey, had been 'much adorned and beautified' by Henry Bagenall and his tenants.[95] Similarly, at Wrexham the incumbent, Rowland Owen, was said to have 'very much adorned and beautified' his church.[96] When Henry Hastings, earl of Huntingdon visited Wrexham in August 1636, he described it as a 'wonderfull faire' church and noted its two organs.[97] It was one of the churches which suffered at the hands of parliamentary soldiers during the Civil War, when Sir William Brereton's forces entered the church in 1643 as well as those at Flint and Holywell, and 'pulled downe the organes, defaced the windowes'.[98] Meanwhile at Hawarden, Flintshire, Captain Byrck wrote in December 1643 of the violence of parliamentary troops towards the images and Laudian apparatus. In the parish church he

> found the common prayer book scattered up and down the chancel ... In windows where there was oriental glass, they broke in pieces only the faces to be as frugal as they could; they left sometimes the whole bodies of painted bishops ... They had pulled down the rails about the table ... and brought down the table into the midst of the church.[99]

The violence against these items came from external sources, and their survival up to this point indicates that, unlike many other areas of the country, there was little popular agitation against such symbols from the local population in the early 1640s. Significantly, Byrck's soldiers, seeing the communion

---

cathedral in 1637: A. I. Pryce (ed.), *The Diocese of Bangor during Three Centuries* (1929), p. xxv.

[94] TNA, PROB 11/321, fo. 138.
[95] TNA, SP16/431/69(i).
[96] Walker, *Sufferings of the Clergy*, ii, p. 322; Lloyd, *Memoires*, p. 570.
[97] Huntington Library, HAP Box 18, item 13. I am grateful to Dr Kenneth Fincham for this reference.
[98] BL, Harleian 2,125, fo. 135ᵛ; Thomas, *St Asaph*, i, p. 107.
[99] Carte, *Ormonde's Papers*, i, pp. 32–3. See also BL, Harleian 2,125, fo. 135ᵛ.

table in the middle of the chancel, 'swore it stood not right . . . and set it close to the east wall again'. The survival of such Laudian innovations in these communities to this point suggests a genuine and deep attachment in Wales to those elements of worship considered anathema by more reformed elements. This appears to gain support from the comments of the royalist soldier Richard Symonds in south Wales; he was surprised to find how 'almost in every parish the crosse or sometime two or three crosses [are] perfect in Brecknockshire, Glamorganshire, & c.'[100]

The architectural expression of the 'high church' principles embodied in Laudianism can be found at their most extreme in the private chapel at Rûg, Merioneth, built in 1637 by the future royalist governor of Denbigh, William Salesbury. Here, the altar was set against the east wall and railed in on three sides. The other adornments of the chapel are more noteworthy, comprising a roof painted to represent the sky and stars, walls covered with colourful paintings, and a credence table on which to place the eucharistic elements.[101] This remarkable building is graphic evidence of the desire of some in Wales for the more visual and ceremonial form of worship which was, in part, satisfied by the Laudian notion of 'beauty of holiness'. Salesbury himself had an attachment to such worship, and was described during the Civil War as 'keeping up the festivals, ministry and prayers of the Church by his example'.[102] One historian has struggled to account for the lack of controversy which surrounded the erection of this structure, offering the hypothesis that such Laudian innovation was 'applied with pastoral sensitivity':[103] it might rather be suggested that it

---

[100] C. E. Long (ed.), *Diary of the Marches of the Royal Army* (Camden Soc., 74, 1859), p. 208.

[101] D. B. Hague, 'Rûg Chapel, Corwen', *Journal of the Merioneth Historical and Record Society*, 3 (1957–60), 178; W. N. Yates, *Rûg Chapel, Llangar Church, Gwydir Uchaf Chapel* (Cardiff, 1993), pp. 10–19.

[102] Lloyd, *Memoires*, p. 660. In the 1650s he requested Rowland Vaughan of Caergai to translate into Welsh a work of William Brough, dean of Gloucester, described as an 'ardent supporter of Laud': *Dictionary of National Biography, s.n.* 'Brough, William'; W. P. Griffith, 'Merioneth and the new and reformed learning in the early modern period', *Journal of the Merioneth Historical and Record Society*, 12 (1997), 339.

[103] Williams, 'Welsh clergy', 352.

harmonized with the conservative religious predilections of many parishioners in the area.

This accumulation of evidence casts new light on the nature of religion in the principality in the years before the Civil War, and suggests that we have neglected the 'conservative conformism' of the country. We should, perhaps, consider more closely the contemporary assertion that Sir Thomas Myddleton obtained his commission to be parliamentary major general of north Wales after informing parliament that the inhabitants of the region were 'grosely ignorant, and of blinde zeale, and havinge soe much ... superstition ... that they had taken upp armes to defend idolatrous pictures which were doomed to bee pulled downe.'[104]

Conclusion

For economic, geographical and linguistic reasons, Wales during the early seventeenth century was a religiously conservative part of Britain. The reception of Protestantism had been slow, and puritan ideals had found fertile ground only amongst a small minority. Although these godly enclaves should not be discounted, it is important to recognize that the 1630s were not a period of incipient puritan activism in Wales. The evidence presented here suggests that the radical programme of the king and Archbishop Laud penetrated parishes throughout the principality. This was not simply the repressive measures against radicals like William Erbery and Walter Cradock, but took a more positive form with an emphasis on church fabric, the altar and the sacraments. Although this survey falls far short of a detailed reconstruction of religion in Wales during the 1630s, it suggests that we need to explain the comparative quiescence of Wales in the 1630s as much as the isolated evidence of dissent.

It is important to note that much of this dissent was voiced by a small group of puritans associated with Sir Robert Harley and a puritan stimulus emanating from England. What we

---

[104] NLW, Wynnstay 54/64.

may term 'indigenous' religion seems to have been of a different order. It has been suggested that the Welsh adopted an Anglican Church which emphasized the symbols and ceremonials of worship rather than the sermonizing and scriptural study of the puritans. Madeline Gray has recently made a powerful assertion of the potency and vibrancy of visual imagery in late medieval Welsh churches, and has demonstrated convincingly how the 'conservative religious practices' managed widespread circumvention of Reformation orders to destroy and remove images in the Church. What is striking about her findings is the extent to which, in Wales, images, symbols and crucifixes survived to the Restoration and beyond, many falling victim only to the Victorian 'restorers' who were particularly ruthless with such survivals.[105] Perhaps it is time to acknowledge that the Laudian emphasis on the physical body of the Church, its ceremonial and its visual majesty, fits more easily into this genealogy than the glosses of post-Restoration evangelical groups.

Moreover, the moderate religious texts available in the vernacular from the mid-sixteenth century helped to forge a form of conservative Anglican conformism which was constructed around the poles of patriotism, monarchy and the Welsh language: none of these was particularly receptive to, or important for, most puritans in England. The Church of England was reconciled to Welsh culture in a manner that allowed it to become a genuinely popular institution, forging a sometimes intense loyalty which seems to have underwritten a number of the political episodes outlined in this book. Philip Jenkins has argued that the Church in Wales by the early seventeenth century had become a 'strongly national and even patriotic' institution.[106] Rather than the 'long sleep' before the evangelical revival reflected in nonconformist mythology, we need to recognize the early seventeenth-century Welsh Church as a vibrant and popular

---

[105] M. Gray, *Images of Piety: The Iconography of Traditional Religion in Late Medieval Wales* (Oxford, 2000), esp. ch. 8.
[106] P. Jenkins, 'The Anglican Church and the unity of Britain: the Welsh experience', in S. G. Ellis and S. Barber (eds), *Conquest and Union: Fashioning a British State, 1485–1725* (1995), pp. 124–5.

body which, though plagued with problems, had set down deep roots and created strong bonds in society. The legacy of the slow and difficult gestation of the Reformation, wherein issues of vernacularization and inculturation were of paramount significance, seems to have encouraged in Wales an emphasis on ceremony, symbols and liturgical practice which were often portrayed by opponents (and often uncritically repeated by historians) as ignorant or popish. For example, the survival of crosses, organs and stained glass in Wales until the later stages of the Civil Wars indicates an absence of spontaneous iconoclasm and a genuine attachment to traditionalist symbols and practices at the heart of much Welsh spirituality. Moreover, fervent support of the Welsh for the Prayer Book and its liturgy was strong enough to become a proverbial gibe in parliamentary satires of the 1640s.[107] Although there is no evidence to suggest that the Laudian experiment was implemented in Wales particularly vigorously or by an especially dogmatic group of bishops, this analysis of pre-war Welsh religion helps to account for the fact that those Laudian elements which manifestly were introduced in Wales did not produce concerted or widespread opposition. It is contended, then, that the religion of most Welsh men and women in the 1630s was closer to that of Charles and Laud than to that of Harley, and that this better explains the politico-religious landscape of the principality at the outbreak of civil war in 1642.

---

[107] See below, pp. 255–7.

6

CIVIL WAR ALLEGIANCE AND WELSH POLITICAL CULTURE

Preceding chapters have explored aspects of early Stuart political culture in Wales, in particular the relationship between centre and locality. It has been suggested that most individuals in Wales, and their representatives at Westminster, remained politically fairly quiescent during the early seventeenth century, even though they were wholly integrated in a wider British polity and fully cognizant of the potential of its parliament. They seem to have paid levies like the forced loan and ship money with comparative alacrity and little dissent, and even appear to have responded positively to the Laudian innovations of the 1630s. Certainly when compared with many regions in England, the Welsh counties demonstrated little in the way of ideologically motivated opposition to Jacobean and Caroline policies, and this chapter seeks to carry these conclusions further with a discussion of allegiance and royalism in the early stages of the Civil Wars which broke out in 1642. It does not claim to be a systematic or comprehensive treatment of the subject,[1] but presents evidence of overt political choice in Wales which helps to clarify and identify some of the more significant elements which shaped Welsh political culture in the early seventeenth century.

This book has adopted the revisionist stricture of examining the political landscape of the early seventeenth century in its own terms rather than through a teleological reading coloured by the knowledge that the country was to divide into opposed camps in the early 1640s. The latter, 'Whiggish', approach has informed most studies of early seventeenth-century Wales, testifying to the enduring legacy of Professor Dodd's pioneering work. This book has not been a contribution to the long-established historical tradi-

---

[1] I hope to pursue this topic more fully on a future occasion.

tion of searching for the causes of the Civil Wars in Wales; but the following survey of allegiance suggests how important connections can be made with the pre-war political landscape. Whilst many 'post-revisionist' scholars are uncovering serious opposition in the political climate of the decades before the war, and are relating this to the form and nature of divisions in the 1640s, this brief chapter suggests some of the ways in which pre-war Welsh politics can be connected with Wales's remarkable royalist unanimity in 1642.

The royalist stance of Wales during the early Civil War is a topic which does not sit easily in a historiography dominated by issues of nonconformity and political radicalism. These preoccupations reflect the prevailing intellectual and political concerns of the formative years of Welsh academic writing of the nineteenth and early twentieth centuries. The mid-seventeenth century saw the effective beginnings of what may be termed a puritan movement in Wales, and although the transition was not a smooth one and the lineages are not always as direct as has sometimes been portrayed, these beginnings fed directly into later Welsh revivalist movements and the flowering of nonconformity and chapel culture in the principality.[2] Most Welsh antiquarians and historians who have studied the seventeenth century have been associated with this nonconformist culture; one consequence has been a marked concentration on the history of dissent and its early advocates such as William Wroth, Walter Cradock and William Erbery.[3]

This martyrological trend in the writing of Welsh religious history has its counterpart in the study of Welsh politics. Here the emphasis has been placed on the champions of the common people, on an interpretation of events from a Liberal rather than a Tory perspective. Welsh royalism, therefore, is a topic concerned with themes which have been neglected in most Welsh historical writing. This has led to the production of textbooks which only acknowledge in

---

[2] P. Jenkins, *A History of Modern Wales, 1536–1990* (Harlow, 1992), pp. 407–12.

[3] See the perceptive comments in S. Roberts, 'Propagating the Gospel in Wales: the making of the 1650 act', *TCS*, NS 10 (2004), 57–9.

passing the royalist sympathies of Wales in the first Civil War, and concentrate far more heavily on the Roundhead martyrs to radical politics, such as the regicide Colonel John Jones of Maesygarnedd. This helps to account for the rather reductive explanations for Welsh royalism which have been perpetuated to the present day, and the lack of detailed research on Civil War allegiance in Wales. Although elaborated in subtle ways, a common thread running through many explanations of Welsh royalism asserts that the principality received considerable benefits from union with England under the 'Welsh' monarchy of the Tudors. The loyalty that this brought about is seen to have been transferred 'virtually undiluted' to the Stuarts, providing reason enough for the Welsh to support the Crown after 1642.[4] This view was espoused most influentially by Professor Dodd, who maintained that Wales was 'too firmly schooled in monarchical instincts ... not to rally round the crown once it seemed in danger of becoming the object of direct attack'.[5] Such an explanation has been accepted by most modern historians who have seen in Dodd's essentially Tudorist analysis a familiar and reassuring restatement of the position that the Welsh were still in a period of political 'apprenticeship' begun under Henry VIII.

The problems with this explanation of a traditional loyalty to the Crown may be seen when it is remembered that a profound attachment to monarchy and the benefits of its patronage in local society were universal phenomena in England as well as Wales, though they did not prevent many English shires from declaring for parliament. In addition, a vague attachment to alleged benefits bestowed by the Tudors 100 years earlier is surely not the best means of accounting for the allegiance of the majority of Welshmen during the Civil War. This chapter offers some new interpretations of popular royalism in Wales at the outbreak of the Civil War, and suggests ways in which these political choices can be seen not simply as functions of an ingrained Welsh loyalty to

---

[4] Versions of this position can be found in most textbooks on early modern Wales; a representative synthesis can be found in G. H. Jenkins, *The Foundations of Modern Wales, 1642–1780* (Oxford, 1987), pp. 4–5.

[5] Dodd, 'Parliaments, 1625–1629', 48.

the Crown, but rather as having important precursors in the political, religious and cultural character of the country.

WALES AND WESTMINSTER, 1640–1642

At the summoning of the Short Parliament in April 1640, Wales did not appear to have been deeply alienated from the policies of the personal rule. There is no doubt, however, that it did experience considerable difficulties in mobilizing the creaking military machine against the Scots Covenanters from 1638: in Denbighshire, for example, a survey revealed that many of the county's corslets had been 'converted ... into friing panns'.[6] In addition, the heavy military charges for the Bishops' Wars compounded the other financial demands such as ship money, and contributed to discordant voices such as the 'heavy groanes of the complayneing inhabitants' of Glamorgan, whilst Lord President Bridgwater spoke darkly of 'some ill spirits' in his lieutenancy.[7]

Yet when the Long Parliament assembled on 3 November 1640, none of Wales's representatives – unlike many MPs – brought a coherent case for reform from their counties, and few demonstrated any enthusiasm for the remedial programme which the Commons adopted in the first year of its existence. No Welsh MP introduced petitions from his county detailing abuses during the personal government, as were forthcoming from a number of other shires, and there is little to suggest that any Welsh member had an agenda for reform.[8] On most of the issues before the Commons during this parliament down to 1642, the position of the Welsh MPs often appears to have been reactive rather than proactive. By contrast, those most vocal in demanding reform were a small group of Welsh puritans headed by William Erbery and Walter Cradock who looked to the Commons to promote a preaching ministry in what they considered to be the reli-

---

[6] NLW, Chirk Castle E1371; Bowen, thesis, 411–29.
[7] TNA, SP16/455/80; 16/466/55.
[8] Some Radnorshire constituents had drawn up a petition of 'divers comon greivances' concerning military charges, but neither the county member, Charles Price, nor the borough member, Philip Warwick, was willing to present it to the House: BL, Add. 70,003, fos 132^v–4, 136^{r-v}.

giously backward principality. Yet what is striking is their lack of support among Welsh MPs in the Commons and from Wales more generally. Rather did this group of radicals look to the Herefordshire puritan, Sir Robert Harley of Brampton Bryan, who had demonstrated an ongoing interest in Wales's spiritual regeneration.[9] A revealing letter to Harley from one of the radicals, Oliver Thomas, in July 1641 enjoined parliamentary action on Welsh religious reform, adding tellingly, 'if the care of provision for us bee comitted to our Welsh parliamentary knights & burgesses, our hopes are gone'.[10] The sole Welsh member who supported the 'root and branch' campaign for abolishing episcopacy was John Bodvel, the member for Anglesey. He spoke against Archbishop Laud and endorsed the Root and Branch Bill, stating that 'we could not expect any fruit of our endeavours except we first cleanse the house of God'.[11] More representative of Welsh opinion were members like Charles Price of Pilleth, Radnorshire, who spoke out against the Welsh puritans, and John Griffith of Cefnamwlch, the member for Beaumaris, who offended the Commons by claiming 'ytt ys distastfull to thys House to speake for the government of the churche.'[12]

Although there was serious disquiet voiced both within the Long Parliament and in the Welsh counties over the influence of prominent Catholic magnates like the earl of Worcester and Lord Powis, this does not seem to have had any straightforward correlation with the political choices which Welsh men and women made to support king or parliament in 1642. Monmouthshire, Montgomeryshire, Anglesey and Pembrokeshire experienced Catholic scares in 1641–2, but only the last showed any real parliamentary impulses, and those small cells of parliamentarians which did spring up, such as those which opposed Worcester in

[9] Hereford Cathedral Library, 6450/3, p. 32; BL, Add. 70,062, unfol.; G. F. Nuttall, *The Welsh Saints, 1640–60* (Cardiff, 1957), pp. 1–17. For Harley, see J. S. Eales, *Puritans and Roundheads* (Cambridge, 1990), and above, pp. 227–8.
[10] BL, Add. 70,106, fo. 155.
[11] BL, Harleian 477, fos 119^v, 586^v.
[12] BL, Harleian 163, fos 279^v, 354^v; 479, fo. 1^v; Add. 14828, fo. 66; Bodleian Library, Rawlinson D1099, fo. 45^v.

Monmouthshire, were fairly isolated and ineffectual in the early stages of the war.[13] It is noticeable that there was a lack of that virulently anti-popish ethic so closely associated with the reformist message of the puritans. Rather than driving people into the arms of the puritans, it would seem that the Catholic scares, on the one hand, and the radical religious programme advocated in the Long Parliament, on the other, drove much of Welsh society to defend traditional religious and political forms. Although Wales was generally conservative in its religious outlook, it was nevertheless solidly Anglican, and as the political crises of 1641–2 mounted, it became clear that the majority in Wales favoured a moderate religious line, distinctly out of step with the inclinations of many English MPs and their constituents. Significantly, no Welsh county petitioned in favour of the removal of episcopacy in 1641, when parliament received pro-abolition representations from nineteen shires in England. It is suggested that this increasingly vocal articulation of moderate religious principles from late 1641 helped to distinguish the Welsh as an ethno-cultural group which manifested an identifiable royalist allegiance in the increasingly polarized political atmosphere. This phenomenon gave long-standing cultural differences a political edge, with the result that the Welsh were stereotyped as ignorant and foolish by the king's opponents; this probably encouraged the decision within many counties of Wales to support the king rather than parliament.

The petitions of 1642

The period after a bloody rebellion of Irish Catholics in October 1641 which electrified England and Wales saw political confusion: episodes such as the king's attempted arrest of the Five Members and his subsequent decision to abandon London polarized political opinion. The stages by which this situation degenerated into civil war by late 1642 were halting and confused, as many in the localities attempted to comprehend the division in the body politic

---

[13] Bowen, thesis, 492–504, 528.

and how they should react. One response adopted by many counties early in 1642 was to petition parliament, often wholeheartedly endorsing the reforms pushed through the Commons by members like John Pym.[14]

The increasing tensions of late 1641 and early 1642 caused a significant sector of Welsh society to call for the restoration of political and religious order, focused on the king and the Established Church. On 12 February 1642 a petition was presented to the Commons on behalf of 'many hundred thousands within the thirteen shires of Wales'.[15] Its claim to represent the whole principality is worthy of note, especially in comparison with other petitions submitted at around this time which were offered in the name of an individual county, city or town. It suggests that its authors believed Wales could be considered as a region which could articulate its own grievances with some concept of uniqueness and homogeneity. Although its claim to speak for such a diverse and disparate community cannot be taken at face value, the petition indicates a contemporary acknowledgement that Wales could be conceived as an entity possessing some degree of rhetorical potency within the prevailing political culture. It suggests that contemporaries recognized Wales as having some form of independent political currency.

Like others of this period, this petition generally supported the reform programme of the Long Parliament; it commended the Commons' 'unwearied labors and uncessant consultations' to reform the 'manifold pressures under which we have groaned these many yeares'. The petitioners included demands for the reform of trade, because the store of cattle 'which is the chiefest mine of our countrey' had been bought and driven into Ireland or England. Such a clause reflected the petition's regional character, and strengthens its claim to represent the concerns of a considerable constituency in Wales.[16] The petitioners further

---

[14] For this petitioning, see A. Fletcher, *The Outbreak of the English Civil War* (1981), pp. 191–227.

[15] *The Humble Petition of Many Hundred Thousands Inhabiting Within the Thirteene Shires of Wales* (1642).

[16] See, for example, the contemporaneous concerns about trade emerging from Carmarthenshire: *A Continuation of the True Diurnall*, 3 (7–14 March 1642), 69.

maintained that the Welsh counties had 'always shown our loyalty to his Majesty, [and] our awfull obedience to you', but they had noticed a disturbing trend towards derision of the Welsh as a people. The petition continued that the Welsh were 'disrespected and shamefully derided with ludibrious contempt more than any other country whatsoever'. This indicates that they were being reviled in the parliamentary press on the basis of their ethnic distinctiveness before the outbreak of the Civil War. This is significant because the anti-Welsh bias of the parliamentary press is well attested, but is often considered to have become a political issue after the outbreak of war and the principality's general declaration for the king. Yet an increasing number of pamphlets were printed from 1641 which drew on long-established themes expressed in a newly politicized manner and ridiculing the Welsh people, aping their forms of speech and national traits.[17] Such portrayals had a long history stretching back into the Middle Ages, but there was a novel political message in these pamphlets which had not been present in previous satirical treatments of the Welsh. In some senses this treatment of Wales and the Welsh may be seen as a corollary of the language of anti-popery which was so pervasive in England. One of the defining characteristics of anti-popery as a discourse by which disturbances in the state could be explained was that these disturbances became ascribed to an alien, external force, a definable 'other' that was 'un-English'.[18] To some degree, the Welsh could fill such a role. At such times of crisis, the English appear to have been moved to ridicule the Welsh as such an 'other', though not with the vitriol that accompanied the attacks on popery.

Though perhaps considered as 'light relief' at times of stress in the body politic, such anti-Welsh pamphlets, which increased in number during 1642, clearly offended and alienated sections of the Welsh community. The petitioners

---

[17] L. Bowen, 'Representations of Wales and the Welsh during the civil wars and Interregnum', *Historical Research*, 77 (2004), 358–64; M. Stoyle, 'Caricaturing Cymru: images of the Welsh in the London press, 1642–6', in D. Dunn (ed.), *War and Society in Medieval and Early Modern Britain* (Liverpool, 2000), pp. 162–79.

[18] P. Lake, 'Anti-popery: the structure of a prejudice', in R. Cust and A. Hughes (eds), *Conflict in Early Stuart England* (Harlow, 1989), pp. 79–80, 82–3, 94.

requested that the 'authors, urgers and suggesters' of such attacks should suffer exemplary punishment for reproaching the Welsh, 'for otherwise we can conceive this epidemicall derision of us to be nothing else but a scorning detestation to our known fidelity ... This grievance, especially unless it be amended, will become a great discouragement to all our countrymen.' The construction of the Welsh as a separate ethnic group of dubious reliability by pro-parliamentarians is an important development of this period. Such anti-Welsh literature has often been seen as a parliamentary response to Wales's royalist support after 1642, but this analysis suggests that such material may help to explain why the principality came to favour the king's party in the first place.

There was little evidence in this petition of support for any programme of 'further reformation' in the country; an important insight into Welsh religious attitudes at this time is another petition presented to the Commons on 5 March 1642 on behalf of the six counties of north Wales.[19] This petition claimed to have been subscribed by thirty thousand people, who asserted their position to be 'the unanimous and undevided request and vote of this whole country', and who had decided to act 'after a long silence and expectation, joyned with some feares'. Again this departed from the presentation of petitions by individual counties in England, and suggests that a wider organizational network was operating here. It is worth recalling that a division between north and south Wales had been institutionalized in the levying of ship money, and that experience may have helped to foster a corporate identity or cooperation among the gentry. This was one of a number of petitions drawn up as a reaction against the attacks on Church government by the Long Parliament and the 'root and branch' petitioning campaign from the localities for the abolition of episcopacy.[20] The attacks on the form of Church government moved the north Wales conformists to defend passionately traditional Prayer Book services. They maintained that the 'mere report' of the

---

[19] *The Humble Petition of the Gentry, Clergy and Other Inhabitants, Subscribed of ... the Sixe Shires of Northwales*, in [T. Aston], *A Collection of Sundry Petitions* (1642), pp. 27–9.

[20] J. Maltby, *Prayer Book and People in Elizabethan and Early Stuart England* (Cambridge, 1998), pp. 83–129.

alteration of church services, 'practised for so many years ... since the blessed time of Reformation', had caused 'no good effect, breeding in the minds of ill disposed persons insolence and contempt'. They were eager, however, to disclaim any pretensions at defending Laudian 'innovation and popish corruption', something which would have been unthinkable in the political climate of the time.

The conformists also defended the embattled bishops. They claimed their office to be of considerable antiquity, and stressed the 'British' dimension of episcopacy, asserting 'it is as wee beleeve that forme which came into this island with the first plantation of religion heere, and God so blessed this island that religion came earely in, with the dawning of the first day, very neere or in the time of the Apostles themselves'. This gives an important Welsh dimension to the petition and helps to support its claims to represent attitudes in the principality to the religious flux of 1641–2.[21] That the Church of England was in fact an ancient 'British' institution given to the original Britons, of whom the Welsh were descendants who had remained faithful to this pure religion despite the corruptions of Rome, was a cherished myth which helped to establish the Church as a genuinely Welsh cultural institution. Bishop Richard Davies had promulgated this idea in his *Epistol at y Cembru*, or 'Letter to the Welsh Nation', which prefaced the Welsh translation of the New Testament of 1567; this served to popularize and naturalize the reformed Church in Wales.[22] Thus, it seems as if the attack on the Church of England was interpreted in parts of Wales as an attack on a Welsh institution. Indeed, the petitioners' assertion that this pure and primitive British religion had 'beene constantly maintained among us, and that without any eminent interruption or gaine-saying, even till these our dayes', articulated a particular sense of Welsh pride and fidelity which helps to understand the role of religion in promoting Welsh loyalty. The petition declared, further, that this antiquity, combined with the 'comfortable

---

[21] Interestingly in this context, an original broadside petition is surmounted by the Welsh insignia of three feathers: Bodleian Library, shelfmark Arch. G.c.5 (12).
[22] G. Williams, *Welsh Reformation Essays* (Cardiff, 1967), pp. 212–13

experience which wee feele ... of the conveniency and moderation of this government', argued for the preservation of episcopacy and the established forms of church service. The inherent conservatism of this representation is clearly visible in the petitioners' claim that they 'cannot without some trembling entertaine a thought of change'. The long experience of Prayer Book services in the vernacular and the generally conservative view of the Church in Wales made for a society which regarded the radical plans for reform at Westminster with considerable anxiety. The petitioners committed themselves to traditional forms of worship, and asked for the Commons to preserve the 'peace and government of the church', which would avoid 'the distractions already too visible'. Such disquieting 'distractions' had indeed already appeared in north Wales, as in the case of John Morgan of Llangollen, who was presented to the court of great sessions, around the time the petition was presented, as 'being one of the sectaries & speaking against the common prayer book'.[23] Such attacks on the Church were viewed with deep concern by many in north Wales, and the same can probably be said of south Wales although the evidence here is lacking. The language of the petition echoes the concerns about 'further reformation' voiced in the Commons by members like John Griffith and Charles Price. Such threats to the Church appear to have encouraged a rallying around familiar forms and the defence of the established order, and it was from impulses such as these that Welsh royalism drew its strength.

Propaganda, debate and the emergence of royalist Wales

The petitions of February and March 1642 were formulated against a backdrop of restiveness and uncertainty in Wales and the kingdom generally as the king and his parliament drew physically as well as ideologically further apart. The increasing conviction among many that a fundamental breach was imminent was fostered by the demands for obedi-

---

[23] NLW, Great Sessions 4/24/1/14.

ence made by king and parliament to the local communities in a propaganda war of claim and counter-claim. The Welsh shires were subject to these propagandist campaigns, though it appears that the king's message was disseminated much more effectively and thoroughly than that of parliament. Arresting evidence for this is found in the letter-book of David Pennant, sheriff of Flintshire in 1642; it reveals how pamphlets supporting the king's position were circulated in the shire.[24] On 27 May 1642, for example, Pennant received from the king's camp forty books about the militia controversy raging between king and parliament, and he was ordered to 'forthwith (by the assistance of the constables, ministers and other officers) publish, disperse and cause to be read in all churches, towns, markets and parishes in that our county all the printed bookes herewith sent'. The leaders of local society were targeted as mouthpieces for the king's message, and the impact of this on the average inhabitant of Flintshire would have been considerable. There may also have been the potential for these individuals to put glosses of their own on the messages, not least because they would certainly have been rendered into Welsh for wider consumption. The use of such vernacular propaganda can be observed in an order of the Flintshire commissioners of array in December 1642 to the hundred of Coleshill which described the need for defence against the parliamentarians of Chester and directed that 'every minister in every parishe church' was to publish the same 'in the vulgar languadge'.[25] It is noteworthy that Pennant was also directed to send his pamphlets to ministers to be read in churches, and it seems likely that similar processes of vernacular dissemination were also employed in these instances.

Parliamentary propaganda may have circulated in Wales, in addition to information concerning the parliament contained in newsletters;[26] but it is a commonplace of Welsh historiography that parliament failed to disseminate its message adequately in Welsh. However, Pennant's letter-

---

[24] Flintshire RO, D/DM 271.
[25] Warwickshire RO, CR2017/TP646.
[26] See, for example, the papers of the Glamorgan gentleman and future parliamentarian, Evan Seys: Glamorgan RO, D/DF/244.

book and the directive of the Flintshire commissioners suggest that it may be more accurate to portray the royalist message as having been promulgated more effectively in the vernacular by leading figures of local society who had already responded positively to the king's position.

The royal propaganda distributed to Pennant, and presumably to other Welsh sheriffs, portrayed Pym and his allies as a destructive clique, and provided nascent royalists in Wales, as elsewhere, with a powerful rhetorical device for combating parliament's claims to authority. In addition, Charles's signature on the letters accompanying the declarations which Pennant received would have endowed them with considerable authority in the eyes of Welsh officials. Among all the uncertainties and debates over fundamental issues of power and authority in the state, the king's own hand invested these messages with an air of legitimacy and authority. Such propaganda, if repeated in the other counties of Wales, would have had a considerable effect in influencing opinion in the early part of 1642. That this is likely to have been the case is suggested by Charles's answer of 4 August 1642 to a loyal petition from Anglesey, in which he referred to the fact that 'the declarations hee hath made, have produced the effects for which they weare intended: the satisfaction, gratitude and confidence of his good subjects'.[27]

It is clear that individuals in Wales were fully aware of the tumultuous events in Charles's kingdoms, and this served to promote political debate and division. A letter written from Lincoln's Inn by Robert Wynn in March 1642 described William Morris of Caernarfonshire as 'that Rowndhead', and suggests a society which was employing polarized language to interpret, and indeed perpetuate, political divisions.[28] Similarly, Samuel Wood of Flintshire informed Sir John Trevor in July 1642 that 'most people grow bold, heady and audatiously violent hereabouts & spare not (many of them) to publish their mindes in dangerous speeches'.[29] One such

---

[27] University College of North Wales, Baron Hill 6721.
[28] NLW, Llanfair-Brynodol C34.
[29] Flintshire RO, D/G 3275.

instance in this political debate which interpreted the king and parliament as opposed forces before the outbreak of hostilities is found in Glamorgan. On 12 April 1642, Matthew Williams was leaving the church at Porthkerry when John Wilson enquired what news he had heard. Williams replied 'that there was much adoe in Parliament concerning the kings prerogative and the priviledges of the subjects'. Wilson responded that 'he wished that the parliament were reconciled to his Majesty', whereupon Williams retorted 'that the parliament hath power to make another king if the king will not complie and agree with the parliament'.[30] It was in this climate of debate on fundamental questions of authority that some individuals began to demonstrate a proclivity for following either the orders of parliament, or those of the king. To suggest, as some historians have, that most Welsh individuals were unaware of what was going on beyond their localities and were ignorant of the fundamental issues at stake, seems to ascribe too great a degree of insularity and disconnection to communities which were in fact wired into the networks of national news, gossip and speculation to a degree which has yet to be appreciated.[31]

It has been argued that most individuals showed the greatest reluctance to choose between king and parliament, only declaring themselves at the last moment when contrary military commissions were before them.[32] However, the widespread circulation of propaganda and the extensive debate over differences between king and parliament encouraged indications of loyalty to manifest themselves before the king issued his commission of array to the Welsh counties in July/August 1642. The principality's support for Charles was considered worthy of comment by the Venetian ambassador as early as May. On 16 May he wrote of a rumour that if the people of Yorkshire (where Charles's court was based) did not support the king sufficiently, 'he contemplates retiring to Newcastle or to Wales, where the people

---

[30] Glamorgan RO, D/D Ess. 4/4. See also ibid., D/D Ess. 4/1–3.
[31] Jenkins, *Foundations of Modern Wales*, p. 6; J. G. Jones, *Early Modern Wales, c.1525–1640* (Basingstoke, 1994), pp. 203–6.
[32] J. Morrill, *Revolt in the Provinces: The English People and the Tragedies of War* (Harlow, 1999), p. 59.

are calling for him'. Little more than a week later, he wrote that 'the people of the province of Wales have offered the king their services beseeching him again to go and live in that corner of the kingdom'. His dispatch of 30 May described how 'in the province of Wales the devotion of the people [to the king] is constantly receiving fresh confirmation'.[33] Some months before Charles called on the military assistance of Wales, then, the country was perceived as loyal to the cause of the Crown.

Such inclinations were also reflected in the way some pamphleteers derided the Welsh affection for the king before the commissions of array brought such loyalties into the open. In a publication of 8 June 1642, for example, one satirist described a fictitious 'resolution' from a Welshman 'against the malignant party'. Although this tract was intended to be offensive and lampooned national traits, it nevertheless drew on images which doubtless had sufficient basis in reality to have a relevance for the reading public. The Welshman claimed to 'protest her [the Welshman's] love to her king from her heart, and will kill all those that are enemies to her Majesty'.[34] He continued that the Welsh 'could never abide the malignant party', and wished 'that all factious Round-heads and the malignant party would hang both together on a Welch gibbet, that her king may be troubled no longer with them'.[35] The image of the Welsh propagated here was one of an unsophisticated loyalty to the king. Wales was not seen as a region of neutrals and prevaricators, then, but one where support for the king had already gathered a considerable head of steam.

These early indicators of Wales's loyalty to Charles proved to be well founded. In the summer of 1642, as the struggle over the militia raged, a petition of support for the king was being drawn up in Wales. It was presented to Charles on 1 August 1642 in the name of the 'gentry, ministers, and freeholders and inhabitants' of the counties of Denbigh,

---

[33] *Calendar of State Papers, Venetian, 1642–3*, pp. 54, 61, 65.
[34] In these satirical publications the Welshman often referred to himself as 'her', a feminizing and sardonic trope probably based on the fact that the Welsh form for 'her' (*hi*) is pronounced in English as 'he': Bowen, 'Representations', 365.
[35] *The Welshmens Prave Resolution* (1642), p. 2.

Anglesey, Glamorgan 'and the whole Principality of Wales'.[36] Referring to the royalist propaganda which had been distributed in counties like Flintshire, the petitioners thanked Charles for 'so full and cleare an account of your actions and intentions', and declared themselves 'thoroughly perswaded of the sincerity and constancy of your Majesties resolution to maintain the true Protestant religion in its primitive purity, the lawes of the land in their genuine sence'. In conclusion, they promised to 'hazard their lives and fortunes for the maintenance and defence' of the king. The prominence of religion is worthy of note, once more indicating the sincere attachment to a 'Prayer Book Protestantism' which scholars like John Morrill and Judith Maltby have suggested should be interpreted as a dynamic political position rather than simply conservative and neutralist rhetoric, empty of conviction and political meaning, something which is often implicit in many accounts of Wales in this period.[37] Such petitions of loyalty encouraged Charles to issue commissions of array to the Welsh shires.

Loyalty and Locality: Explaining Welsh Royalism

There were various responses which individuals might make to the competing military commissions of the king and parliament. Yet for all the caveats which can be applied to the statement, most of Wales was solidly royalist at the outbreak of the Civil War. In most counties the commission of array was executed without any serious challenge from parliament's militia ordinance. Samuel Wood wrote in August 1642 of the commission of array in Denbighshire and Flintshire: 'all the country follows the gentry's direction except some few which are no considerable party'.[38] In

---

[36] *Two Petitions Presented to the Kings Most Excellent Majestie at Yorke, the First of August 1642* (York, 1642). Three days later another was presented by the inhabitants of Flintshire which contained exactly the same wording, suggesting that a *pro-forma* petition was agreed among the north Wales counties: *A Petition of the Gentry, Ministers and Freeholders of the County of Flint* (1642); BL, Harleian 1970, fo. 77ᵛ. For the organization of this petition, see Bowen, thesis, 522–4.

[37] Maltby, *Prayer Book and People*; J. Morrill, 'The Church in England, 1642–9', in idem (ed.), *Reactions to the English Civil War* (Basingstoke, 1982), pp. 89–114.

[38] Flintshire RO, D/G 3275.

October, Anne Petre wrote to her cousin in Caernarfonshire, Owen Wynn, that the parliamentarian army officer John Hotham would soon march into Wales, and that he would direct his forces to the two counties of Flint and Denbigh 'in regards that the gentry of both these counties have so firmly stood for his Majesty at the commission of array'.[39] In early September, one observer recorded that 'all north Wales begins to stir, and were it not harvest time, they would flock to the [king's] standard like wilde geese'.[40] Some of this enthusiasm must be attributable to the physical presence of the king, who visited the Welsh borders late in 1642.[41] A later account noted how the king's army grew slowly in the north, 'but when he was come to Shrewsbury, the Welsh-men came running down the mountains in such multitudes that their example did much animate the English'.[42] Clarendon made it clear that Charles resolved to come to the Welsh borders because it was there that 'the power of the parliament had been the least prevalent'.[43]

Most of south Wales also demonstrated loyalty to the king in 1642. Richard Symonds wrote in his diary that Glamorgan had 'never dealt with the militia [ordinance]. Never admitted'.[44] Breconshire opinion for the king was mobilized rapidly, and in mid-August 1642 a parliamentary official informed the Commons that he found it impossible to discharge his duties in the county as 'at that time they beat up drums for Prince Charles'.[45] In Monmouthshire, meanwhile, the earl of Worcester and his son were overseeing the implementation of the array, and it was reported in the Commons that those 'well affected to the parliament ... wanted some assistance'. Any resistance to Raglan appears to have quickly collapsed, however, and one diarist reported that the royalists of the county had 'set up gallows in every

---

[39] NLW, MS 9063E/1716.
[40] *Speciall Passages*, 3 (6–13 Sept. 1642), 39.
[41] See, for example, Warwickshire RO, CR2017/TP29.
[42] *The True Informer* (Oxford, 1643), p. 40.
[43] Edward Hyde, earl of Clarendon, *The History of the Rebellion*, ed. W. D. Macray (Oxford, 1888), ii, p. 310.
[44] C. E. Long (ed.), *Diary of the Marches of the Royal Army* (Camden Soc., 74, 1859), p. 218.
[45] TNA, SP23/82/881.

town to terrify others'.[46] By December Arthur Trevor was confident in reporting to the duke of Ormonde that 'north Wales & south Wales (except a very few) are his Majestys'.[47]

Pembrokeshire was the only county in Wales to declare for parliament with any considerable backing, and it was clearly in a minority among south Wales counties. In a letter of 2 November 1642, the leading pro-parliament gentlemen there wrote to the earl of Stamford

> that this county wherein we live is only in amongst those of Wales which standeth firm and faithful to the Parliament's cause, whereby we are so much environed with ill neighbouring counties, that we cannot possibly address our letters unto your honour without search and discovery.[48]

Generally, then, the counties of Wales, with the exception of Pembroke, came out in support of the king in 1642.[49] This is not to deny that there were shades of royalism in Wales or even within counties; the north appears to have contained more enthusiastic royalists than the south. Difficulties were encountered as might be expected in such fraught circumstances, and there was significant pro-parliamentary sentiment in many counties. For a balanced view of the outbreak of war in Wales, these opinions need to be acknowledged and are important in explaining later fissures in the royalist phalanx.[50] However, even in these cases we should be wary of a historiography which teleologically reads back divisions within the royalist movement dating from 1645–6 to the decisions of 1642, weakening the claim of genuine conviction among the participants at the moment of decision. In acknowledging that the royalist position was a

---

[46] W. H. Coates, A. S. Young and V. F. Snow (eds), *The Private Journals of the Long Parliament* (New Haven, 1982–92), iii, pp. 353, 287–8; *CJ*, ii, pp. 708, 785; C. Thompson (ed.), *Walter Yonge's Diary of Proceedings in the House of Commons, 19 September 1642–7 March 1643* (Wivenhoe, 1986), p. 21.

[47] Bodleian Library, Carte 4, fo. 145ᵛ.

[48] *LJ*, v, p. 441.

[49] To say that Pembrokeshire was wholly parliamentarian is, of course, an oversimplification: Bodleian Library, Tanner 59, fo. 424; TNA, SP19/126/105–6; A. L. Leach, *The History of the Civil War (1642–1649) in Pembrokeshire and on its Borders* (1937), pp. 34–5; R. Hutton, *The Royalist War Effort, 1642–1646* (Harlow, 1982), pp. 68–74.

[50] Bowen, thesis, 530–2.

coalition which encompassed various shades of opinion, we should not ignore the fact that 1642 witnessed an unique unity of political purpose in most communities of Wales. This remarkable unanimity requires a more convincing explanation than has been offered previously.

One persuasive explanation of Welsh royalism relies on the belief that most aristocratic and gentry families declared for the king and took their tenants with them, exploiting ties of loyalty and deference. There is doubtless an element of truth in this model. Sir Thomas Myddleton, for example, wrote that he found it difficult to reduce much of royalist Wales, in part because of 'the severe power which some gentlemen have and do exercise over the common people', whilst the comments of Samuel Wood and Anne Petre support his opinion.[51] There are difficulties in accepting this explanation, however, and doubts have been voiced as to the extent to which the allegiance of the upper classes determined that of those beneath them. A recent study of Monmouthshire Catholics, for example, has concluded that, despite the presence of the powerful lords of Raglan, there is no significant evidence for the seigneurial determination of allegiance.[52] The support for Charles among the communities of many regions of Wales seems to have been genuinely popular rather than deriving solely from the activism of aristocrats like Worcester; one parliamentarian noted that he found 'the inclinations of most men [in Monmouthshire] averse and a malignant party very predominant'.[53] It is difficult to account otherwise for the zeal shown by Welsh royalists lower down the social scale. Robert Mathews of Vivod in Llangollen, Denbighshire, a shoemaker, asserted that he had been constant in his loyalty to Charles, and maintained that 'he would choose rather to die in the service of his Majesty if occasion were offered ... than

---

[51] Bodleian Library, Tanner 60, fo. 41. For recent studies which emphasize the role of aristocratic influence in Welsh allegiance, see S. Roberts, 'How the west was won: parliamentary politics, religion and the military in south Wales, 1642–9', *WHR*, 21 (2002–3), 646–74; idem, 'Office-holding and allegiance in Glamorgan in the civil war and after: the case of John Byrd', *Morgannwg*, 44 (2000), 13–16.

[52] R. P. Matthews, 'Roman Catholic recusancy in Monmouthshire, 1603–1689: a demographic and morphological analysis' (Ph.D. thesis, University of Wales, 1996), 333, 355.

[53] Bodleian Library, Tanner 60, fo. 440.

to live in other condition contrary to his Majesty's crown and dignity'.[54] The simple top–down model of allegiance also makes it difficult to account for the actions of Mathew Roberts, an independent tailor of Denbigh, who 'at the first riseing of the rebels in this kingdom against his lat[e] Majesty ... did voluntarily retaine himself a privat souldier [for the king]'.[55] The work of David Underdown and Mark Stoyle has shown that such acts by the 'common sort', independent of the gentry, were important in the political complexion of many areas during the wars.[56] Yet even if we accept the picture of the masses following their social superiors, the original question remains unanswered, for we have only considered allegiances within Wales and not addressed the question of why Wales as a whole demonstrated a homogeneous attitude in support of the king. We still need to explain why the Welsh elites supported the king in the early 1640s with an unanimity not replicated over such a large region of England.

It would appear that one of the more important determinants of Welsh allegiance was religion. Change in religion was exactly what the parliamentarians represented, and Welsh support for the king appears to have been in no small measure a reaction to this, namely, as a means of defending the Church. Chapter 5 and the previous discussion of the Welsh petitions of 1642 have suggested how the Church of England in Wales had become a national, even a patriotic, Welsh institution by this period; such a rallying point may well help to explain why Wales, almost in its entirety, supported Charles in 1642. The parliamentarian conception of Wales disseminated in pamphlets and newsbooks was dominated by the view that it was corrupted with 'popery', but this was often used as a euphemism for an attachment to a ritualized, conservative Protestantism. Although one must be aware of the dangers of using partisan sources based on negative stereotypes, the link they suggest between support for the king and the defence of traditional religious prac-

[54] NLW, Chirk Castle B86/20.
[55] NLW, Chirk Castle B86/69.
[56] D. Underdown, *Revel Riot and Rebellion: Popular Politics and Culture in England, 1603–1660* (Oxford, 1985); M. J. Stoyle, *Loyalty and Locality: Popular Allegiance in Devon during the English Civil War* (Exeter, 1994).

tices is significant. For example, a parliamentary newsbook wrote that for the Welsh

> paganisme and popery are alike to them, they find no fault with any religion but round-headisme; nor hate any man but him that will preach against her good-fellowship on Sunday about the May-poll: they know no God but nature and their King; and for their king they will live or die.[57]

Contemporaries perceived that there was an explicit link between traditional religion in Wales and support for Charles. As another author observed, 'they [the Welsh] have no religion yet but letanies ... they followed the King in the darke and knew nothing'.[58] Parliamentary commentators mocked the Welshman's love of ceremonies in the worship of God. When surprised by the parliamentary commander, Col. Mytton, Sir William Vaughan was described as being 'upon his knees receiving the sacrament'. The diurnalist observed that this was 'a judgement upon the silly idolatrous Welsh knight, who like some other of his country-men is infected with a hotch-potch of paganism and popery; they were (I warrant you) idolizing the bread, according to the tradition of their fathers'.[59]

Throughout the war the Welsh were portrayed as possessing a deep affinity for the Book of Common Prayer, a text which included prayers for, and enjoined obedience to, the monarch.[60] One account described how Archdeacon Rudd, 'a notable Cavalier', commended a congregation in Pembrokeshire for 'keeping the Book of Common Prayer and not using the [parliament's] Directory that was out'.[61] A pro-parliament pamphleteer claimed that the Welsh had 'scarce had any more reformation then the Common Prayer Book, a masse-book junior', while satirical parliamentary publications caricatured the Welsh as demanding 'to have

---

[57] *The Scottish Dove*, 17 (2–7 February 1644), 134.
[58] *Mercurius Britanicus*, 45 (22–9 July 1644), 355.
[59] *Mercurius Britanicus*, 67 (16–22 December 1644), 490.
[60] See J. Maltby, '"The good old way": prayer book Protestantism in the 1640s and 1650s', in R. N. Swanson (ed.), *The Church and the Book* (Studies in Church History, 34, 2004), pp. 233–56.
[61] *An Answer ... Against A Scandalous Pamphlet Published by One John Poyer* (1646), p. 17.

t[h]e Book of Common Prayer in referent ant pious observation'.[62] That there was a strong affection for the Book of Common Prayer among the Welsh is also indicated by the complaints of the 'Peaceable Army' in Glamorgan which lamented that 'the book of common prayer hath been traduced, and several Sundays omitted in Cardiff, which we apprehend as a forerunner of its final rejection had some their desires, and were we not resolved by the help of God to continue it'.[63] Rowland Laugharne, a parliamentarian army officer, had to reassure the Glamorgan men that 'for the common prayer book, we shall not disturb any in the use of it'.[64]

The continuity of such rites during the war is difficult to recover, but some telling indications can be found. Rees Davies of Llandaff, for example, was recorded as having 'by stealth performed the duty and office of priesthood according to the liturgy of the Church of England' after the parliamentarians came to power.[65] Another Glamorgan churchman, Thomas Bassett, was imprisoned as a delinquent during the war, and he wrote to a friend from gaol that his offence 'was my high insolence of christening a child according to the superstition of the Comon Prayer Booke (as they call it)'. He continued: 'I can not deny but that I set out my flagg of defyance too'.[66] Bassett was a wholehearted supporter of Charles I, basing his royalism squarely on his religious beliefs; he was part of a 'high-church' group, identified by Philip Jenkins, of gentry and clergy in south Wales who defended the Church of Charles I throughout the 1640s and 1650s.[67] This attachment to traditional forms of worship appears to have been an important aspect of the Welsh *mentalité* during this period. Significantly in this respect, a

---

[62] *Mercurius Britanicus*, 26 (5–12 March 1645), 202; *The Welshmens Prave Resolution* (1642), p. 3.

[63] Quoted in Morrill, *Revolt in the Provinces*, p. 151, n. 72. Cf. B. Willis, *Survey of ther Cathedral Church of Llandaff* (1719), p. 32.

[64] HMC, *Portland MSS*, i, p. 352; Roberts, 'How the west was won', 662–5.

[65] P. Jenkins (ed.), '"The sufferings of the clergy": the church in Glamorgan during the Interregnum, part two: the account of Francis Davies', *Journal of Welsh Ecclesiastical History*, 4 (1987), 20.

[66] Cardiff Central Library, 1.223, pp. 35–6.

[67] P. Jenkins, 'Welsh Anglicans and the Interregnum', *Journal of the Historical Society of the Church in Wales*, 32 (1990), 54.

good deal of the political poetry produced in Welsh during the 1640s and 1650s lamented parliament's attacks on the Church of England and the cherished Welsh Prayer Book.[68] Loyalty to the Church and the Book of Common Prayer in Wales may go some way towards explaining why, in 1642, the principality looked to Charles I as defender of the Church, rather than to the Long Parliament. Clarendon's observation on the relationship between attachment to the Prayer Book and royalism appears to hold a good deal of relevance to the Welsh experience:

> a love of the established government of the church and state, especially to that part of the church as concerned with the liturgy, or Book of Common Prayer ... was a most general object of veneration with the people; and the jealousy and apprehension that the other party intended to alter it, was a principal advancement of the King's service.[69]

As suggested earlier, the conservatism of Welsh religion had much to do with the barrier of language, and linguistic patterns in Wales appear to have been an important variable in determining Civil War allegiance. It is significant, for example, that the only area of Wales which showed any enthusiasm for parliament, Pembrokeshire, contained large wholly Anglophone communities.[70] It is surely significant that the most Anglicized hundred of Castlemartin in the south of the county was seen by contemporaries as a stronghold of parliamentarianism. One parliamentary newsbook of 1645 described how royalists in Pembrokeshire 'came first to Castle Martin to consume that hundred by fire and sword'.[71] Important too was a tightly knit group of families centred on the hundred; they were closely associated with the family of the parliamentary commander, the earl of Essex.[72] This group of families, in an English-speaking area, and with a

---

[68] See, for example, *Hen Gerddi Gwleidyddol* (Cymdeithas Llên Cymru II, Cardiff, 1901), p. 33; L. Bowen, '"This murmuring & unthankful peevish land": Wales and the Protectorate', in P. Little (ed.), *The Cromwellian Protectorate* (forthcoming, 2007).
[69] Clarendon, *Rebellion*, ii, p. 449.
[70] G. Owen, *The Description of Pembrokeshire*, ed. H. Owen (1892–1936), iii, pp. 100–1.
[71] *The City Scout*, 7 (9 September 1645), 3.
[72] R. Mathias, 'The first civil war', in B. E. Howells (ed.), *Early Modern Pembrokeshire, 1536–1815* (Aberystwyth, 1987), pp. 160–8.

history of attachment to reforming Protestantism, in many ways represented much of what the rest of Wales was not.

The case of Pembrokeshire suggests another factor influencing allegiance which stems naturally from the question of language, namely ethnicity.[73] The nascent parliamentarians saw Wales as a potential threat many months before the outbreak of hostilities, and with the outpouring of anti-Welsh diatribes from the parliamentary presses in London, it is not perhaps surprising that they had such little initial success in the principality. This antipathy towards the Welsh by the parliamentarian camp probably helped to coalesce Wales behind the king. However, a more positive royalist response may have arisen from the ethnic distinctiveness of the principality. It is natural for distinct cultural communities to band together against a potential threat, and it has been seen how the Welsh petition of February 1642 demonstrated a strong reaction against these negative representations. In this atmosphere, there would have been a strong impulse towards a collective response from the Welsh against hostility that was evidently generated in England. In a letter of 6 August 1642, Samuel Wood observed a distinctive 'national' position when discussing Welsh troops who had been raised by the array but who were exercising in Shropshire. He noted that 'they are all there devided and the Welch party violently bent for warre, the other side not'.[74] Wood suggests a separation based on ethno-cultural lines; even at this early stage the Welsh were seen as passionate royalists.

They were seen as a distinctive group by both the royalist and parliamentarian presses, to one truly loyal, to the other ignorant and disloyal. The operation of a linguistic/ethnic divide between Welsh and English communities as a factor in matters of allegiance is best illustrated by the case of Pembrokeshire. To the parliamentary press these were 'honest Brittaines', yet the royalists termed them 'Pembrokian rebels'. The county's claim to be Welsh was

---

[73] On this theme, see Bowen, 'Representations'; Stoyle, 'Caricaturing Cymru'; idem, 'English "nationalism", Celtic particularism and the English civil war', *Historical Journal*, 43 (2000), 1113–28.

[74] Flintshire RO, D/G 3275.

disputed by the royalist newspaper *Mercurius Aulicus*, which noted that Pembrokeshire was 'the most seditious county of all Wales, or rather of England, for the inhabitants live like English corporations, very unlike the loyall Welchmen'.[75] One contemporary observed that this kind of characterization was also present within Welsh society: 'it was ... commonly spoken by the best sort of gentlemen that the Welsh were the true Brittaines, and his Majesty's best and only orthodox subjects, and Pembrokeshire for the most part Saxons and bastards'.[76] This was indeed 'little England beyond Wales', its loyalty to parliament being perceived as distinctly 'un-Welsh'.

These examples suggest that there was something about the Welsh national character that encouraged royalism. The most obvious components were the cultural and linguistic distinctiveness of the region, as well as its attachment to the Church of England. Religion, deeply informed by language, was at the heart of Welsh loyalism. Religious zeal as a motivating factor in political choice was not, it seems, the preserve of the parliamentarians alone. It was for this reason that the parliamentarians stressed the need for preaching ministers to be planted in Wales. They appear to have been correct that the 'disaffection' of the Welsh stemmed from the lack of a puritan ministry. Remedies were offered by men like Erbery and Cradock soon after the opening of the Long Parliament, but the need became more pressing as the war progressed, leading in 1646 to the parliamentary directive that itinerant ministers be ordered to Wales. It was no longer simply a question of bringing the Word of God to the ignorant, it was also a political decision to address the innate royalism which such a religious outlook promoted.[77] The Commission for the Propagation of the Gospel in Wales (1650–3) was not a spontaneous manifestation of inherent Welsh radicalism, but rather a reaction against what Major General Fleetwood termed Wales's 'cavaleering spiritt'.[78]

---

[75] Bowen, 'Representations', 366–7.
[76] *Some Particular Animadversions of Marke for Satisfaction of the Contumatious Malignant* (1646), p. 11.
[77] Bowen, 'Representations', 367–76.
[78] T. Birch (ed.), *A Collection of the State Papers of John Thurloe* (1742), ii, p. 256.

Conclusion

This brief assessment of allegiance and royalism in Wales during the first Civil War suggests a remarkably coherent response from this large and diverse region which was not paralleled elsewhere in England. This particularism appears to have stemmed largely from the region's linguistic and cultural distinctiveness, and suggests parallels with Mark Stoyle's recent work on another 'particularist' region of solid royalism, Cornwall.[79] The antagonism towards Wales and the Welsh in the satirical pamphlets produced by parliamentarian presses in 1642–3 promoted a backlash from significant elements in Welsh society. Yet we should be aware that these satirical pamphlets themselves appear to have been a response to a perceived Welsh loyalism rather than simply being the creators of it. The image of the Welsh as stalwart supporters of the king found in the parliamentary pamphlets of 1641–2 was doubtless composed in part from traditional rhetoric of their allegiance to the 'British Crown', an image invoked since the accession of Henry Tudor. Indeed, this analysis would not discount the potency of this discourse of Wales's monarchical affinity in configuring patterns of loyalty. But could such ideas be sufficient explanation for the patterns of allegiance?

A more powerful and convincing explanation acknowledges the strength and influence of Welsh religious conformism in this period, and the revulsion many demonstrated towards the puritan reforms of the Long Parliament. The analysis of Welsh responses to the political tensions of the 1620s and 1630s (in Chapters 3 and 4), along with the discussion of religious policies of the 1630s (in Chapter 5), suggests that the absence of a strong puritan presence, or indeed any political discourse informed by vigorously Calvinist or anti-popish language, combined with a strong commitment to the Church of England in Wales to encourage a 'politics of conformity'. Voices of reform or opposition were muted, and we find comparative compliance with policies which engendered deep controversy and resistance elsewhere.

---

[79] M. Stoyle, *West Britons: Cornish Identities and the Early Modern British State* (Exeter, 2002).

In reconnecting the Civil War with developments earlier in the century, 'post-revisionist' scholars have recently emphasized continuities of political and religious discontent across the early Stuart period, whereby the fractured political discourses found in the language of 'court' and 'country', and the dwindling political stock of the Court in the 1620s, have direct links with the breakdown of the early 1640s. The analysis offered here suggests that such connections between the political culture of the early seventeenth century and the Civil War period may not be restricted simply to issues of opposition and dissent. In places such as Wales where resistance – especially organized resistance – to royal policies in the 1620s and 1630s is very difficult to locate, there may be important complexes of compliance and conformity which contribute to the pattern of allegiance in the Civil War. If the seeds of radicalism which germinated to produce parliamentarianism and republicanism were sown earlier in the seventeenth, or even the sixteenth, century, it is possible to make a case for placing popular royalism in a region like Wales in the context of a prevailing political culture of conformism.

The historiography of such episodes in Wales has traditionally highlighted the isolated voices of criticism and the lineages of nonconformity and parliamentarianism to a degree that has misrepresented the experience of the region during the early Stuart period. We need to explain the remarkable ubiquity of royalism in early Civil War Wales as much as the appearance of a small band of nonconformists who spoke out against the king and his religious innovations. That these nonconformists were to dominate the political scene after the ending of the wars has given them a historiographical stature out of proportion to their numbers and influence in the 1630s and early 1640s. Conversely, the majority of Welshmen who fought for the king have left little trace in the record, their papers have not survived, and the ensuing centuries have not been disposed to look upon them kindly. Yet we should accord them a prominent place in the story of Welsh politics under the early Stuarts, and seek to understand the imperatives which drove them to support Charles I, and the contexts in which they did so.

CONCLUSION: A 'WELSH POLITICS'?

Until quite recently historians have been content to accept the model of early modern Welsh politics popularized by Professor Dodd in the 1940s. Here Welsh politics is presented as a clearly identifiable phenomenon based on a distinct set of 'principles' manifesting a 'sense of national solidarity', and is recoverable largely through the speeches and actions of Welsh MPs at Westminster.[1] In a stimulating recent re-evaluation of seventeenth-century Wales, Professor Philip Jenkins challenged such a view, asserting that 'there was no such thing as Welsh politics in the seventeenth century'.[2] He argued instead that, on account of the close integration of England and Wales after the Acts of Union, Welsh politics by the seventeenth century was indistinguishable from 'British politics', and was of the same tenor as the local politics found in an English county such as Norfolk or Lancashire.[3] There was simply no specifically Welsh dimension to political life. The present study provides a good deal of support for Professor Jenkins's thesis, but episodes such as the principality's support for the king in 1642 should give us pause to suggest that things were more complex than he allowed. Indeed, his characterization of 'Welsh politics' is somewhat of a caricature, interpreting the term only in the sense of a nationalist or separatist discourse. The foregoing analysis has offered a more nuanced set of categories by which to understand Welsh political life under the early Stuarts, suggesting that we may comprehend a 'politics of

---

[1] Dodd, 'Pattern of politics', 9, 20–7, 88. It is also revealing that Dodd could identify those MPs who did or did not represent 'the mind of Wales': ibid., p. 48.

[2] P. Jenkins, 'Seventeenth century Wales: definition and identity', in B. Bradshaw and P. Roberts (eds), *British Consciousness and Identity: The Making of Britain, 1533–1707* (Cambridge, 1998), p. 215.

[3] Jenkins's view has been influential in the recent literature on Wales's position in the early modern British state: J. Morrill, 'The fashioning of Britain', in S. Ellis and S. Barber (eds), *Conquest and Union: Fashioning a British State, 1485–1725* (1995), p. 18; M. Braddick, *State Formation in Early Modern England, c.1550–1700* (Cambridge, 2000), p. 352.

the principality' without returning to Dodd's set of Welsh political principles or Jenkins's politics-as-nationalism model.

This book acknowledges that the monolithic category of Welsh politics breaks down the closer one scrutinizes the political actions of Welsh MPs and gentry governors in the Welsh shires, but it also suggests that the entity of 'Wales' did have some purchase in early modern political discourse, and that a notion of Welsh politics can be constructed from the experience of early Stuart policies in the country. We are better served by the notion of a composite regional political culture, which was integrated fully in wider political networks while retaining a certain distinctiveness which transcended mere localism. In an attempt to identify this more capacious and inclusive understanding of early modern Welsh political culture, this study suggests a multifaceted approach, examining politics at a number of discrete levels ranging from the local to the national. It does not assert that a coherent and stable Welsh political perspective was articulated by contemporaries. Rather does it suggest that the counties comprising Wales often demonstrated a shared distinctiveness in political matters, but that this was mutable and shifting rather than a fixed nationalistic position; at the core of such a political culture is the manner in which local communities in Wales interacted with the centre, especially through the institution of parliament.

The examination of elections and parliamentary business in early Stuart Wales reveals how honour, credit and the rhetoric of service were of paramount importance in understanding the moral economy of interrelationships between MPs and their constituencies. Patterns of aristocratic and gentry patronage have been seen as overriding factors in configuring the electoral landscape of early Stuart Wales, and a close examination of Welsh elections suggests ways in which conventions of reciprocity and community underwrote the exercise of political power. These notions of service and accountability were a key to structuring Welsh identities in parliament which can be recovered through an examination of local lobbying and representation. It is suggested that Dodd's limited idea of a 'Welsh interest' in parliament misses much of the subtlety and elasticity of local and regional business which members conducted there. In the Commons local identities were reflected and deployed by drawing on vocabularies of community interest and accountability which helped to legitimate and promote the causes being pursued.

The kaleidoscope of Welsh interest groups and their alliances and coalitions which were developed in promoting regional business, underlines the complex pattern of local identities present in the Commons, and suggests the need for a more comprehensive framework by which to understand the realities of political life. It is important to recognize, however, that one of the identities which could occasionally spring to life in the Commons was that of a collective Welsh presence. The rhetorical potency of presenting a cause or petition in the name of 'Wales' was noted by contemporaries, who recognized the value of claiming a wide representation of opinion to promote an issue. Sometimes such causes were wholly partisan affairs, as in the case of the petition presented in 1624 in the name of 'the inhabitants of Wales' against the lease of Welsh greenwax fines by Sir Richard Wynn. However, this petition carried only the names of fifteen Welsh MPs, and was, in fact, engineered by one of Wynn's opponents, Sir Euble Thelwall.[4] This was evidently another 'interest group' in the Commons which realized the power of claiming to represent Wales in order to further its concerns. A more genuinely representative Welsh interest group could be manufactured, as was seen in the debates on purveyance and the 'Henry VIII clause', matters which were of interest to all Welsh counties. Although 'Wales' may have been an ephemeral presence in the Commons, it was potentially a powerful one, and an analysis of early Stuart parliamentary business prior to the personal rule suggests some of the ways by which a shifting conception of broadly conceived Welsh interest groups could both fragment and coalesce.

A study of elections in early Stuart Wales brings into sharper relief a thread which runs through this book, and

---

[4] NLW, MSS 9059E/1217, 1228.

which may be characterized as a 'politics of conformity'. Unlike many electoral divisions in the early seventeenth century, Welsh constituencies showed no sign of protesting against candidates who were closely associated with the Court or its policies; nor did the Welsh hustings become occasions of ideological choice during the wars of the 1620s or in the politically charged atmosphere of 1640. Further, the analysis of prerogative financial expedients such as the forced loan and ship money demonstrates a considerable degree of compliance and obedience on the part of Welsh shires, something which has been commented upon but not explained in other studies. Similarly, the Laudian experiment caused no great reaction from the principality, while the most striking manifestation of this kind of conservative conformism may be seen in the remarkably unanimous support for the king in Wales in 1642. This study does not suggest that a static or inflexible 'politics of conformity' should be substituted for Dodd's idea of what constituted Welsh politics, but it does offer a framework within which we can comprehend Wales's experience of early Stuart policy without reducing it to a set of 'distinct political principles'.[5] The conclusion of this book suggests some of the elements which help to interpret and explain such a political culture of conformism, whilst remaining fully cognizant that we are discussing a diverse region which could often demonstrate a whole range of responses. The foregoing analysis nevertheless indicates that it is the very homogeneity of these responses which is striking, and merits a more satisfactory explanation than historians have offered hitherto.

It may be suggested that Wales's geographical position and comparative remoteness from the centre of national political power were among the more significant elements shaping its political culture. For all their internal geographical divisions and dissimilarities, the Welsh counties were on the western edge of mainland Britain and broadly the country was composed of upland pastoral communities, although we must not ignore the tracts of lowlands and the strategically

---

[5] J. G. Jones, *Early Modern Wales, c.1525–1640* (Basingstoke, 1994), p. 177, following Dodd, 'Pattern of politics'.

important urban centres found in every county. Although the Council in the Marches was intended to serve as a 'superintendant'[6] of the Welsh shires, there is evidence of the difficulties which this agency of central government experienced in imposing close supervision throughout the territories under its jurisdiction. This is seen graphically in Bridgwater's lament in 1640 that 'I live here with suche intelligence that I do not knowe what to thinke'.[7] William Vaughan of Llangyndeyrn, Carmarthenshire, referred to the Council in the Marches as 'that remote place' in 1626, while the problems of administration and control from the Marches were discussed in a different context by a parliamentary tax-collector in 1647, who described the difficulties he was facing because 'the Welch iourneyes are scattered and wilde'.[8]

If supervision from Ludlow was difficult, things in London were even worse. Welsh counties and place names were not infrequently mistaken in memoranda and official correspondence.[9] Errors, such as confusing Glamorgan with Montgomeryshire in the ship money accounts of February 1636, or placing Denbighshire in south Wales in the 1640 accounts, reflected a lack of knowledge and familiarity.[10] Conciliar perspectives on Wales's distance seeped into official directives, such as the Privy Council letters to Bridgwater of 1637 and 1639 which referred to 'those counties [of Wales] being soe farr remote'.[11] That the government was unfamiliar with the Welsh shires is indicated by maps of the west coast of Britain produced by John Norden to assist the secretary of state, Robert Cecil, around 1610. Cecil was apparently unaware that Norden's finished map wrongly labelled Glamorgan as Monmouthshire, located Radnorshire in the wrong place and placed Aberystwyth and Caernarfon in Merioneth.[12] Such 'blind-spots' were often exposed, for

[6] Huntington Library, Ellesmere 7466.
[7] TNA, SP16/466/55.
[8] W. Vaughan, *The Golden Fleece* (1626), ii. 33; BL, Add. 46,931A, fo. 79.
[9] For example, TNA, PC2/47, p. 17.
[10] TNA, SP16/314/100; 16/450/29.
[11] TNA, PC2/48, p. 121; 2/50, p. 292.
[12] TNA, MPF1/65.

example, during the military preparations of the 1620s, when it was revealed that the Privy Council did not know the strength of the trained bands in Wales.[13] Even a north Wales native like William Wynn began to adopt these perspectives after being employed in the London household of Lord Keeper Williams for some years; writing from Isleworth, Middlesex, in September 1626, he referred to the western parts of his own Caernarfonshire as 'a corner out of the worlde'.[14]

For officials in south-eastern England with a London-centred view of government and administration, the Welsh counties occupied both a geographical and informational periphery. George Owen testified to such problems in his account of Pembrokeshire when he averred that the county had been overburdened with demands by central government because they believed it to be larger than it actually was. Officials relied on Christopher Saxton's maps for their information about Wales; when 'vywed superficiallie', these made it appear that Pembrokeshire was the largest county, occupying a whole sheet to itself. This contrasted with the representation of neighbouring Cardiganshire, Carmarthenshire, Breconshire and Radnorshire, which were gathered together on another sheet. This gave the impression that the 'poore countrey' of Pembrokeshire could shoulder a greater part of central government demands. Owen concluded plaintively, 'I would hartely wishe theire honours would be truelye and throwely enformed of the state thereof'.[15] This sentiment was surely not shared by the inhabitants of the other shires. This is not to say that the Welsh gentry and those beneath them were correspondingly ignorant of London or wider political events. There is abundant evidence that Welsh communities were fully aware of the most recent national news and gossip and had strong links with powerful courtiers and influential families in the capital and elsewhere in England.[16] It seems, however, that they were more aware of developments in London than the

[13] TNA, SP16/6/65.
[14] NLW, MS 9061E/1436.
[15] G. Owen, *Description of Pembrokeshire*, ed. H. Owen (1892–1936), i, pp. 2–4.
[16] Bowen, thesis, 117–31.

London government was of them, and this study suggests that it was advantageous for them to have kept it that way.

Remoteness from the political centre appears to have had a bearing on the Welsh experience of the financial levies of the early Stuart era and perhaps helped to mitigate their impact. Although we do not possess enough detailed studies of the Welsh economy in this period to allow accurate comparisons to be made, it appears as though the Welsh counties were under-assessed in terms of taxation and other financial demands made by the Jacobean and Caroline authorities. Although the Welsh only became liable for regular taxation in the Tudor era, they learned quickly from their English counterparts the possibilities of evasion and under-assessment which helped to undermine the yield of parliamentary subsidies.[17] On the 1545/6 subsidy, for example, Caernarfonshire produced some 842 taxpayers, yet by 1597/8 this figure had fallen to 211. The 1545/6 subsidy in the county yielded £253, but this had fallen to £73 by the end of Elizabeth's reign, and Caernarfonshire was only paying around £49 per subsidy in the 1620s; this decline was even more significant in a period of rampant inflation and in spite of the fact that the later subsidies were taxed at heavier rates.[18] The London authorities seem to have been poorly apprised of the economic potential of the Welsh counties and they were more reliant on information provided by, and the administrative performance of, the gentry governors of this distant region compared with shires closer to the capital. As a consequence, relative under-assessment combined with the country's remoteness to produce a situation in which the demands of the Stuart state do not appear to have pressed sufficiently heavily on the Welsh taxpayers to cause the resentment, alienation and politicization apparent elsewhere in the kingdom. For example, it appears that Merioneth never paid anything towards the forced loan, and the pressure from the Council for payment

[17] H. A. Lloyd, *The Gentry of South-West Wales* (Cardiff, 1968), pp. 25–6; M. Braddick, *Parliamentary Taxation in 17th Century England* (Woodbridge, 1994).

[18] E. G. Jones, 'Caernarvonshire subsidy roll, 1597/8', *BBCS*, 8 (1935–7), 336–44; R. Stephens, 'Gwynedd, 1528–1547' (Ph.D. thesis, University of California, 1975), 83, 146; S. Healy, 'Oh, what a lovely war? War, taxation and public opinion in England, 1624–29', *Canadian Journal of History*, 38 (2003), 452–5.

was minimal. This is perhaps not surprising, however, when we consider the paltry sum involved (*c.* £250) which was probably not worth pursuing.[19] The fact that the official assessments for the yield of the loan contained a blank space for Merioneth could not have helped matters, but this again seems to reflect the poor informational awareness of the condition of Wales on the part of central administrators.[20]

Such factors appear to have encouraged a culture of evasion among the Welsh gentry which is well brought out in the Wynn correspondence dealing with the demands of the 1620s. Here we encounter what may be characterized as the creative use of a 'rhetoric of poverty' which was deployed in communications with central authorities, which were at best sketchily informed about the condition of the Welsh shires and the potential burdens they could bear. This 'ould generall plea' of the 'extreame povertie of those remote partes' seems to have served well the taxpayers of counties like Caernarfonshire throughout the 1620s and 1630s.[21] Evocative language referring to 'theise poore and remote partes of the kingdome' may have reflected real experiences in Wales, but its general currency equally indicated opportunities which could be exploited in communications with the central government.[22] When the lord president of the Council in the Marches was commenting on the poor return on the Privy Seal loans of 1605 in Welsh counties, a Caernarfonshire man immediately responded that he 'hoped his lordshipp would not expecte out of our cuntrey such great soms as he had out of other shires within the marches, in respect wee wear generally poore'.[23]

---

[19] Similarly, a memorandum of 1622 regarding arrears of the Palatinate benevolence noted 'all Wales' to be behind with its contribution, but no concerted pressure for payment from the political centre was forthcoming: Centre for Kentish Studies, U269/1 OE1520; NLW, MS 9058E/1043. Cf. Chandaman's comments concerning the efficiency of the hearth tax, whereby greater returns from the regions were a product of more detailed surveys. This was not the case in Wales and the four northern counties of England, 'where the potential gain did not presumably appear to justify the effort': C. D. Chandaman, *The English Public Revenue, 1660–1688* (Oxford, 1975), p. 109.

[20] TNA, SP16/84/89.
[21] NLW, MS 9061E/1424.
[22] TNA, SP16/25/37.
[23] NLW, MS 9052E/335; see also NLW, Add. 465E/322.

The languages of poverty and remoteness provided a useful vocabulary in dealing with the state's demands, and when presented with calls for men and money, several Welsh counties manœuvred to present themselves as the poorest in the kingdom as a way of moderating and ameliorating the requests. Such claims were, of course, particularly effective from a region which was but dimly perceived by councillors and administrators who, for the most part, had little or no personal knowledge of Wales. Thus, the Anglesey JPs could respond to a request by the Privy Council for a greater subsidy yield with the claim that they paid as much as they could, and cited the authors of the Henrician union legislation who, 'knowing the povertie of Wales ... whereof this countie is the least & poorest', had waived the £20 property qualification for Welsh JPs.[24] The economic perceptions of pre-union Wales provided the Anglesey JPs with a useful set of precedents for alleviating the demands of the Caroline Privy Council.[25] Did a group of Flintshire petitioners in 1640 perhaps let the cat out of the bag when they mentioned that, before ship money, levies were 'small and therefore little heede & respect ... [was] taken of every particular assessment'?[26] Such an argument should not be pushed too far, however, for Welsh officeholders were well aware that their local authority depended in no small measure on the continued approbation of officials in Ludlow and London: the interests of the central and local elites were interdependent rather than in conflict. Claims of indigence rarely extended into full non-compliance, and acceptable administrative performance was essential for continued tenure as a justice. The suggestion offered here is that the language of poverty found in communications with the centre may have helped to circumscribe, and limit the scale of, financial demands in the first instance.

To suggest that the Welsh squirearchy may have helped to

[24] TNA, SP16/25/37.
[25] It is worth noting that, as early as Elizabeth's reign, gentlemen like David Lewis and George Owen were complaining that the waiving of the property qualification for Welsh JPs needed to be rethought as it no longer reflected economic realities: TNA, SP12/107/4; Owen, *Pembrokeshire*, iii, pp. 54, 58, 117.
[26] NLW, Great Sessions 4/982/8/5.

mitigate the impact of the burdens of the 1620s and 1630s is not, however, to deny that many communities experienced severe hardship or that the scale of the demands for the wars of the 1620s and for ship money were often heavy. In the 1620s there were clear signs in places such as Pembrokeshire and Monmouthshire of an attachment to taxation by parliament, and ship money evidently represented a different scale of imposition and engendered deep resentment because it reached sections of society never before burdened with taxes. The persistence of rating disputes and the experience of the final writ of 1639–40 show clearly the disruptive capability of ship money in Wales. Yet there are doubts about the degree to which even ship money exploited the real wealth of the region, especially when we compare Welsh assessments with those of neighbouring counties in England.

In addition to this financial aspect, the scale of recruitment in Wales for the military expeditions of the 1620s, though significant and yet barely noticed by historians, was not of the same order as the much more disruptive impressment for the Irish wars of the 1590s. It also seems that geography helped to spare Wales the most contentious aspects of war in the 1620s, namely, billeting and martial law which blighted the southern coasts of England and generated some of the most vehement opposition to Charles's and Buckingham's war. The region's geography may also have helped to secure compliance in the payment of ship money, as the country's long coastline and problems with piracy in the 1630s rendered the levies more palatable to the people of Wales.

Such conclusions about Wales's relationship with the political centre in this period are particularly significant when we consider Tom Cogswell's recent reappraisal of the key role played by an intrusive and burdensome early Stuart state in engendering the resentment and bitterness which helped to alienate many communities from the king by the early 1640s.[27] Although the state was certainly not an abstraction for those Welshmen burdened with ship money and

---

[27] T. Cogswell, *Home Divisions: Aristocracy, the State and Provincial Conflict* (Manchester, 1998), pp. 305–18.

military levies, it had not perhaps alienated communities in Wales to the degree experienced in Cogswell's Leicestershire. It may be that remoteness from the political centre mitigated the negative effects of Charles's financial and military demands, and that this helped to keep the stock of the monarchy at a higher level than was so in many regions of England. The early Stuart state was certainly a reality for the gentry governors of Wales, but they seemed able to accept it on their own terms to a greater degree than their fellows in many English shires. Brendan Bradshaw's arguments that the Tudor 'revolution' in government and religion was mediated and modified by the Welsh gentry in line with their own predilections can, perhaps, be extended to encompass their experience of the Stuart state too.[28] This goes some way to answer Professor Jenkins's call for a better understanding of how Welsh elites accepted all elements of the British state system but 'shaped them to fit local concerns'.[29] The British state may have been more acceptable in early Stuart Wales because local interests mediated and mitigated its impact on issues such as prerogative taxation more successfully than elsewhere.

In highlighting the role of local Welsh elites and their relationship with the centre in this period, it is relevant to note the degree to which aristocratic influence failed to make a significant impression on the political culture of Wales beyond the southern and eastern lowlands, something which is reflected in the electoral topography of the principality. The earls of Worcester were the only resident aristocratic family in Wales for the majority of this period, and it has been suggested in Chapter 3 that their role in enjoining compliance with the government's demands in Glamorgan and Monmouthshire during the 1620s was not inconsiderable. Beyond these counties, however, the absence of aristocratic power may also have diluted the immediacy of conciliar authority in Wales, because the Council could not call on many resident peers and lords

---

[28] B. Bradshaw, 'The English Reformation and identity formation in Wales and Ireland', in Bradshaw and Roberts, *British Consciousness and Identity*, pp. 72–83.

[29] Jenkins, 'Seventeenth century Wales', p. 235.

lieutenant. In a period when government and communication through the aristocracy were important for the implementation of policy, this meagre aristocratic influence served to temper the Privy Council's capacity for compulsion in Wales.[30] A weak aristocratic presence may also have insulated Wales somewhat from the political divisions engendered by Buckingham's hegemony in the 1620s. Aristocratic dissatisfaction with the favourite and his policies was channelled in several English counties through the patronal networks of leading magnates. The earl of Warwick, for example, was a leading opponent of Buckingham and encouraged more widespread resistance to government policy in Essex where his influence was strong.[31]

Another component of this complex political culture of conformity was the discourse of Britishness and Welsh antiquity which helped to legitimate the rule of the monarch and the Church of England in Wales. Although too much can be made of abstract loyalty to the Tudors being transferred to the Stuarts, it appears that the identification of the Welsh with the ancient Britons had important implications for the political culture of the early Stuart principality. The Anglo-Scottish union of 1603 was interpreted by Welsh MPs like Sir William Maurice of Clenennau primarily in terms of Welsh prophecies of the reunification of an ancient British kingdom. It does indeed appear that Welsh loyalties to the Crown were strengthened by this identification of the Stuarts as inheritors of the mantle of British kings. In the polarized atmosphere of civil war, Welsh attachment to ideas of Britishness featured prominently, for example in satirical parliamentary publications which spoke slightingly of Welsh pretensions to be 'old Brittaines'.[32] A more positive portrait of the connections between the Welsh people and the British monarchy is found in a striking description of an entertainment given to Prince Charles at Raglan by the earl of Worcester in 1642. The entertainment was redolent of

---

[30] K. Sharpe, 'Crown, parliament and locality: government and communication in early Stuart England', *English Historical Review*, 101 (1986), 321–50.

[31] R. Cust, *The Forced Loan and English Politics, 1626–1628* (Oxford, 1987), pp. 198–201, 229–32.

[32] *The Welch-mans Publike Recantation* (1642), sig. A3v.

Welsh pride in a British heritage, and the visiting prince was assured that

> It is the glory of the Britaines that we are the true remaining and only one people of this land, and we have alwayes been true in our affections to our king and countrey ... We know no sun that can with the influence of royall beames cherish and warme our true British hearts, but the sun of our gracious sovereigne ... In what true and ancient Britaines may serve you, you may command us to our uttermost strength, our lives and fortunes to be ready to assist you.[33]

These examples suggest that Jenkins's observation that there was 'a definite sense of ethnic self-recognition in seventeenth century Wales and this had political ramifications' should be given greater weight than he allows in fostering a distinct political culture of loyalism.[34] Although ideas of a discrete cultural identity did not translate into a separatist political agenda, the fact that they fostered discourses of assimilation and integration appears to offer significant insights into the nature of Welsh politics in this period and to underline the fact that we are dealing with something distinctive.

If the idea of Britishness adds another lexical layer to the politics of conformity, it equally reveals a cultural cleavage in the British state with political consequences. Some English MPs were ready to traduce the Welsh as 'the most base, pesantly perfidious people of the world', while discussions early in James I's reign about the abolition of the Council in the Marches of Wales stressed that its removal would 'make the Welsh men despised by the English ... and so will ere longe revive the aunceient enmyitie betweene these two people and bring all to the old confusion againe'.[35] Even the chief justice of King's Bench, Sir Thomas Richardson, could be accused in 1633 of 'words ... in reproach & derogacon of the peoples or subiects in generall of the principallitie of Wales'.[36] Although Wales had been integrated successfully in the British state, simmering traces of cultural and ethnic division could still be discerned, and they appear to have been

---

[33] *A Loyal and Loving Speech ... at Raglan Castle* (1642), pp. 1–2.
[34] Jenkins, 'Seventeenth century Wales', p. 221.
[35] TNA, SP14/24/23; 14/19/35.
[36] TNA, PC2/43, p. 59.

important in configuring Welsh allegiances in the early stages of the Civil War when anti-Welsh squibs began rolling off the London presses. Mark Stoyle has suggested that Charles I's claims to represent an inclusive and culturally heterogeneous British monarchy, rather than the parliamentarians' 'narrowly English interest', encouraged the royalism of the culturally and linguistically distinct Cornish.[37] His observation may also be relevant to the Welsh who, like the Cornish, became passionate royalists.[38]

This notion of Britishness was related to an even more significant aspect of Welsh political culture which has been almost entirely ignored by historians: the strong attachment to an inculturated Church of England. Emphasis on the beginnings of Welsh nonconformity has led us seriously to underestimate the affection in Wales for the Church and its influence on political culture. Important here was the successful fusion of the Elizabethan religious settlement with powerful native traditions of a distinctive British Church by scholars such as Bishop Richard Davies; this helped to forge a national institution whose potency and popularity in the early seventeenth century have not been sufficiently recognized. Although wary of collapsing Laudianism and Prayer Book conformity into a single category, this study has argued that there are important parallels between the absence of religious protest in Wales during the 1630s and Welsh affection for the Anglican Church and its Prayer Book which became proverbial in the polemical literature of the early 1640s. The Welsh petitions of 1642 suggest how this religious complexion helped to give a particularist, rather than a separatist, dimension to the political culture of the country.

Perhaps even more important is the degree to which the tenor of early seventeenth-century Welsh spirituality presented formidable barriers to the reception and propagation of puritan ideas before the Civil Wars. The large number of books and articles written on the progenitors of

---

[37] M. Stoyle, *West Britons: Cornish Identities and the Early Modern British State* (Exeter, 2002), pp. 150, 50–65.
[38] See the comments in T. Thornton, 'Dynasty and territory in the early modern period: the princes of Wales and their western British inheritance', *WHR*, 20 (2000–1), 24–5.

the puritan movement in Wales has obscured the fact that these puritans were few in number and, before 1640, had little influence. The absence of a radical discourse of puritanism is important in configuring the notion of a political culture of Welsh conformity, and helps to explain more satisfactorily the muted resistance to early Stuart policies in Wales. In recent studies, opposition to the wars of the 1620s and to prerogative taxation, resistance to ship money and the more general opposition to Caroline rule, have all been linked intimately to a critical puritan ethic.[39] The comparative lack of such a body of godly opinion in Wales, therefore, seems highly significant in accounting for the comparative quiescence of the principality. Puritanism was also, of course, a central element of parliamentarianism, whose weakness in Wales during the early 1640s seems in no small measure due to the fact that the country was not a fertile ground for the godly.

Conformity presents evidential problems; by its very nature it does not produce much by way of historical records. Judith Maltby has shown that 'prayer book conformists' were most visible during periods of persecution such as 1640-2, when they were driven publicly to defend their deeply held beliefs and traditions.[40] Examining the evidence for the political culture of early seventeenth-century Wales also requires some reading against the grain, in order to account for what was not being said as well as what was being said. Rather than discussing isolated episodes of dissent and opposition, this study argues that we need to better explain the comparative compliance of the Welsh shires with the policies of the early Stuarts, and it suggests that a political culture of conformity may be a fruitful way forward. Not that it was a coherent creed, or was articulated consistently through informal or institutional bodies, but it does provide

---

[39] For example, Cust, *Forced Loan*; T. Cogswell, *The Blessed Revolution* (Cambridge, 1989); Gill, 'Ship money'; A. Hughes, 'Thomas Durgard and his circle in the 1630s: a parliamentary–puritan connection?', *Historical Journal*, 29 (1986), 771–93; J. Fielding, 'Opposition to the personal rule of Charles I: the diary of Robert Woodford, 1637–41', *Historical Journal*, 31 (1988), 769–88.

[40] J. Maltby, *Prayer Book and People in Elizabethan and Early Stuart England* (Cambridge, 1998).

an useful interpretative matrix of religious, political and cultural traditions through which we may better understand how the demands of the early Stuart state were experienced and interpreted in Wales.

Such findings have wider implications for early modern local and regional historiographies. As Tom Cogswell has noted, the attack on the localist thesis of scholars such as Alan Everitt has undermined the very vitality of local studies in this period.[41] Supporting Cogswell's call 'to return the prominence and lustre to local studies', this book urges the continued utility of local, regional history, in a manner which moves beyond the insularities of the county community model, in order to test some of the larger hypotheses of recent historical works. In acknowledging the interdependence of locality and centre through a dialogue of parliamentary, financial and religious discourses, the success of Wales's integration in the English body politic by the early seventeenth century can be clearly discerned. Nonetheless, it is argued that this integration did not preclude a degree of particularism in the political culture of Wales, or that a distinctive Welsh 'accent' can still be detected in the political languages of the early modern British state.

In studying a region rather than a county, this book has also suggested that the politics of cultural regions in the early modern British state repays further investigation. This is especially the case with areas beyond the south-east of England which are usually considered to be integrated unproblematically in the unitary state. In an unjustly neglected article of 1981, Brian Quintrell explored some of the ways in which Lancashire's relations with the Privy Council between 1570 and 1640 demonstrated the latter's myopia when it came to demanding taxes and enjoining compliance.[42] Furthermore, Mark Stoyle's pioneering researches into the political ramifications of Cornishness and Cornwall's comparative isolation from the centre offer new opportunities for reinterpreting the nature of centre–

---

[41] Cogswell, *Home Divisions*, pp. 1–9.
[42] B. Quintrell, 'Government in perspective: Lancashire and the Privy Council, 1570–1640', *Transactions of the Historical Society of Lancashire and Cheshire* 13 (1981), 35–62.

locality relationships in the peripheries of the English state and their implications for understanding regional political cultures. Tim Thornton has also offered a reappraisal of the particularism of Cheshire during the Tudor period, making important suggestions as to how 'strong local identities did not necessarily mean that localist or even separatist opposition were dominant in politics'.[43] Many of these themes find echoes in these pages. Distinct historical traditions and linguistic topographies exacerbate the apparent differentiation of Wales, whereas the experience of early Stuart politics emphasizes the powerful integrative and conservative continuities which characterize the Welsh reaction to Jacobean and Caroline rule. Studies of the manner in which political cultures on the peripheries of the early modern English state adapted to, and were altered by, the demands of the centre add another dimension to our understanding of the expansion of state power in the early modern period.

Early Stuart Wales has revealed itself as a somewhat anomalous and contradictory component of the wider realm, at once intimately connected to the political and administrative rhythms of its more powerful English partner, yet manifesting unique qualities that made it distinct. Although 'Welsh politics' remains a nebulous and problematic idea, it is contended that such a phenomenon is recoverable from the early seventeenth century. This ought not to be seen as the unified voice of a nation, but rather as the composite and shifting responses by a culturally differentiated region to the policies of the centre. Wales was very closely integrated with the kingdom of England, but was never completely subsumed in it, and its political culture reflects the extent to which Wales had become a part of a larger governmental entity without sacrificing its peculiar character.

---

[43] T. Thornton, *Cheshire and the Tudor State, 1480–1540* (Woodbridge, 2000), p. 62.

BIBLIOGRAPHY

MANUSCRIPT SOURCES

(i) The National Archives, Kew

C2/ChasI	Chancery pleadings, Charles I
C54	Close rolls
C66	Patent rolls
C115	Chancery Masters' Exhibits, Scudamore MSS
C193/12/2	Forced loan commission book, 1626–7
C205/14/11	Papers of commission of enquiry, south Wales, 1635–6
C212	Lists of subsidy commissioners
C219	Original writs and returns of members to parliament
C231/5	Crown Office, docquet book, 1629–1643
E101	Exchequer, various accounts
E112	Exchequer, bills and answers
E134	Exchequer, depositions by commission
E178	Special commissions of the Exchequer
E179	Lay subsidy rolls and assessments of benevolences/forced loans
E331	Bishops Institution Books, Series A, 1566–1660
E351	Pipe Office, declared accounts
E359	Pipe Office, enrolled subsidy accounts
E401	Exchequer receipts
E403	Exchequer payments
E407	Exchequer miscellanea
HCA14	High Court of Admiralty, miscellaneous drafts
HCA30	High Court of Admiralty, examinations
LR2	Land Revenue, miscellaneous
LS13/279	Lord Stewards' department, purveyance material
MPF1/65	John Norden's map of western England and Ireland
30/53	Gifts and Deposits, Powis MSS
PC2	Privy Council registers, 1631–42
PSO5/2	Privy Seal Office, docquet book, 1601–9
PROB11	Prerogative Court of Canterbury, wills
SO1/1–3	Signet Office, 'Irish letter books'
SO3/4	Signet Office, docquet book, 1608–10
SP12	State Papers, Elizabeth I
SP14	State Papers, James I

SP16	State Papers, Charles I
SP19	Papers of the Committee for the Advance of Money
SP23	Papers of the Committee for Compounding with Delinquents
SP28	Commonwealth Exchequer Papers
SP38	State Papers, Docquets
SP46	State Papers, Supplementary
SP63	State Papers, Ireland
STAC8	Star Chamber cases, James I

(ii) British Library, London

Additional MSS

5,847	Cole papers, copy of Welsh petition on purveyance, 1604
10,609	Breconshire lieutenancy papers, 1608–1637
11,045	Scudamore papers
12,496	Papers of Sir Julius Caesar
14,828	Parliamentary diary of Framlington Gawdy, 1641
18,597	Parliamentary diary of Sir Walter Earle, 1624
34,274	Miscellaneous letters
37,817	Papers of Sir Edward Nicholas
64,882–64,981	Papers of Sir John Coke
70,001–3, 70,062, 70,106–9	Papers of Sir Robert Harley

Harleian MSS

163–4	Parliamentary diary of Sir Simonds D'Ewes, 1641–2
286	Miscellaneous state papers
477,479	Parliamentary diary of John Moore, 1640–2
1314	Papers on the Anglo-Scottish Union, 1606
1970	Miscellaneous tracts including Welsh material
2125	Civil War MSS
4220	Book of fines for the Council in the Marches of Wales, 1616–37
4931	Miscellaneous parliamentary and state papers

Lansdowne MSS

216	Tract on the government of Wales

Cotton MSS
Vitellius C.i.   Documents relating to the Council in the Marches of Wales
Titus B.viii   Council of Wales papers

Egerton MSS
2882   Register of the Council in the Marches of Wales, 1586–1644

Microfilm
M.485   Hatfield House, Cecil MSS

(iii) National Library of Wales, Aberystwyth

National Library of Wales MSS
1546(iii)	Papers relating to Anglesey
1572C	Transcripts by Angharad Llwyd, with some original papers
1575B	Extracts from Lleweni papers
1595E	Miscellaneous papers, including Flintshire correspondence
1600E	Kinmel MSS, including Flintshire material
5390D	Commonplace book of Sir Thomas Salusbury
5666C	'A Politike Discourse', by Sir John Stradling (1625)
6285E	Copy of Flintshire lieutenancy papers from Mostyn Hall
9052E-9069E	Wynn of Gwydir papers
17012D	Llangibby Castle MSS
17156D	Gwysaney papers
Add. 339F	Deeds and documents of the Council in the Marches of Wales
Add. 465E–467E	Wynn of Gwydir papers

Local Collections and Family Papers
Badminton	Monmouthshire papers including accounts for rebuilding Chepstow bridge
Bodewryd	Papers of Edwards family, Bodewryd, Anglesey
Brogyntyn (Clenennau)	Papers of Sir William Maurice and Sir John Owen
Bronwydd	Pembrokeshire papers
Bute	Papers of William Herbert, Glamorgan

Carreglwyd Series I and II	Correspondence of Griffith family and papers concerning Anglesey
Chirk Castle B	Denbighshire quarter sessions papers
Chirk Castle E, F	Correspondence and papers of the Myddleton family, Denbighshire
Duchy of Cornwall	Duchy of Cornwall lands in Wales
Edward Owen Deeds 39	Bromfield and Yale material
Great Sessions 4	Courts of Great Sessions, Gaol files
Ll/Ch/4	Llandaff Cathedral, Chapter Act Book.
Llanfair-Brynodol C	Correspondence of Griffiths of Llanfair, Caernarfonshire
Lleweni	Papers of the Salusbury family of Lleweni, Denbighshire
Peniarth 410 (ii)	Merioneth material
Peniarth 430E	Merioneth ship money assessments, 1637–8
Peniarth Estate CA/52–3	Papers re-ship money, Flintshire, 1635
SA/Misc.	Church in Wales MSS, St Asaph miscellaneous SD/Ch/B/4
St David's Cathedral	Chapter Act Book, 1621–1660
SD/Probate	Original wills, St David's diocese
Tredegar Park	Papers of the Morgan family of Tredegar, Monmouthshire.
Wynnstay	Denbighshire MSS

(iv) Bodleian Library, Oxford

Bankes 43	Papers of Sir John Bankes, attorney general
Carte 4	Ormonde papers
Rawlinson D932, D1099	Parliamentary diary of Sir John Holland, 1641
Rawlinson D1100	Parliamentary diary of Sir Thomas Holland, 1624
Tanner 58–60, 66	Lenthall correspondence, 1640s
Tanner 91	Miscellaneous collection
Tanner 169	Commonplace book of Sir Stephen Powle
Tanner 392	Parliamentary diary of Sir Thomas Holland, 1624

(v) Caernarfonshire Record Office, Caernarfon

XQS	Caernarfonshire quarter sessions records

(vi) Cardiff Central Library

1.223	'A Caveat for Subjects' by Thomas Bassett (1649)
3.42	Commonplace book of Philip Powell

BIBLIOGRAPHY

4.56	Gwysaney papers
4.58	Wynn of Gwydir papers
4.69	Wynn of Gwydir papers
5.50	Flintshire miscellanea, copies of lieutenancy material

(vii) Carmarthenshire Record Office, Carmarthen

Dynevor Muniments, Box 154/1	Correspondence of Rice and Mansell families

(viii) Centre for Kentish Studies, Maidstone

U269/1	Cranfield MSS

(ix) Cheshire and Chester Archives, Chester

ZM/L/2/277	Mayors' papers, schedule of ship money assessments, 1635

(x) Denbighshire Record Office, Ruthin

BD/A/1	Denbigh corporation minute book
BD/A/22–3	Letters to Denbigh corporation
PD/78/1/39	Churchwarden accounts of Llanynys, Denbighshire

(xi) East Sussex Record Office, Lewes

GLY 554, 559	Glynde Place MSS, Papers of the Trevors of Trevalyn and Plas Teg

(xii) Flintshire Record Office, Hawarden

D/DM/271	Civil War pamphlet collection of David Pennant
D/G	Papers and correspondence of Trevor family of Trevalyn and Plas Teg
D/GW	Davies of Gwysaney papers
D/HE/733	Paper supporting bill for free trade of Welsh cloth, 1621
D/PT	Papers of Trevor family of Trevalyn and Plas Teg

(xiii) Glamorgan Record Office, Cardiff

D/D/Ess. 4/1–4	Informations before Glamorgan JPs, 1642
D/DF/244	Letters of the Seys family, Glamorgan
P/38/CW/1	Parish register of Llantrithyd

(xiv) Gloucester Public Library
16,524　　　　　Smyth of Nibley MSS

(xv) Guildhall Library, London
15842, 15874　　Papers of the Haberdashers' Company
25475/1　　　　Papers re – the collection for St Paul's, 1630s

(xvi) Gwent Record Office, Cwmbran
Misc. MS 648　　Letter book of Richard Herbert

(xvii) Hereford Cathedral Library
6450/3　　　　　Transcript survey of the diocese of Hereford, 1640/1

(xviii) Herefordshire Record Office, Hereford
AE62/1　　　　　Parish register of Presteigne, Radnorshire

(xix) Houghton Library, Harvard University
Eng. 980　　　　Parliamentary diary of William Spring, 1624

(xx) House of Lords Record Office, London
Main Papers, 1614–1647
Parchment Collection
Original Acts

(xxi) Henry E. Huntington Library, San Marino, California
Ellesmere　　　　Papers of John Egerton, 1st earl of Bridgwater

(xxii) Lambeth Palace Library, London
Misc. 943　　　　Papers of Archbishop William Laud

(xxiii) Library of the University College of North Wales, Bangor
Baron Hill　　　　Papers of the Bulkeley family, Anglesey

(xxiv) Longleat House, Wiltshire
Whitelocke II　　Papers of Sir James Whitelocke

(xxv) Northamptonshire Record Office, Northampton
Finch-Hatton 50　Parliamentary diary of John Pym, 1624

(xxvi) Oswestry Town Hall, Oswestry
A75/1/9, 12　　　Papers regarding the Welsh wool trade, 1620s

(xxvii) Pembrokeshire Record Office, Haverfordwest
Haverfordwest Corporation   Corporation muniments, and papers of St Mary's church
D/RTP/HAM/96   Haverfordwest expenditure on weapons, 1619

(xxviii) Sheffield City Archives
Wentworth Woodhouse
Collection, Str. P.   Papers of the earl of Strafford

(xxix) Shropshire Archives, Shrewsbury
212/364   Bridgwater correspondence
1831/6   Minute Book of Shrewsbury Drapers' Company, 1607–1740
1831/10   Petitions of Shrewsbury Drapers' Company
1831/20   Miscellaneous box including letters of John Prowde to Shrewsbury Drapers' Company, 1621

(xxx) Somerset Record Office, Taunton
DD/L 1/55/1   Luttrell papers, draft of Minehead harbour bill, 1610

(xxxi) Tenby Museum, Pembrokeshire
TEM/Box 16   Account of money disbursed by corporation, 1626

(xxxii) Warwickshire Record Office, Warwick
CR2017/TP   Feilding of Newnham Paddox MSS

(xxxiii) West Glamorgan Archives Service, Swansea
B2   Swansea corporation, Book of Orders
D2   St Mary's, Swansea, churchwarden accounts, 1558–1694

Printed primary sources

Place of publication is London unless otherwise stated.

(i) Contemporary books and tracts
Davies, E., *Millitary Directions, or the Art of Trayning* (1618).
Dodderidge, Sir John, *The History of the Ancient and Moderne Estate of the Principality of Wales* (1630).
Hacket, John, *Scrinia Reserata* (1693), 2 vols.

Harry, George Owen, *The Genealogy of the High and Mighty Monarch, James* (1604).
Heylyn, Peter, *Cyprianus Anglicus* (1671), 2 vols.
Heyward, J., *A Treatise of Union* (1604).
Holland, Robert, *Basilicon Doron ... Translated into the True British Tongue* (1604).
Jones, Thomas, *Mercy Triumphing Over Judgement, or a Warning for Sabbath-Breakers* (1640).
Lloyd, David, *Memoires* (1662).
Perrot, Sir James, *An Invitation Unto Prayer* (1624).
Prynne, William, *Canterburies Doome* (1644).
Stradling, Sir John, *Beati Pacifici: A Divine Poem Written to the Kings Most Excellent Maiestie* (1623).
Thornborough, J., *A Discourse Plainely Proving the Evident Utilitie and Urgent Necessitie of the Desired Happie Union* (1604).
Vaughan, William, *The Spirit of Detraction ... in Seven Circles* (1611).
— *The Golden Fleece* (1626).
Williams, Griffith, *The Delights of the Saints* (1622).

(ii) Anonymous works
A Loyal and Loving Speech ... at Raglan Castle (1642).
An Answer in Just Vindication of Some Religious and Worthy Gentlemen of Pembrokeshire Against a Scandalous Pamphlet Published by One Iohn Poyer (1646).
The Humble Petition of Many Hundred Thousands Inhabiting Within the Thirteene Shires of Wales (1642).
The Humble Petition of the Gentry, Clergy and Other Inhabitants, Subscribed of ... the Sixe Shires of Northwales (1642).
His Majesties Speech to the Inhabitants of Denbigh and Flintshire, 27 September 1642 (1642).
The Miraculous and Happie Union of England and Scotland (1604).
A Petition of the Gentry, Ministers and Freeholders of the County of Flint (1642).
Some Particular Animadversions of Marke for Satisfaction of the Contumatious Malignant (1646).
Two Petitions Presented to the Kings Most Excellent Majestie at Yorke, the First of August 1642 (York, 1642).
The Welshmens Prave Resolution: In Defence of Her King, Her Prittish Parliament, and Her Country Against te Malignant Party (1642).

(iii) Later editions and compilations
Acts of the Privy Council of England, 1618–1631 (1929–64), 11 vols.
'Llanllyfni papers', *Archaeologia Cambrensis*, 3rd series, 6 (1863).
Ballinger, J. (ed.), *Calendar of Wynn (of Gwydir) Papers, 1515–1690* (Cardiff, 1926).

Birch, T. (comp.), *The Court and Times of Charles I* (1848), 2 vols.
Birch, T. (ed.), *A Collection of the State Papers of John Thurloe* (1742), 7 vols.
Bowen, L. (ed.), *Family and Society in Early Stuart Glamorgan: The Household Accounts of Sir Thomas Aubrey of Llantrithyd, c.1565–1641* (Llandybïe, 2006).
Calendar of State Papers, Domestic.
Calendar of State Papers, Venetian.
Carte, T. (ed.), *A Collection of Original Letters and Papers Concerning the Affairs of England ... Found Among the Duke of Ormonde's Papers* (1739), 2 vols.
Clark, G. T. (ed.), *Limbus Patrum Morganiae et Glamorganiae* (1886).
Coates, W. H., Young, A. S., and Snow, V. F. (eds), *The Private Journals of the Long Parliament* (New Haven, 1982–1992), 3 vols.

Commons Journals
Curll, E., *The Life of ... Robert Price, esq.* (1734).
'D.R.T.', 'The registers of Trefeglwys', *Montgomeryshire Collections*, 32 (1902).
Fincham, K. (ed.), *Visitation Articles and Injunctions of the Early Stuart Church* (Woodbridge, 1994–8), 2 vols.
Foster, E. R. (ed.), *Proceedings in Parliament, 1610* (New Haven, 1966), 2 vols.
Galloway, B. R., and Levack, B. P. (eds), *The Jacobean Union: Six Tracts of 1604* (Scottish History Society, 4th series, 21, 1985).
Gardiner, S. R. (ed.), *Notes of Debates in the House of Lords ... 1624 and 1626* (Camden Soc., NS, 24, 1879).
Green, M. A. E. (ed.), *The Diary of John Rous* (Camden Soc., 66, 1856).
Hawarde, J., *Les Reportes del Cases in Camera Stellata, 1593–1609*, ed. W. P. Baildon (1894).
Hyde, Edward, earl of Clarendon, *The History of the Rebellion and Civil Wars in England*, ed. W. D. Macray (Oxford, 1888), 6 vols.
J. Jacobs, (ed.) *Epistolae Ho-Elianae: The Familiar Letters of James Howell* (1892), 2 vols.
Jansson, M., and Bidwell, W. B. (eds), *Proceedings in Parliament, 1625* (New Haven, 1987).
Jansson, M. (ed.), *Proceedings in Parliament, 1614 (House of Commons)* (Philadelphia, 1989).
Jansson, M. and Bidwell, W.B. (eds), *Proceedings in Parliament, 1626* (New Haven, 1992–6), 4 vols.
Jenkins, P. (ed.), '"The sufferings of the clergy": the Church in Glamorgan during the Interregnum, part two: the account of Francis Davies', *Journal of Welsh Ecclesiastical History*, 4 (1987).
Jones, E. D., 'The Brogyntyn Welsh manuscripts', *NLWJ*, 6 (1949–50).
Jones, E. G. (ed.), *Exchequer Proceedings (Equity) Concerning Wales, Henry VIII–Elizabeth* (Cardiff, 1939).

Jones, T. I. Jeffreys (ed.), *Exchequer Proceedings Concerning Wales in Tempore James I* (Cardiff, 1955).
Keeler, M. F., Johnson, R. C., Cole, M. J. and Bidwell, W. B. (eds), *Commons Debates, 1628* (New Haven, 1977–8), 4 vols.
Larkin, J. F. and Hughes, P. L. (eds.) *Stuart Royal Proclamations* (Oxford, 1973–83), 2 vols.
Laud, William, *The Works of William Laud*, ed. J. Bliss and W. Scott (Oxford, 1847–60), 7 vols.
Lewis, Rice, 'A Breviat of Glamorgan', ed. William Rees, *South Wales and Monmouth Record Society*, 3 (1954).
Lloyd, J. Y. W. (ed.), 'Survey of the Lordship of Bromfield and Yale', *Original Documents (Archaeologia Cambrensis Supplement)* (1877).
Long, C.E. (ed.), *Diary of the Marches of the Royal Army* (Camden Soc., 74, 1859).

Lords Journals
McGrath, P. (ed.), *Records Relating to the Society of Merchant Venturers and the City of Bristol in the Seventeenth Century* (Bristol Record Society, 17, 1951).
Matthews, J. H. (ed.), *Records of the County Borough of Cardiff* (Cardiff, 1898–1911), 6 vols.
McClure, N. E. (ed.), *Chamberlain Letters* (Philadelphia, 1939), 2 vols.
Notestein, W., Relf, F. H., and Simpson, H. (eds), *Commons Debates, 1621* (New Haven, 1935), 7 vols.
Owen, George, *The Description of Pembrokeshire*, ed. H. Owen (1892–1936), 4 vols.
Owen, H. (ed.), 'The diary of Bulkeley of Dronwy, Anglesey, 1630–1636', *Transactions of the Anglesey Antiquarian Society* (1937).
Perrot, Sir James, *The Chronicle of Ireland, 1584–1608*, ed. H. Wood (Dublin, 1933).
Phillips, J. R. S. (ed.), *The Justices of the Peace in Wales and Monmouthshire, 1541–1689* (Cardiff, 1975).
Pryce, A. I. (ed.), *The Diocese of Bangor During Three Centuries* (1929).
Roberts, S. K. (ed.), *The Letter Book of John Byrd* (South Wales Record Society, 14, 1999).
Scott, D. (ed.), '"Particular businesses" in the Long Parliament: the Hull letters, 1644–1648', in C. R. Kyle (ed.), *Parliaments, Politics and Elections, 1604–1648* (Camden Soc., 5th ser. 17, 2001).
Spedding, J., et al. (eds), *The Works of Francis Bacon* (1857–74), 14 vols.
Statutes of the Realm (1810–28), 10 vols.
Thomas, D. R. (ed.), *Y Cwtta Cyfarwydd* (1883).
Thompson, C., (ed.), *The Holles Account of Proceedings in the House of Commons in 1624* (Wivenhoe, 1985).
—— (ed.), *Walter Yonge's Diary of Proceedings in the House of Commons, 19 September 1642–7 March 1643* (Wivenhoe, 1986).

—— (ed.), *Obseruatyones of the Proceedinges in the Ple=mente held at Westeminster An⁰ Primoe et Secundo Jacobi Regis* (Wivenhoe, 1990).
Walker, J., *An Attempt Towards Recovering an Account of the Numbers and Sufferings of the Clergy* (1714), 2 vols.
Willson, D. H. (ed.), *The Parliamentary Diary of Robert Bowyer, 1606–1607* (Minneapolis, 1931).
Winwood, Ralph, *Memorials of Affairs of State* (1725), 3 vols.
W[ynne], W. W. E. (ed.), 'Documents relating to the town of Harlech', *Archaeologia Cambrensis*, 1 (1846).
Yardley, E., *Menevia Sacra*, ed. F. Green (1927).

(iv) Newsbooks
The City Scout
A Continuation of the True Diurnall
Mercurius Britanicus
The Scottish Dove
Speciall Passages
The True Informer

(v) Historical Manuscripts Commission, Reports
Hastings MSS
Mar and Kellie MSS (Supp.)
Portland MSS
Salisbury MSS
Skrine MSS
Fourth Report

SECONDARY SOURCES

Addleshaw, G. W. O., and Etchells, F., *The Architectural Setting of Anglican Worship* (1948).
Atherton, I., 'Viscount Scudamore's "Laudianism": the religious practices of the first Viscount Scudamore', *Historical Journal*, 34 (1991).
—— *Ambition and Failure in Early Stuart England: The Career of John, First Viscount Scudamore* (Manchester, 1999).
Aylmer, G. E., 'The last years of purveyance, 1610–1660', *Economic History Review*, 2nd series, 10 (1957–8).
Ballinger, J., *The Bible in Wales* (1906).
Barnes, T. G., *Somerset, 1625–1640* (Cambridge, MA, 1961).
Bowen, L., 'Wales at Westminster: parliament, principality and pressure groups, 1542–1601', *Parliamentary History*, 22 (2003).
—— 'Representations of Wales and the Welsh during the civil wars and Interregnum', *Historical Research*, 77 (2004).

Braddick, M. J., *Parliamentary Taxation in 17th Century England* (Woodbridge, 1994).
—— *State Formation in Early Modern England, c.1550–1700* (Cambridge, 2000).
Bradney, J. A., *A History of Monmouthshire* (1904–33), 4 vols.
Bradshaw, B., 'The English Reformation and identity formation in Wales and Ireland', in idem and P. R. Roberts (eds), *British Consciousness and Identity* (Cambridge, 1998).
Chandaman, C. D., *The English Public Revenue, 1660–1688* (Oxford, 1975).
Cogswell, T., 'England and the Spanish match', in R. Cust and A. Hughes (eds), *Conflict in Early Stuart England* (1989).
—— *The Blessed Revolution* (Cambridge, 1989).
—— *Home Divisions: Aristocracy, the State and Provincial Conflict* (Manchester, 1998).
Cressy, D., 'Purification, thanksgiving and the churching of women in post-Reformation England', *Past and Present*, 141 (1993).
Croft, P., 'Parliament, purveyance and the City of London, 1589–1608', *Parliamentary History*, 4 (1985).
—— 'The parliamentary installation of Henry, Prince of Wales', *Historical Research*, 65 (1992).
Cust, R., 'News and politics in early seventeenth century England', *Past and Present*, 112 (1986).
—— *The Forced Loan and English Politics, 1626–1628* (Oxford, 1987).
—— 'Election and selection in Stuart England', *Parliamentary History*, 7 (1988).
—— 'Honour, rhetoric and political culture: the earl of Huntington and his enemies', in S. D. Amussen and M. Kishlansky (eds), *Political Culture and Cultural Politics in Early Modern England* (Manchester, 1995).
—— and Hughes, A. (eds), *Conflict in Early Stuart England* (1989).
——, and Lake, P., 'Sir Richard Grosvenor and the rhetoric of magistracy', *Bulletin of the Institute of Historical Research*, 54 (1981).
Davies, D. L., 'The historical development of Gresford Church', *Denbighshire Historical Society Transactions*, 7 (1958).
Davies, J., *The Caroline Captivity of the Church: Charles I and the Remoulding of Anglicanism* (Oxford, 1992).
Davies, R. R., 'The peoples of Britain and Ireland, 1100–1400. IV. Language and historical mythology', *Transactions of the Royal Historical Society*, 6th series, 7 (1997).
Dean, D. M., 'Public or private? London, leather and legislation in Elizabethan England', *Historical Journal*, 31 (1988).
—— 'Parliament and locality', in idem and N. L. Jones (eds), *The Parliaments of Elizabethan England* (1990).
—— 'Pressure groups and lobbies in the Elizabethan and early Jacobean parliaments', *Parliaments, Estates and Representation*, 11 (1991).

—— *Law-Making and Society in Late Elizabethan England: The Parliament of England, 1584–1601* (Cambridge, 1996).
Dodd, A. H., 'Wales's parliamentary apprenticeship (1536–1625)', *TCS* (1942).
—— 'Wales in the parliaments of Charles I: I (1625–1629)', *TCS* (1945).
—— 'Wales in the parliaments of Charles I: II (1640–1642)', *TCS* (1946–7).
—— 'The pattern of politics in Stuart Wales', *TCS* (1948).
—— 'Caernarvonshire elections to the Long Parliament', *BBCS*, 12 (1948).
—— 'The Caernarvonshire election dispute and its sequel', *BBCS*, 14 (1950).
—— 'Wales under the early Stuarts', in A. J. Roderick (ed.), *Wales through the Ages* (Llandybie, 1960).
—— *Studies in Stuart Wales* (Cardiff, 1952; 2nd edn, 1971).
Durston, C., and Eales, J. (eds), *The Culture of English Puritanism, 1560–1700* (1996).
Eales, J., *Puritans and Roundheads: The Harleys of Brampton Bryan and the Outbreak of the English Civil War* (Cambridge, 1990).
Elton, G. R., *The Parliament of England, 1559–1581* (Cambridge, 1986).
—— 'Wales in parliament, 1542–1581', in his *Studies in Tudor and Stuart Politics and Government* (Cambridge, 1992).
Emery, F. V., 'The farming regions of Wales', in J. Thirsk (ed.), *The Agrarian History of England and Wales, IV, 1500–1640* (Cambridge, 1967).
Fielding, J., 'Opposition to the personal rule of Charles I: the diary of Robert Woodford, 1637–41', *Historical Journal*, 31 (1988).
Fincham, K., 'William Laud and the exercise of Caroline ecclesiastical patronage', *Journal of Ecclesiastical History*, 51 (2000).
—— 'The restoration of altars in the 1630s', *Historical Journal*, 44 (2001).
Fletcher, A., *A County Community in Peace and War: Sussex, 1600–1660* (1975).
—— *The Outbreak of the English Civil War* (1981).
Foster, A., 'Church policies of the 1630s', in R. Cust and A. Hughes (eds), *Conflict in Early Stuart England* (1987).
Gordon, M. D., 'The collection of ship money in the reign of Charles I', *Transactions of the Royal Historical Society*, 3rd series, 4 (1910).
Gray, M., 'Power, patronage and politics: office-holding and administration on the Crown's estates in Wales', in R. W. Hoyle (ed.), *The Estates of the English Crown, 1558–1640* (Cambridge, 1992).
—— *Images of Piety: The Iconography of Traditional Religion in Late Medieval Wales* (Oxford, 2000).
Griffith, W. P., 'Merioneth and the new and reformed learning in the early modern period', *Journal of the Merioneth Historical and Record Society*, 12 (1997).

Gruenfelder, J. K., 'The Wynns of Gwydir and parliamentary elections in Wales, 1604–1640', *WHR*, 9 (1978–9).
—— 'Radnorshire's parliamentary elections, 1604–1640', *Transactions of the Radnorshire Society*, 47 (1977).
—— *Influence in Early Stuart Elections, 1604–1640* (Columbus, Ohio, 1981).
Gruffydd, R. G., *'In That Gentile Country ...': The Beginnings of Puritan Nonconformity in Wales* (Bridgend, 1975).
—— (ed.), *A Guide to Welsh Literature, c.1530–1700* (Cardiff, 1997).
Hague, D. B., 'Rug Chapel, Corwen', *Journal of the Merioneth Historical and Record Society*, 3 (1957–60).
Ham, R. E., 'The Four Shire Controversy', *WHR*, 8 (1976–7).
—— *The County and the Kingdom: Sir Herbert Croft and the Elizabethan State* (Washington, DC, 1977).
Hasler, P. W., (ed.) *The House of Commons, 1558–1603* (1981), 3 vols.
Healy, S., 'Oh, what a lovely war? War, taxation and public opinion in England, 1624–29', *Canadian Journal of History*, 38 (2003).
Hill, C., 'Puritans and the dark corners of the land', in idem, *Change and Continuity in Seventeenth Century England* (1974).
Hirst, D., *The Representative of the People? Voters and Voting in England under the Early Stuarts* (Cambridge, 1975).
—— 'The Privy Council and problems of enforcement in early Stuart England', *Journal of British Studies*, 18 (1978).
Howells, B. (ed.), *Early Modern Pembrokeshire, 1536–1815* (Aberystwyth, 1987).
Hoyle, R. W., '"Shearing the hog": the reform of the estates, c.1598–1640', in idem (ed.), *The Estates of the English Crown, 1558–1640* (Cambridge, 1992).
Hughes, A., *Politics, Society and Civil War in Warwickshire, 1620–1660* (Cambridge, 1987).
—— 'Thomas Durgard and his circle in the 1630s: a parliamentary-puritan connection?', *Historical Journal*, 29 (1986).
Hutton, R., *The Royalist War Effort, 1642–1646* (Harlow, 1982).
Jenkins, G. H., *The Foundations of Modern Wales, 1642–1780* (Oxford, 1987).
—— *Protestant Dissenters in Wales, 1639–1689* (Cardiff, 1992).
——, Suggett, R., and White, E. M., 'The Welsh language in early modern Wales', in G. H. Jenkins (ed.), *The Welsh Language Before the Industrial Revolution* (Cardiff, 1997).
Jenkins, P., 'A new history of Wales', *Historical Journal*, 32 (1989).
—— 'Welsh Anglicans and the Interregnum', *Journal of the Historical Society of the Church in Wales*, 32 (1990).
—— *A History of Modern Wales, 1536–1990* (Harlow, 1992).
—— 'The Anglican Church and the unity of Britain: the Welsh experience, 1560–1714', in S. G. Ellis and S. Barker (eds), *Conquest and Union: Fashioning a British State, 1485–1725* (1995).

—— 'Seventeenth century Wales: definition and identity', in B. Bradshaw and P. Roberts (eds), *British Consciousness and Identity: The Making of Britain, 1533–1707* (Cambridge, 1998).

Johnson, A. M., 'Wales and the Protectorate', in D. Pennington and K. Thomas (eds), *Puritans and Revolutionaries* (Oxford, 1978).

Jones, E. G., 'Catholic recusancy in the counties of Denbigh, Flint and Montgomery, 1581–1625', *TCS* (1945).

—— 'Anglesey and invasion', *Transactions of the Anglesey Antiquarian Society* (1947).

—— *Cymru a'r Hen Ffydd* (Cardiff, 1951).

Jones, J.G., 'The Welsh poets and their patrons, c.1550–1640', *WHR*, 9 (1978–9).

—— *Concepts of Order and Gentility in Wales, 1540–1640* (Llandysul, 1992).

—— *Early Modern Wales, c.1525–1640* (Basingstoke, 1994).

—— *Law, Order and Government in Caernarfonshire, 1558–1640* (Cardiff, 1996).

—— *The Welsh Gentry, 1536–1640* (Cardiff, 1998).

—— 'The Welsh gentry and the image of the "Cambro-Briton", c.1603–25', *WHR*, 20 (2000–1).

—— 'Some puritan influences on the Anglican Church in Wales in the early seventeenth century', *Journal of Welsh Religious History*, NS, 2 (2002).

Kennedy, M. E., 'Legislation, foreign policy and the "proper business" of the parliament of 1624', *Albion*, 23 (1991).

Kishlansky, M. A., *Parliamentary Selection: Social and Political Choice in Early Modern England* (Cambridge, 1986).

Kyle, C. R., 'Parliament and the politics of carting in early Stuart London', *The London Journal*, 27 (2002).

—— '"It will be a scandal to show what we have done with such a number": House of Commons committee attendance lists', in idem (ed.), *Parliaments, Politics and Elections, 1604–1648* (Camden Soc., 5th series, 17, 2001).

—— 'Attendance, apathy and order? parliamentary committees in early Stuart England', in idem and J. T. Peacey (eds), *Parliament at Work: Parliamentary Committees, Political Power and Public Access in Early Modern England* (Woodbridge, 2002).

Lake, P., 'The collection of ship money in Cheshire during the sixteen-thirties: a case study of relations between central and local government', *Northern History*, 17 (1981).

—— 'Constitutional consensus and puritan opposition in the 1620s: Thomas Scott and the Spanish Match', *Historical Journal*, 25 (1982).

—— 'Anti-popery: the structure of a prejudice', in R. Cust and A. Hughes (eds), *Conflict in Early Stuart England* (1989).

—— 'Lancelot Andrewes, John Buckeridge and *avant-garde* conformity at the court of James I', in L.L. Peck (ed.), *The Mental World of the Jacobean Court* (Cambridge, 1991).

—— 'The Laudian style', in K. Fincham (ed.), *The Early Stuart Church, 1603–1642* (1993).

Lambert, S., 'Procedure in the House of Commons in the early Stuart period', *English Historical Review*, 95 (1980).

Laurence, A., *Women in England, 1500–1760* (London, 1994).

Lindquist, E. N., 'The king, the people and the House of Commons: the problem of early Jacobean purveyance', *Historical Journal*, 31 (1988).

Lloyd, H. A., *The Gentry of South West Wales, 1540–1640* (Cardiff, 1968).

Lloyd, J. E., et al. (eds), *The Dictionary of Welsh Biography down to 1940* (1959).

Maltby, J., *Prayer Book and People in Elizabethan and Early Stuart England* (Cambridge, 1998).

—— '"The good old way": prayer book Protestantism in the 1640s and 1650s', in R. N. Swanson (ed.), *The Church and the Book* (Studies in Church History, 34, 2004).

Marsh, C., 'Sacred space in England, 1560–1640: the view from the pew', *Journal of Ecclesiastical History*, 53 (2002).

McGee, J. S., 'William Laud and the outward face of religion', in R. L. DeMachen (ed.), *Leaders of the Reformation* (Susquehanna Univ. Press, 1984).

Mendenhall, T. C., *The Shrewsbury Drapers and the Welsh Wool Trade in the XVI and XVII Centuries* (Oxford, 1953).

Merritt, J. F. (ed.), *The Political World of Thomas Wentworth, Earl of Strafford, 1621–1641* (Cambridge, 1996).

—— 'Puritans, Laudians and the phenomenon of church-building in Jacobean London', *Historical Journal*, 41 (1998).

Meyrick, S. R., *History and Antiquities of the County of Cardigan* (Brecon, 1907).

Morrill, J. S., 'The church in England, 1642–9', in idem (ed.), *Reactions to the English Civil War, 1642–1649* (Basingstoke, 1982).

—— *Revolt in the Provinces: The People of England and the Tragedies of War, 1630–1648* (Harlow, 1999).

Newman, K. A., 'Holiness in beauty? Roman Catholics, Arminians, and the aesthetics of religion in early Caroline England', in D. Wood (ed.), *The Church and the Arts* (Studies in Church History, 28, 1992).

Nuttall, G. F., *The Welsh Saints, 1640–1660* (Cardiff, 1957).

Orrin, G. R., *Medieval Churches of the Vale of Glamorgan* (Cowbridge, 1988).

Owen, G. D., *Wales in the Reign of James I* (Woodbridge, 1988).

Palmer, A. N., and Owen, E., *A History of Ancient Tenures of Land in Wales and the Marches* (2nd edn, Wrexham, 1910).

Quintrell, B. W., 'Government in perspective: Lancashire and the Privy Council, 1570–1640', *Transactions of the Historic Society of Lancashire and Cheshire*, 131 (1981).
Rees, T., *History of Protestant Nonconformity in Wales* (1861).
Rees, W., *Cardiff: A History of the City* (Cardiff, 1962).
Reid, R., *The King's Council in the North* (1921).
Richards, T., *The Puritan Movement in Wales, 1639–53* (1920).
Ridgeway, M. H., *Church Plate of the Diocese of St Asaph* (Denbigh, 1997).
Roberts, P. R., 'Wales and England after the Tudor "union": crown, principality and parliament, 1543–1624', in C. Cross, D. Loades and J. J. Scarisbrick (eds), *Law and Government under the Tudors* (Cambridge, 1988).
—— 'The "Henry VIII clause". Delegated legislation and the Tudor principality of Wales', in T. G. Watkin (ed.), *Legal Record and Historical Reality: Proceedings of the 8th British Legal History Conference* (1989).
—— 'The English Crown, the principality of Wales and the Council in the Marches, 1534–1641', in J. Morrill and B. Bradshaw (eds), *The British Problem, c.1534–1707: State Formation in the Atlantic Archipelago* (1996).
—— 'Tudor Wales, national identity and the British inheritance', in idem and B. Bradshaw (eds), *British Consciousness and Identity: The Making of Britain, 1533–1707* (Cambridge, 1998).
Roberts, S. K., 'Office-holding and allegiance in Glamorgan in the civil war and after: the case of John Byrd', *Morgannwg*, 44 (2000).
—— 'How the west was won: parliamentary politics, religion and the military in south Wales, 1642–9', *WHR*, 21 (2002–3).
Rowe, V. A., 'The influence of the earls of Pembroke on parliamentary elections', *English Historical Review*, 50 (1935).
Royal Commission on Ancient and Historical Monuments in Wales and Monmouthshire (Anglesey) (1937).
Royal Commission on Ancient and Historical Monuments in Wales and Monmouthshire (Caernarfonshire) (1956).
Ruigh, R. E., *The Parliament of 1624* (Cambridge, MA, 1971).
Russell, C. S. R., *Parliaments and English Politics, 1621–1629* (Oxford, 1979).
—— *The Fall of the British Monarchies, 1637–1642* (Oxford, 1991).
Salt, S. P., 'Sir Simonds D'Ewes and the levying of Ship Money, 1635–1640', *Historical Journal*, 37 (1994).
Salter, M., *The Old Parish Churches of Gwent, Glamorgan and Gower* (Malvern, 1991).
Schofield, R., *Taxation under the Early Tudors, 1485–1547* (Oxford, 2004).
Schwarz, M. L., 'Lord Saye and Sele's objections to the Palatinate benevolence of 1622', *Albion*, 5 (1971).
Sharpe, K. (ed.), *Faction and Parliament* (Oxford, 1978).
—— 'Crown, parliament and locality: government and communication in early Stuart England', *English Historical Review*, 101 (1986).

—— *The Personal Rule of Charles I* (New Haven 1992).
Skeel, C. A. J., *The Council in the Marches of Wales: A Study in Local Government during the Sixteenth and Seventeenth Centuries* (1904).
Smith, D. L., *The Stuart Parliaments, 1603–1689* (1999).
Spurr, J., *The Restoration Church of England, 1646–1689* (New Haven and London, 1991)
Stoyle, M. J., *Loyalty and Locality: Popular Allegiance in Devon during the English Civil War* (Exeter, 1994).
—— '"Pagans or paragons?": images of the Cornish during the English civil war', *English Historical Review*, 111 (1996).
—— 'Caricaturing Cymru: images of the Welsh in the London press, 1642–6', in D. Dunn (ed.), *War and Society in Medieval and Early Modern Britain* (Liverpool, 2000).
—— 'English "nationalism", Celtic particularism and the English civil war', *Historical Journal*, 43 (2000).
—— *West Britons: Cornish Identities and the Early Modern British State* (Exeter, 2002).
Supple, B. E., *Commercial Crisis and Change in England, 1600–1642* (Cambridge, 1964).
Thomas, D. R., *The History of the Diocese of St Asaph* (Oswestry, 1908–13), 3 vols.
Thomas, W. S. K., 'Municipal government in Swansea, 1485–1640', *Glamorgan Historian*, 1 (1963).
Thornton, T., *Cheshire and the Tudor State, 1480–1560* (Woodbridge, 2000).
—— 'Dynasty and territory in the early modern period: the princes of Wales and their western British inheritance', *WHR*, 20 (2000–1).
Thrush, A., 'Naval finance and the origins and development of ship money', in M. C. Fissel (ed.), *War and Government in Britain, 1598–1650* (Manchester, 1991).
Tibbott, G., 'Welshmen with Prince Charles in Spain, 1623', *NLWJ*, 1 (1939–40).
Tucker, N., 'Volunteers in the Thirty Years' War', *NLWJ*, 16 (1969–70).
Tyacke, N., 'Lancelot Andrewes and the myth of Anglicanism', in P. Lake and M. Questier (eds), *Conformity and Orthodoxy in the English Church, c.1560–1660* (Woodbridge, 2000).
Underdown, D., *Revel, Riot and Rebellion: Popular Politics and Culture in England, 1603–1660* (Oxford, 1985).
Wakeman, H. O., 'The Laudian movement in Wales', *Cymru Fydd*, 3 (1890).
Walker, D. G., 'The Reformation in Wales', in idem (ed.), *A History of the Church in Wales* (Bridgend, 1976).
Walsham, A., 'The parochial roots of Laudianism revisited: Catholics, anti-Calvinists and "parish Anglicans" in early Stuart England', *Journal of Ecclesiastical History*, 49 (1998).

Williams, G., *Welsh Reformation Essays* (Cardiff, 1967).
—— *Renewal and Reformation Wales, c.1415–1642* (Oxford, 1987, pbk 1993).
—— *The Welsh and their Religion* (Cardiff, 1991).
—— 'Unity of religion or unity of language? Protestants, Catholics and the Welsh language, 1536–1660', in G. H. Jenkins (ed.), *The Welsh Language Before the Industrial Revolution*, (Cardiff, 1997).
Williams, P., *The Council in the Marches of Wales under Elizabeth I* (Cardiff, 1958).
—— 'The activity of the Council in the Marches under the early Stuarts', *WHR*, 1 (1960–3).
—— 'The attack on the Council in the Marches', *TCS* (1961).
Wood, A., *Athenae Oxoniensis*, ed. P. Bliss (Oxford, 1813–20), 4 vols.
Woodworth, A., *Purveyance for the Royal Household in the Reign of Queen Elizabeth* (Philadelphia, 1945).
Yates, W. N., *Rûg Chapel, Llangar Church, Gwydir Uchaf Chapel* (Cardiff, 1993).
Young, M. B., 'Buckingham, war and parliament: revisionism gone too far?', *Parliamentary History*, 4 (1985).
—— 'Revisionism and the council of war, 1624–1626', *Parliamentary History*, 8 (1989).
Yule, G., 'James VI and I: furnishing the churches in his two kingdoms', in A. Fletcher and P. Roberts (eds), *Religion, Culture and Society in Early Modern Britain* (Cambridge, 1994).

UNPUBLISHED DISSERTATIONS

Bowen, L., 'Wales in British politics, c.1603–42' (Ph.D. thesis, University of Wales, 1999).
Gill, A. A. M., 'Ship money during the personal rule of Charles I: politics, ideology and the law, 1634 to 1640' (Ph.D. thesis, University of Sheffield, 1990).
Hodges, V. J., 'The electoral influence of the aristocracy, 1604–41' (Ph.D. thesis, Columbia University, 1977).
Hughes, C. E., 'Wales and piracy: a study in Tudor administration, 1500–1640' (MA thesis, University of Wales, 1937).
Jones, M. E., 'Glamorgan, 1540–1640: aspects of social and economic history' (MA thesis, University of Wales, 1973).
Kyle, C. R., '*Lex loquens*: legislation in the parliament of 1624' (Ph.D. thesis, Auckland University, 1994).
Langelüddeke, H. A., 'Secular policy enforcement during the personal rule of Charles I' (D.Phil. thesis, University of Oxford, 1995).
O'Farrell, B., 'Politician, patron, poet, William Herbert, 3rd earl of Pembroke' (Ph.D. thesis, University of California, 1966).

Matthews, R. P., 'Roman Catholic recusancy in Monmouthshire, 1603–1689: a demographic and morphological analysis' (Ph.D. thesis, University of Wales, 1996).

Williams, B., 'The Welsh clergy, 1558–1642' (Ph.D. thesis, Open University, 1998).

INDEX

Abbot, George, archbishop of Canterbury 224
Aberavon (Glam.) 17
Abergwili (Carms.) 214, 216, 222–3
Aberhafesb (Montgom.) 218
Abermarlais (Carms.) 118
Aberystwyth (Cards.) 266
Acts of Union 1, 5–6, 12, 70, 75, 80, 162n.32, 237, 262, 270
altar policy 209–210, 222–32
Alured, Thomas 98, 172n.72
Andrewes, Lancelot, bishop of Winchester 222–3
Anglesey 105, 114, 122–3, 145, 149, 154, 156, 239, 247, 250, 270
   benevolence (1622) 93–4, 97, 139
   cattle trade 68n.110, 93
   commission of the peace 22–4, 39, 68n.110, 92–3
   deputy lieutenants 104–5, 122–3
   elections 18–19, 22–3, 39
   forced loan 136, 139–40
   impressment 104–6, 122, 141
   musters 103–4
   Privy Seal loan (1625–6) 118, 154
   ship money 160n.25, 169, 173, 186, 201–6
Anglicanism 207 and n.1, 209, 233–4
   see also Church of England in Wales; religion in Wales
Anglo-Scottish Union (1603) 7, 41, 70–4, 80, 273
anti-popery 34, 89, 91, 98–102, 123, 150, 239–40, 242, 244, 260
anti-Welshness 72, 240, 242–3, 258, 260, 274–5
   see also ethnicity; satires on the Welsh
Anwyll, William Lewis (Parc, Merion.) 178–9
Arllechwedd Isaf (Caern.) 159
Arllechwedd Uchaf (Caern.) 94–5
Arminianism 143
Arnold, Nicholas (Llanthony, Mon.) 33
Aubrey, Sir Thomas (Llantrithyd, Glam.) 132–3, 229

Bacon, Francis 42
Bagenall, Henry (Anglesey) 230
Bagenall, Magdalen (Flints.) 21–2
Bagg, Sir James (Devon) 124
Bangor Cathedral 219, 229–30
Bangor diocese 214–15
Bangor, bishops of *see* Bayly, Lewis; Griffith, Edmund; Roberts, William
bardic poetry 35
Barlow, George (Narberth, Pembs.) 102
Bassett, Thomas (Llantrisant, Glam.) 256
Bayly, Lewis, bishop of Bangor 79, 102, 122–3, 148
beacons 120–1
Beaumaris (Anglesey) 23, 107, 239
   elections 24
Beaumaris Castle 122

'beauty of holiness' 222–32
Beibl Bach 211
benevolences
   (1614) 94, 96
   (1620: 'Palatinate benevolence') 86–7, 139, 170, 269n.19
   (1622–3) 92–7
   (1626) 9, 128–31, 143
   repair of Bangor Cathedral 219
Berkeley (Glos.) 42–3
Bettws (Carms.) 175
billeting 119–20, 142, 145–6, 271
Bishops' Wars 184–6, 188, 238
Bodvel, Sir John (Bodvel, Caern.) 23, 104, 239
Bohemia *see* Palatinate
Bold, William (Trerddol, Anglesey) 229
Bowen, William (Haverfordwest, Pembs.) 179–80
Bowyer, Robert (parliamentary diarist) 44
Bradshaw, Brendan (historian) 210, 272
Brampton Bryan (Herefs.) 228
Breconshire 96, 104–5, 149, 224, 226, 231, 251, 267
   elections 13
   forced loan 136
   impressment 108
   musters 104
   Privy Seal loan (1625–6) 116–18
   ship money 161, 168, 183n.112, 186n.123, 198, 201–6
Brereton, Andrew (Denbs.) 21, 24
Brereton, Sir William (Ches.) 230
Bridgeman, Sir John (chief justice of Chester) 157–9, 167–8, 172
Bridgwater, earl of *see* Egerton, John, 1st earl of Bridgwater
Brinsley, John (Great Yarmouth, Norf.) 227
Bristol 6, 45, 65, 212
Bristol Merchant Venturers 65
Britain
   rhetorical significance of in Wales 7, 70–3, 244, 273–4
   Welsh parliamentary interest in 41, 70–80, 273
Bromfield and Yale (Denbs.) 49–51
Buckingham, duke of *see* Villiers, George, 1st duke of Buckingham
Bulkeley family (Beaumaris and Baron Hill, Anglesey) 18–19, 23, 156
Bulkeley of Dronwy (Anglesey) 220
Bulkeley, Richard (Baron Hill, Anglesey) 186
Bulkeley, Sir Richard (Baron Hill, Anglesey) 23, 53n.50, 57, 73n.130
Butler, James, 1st duke of Ormonde 252
butter, export of *see* Welsh butter trade
Byrck, Captain 230–1

Cadiz 105, 107, 109, 118–19, 127, 132, 141, 145
Cadoxton-juxta-Barry (Glam.) 226

INDEX

Caernarfon 51, 107, 142, 212, 266
Caernarfonshire 47, 52, 58, 59, 80, 91, 104–5, 122–3, 143, 147, 150, 226, 267–9
   benevolence (1622) 94–7
   benevolence (1626) 128–9
   commissioners of the peace 94
   declining yield of subsidy in 268
   deputy lieutenants 106–7, 113
   elections 21–2, 27–31, 33, 35, 38
   forced loan 134n.190, 135–6
   impressment 106–7
   Privy Seal loan (1625–6) 113–17
   ship money 159, 160n.25, 168, 169–70, 178, 186n.123, 195–6, 197, 201–6
Canon, Sir Thomas (Haverfordwest, Pembs.) 27, 32
Cardiff (Glam.) 14, 133, 157–8, 185n.122, 212, 256
   elections 15–18
Cardiganshire 96, 105, 108, 121, 267
   deputy lieutenants 108
   forced loan 133, 134n.190, 135–7
   impressment 108
   Privy Seal loan (1625–6) 117
   ship money 160n.25, 165–7, 169, 181–4, 190–1, 201–6
Carmarthen 134n.190, 137, 158, 171
Carmarthenshire 95–6, 105, 121, 267
   collection for repair of St Paul's Cathedral 220
   commission of the peace 95–6
   elections 18–19
   forced loan 133–4 and n.190, 136
   Palatinate benevolence 87, 170
   ship money 158, 160n.25, 165, 170–1, 175, 183n.112, 186n.123, 188, 195, 196, 201–6
Castlemartin hundred (Pembs.) 257
catholics/catholicism 31–2, 34, 89–90, 94, 97, 100–2, 122–3, 139, 210, 223–4, 239–40, 253
cattle trade 68–9, 93, 160, 163, 241
   see also Irish cattle
Cecil, Sir Robert (later earl of Salisbury; secretary of state) 54, 74, 266
Charles I 34, 67, 81, 108, 110, 112, 118, 122–4, 127–33, 141–2, 145, 150–5, 159, 161, 164, 170–1, 178, 183–4, 199, 207–8, 213–14, 216, 220, 222, 232, 234, 240, 247–58, 260–1, 265, 271–2, 275
   as Prince of Wales 49–50, 56–7, 80, 98–101, 131
Charles II (as Prince of Wales) 251, 273–4
Cheadle, Thomas (Anglesey) 157
Chepstow (Mon.) 44
Chepstow Bridge 8, 42–6, 84
Cheshire 146, 157, 278
Chester 158, 167, 212, 246
Chirk (Denbs.) 216–17
Church of England in Wales 7, 9–10, 200, 210, 212, 213, 222, 232–4, 254–7, 260, 275
   as popular institution 233–4, 243–5, 254–7, 275
   emphasis on sacraments 229–30, 255–7
   historical mythology relating to 7, 244–5, 273, 275
   metropolitical visitation (1636) 224, 226
   painting of churches 223–4
   poverty of 212, 213–15, 232
   refurbishment of church buildings 215–20, 230–2

   see also 'beauty of holiness'
   stained glass in churches 230, 234
   see also religion in Wales; Wales, royalism, significance of religion
church organs 230, 234
church plate, donations of 229–30
churchwardens 216–19, 225–6
Civil Wars 152, 231, 234, 235–61 passim, 273–5
   distribution of propaganda 246–8, 250
   patterns of allegiance in Wales 8, 10, 234, 235–61
   see also Wales, royalism
Clarendon, earl of *see* Hyde, Edward, 1st earl of Clarendon
cloth *see* Welsh cloth trade
coastal defence 103, 120–1, 125, 142, 155–6, 198, 271
coat and conduct money 106–8, 119, 132, 139, 185, 186, 189
Cogswell, Thomas (historian) 114, 148, 271–2, 277
Coke, Sir John (secretary of state) 159
Coleshill hundred (Flints.) 246
commission for preserving the king's revenues in north Wales (1633) 155
Commission for the Propagation of the Gospel in Wales (1650–3) 259
commissions/commissioners of array 246–7, 248, 250–1
communion rails/tables *see* altar policy
Compton, Sir William, 1st earl of Northampton (lord president of the Council in the Marches) 78–80, 86–7, 103–4, 111–14, 120–1, 123, 147–9
contributory boroughs *see* elections, outboroughs (contributory boroughs)
Conway, Edward (secretary of state) 104, 120, 214
Conway, Sir John (Bodrhyddan, Flints.) 187, 192
Coote, Mr (Montgomery, Montgoms.) 227–8
Cornwall 10, 150, 260, 277
Council in the Marches of Wales 5–6, 32, 41, 42, 45, 48, 69, 73–5, 77–80, 86, 107, 140, 147–8, 156–7, 159, 168, 182, 199, 266, 269, 274
   lord president 69, 156–7, 269 *see also* Eure, Lord Ralph; Egerton, John, 1st earl of Bridgwater; Compton, Sir William, 1st earl of Northampton
   opposition to 73–5, 274
   problems of close supervision in Wales 147–8, 172–4, 199, 266
Council in the North 74
Council of War 106, 109
'Court' and 'Country' 31, 33, 35–6, 261
Court (royal) 48, 51, 62, 128, 152
Court of Arches 217
Coventry, Baron *see* Coventry, Thomas, 1st Baron Coventry
Coventry, Thomas, 1st Baron Coventry (attorney general/lord keeper) 59, 172, 180
Cowbridge (Glam.) 16–17
Coytmor, Richard (Caern.) 169–70
Cradock, Walter 232, 236, 238, 259
Cranfield, Lionel, 1st earl of Middlesex (lord treasurer) 66–7
credit *see* elections, honour and social standing in
Criccieth (Caern.) 170
Croft, Sir Herbert (Croft Castle, Herefs.) 73–4

INDEX

crucifixes/crosses 210, 229, 233, 231, 234
Cumberland 157
Cust, Richard (historian) 30–1, 34, 38, 149
Cwmcarvan (Mon.) 226

Davies, John Harris (Llanfynydd, Carms.) 196
Davies, Julian (historian) 215
Davies, Matthew (Cardiff, Glam. and Mdx.) 17, 43, 46, 68, 77
Davies, Rees (Llandaff, Glam.) 256
Davies, Richard, bishop of St David's 244, 275
Davies, Robert (Conwy, Caern.) 195–6
Davies, Robert (Gwysaney, Flints.) 35–6
Denbigh 217, 231
  elections 19, 37
Denbighshire 49–51, 57, 94, 105, 128–9, 217, 238, 249–51, 266
  benevolence (1626) 128–30
  clothiers 63
  deputy lieutenants 112
  elections 21, 24
  forced loan 136, 138–9
  Privy Seal loan (1625–6) 112, 115–17
  ship money 160n.25, 167, 168–9, 178, 180, 183n.112, 201–6
Derby, earls of *see* Stanley family, earls of Derby
Derllys (Carms.) 96
Devereux family, earls of Essex 13, 32, 257–8
Devon 161
Digges, Sir Dudley 89
Dindeathwy (Anglesey) 103–4
Directory of Worship 255
Diserth (Flints.) 192
Dodd, A. H. (historian) 2–4, 40–2, 61, 81–5, 87, 144, 152–3, 170, 173, 235, 237, 262–3, 265
Dodderidge, John 70
Dohna, Baron von 86
Dolgellau (Merion.) 225
drovers 160, 178

Edeirnion (Merion.) 176–7
Edward I 75
Egerton, John, 1st earl of Bridgwater (lord president of the Council in the Marches) 13, 50–1, 148, 157, 159, 168, 171–4, 179–80, 182, 185, 199, 238, 266
Egerton, Thomas, 1st Viscount Brackley and Baron Ellesmere 13
Eifionydd (Caern.) 169–70
elections 12–39 passim, 263–5 (for individual elections, *see* respective shire and borough entries)
  aristocratic patronage 13–19, 263
  commission of the peace, role in 22–4
  consensus, ideal of 20, 24–5
  contests 25–34, 38
  franchise arrangements 12–13
  historiography 30, 34, 38
  honour and social standing in 16, 18, 20–2, 27–30, 34–5, 38–9, 69, 263
  ideological divisions in 19, 30–4, 265 *see also* 'Court' and 'Country'
  freeholders 26, 28–30, 34–5
  kinship and 21–2, 35
  pre-election negotiations 20–5
  outboroughs (contributory boroughs) 13, 16–18, 24
  reciprocity 16, 18, 38, 263

representation and accountability 19, 30, 35–40, 64, 67–9, 263
Eliot, Sir John (St German's, Cornw.) 143–4
Elizabeth I 49, 52, 73, 167
Elizabeth of the Palatinate and Bohemia 85–6, 89, 91
Ellesmere, Baron *see* Egerton, Thomas, 1st Viscount Brackley and Baron Ellesmere
Elton, Geoffrey (historian) 40, 84
Epistol at y Cembru (1567) 244
Erbery, William (Cardiff, Glam.) 232, 236, 238, 259
escheators *see* ship money, escheators
Essex 273
Essex, earls of *see* Devereux family, earls of Essex
ethnicity 7–8, 10, 240, 242–3, 258–9, 274–5
Eure, Sir Francis (Salop and London) 78n.153
Eure, Lord Ralph (lord president of the Council in the Marches) 32, 48
Evans, Michael (Llanfihangel-y-traethau and Llandecwyn, Merion.) 185
Everitt, Alan (historian) 277
Exchequer 95–6, 114, 116, 118–20, 128, 132, 134–5, 140, 145, 147, 170
Eyton, John (Leeswood, Flints.) 186–7
Field, Theophilus, bishop of Llandaff and St David's 213–14, 216, 223
fifteenths and tenths 147
Fincham, Kenneth (historian) 224
Fleetwood, Major General Charles 259
Flint 80, 91, 230
Flintshire 86–7, 94, 96, 105, 128–9, 146, 149, 246–7, 250–1, 270
  benevolence (1626) 128–30
  deputy lieutenants 86–7, 104, 111
  elections 13, 21–2, 35–6
  forced loan 134n.190, 136
  impressment 107–8
  musters 104
  Palatinate benevolence 86–7
  Privy Seal loan (1625–6) 111, 117
  ship money 160n.25, 163, 166–8, 173–4, 180, 183, 186–8, 191–6, 201–6
Foot, Michael 1
forced loan (1626–8) 9, 85, 119, 130–41 passim, 144, 147, 149, 200, 265
  commissioners 131–2
  refusers and defaulters 134–5, 138–9, 144
  yield of in Wales 133, 136–7, 140–1
  see also under individual counties; taxation, resistance to non-parliamentary taxation
forest fines 155
'four propositions' 103, 109
France 67, 85, 124, 141
  see also Ile de Rhé
Frederick V of the Palatinate and Bohemia 85–6, 91

Gardiner, S. R. (historian) 2–3
Gill, Alison (historian) 162, 199–200
Glamorgan 65, 97, 101, 105, 107, 109, 125, 148, 231, 238, 250, 251, 256, 266, 272
  butter trade 65–8
  deputy lieutenants 110–11, 125, 145
  elections 14–15
  forced loan 133, 137
  impressment 109
  Privy Seal loan (1625–6) 111–13, 118, 125
  ship money 157–8, 160n.25, 170, 185, 201–6

INDEX

taxation 109, 145–6
trade with Minehead 68
Gloucestershire 6, 42–6, 73, 77, 140
Gooch, Dr Barnaby 78
Gordon, M. D. (historian) 188, 195
Gray, Madeline (historian) 233
'Great Contract' (1610) 55, 75–6
great sessions, courts of 5–6, 23, 47n.32, 51, 66, 181–2, 187, 192–3, 199
  judges 50, 51, 66, 69, 156n.15, 172, 179–80, 182, 185
  see also ship money, great sessions
Gresford (Denbs.) 217, 225
Grey, Henry, 1st earl of Stamford 252
Griffith family (Cefnamwlch, Caern.) 27–30, 150
Griffith, Edmund, bishop of Bangor 214–15, 224n.68
Griffith, John (Cefnamwlch, Caern.) 22, 28–9, 31, 36, 125–6, 143–5, 150, 155–6, 239, 245
Griffith, Peter (Flints.) 163
Griffiths, Richard (Sutton, Montgom.) 227–8
Grosvenor, Sir Richard (Eaton Hall, Ches.) 25
Gwyn, Evan (Cards.) 173–4

Haberdashers' Company 46–7
Hampden, John 141, 180, 183, 198
Hanmer, John, bishop of St Asaph 218
Hanmer, Sir John (Hanmer, Flints.) 22, 96
Harlech (Merion.) 47–8
Harley, Sir Robert (Brampton Bryan, Herefs.) 227–8, 232, 239
Harry, George Owen (Whitchurch, Pembs.) 70–1
Harry, John (Mon.) 150
Hastings, Henry, 5th earl of Huntington 114, 230
Hatcham Barnes (Kent) 46
Haverfordwest (Pembs.) 54–5, 57, 66, 88, 99, 120–1, 137, 145
  elections 12, 27
  ship money 158, 179–80
  St Mary's Church 218, 225
Hawarden (Flints.) 226, 230
Heath, Sir Robert (solicitor general) 88
Henllan (Denbs.) 139
Henry VII 73, 76, 260
'Henry VIII' clause 41, 55, 75–80, 84, 88–9, 264
Henry, Prince of Wales 56, 74–5, 128
Herbert family (Montgom. and Glam.) 13–14
Herbert family (Montgomery Castle, Montgom.) 18
Herbert family (Powis Castle, Montgom.) 18, 32, 180
Herbert, Lord, of Raglan *see* Somerset, Henry, 5th earl and 1st marquess of Worcester
Herbert, Lord Edward, of Cherbury 227
Herbert, Sir Edward (Montgomery Castle, Montgom.) 47n.30
Herbert, Henry (Coldbrook, Mon.) 32
Herbert, John (Brecs.) 169
Herbert, Mary, dowager countess of Pembroke 14
Herbert, Philip, 4th earl of Pembroke and Montgomery 32–3
Herbert, William, 3rd earl of Pembroke 14–18, 79, 91, 120
  Welsh clientage in the Commons 91, 99–102, 109–10, 124–5, 127, 143, 150
Herbert, William (Grey Friars, Glam.) 16–18
Herbert, William (Cogan Pill, Glam.) 16, 17n.17, 67

Herbert, Sir William (Powis Castle, Montgom.; later Lord Powis) 18–19, 60–2, 64, 68, 83, 91, 101, 124, 150, 239
Hereford diocese 227
Herefordshire 6, 73, 77, 140, 162, 198
Heylin, Rowland 211
Hirst, Derek (historian) 30, 34, 37–8, 104
History of England from the Accession of James I to the Outbreak of the Civil War 2
Holywell (Flints.) 230
Holland, Robert (Pembs.) 70
Holland, Thomas (Berw, Anglesey) 103–4
Holland, William (Conwy, Caern.) 96–7
homilies *see* religion in Wales, Welsh homilies
honour *see* elections, honour and social standing in
Hookes, William (Conwy, Caern.) 195
Hotham, John 251
Howell, Howell (Brynaman, Carms.) 196
Hughes, Ralph (Diserth, Flints.) 191–5
Huguenots 141
Huntington, earl of *see* Hastings, Henry, 5th earl of Huntington
Hyde, Edward, 1st earl of Clarendon 251, 257

Ile de Rhé 135, 143, 145
impeachment 123–7
impressment 8, 103–8, 113, 141–2, 150, 271
invasion, fear of 106, 120–3, 145
Invitation Unto Prayer (1624) 89
Ireland 32, 85, 87, 90, 103–4, 107, 123, 125, 142, 156, 241, 271
Irish cattle 68–9
Irish Rebellion (1641) 240
Is Aled (Denbs.) 138
Is Aeron (Cards.) 181–3, 191
Is Dulas (Denbs.) 138
Is Gwyrfai (Caern.) 94–5

Jackson, Eleazer (Abergavenny, Mon.) 90
James I 7, 13, 41, 52–3, 55–7, 62, 65–6, 70–4, 76–7, 81, 83, 85, 87–8, 91–2, 94–5, 97–9, 107, 110–11, 118, 151
James, Edward 210
James, Richard (Newport, IOW) 72
Jenkins, John (Cards.) 135
Jenkins, Philip (historian) 233, 256, 262–3, 272, 274
Johnson, Sir Robert (Bucks. and London) 44, 46, 54
Jones, Charles (Castellmarch, Caern.) 125
Jones, Edward (Mold, Flints.) 96
Jones, Harry (Merion.) 176–7
Jones, Sir Henry (Abermarlais, Carms.) 118, 170, 173
Jones, John (Maesygarnedd, Merion.) 237
Jones, Thomas (Hereford) 223–4
Jones, William (Beaumaris, Anglesey) 77
Jones, William (London haberdasher) 46–7
justices of the peace 5, 23–4, 36, 39, 42, 63, 78, 86, 92–6, 119, 129–30, 132–3, 162n.32, 164–6, 170, 172, 175, 178, 182, 187, 270 and n.25
Juxon, William (lord treasurer) 194, 195

Kemeys, Sir Nicholas (Llanfair Discoed, Mon. and Cefn Mabli, Glam.) 32
Kent 128

INDEX

Kidwelly hundred (Carms.) 175
Kishlansky, Mark (historian) 30, 33–4, 38
knighthood composition 154–5, 162n.32
Knollys, Sir Robert (Porthamel, Brec. and London) 53n.50, 54

La Rochelle 143–4
Lambe, Sir John 218
Lancashire 147, 157, 262, 277
Laud, William, archbishop of Canterbury 9–10, 154, 156, 207–11, 213–16, 219–20, 222, 225, 227, 229, 232, 234, 239
  as bishop of St David's 102, 215–16, 222–4, 232
Laudianism 10, 153, 184, 207 and n.2, 209, 213, 222, 231, 234, 235, 244, 265, 275
Laugharne (Carms.) 175
Laugharne, Col. Rowland (Pembs.) 256
Leicestershire 114, 150, 272
Lewis, Anthony (Burton, Denbs.) 217
Lewis, David 65
Lewis, Rowland (Carms.) 171
Lincolnshire 146, 161
Littleton, Sir Edward (Henley, Salop and London) 51, 142
Llanbadarn Fawr (Cards.) 138
Llandaff, bishops of see Field, Theophilus; Morgan, William; Murray, William; Owen, Morgan
Llandaff Cathedral 220
Llanfihangel Esceifiog (Anglesey) 230
Llangathen (Carms.) 175
Llangelynin (Caern.) 226
Llanidloes hundred (Montgom.) 174
Llanrheader (Denbs.) 227
Llanrhychwyn (Caern.) 226
Llansilin (Denbs.) 225–6
Llantrisant (Glam.) 4, 16–17
Llanynys (Denbs.) 225
Llechcynfarwy (Anglesey) 229
Llewerllyd (Flints.) 192
Lloyd, David (Forest, Carms.) 170
Lloyd, Edward (Llwyn-y-Maen, Salop) 91
Lloyd, Griffith (Maes-y-coed, Merion.) 186
Lloyd, Griffith (Ynyswen, Carms.) 87, 170
Lloyd, H. A. (historian) 83
Lloyd, Hugh (Foxhall, Denbs.) 169
Lloyd, Hugh (Rossindale, Denbs.) 169
Lloyd, Sir John (Rhiwaedog, Merion.) 139
Lloyd, Marmaduke (Maesyfelin, Cards. and Ludlow) 180, 182, 185, 266
Lloyd, Oliver David (Montgom.) 107
Llŷn (Caern.) 104
lobbies see parliament, lobbies and sectional interests
London 5, 45, 48, 52–3, 80, 108, 115–16, 128, 139, 159, 165, 168–9, 171, 172, 178, 179, 195, 196, 209, 220, 240, 258, 266–8, 270, 275
London companies 41, 58
  see also Haberdashers' Company
Long Parliament see parliaments, (Long Parliament, 1640–53)
Lostwithiel (Cornw.) 124
Lougher, William (Glam.) 170
Loughor (Glam.) 17
Ludlow (Salop) 6, 78, 123, 148, 157–9, 167, 266, 270

Mainwaring, Roger, bishop of St David's 208, 214, 226

Maltby, Judith (historian) 250, 276
Mansell, Sir Lewis (Margam, Glam.) 174
Mansell, Sir Robert (Margam, Glam. and London) 73n.130, 101, 109–10, 124–5, 127–8, 143, 150
Mansfeldt, Count Peter 105, 109
marcher lordships/Welsh Marches 6, 77, 217
  see also Gloucestershire, Herefordshire, Shropshire, Worcestershire
martial law 142, 146, 271
Matthews, Robert (Llangollen, Denbs.) 253
Maurice, Sir William (Clenennau, Caern.) 7, 22, 36, 47–8, 52, 55, 58, 71–4, 273
Melcombe Regis (Dorset) 25
Merioneth 47–8, 94, 105, 154, 266
  clothiers 63
  elections 12, 20–1
  forced loan 134n.190, 137, 139, 268–9
  Privy Seal loan (1625–6) 114, 116–17, 139, 154
  ship money 176, 183, 186, 197, 201–6
Milborne, John (Wonastow, Mon.) 189–90
Milford Haven (Pembs.) 102, 119–22, 143, 156
Militia Ordinance (1642) 246, 249–51
militia rates 145
Minehead (Som.) 68
mises and 'Prince's mise' 56–7, 88, 114, 128, 146, 187, 192–3
Mold (Flints.) 96
Monmouth 43–6, 147
  manor 46
  see also Johnson, Sir Robert; Monmouth School
Monmouth School 46–7
Monmouthshire 4n.6, 42–4, 95, 100, 105, 132, 146, 148, 221, 251, 253, 266, 271–2
  benevolence (1626) 130
  catholicism in 31–2, 34, 100, 239–40, 253
  elections 12, 13, 31–2
  forced loan 131–2, 137
  Privy Seal loan (1625–6) 114, 116–17
  ship money 157–9, 160n.25, 161–2, 189–90, 196, 201–6
monopolies and patentees 57–68
  see also Welsh butter trade; Welsh cloth trade
Monopolies Act (1624) 66n.104
Montgomery 227–8
  elections 18
Montgomeryshire 95, 105, 180, 239, 266
  clothiers/cloth trade 60, 63
  elections 18–20, 32, 34
  forced loan 137, 139–40
  ship money 161, 167, 174, 186n.123, 188, 195–6, 201–6
Morgan, Sir Edmund (Penhow, Mon.) 33, 91
Morgan, John (Llangollen, Denbs.) 245
Morgan, William, bishop of Llandaff and St Asaph 210
Morgan, Sir William (Tredegar, Mon.) 31–2, 100, 102
Morrill, John (historian) 181, 250
Morris, Edward (Llansilin, Denbs.) 225
Morris, William (Caern.) 247
mortmain legislation 46, 47n.28
Mostyn, John (Tregarnedd, Anglesey) 23, 39
Mostyn, Sir Roger (Mostyn, Flints.) 22, 113, 128–9
Mostyn, Thomas (Mostyn, Flints.) 22, 35, 174
Murray, William, bishop of Llandaff 214
Mutton, Peter (Llanerch, Denbs.) 28, 50–1, 53n.50, 54, 79

INDEX

Myddleton, Sir Hugh (Denbigh and London) 19, 37
Myddleton I, Sir Thomas (Chirk Castle, Denbs.) 21, 24
Myddleton II, (Sir) Thomas (Chirk Castle, Denbs.) 25, 36, 211, 216–17, 218, 232, 253
Mytton, Col. Thomas 255

Nanney, Hugh (Nannau, Merion.) 21, 183–4, 197
Narberth (Pembs.) 102
Neale, Sir John (historian) 83
Neath (Glam.) 17
'New British History' 2
New Radnor (Rads.) 143, 165n.43, 177–8
Newcastle 248
Newport (Mon.) 44n.15, 157–8
Nicholas, Edward (secretary of the Admiralty) 157, 176, 185, 191–5
nonconformists/nonconformity see puritans/puritanism
Norden, John 49, 266
Norfolk 128, 262
north Wales 51, 61–2, 92, 155–6, 168, 185, 243, 251–2
Northampton, earl of see Compton, Sir William, 1st earl of Northampton
Notestein, Wallace (historian) 83

Old Sarum (Wilts.) 15
Ormonde, duke of see Butler, James, 1st duke of Ormonde
Oswestry (Salop) 61–3
outboroughs see elections, outboroughs (contributory boroughs)
Owen, George (Henllys, Pembs.) 81, 267
Owen, George (Pembs.) 119–20
Owen, Hugh (Gwenynog, Anglesey) 94, 122
Owen, Dr John, bishop of St Asaph 187, 214, 217–18, 225, 227–8
Owen, Morgan, bishop of Llandaff 209, 220n.53
Owen, Richard (Gwenynog, Anglesey) 94
Owen, Sir Roger (Condover, Salop) 44–5, 74
Owen, Rowland (Wrexham, Denbs.) 230

Palatinate 8, 85–8, 90–2
Parliament and English Politics, 1621–1629 1
parliaments
    (1604–10) 41–9, 52–8, 68, 71–6
    (1614) 44, 46–7, 58, 76–7
    (1621) 57–66, 68–9, 77–9, 87–92
    (1624) 63–4, 66–7, 79–80, 99–103
    (1625) 108–10
    (1626) 49–50, 67, 123–7, 132
    (1628–9) 50–1, 140–5
    (Short Parliament, 1640) 194–5, 197, 238
    (Long Parliament, 1640–53) 196, 238–48, 250–2, 257, 259
    elections to see elections
    lobbies and sectional interests 40–80 passim, 264 see also Bromfield and Yale; Chepstow Bridge; Glamorgan, butter trade; Glamorgan, trade with Minehead; Harlech; 'Henry VIII clause'; Ireland, cattle trade; mises; Monmouth School; purveyance; Shrewsbury Drapers' Company; Welsh butter; Welsh cloth trade
parliamentarians/ism 239, 243, 251–4, 256–61
Parry, Richard, bishop of St Asaph 79

Parry, Thomas (Cards.) 191
'Peaceable Army' 255
Pembroke 119
Pembroke, earls of see Herbert, William, 3rd earl of Pembroke; Herbert, Philip, 4th earl of Pembroke and Montgomery
Pembrokeshire 12, 66, 68, 90, 102, 105, 107, 119–21, 144–5, 149, 154, 239, 252, 255, 257–9, 267, 271
    benevolence (1626) 129–30, 143
    deputy lieutenants 119, 156
    elections 13, 107
    forced loan 134 and n.190, 137
    impressment 108n.89, 141
    Palatinate benevolence 87
    parliamentarian impulses in 252, 257–9
    ship money 165, 171, 179–80, 183n.112, 186n.123, 201–6
Penmynydd (Anglesey) 23
Pennant, David (Downing, Flints.) 246–7
Perrot, Sir James (Haroldston, Pembs.) 55, 57, 66, 68, 82–3, 87, 99, 147
    activity in parliament 150
        (1621) 89–90, 100
        (1624) 100–1
        (1628–9) 142–4
    anti-catholic sentiment 89–90, 142–3, 150
    attitude to war 90, 121, 142–4, 150
    concern for fortification of Haverfordwest and Milford Haven 120–2, 143
    election contests in 1620s 27, 32
    see also *Invitation Unto Prayer* (1624)
Perrot, Sir John (Haroldston and Carew Castle, Pembs.) 27, 90
Petition of Right (1628) 142, 144
petitions 238, 241
    Anglesey (Aug. 1642) 247
    Cardiff charter 18
    Chepstow Bridge 43
    clothiers of north Wales 60n.78, 62–3
    Eleazer Jackson (Mon.) 90
    Glamorgan gentry (Welsh butter trade) 65–7
    Harlech (great sessions) 47n.32, 48
    Is Aeron (Cards.; ship money) 181
    'many hundred thousands' in Wales (Feb. 1642) 241–3, 258, 275
    privy seal loan (1625–6) 114, 116
    pro-episcopacy (Mar. 1642) 243–5, 275
    purveyance (1604) 52–4
    Rhuddlan (Flints.; ship money) 187
    Richard Price (Cards.; ship money) 190
    Shrewsbury Drapers' Company 61
    tenants of Bromfield and Yale 50
    Radnorshire grievances (1640/1) 36, 238n.8
    Welsh MPs ('Henry VIII clause') 75–6 (1610); 75, 77 (1621)
    Wales (Aug. 1642) 249–50
Petre, Anne 251, 253
Pierce, Lloyd (Maesmawr, Montgom.) 174
pirates 111, 118, 121, 125, 155–6, 198, 271
plague see ship money, plague affecting
Plymouth (Devon) 121
Porthkerry (Glam.) 248
Portsmouth (Hants.) 127
post-revisionism 2–3, 153, 197, 236, 261
Powell, Philip (Brecon) 98
Powell, Thomas (Caern.) 28–9
Powell, Thomas (Horsley, Denbs.) 186

INDEX

Powis Castle (Montgom.) 180
  see also Herbert family (Powis Castle, Montgom.)
Powis, Lord, see Herbert, Sir William
'Prayer Book Protestantism' 209, 211, 213, 234, 243–5, 250, 275–6
Prestatyn hundred (Flints.) 163
Presteigne (Rads.) 177–8
Prichard, Rhys (Llandovery, Carms.) 98–9
Price family (Pilleth, Rads.) 26
Price, 'Mr' 91
Price, Charles (Pilleth, Rads.) 36, 126–7, 143, 150, 238n.8, 239, 245
Price, Dame Gwen (Gogerddan, Cards.) 138
Price, Herbert (The Priory, Brecon) 223
Price, James (Mynachdy, Rads.) 26
Price John (Gogerddan, Cards.) 138
Price, Sir John (Newton, Montgom.) 32
Price, Richard (Gogerddan, Cards.) 190–1
Price, Thomas (Brecs.) 116
Price, Thomas (Gogerddan, Cards.) 138
Price, Thomas (Pembs.) 134
Price, William (Britton Ferry, Glam.) 66
Prince's mise see mises and 'Prince's mise'
principality see Wales, principality of
private bills 43, 47, 50
Privy Council 3, 5, 15, 48, 52, 55, 59, 62–4, 69, 92, 95–6, 104, 106–9, 111–13, 116, 119–21, 124, 127, 129–32, 134–5, 139–41, 145–9, 152, 154, 156–7, 160–1, 164–71, 173–4, 177–8, 180–3, 186, 188–93, 196–7, 199, 217, 266–70, 272–3, 277
  perspectives on Wales 104, 146, 148–9, 157, 167–8, 266–7, 270
Privy Seal loans
  (1604) 117–18, 149n.236, 269
  (1625–6) 110–18, 125, 135, 147–9, 154, 170
  see also under individual counties
  (1626) 131
proclamations 65–6, 72n.126
propaganda see Civil Wars, distribution of propaganda
prophecy 71–2
Prowde, John (Shrewsbury, Salop) 58, 60–1, 64
Prynne, William 212, 222–3
Prys, Edmwnd (Maentwrog, Merion.) 211
Puleston, Roger (Emral, Flints.) 53n.50, 54, 57
puritans/puritanism 34, 149–50, 200, 207–9, 212, 227–8, 232–3, 236, 238–40, 245, 259–61, 276
  activity in the Long Parliament 238–9, 259
  influence from England 212, 227–8, 232–3
  limited presence in Wales 208, 210–13, 260, 276
  see also religion in Wales, historiography of; ship money, puritanism and opposition
purveyance 41, 52–6, 80, 164, 187, 192–3, 264
Pwllheli (Caern.) 115
Pye, Sir Walter (The Mynde, Herefs.) 51, 66
Pym, John 241, 247

Quintrell, Brian (historian) 147, 277

Radnorshire 105, 238n.8, 266, 267
  elections 13, 26
  forced loan 134n.190, 135, 137
  impressment 108n.90
  Privy Seal loan (1625–6) 117, 135, 154

ship money 161, 164–5, 174, 177–8, 183n.112, 201–6
Raglan Castle (Mon.) 13, 251, 253, 273
Raglan hundred (Mon.) 221
rating disputes see ship money, rating disputes
Ravenscroft, Robert (Bretton, Flints.) 35
Ravenscroft, William (Bretton, Flints. and London) 80, 91
recusants see catholics/catholicism
Rees, Thomas (historian) 208
Reformation, the 210, 213, 233–4, 244
religion in Wales 34, 207–34 passim, 239–40, 243–5, 254–8
  'conservative conformism' 209–10, 213, 232–4, 240, 243–5, 254–7
  historiography 207–10, 222
  liturgy, centrality of 209–10, 211, 228–32, 234, 244–5, 255
  problems of source material in 1630s 209 and n.7, 213
  Welsh Bible 210–11, 233, 244
  Welsh homilies 210
  Welsh Prayer Book 210–11, 213, 233–4, 243–4, 254–7
  Welsh language 209–13, 232–4, 275
  see also Church of England in Wales; puritans/puritanism; catholics/catholicism
revisionism 2–3, 10, 153, 235
Rhuddlan hundred (Flints.) 187, 192–3
Rich, Robert, 2nd earl of Warwick 273
Richards, Thomas (historian) 208
Richardson, Thomas (chief justice of King's Bench) 274
River Wye 42
Roberts, Mathew (Denbigh, Denbs.) 254
Roberts, Peter (St Asaph, Denbs.) 219
Roberts, Peter (historian) 75
Roberts, Stephen (historian) 2
Roberts, William, bishop of Bangor 208–9, 215, 219, 226, 229–30
'root and branch' reform/bill 239–40, 243–4
royal prerogative 91, 100
royalists/royalism see Wales, royalism of
Rudd, Archdeacon 255
Rudd, Rice (Aberglasney, Carms.) 175
Rûg (Merion.) 231
Russell, Conrad (historian) 1, 40, 90
Russell, Sir William (treasurer of the navy) 162, 179n.96, 188
Ruthin (Denbs.) 115–16
Rutland 146

St Albans (Herts.) 212
St Asaph, bishops of see Hanmer, John; Morgan, William; Parry, Richard
St Asaph Cathedral 219–20
St Asaph diocese 214, 217, 225, 229
St David's, bishops of see Field, Theophilus; Laud, William, as bishop of St David's; Mainwaring, Roger
St David's Cathedral 215–16, 227
St David's diocese 213–14, 222–4
St Donats (Glam.) 14
St Paul's Cathedral, collections for repair of 220–1
Salisbury, earl of see Cecil, Sir Robert (later earl of Salisbury)

INDEX

Saltash (Cornw.) 57
Salusbury, (Sir) Henry (Lleweni, Denbs.) 24, 138
Salusbury, John (Lleweni, Denbs.) 86, 217
Salusbury, William (Bachymbyd, Denbs. and Rûg, Merion.) 21, 91, 231
satires on the Welsh 211, 234, 240, 242–3, 249, 254–6, 258–60, 273
Saxton, Christopher 267
Scotland 184, 188, 238
Scott, Thomas 98
Scottish wars *see* Bishops' Wars
Scudamore, Sir John (Holme Lacy, Herefs.) 224n.67
Scurfield, John (Pembs.) 171
Selden, John 125
Seys, Evan (Boverton, Glam.) 246n.26
ship money 4, 9, 152–206 passim, 243, 265, 271
 administrative problems 157–60, 168, 171–4, 180
 arrears and defaulting 170–1, 178–80, 183–4, 185–7, 193, 195–6, 202–6
 assessment 157–8, 160, 161–2, 163–6, 173, 170, 174–6, 180–2, 186–7, 191–3, 197, 201–6 *see also* ship money, rating disputes; ship money, sheriffs, rating
 division of Wales into northern and southern blocs for purposes of 159, 161, 166, 168, 180, 243
 traditional local rates employed 163–4, 174, 176, 181–2, 187–8, 192–3 *see also* prince's mise; purveyance
 attempt to levy in 1626 131, 165
 burden of 157, 159, 161–2, 170, 175, 184–5, 192–3, 197–9
 compliance in Wales 157, 162, 188, 197–200
 corporations 157–8, 165n.43, 171, 185n.122
 declared accounts, problems with and errors of 162, 188, 195–6, 205
 difficulty of opposing directly 164, 183
 distraint 183n.113, 187, 190–1, 193, 197
 dynamics of payment 160, 162–3, 169–71, 184, 185–7, 197–8, 201–6
 escheators 191, 194–6
 great sessions 172, 181–2, 187, 192–3, 199
 hundredal/parish officials 163, 175–7, 183, 186, 189, 193
 mayors 157–8, 171, 179
 nature of opposition to 170, 173, 177, 179, 183–4, 186, 188, 189–96, 197–200
 parliament 189, 194–6
 plague affecting 172, 177–8, 188
 poverty 186, 189–94, 196
 problems of transporting money 159–60, 168–9, 178
 puritanism and opposition 199–200, 276
 rating disputes 164, 170, 173–4, 180–4, 187–8, 189, 191, 192–3
  as opposition 183–4, 189
  between counties 165–8, 173, 180
 sheriffs 156–7, 161, 163–5, 168–9, 170, 174, 177, 183–4, 190, 191
  choice of 171–4, 179, 180, 185
  evasion of office 156–7, 171, 180
  rating 163–4, 174–5, 180, 182, 187, 191
 ships or money 155, 158–9
 underassessment in Wales 157, 198
 Welsh counties joined with English counties (1634) 157–60, 161

writs of
 (1634) 155–60, 201
 (1635) 161–7, 168–71, 173, 187, 202
 (1636) 167–8, 171–80, 187, 203
 (1637) 168, 180–4, 187, 204
 (1638) 184–8, 195, 205
 (1639) 188–96, 199, 206
 see also entries under individual counties; pirates; Wales, political culture of
sheriffs *see* ship money, sheriffs
Short Parliament *see* parliaments, (Short Parliament, 1640)
Shrewsbury (Salop) 6, 59n.72, 60, 62–3, 251
Shrewsbury Drapers' Company 58–64, 83
Shropshire 6, 73, 77, 140, 258
Skenfrith hundred (Mon.) 221
soldiers 107, 119
 see also impressment
Somerset family, earls of Worcester 13, 17, 31, 272
Somerset, Edward, 4th earl of Worcester 44, 46–7, 79, 131–3
 as lord lieutenant (Glam. and Mon.) 103, 111, 114, 148, 272
Somerset, Henry, 5th earl and 1st marquess of Worcester 32, 47n.27, 131–3, 148, 220, 239–40, 251–3, 273–4
Somerset, Sir Thomas (Mon.) 33, 73n.130
Somersetshire 125, 161, 197
South Phoenix, The 119
south Wales 43, 45, 65, 67, 107, 166, 168, 180, 231, 243, 251–2
Spain 8, 85, 87
 war against 90–1, 97–102, 120
Spanish Match 97–103
Stamford, earl of *see* Grey, Henry, 1st earl of Stamford
Stanley family, earls of Derby 13
Star Chamber 138
Steadman, John (Strata Florida, Cards.) 181–2
Stepney, Dame Jane (Prendergast, Pembs.) 179
Stepney, Sir John (Prendergast, Pembs.) 179
Stoyle, Mark (historian) 254, 260, 275, 277
Stradling, Sir John (St Donats, Glam.) 14–15, 67, 97–8, 100–2, 109–10, 125, 150
Studies in Stuart Wales 2
subsidies 56–7, 80, 87–9, 92–3, 97, 103–4, 107–12, 114–15, 119–20, 124, 127–30, 138, 143–4, 146, 162, 165, 175–6, 268, 270
Swansea (Glam.) 17
Symonds, Richard 231, 251

taxation
 burden of in 1620s 145–50
 relative under-assessment of Wales 140–1, 142–3, 146–9, 161–2, 268
 resistance to non-parliamentary taxation 93–4, 96, 111–13, 128–31, 133, 146, 271
 see also benevolences; coat and conduct money; forced loan; knighthood composition; militia rates; mises; Privy Seal loans; ship money; subsidies; Wales, language of poverty in
Thelwall, Sir Euble (Denbs. and London) 25, 50–1, 79, 264
Thelwall, Simon (Plas-y-Ward, Denbs.) 24
Theodor, David Owen (Penmynydd, Anglesey) 23

INDEX

Thirty Years' War 8–9, 31, 33–4, 85–151 passim
Thomas ap Humfffrey (Merion.) 176–7
Thomas ap John Hugh (Talley, Carms.) 227
Thomas, David Lloyd (Rhuddlan, Flints.) 187
Thomas, James (Dyffryn Clydach, Cards.) 138
Thomas, Oliver (West Felton, Salop) 239
Thomas, Sir William (Caernarfon and Aber, Caern.) 21, 28, 94–5, 107, 114–16, 118, 197
Thornton, Tim (historian) 278
Tomme, Richard (Haverfordwest, Pembs.) 225
Townshend, Sir Henry (Ludlow, Salop) 78n.153
trained bands 103–4, 120–1, 147, 267
Tre'r Castell (Flints.) 192
Trefeglwys (Montgom.) 224–5
Trellech hundred (Mon.) 221
Trevor, Arthur 252
Trevor, Sir John, jun. (Trevalyn, Denbs.) 22, 247
Trevor, Sir Richard (Trevalyn, Denbs.) 21, 126
Trevor, Sir Sackvill (Plas Newydd, Anglesey and London) 39
Trevor, Sir Thomas (Trevalyn, Denbs. and London) 50–1, 57, 87–8
Tudor dynasty 1, 10, 199, 237, 260, 273
Turks 98, 111

Underdown, David (historian) 254
Uwch Aeron (Cards.) 181–3, 191

Vaughan family (Golden Grove, Carms.) 18–19
Vaughan, Sir John (Golden Grove, Carms.) 96n.42, 131
Vaughan, Morgan (Rads.) 164
Vaughan, Rice (Pembs.) 179
Vaughan, Thomas (Carms.) 171
Vaughan, William (Corsygedol, Merion.) 21
Vaughan, William (Llangyndeyrn, Carms.) 227, 266
Vaughan, William (Llowes, Rads.) 26
Vaughan, Sir William (royalist colonel) 255
Venetian ambassador 248–9
Villiers, George, 1st duke of Buckingham 4, 31, 34, 65, 98–101, 108–10, 112, 118, 123–8, 131, 135, 141, 143–5, 150, 271–2
  Welsh clientage in the Commons 125–7, 143–5, 150

Wales
  aristocratic presence, absence of 13–14, 18, 127, 147, 150, 272–3
  communications in 6, 41, 157–60, 169, 266
  concept of 'Welsh politics' 4–5, 10–11, 262–78
  deputy lieutenants 110–18, 148, 175
  see also under individual counties
  economic lobbies 52–70
  economy 53, 68, 160, 161–2, 209, 268, 271
    depression in 58, 60–3, 65, 69, 92–7, 241
    lack of ready money 160, 163
  geographical heterogeneity 6, 265–6
  greenwax fines 264
  historiography of 1–4, 81–4, 152–4, 236–8, 252, 262–3, 277–8
  language of poverty in 111–18, 128–9, 141, 146–9, 154, 161–2, 164, 166, 269–71
  lieutenancy 85, 103–4, 111–14, 122–3, 147–8, 238 see also Compton, William, 1st earl of Northampton; Somerset, Edward, 4th earl of Worcester, as lord lieutenant (Glam. and Mon.)
  MPs
    as a 'Welsh party' 40, 80–4, 263
    as constituency representatives 35, 39–70 passim, 102–3, 125, 238, 263–4 see also Bromfield and Yale; Chepstow Bridge; Glamorgan, butter trade; Glamorgan, trade with Minehead; Harlech; 'Henry VIII clause'; Ireland, cattle trade; mises; Monmouth School; purveyance; Shrewsbury Drapers' Company; Welsh butter; Welsh cloth trade
    attitudes to war (1620s) 88, 91–2, 99–103, 142–4
    collective action by 41, 52–7, 58–62, 64–5, 75–80, 87–9
    ideological motivations 84
    inactivity in the Commons 37, 39, 51, 69–70, 83, 91–2
    nomination to committees 46, 50, 68, 69, 77, 81–2
    regional coalitions 46, 60–3, 64–8
    patronage ties 99–102, 109–10, 142–5
    resistance to puritan reforms (1640–2) 238–9
    serving 'apprenticeship' 41–2, 51, 69, 83–4, 237
    Tudor parliaments 81
  news and political information in 245–8, 267–8
  perceptual distance from political centre 115, 122–3, 128, 146–9, 161–2, 167–8, 171–4, 199, 265–73
  political culture of 3–5, 8, 10–11, 34, 153, 197–200, 235, 240, 241, 260–1, 262–78
  principality of 6, 74
  religion see religion in Wales
  rhetorical force of in parliament/political culture 81, 241, 250, 263–4
  royalism 153, 199, 211, 235–7, 240, 243, 246–61 passim
    ethnicity 258–9, 274–5
    fissures within royalist phalanx 252–3
    loyalty to 'British' monarchy 237–8, 260, 273
    role of language 257–8
    popular 253–4
    role of gentry/aristocracy 251–2, 253–4
    significance of religion 254–8, 260–1
    unanimity of 250–4, 260–1
  see also Civil Wars; commissions/commissioners of array
  see also Acts of Union; anti-Welshness; Britain, rhetorical significance of; taxation, burden of in Wales; north Wales; south Wales
Warwick, earl of see Rich, Robert, 2nd earl of Warwick
Warwick, Philip 238n.8
Welsh butter trade 64–68
Welsh cloth trade 8, 57–64, 96
Welsh history and mythology 7
Welsh language 7, 10, 99, 198, 209–11, 224, 233, 246, 257–8, 275
  see also religion in Wales, Welsh language
Wentloog hundred (Mon.) 221
Whitelocke, Sir James (chief justice of Chester) 23, 78, and n.153
Whitley, Thomas (Aston, Flints.) 183

INDEX

Williams, Charles (Llangibby, Mon.) 32
Williams, Glanmor (historian) 152
Williams, Griffith (Llanllechid, Caern.) 92n.29
Williams, Gwyn Alf (historian) 1
Williams, Sir Henry (Gwernyfed, Brecs.) 79
Williams, John (bishop of Lincoln and lord keeper) 31, 106, 150, 267
Williams, John (Caern.) 185
Williams, Matthew (Porthkerry, Glam) 248
Williams, Penry (historian) 148
Williams, Richard (Glam.) 65, 67
Wilson, John (Porthkerry, Glam.) 248
Windebank, Sir Francis (secretary of state) 148
Wogan, John (Wiston, Pembs.) 107, 171
Wood, Owen (Rhosmor, Anglesey) 94, 156
Wood, Samuel (Trevalyn, Denbs.) 247, 250, 253, 258
Worcester, earls of *see* Somerset family; Somerset, Edward, 4th earl of Worcester; Somerset, Henry, 5th earl and 1st marquess of Worcester
Worcestershire 6, 73, 77, 140
Wrexham (Denbs.) 212, 218, 226, 230
Wroth, William (Llanfaches, Mon.) 236
Wynn family (Gwydir, Caern.) 96, 114, 150, 269
  electoral activities in 1620s 27–30

Wynn, Henry (Gwydir, Caern. and London) 20, 80, 110–11
Wynn, John (Cards.) 194
Wynn, Sir John (Gwydir, Caern.) 21, 28–9, 35, 59, 69, 80, 91–2, 94–5, 114, 128, 148–9
  benevolence (1622) 96–7
  impressment 106–7
  Privy Seal loan (1625–6) 113–15
Wynn, Owen (Gwydir, Caern. and London) 23, 29, 62, 91, 114–16, 126, 128, 148–9, 251
Wynn, Sir Richard (Gwydir, Caern. and London) 20, 22, 28, 69, 92, 264
Wynn, Robert (Conwy, Caern. and Lincoln's Inn) 247
Wynn Robert (Maes Mochnant, Denbs.) 25
Wynn, Thomas (Melai, Denbs.) 86
Wynn, William (Glyn Cywarch, Merion.) 185
Wynn, William (Gwydir, Caern. and London) 28, 59, 267
Wynne, William (Llanfair, Denbs.) 167, 176

Yorkshire 248

Zouche, Edward 149n.236